Philosophical Essays on Curriculum

THE LIPPINCOTT FOUNDATIONS
OF EDUCATION SERIES

Under the Editorship of
John Hardin Best and James E. Wheeler
Rutgers University

Philosophical Essays on Curriculum

edited by

Robert S. Guttchen
Hofstra University

Bertram Bandman
Long Island University

J. B. Lippincott Company
Philadelphia · New York

To Our Children
Peter and David Guttchen
and
Nancy Susan Bandman

When one considers in its length and in its breadth the importance of this question of the education of a nation's young, the broken lives, the defeated hopes, the national failures, which result from the frivolous inertia with which it is treated, it is difficult to restrain within oneself a savage rage. In the conditions of modern life the rule is absolute, the race which does not value trained intelligence is doomed. Not all your heroism, not all your victories on land or at sea, can move back the finger of fate. To-day we maintain ourselves. To-morrow science will have moved forward yet one more step, and there will be no appeal from the judgment which will then be pronounced on the uneducated.

Alfred North Whitehead

Preface

The curricula in schools and colleges have been the subject of considerable discussion and debate. We think philosophy is relevant and important to this debate. We have accordingly selected philosophical writings on the subjects taught as well as philosophical materials on the teaching of those subjects. We have thereby hoped to draw philosophical attention to two important curricular questions: (1) How should a curriculum be organized? and (2) What should be the elements of a curriculum?

This work is a collaborative one for which we assume full responsibility. We wish to thank the contributing authors and publishers for their cooperation. We are grateful for a grant from the Research Fund of the School of Education of Hofstra University, and for the assistance of Helen Lipp, Barbara Kohn, Euniceteen Pittman and James Dahl of Hofstra, and Henrietta Weinstein of Long Island University. The advice of our colleagues, William J. McKeough of Hofstra University, and Alex Orenstein of Queens College of the University of the City of New York, was greatly appreciated. Our thanks go to James E. Wheeler of Rutgers University, an editor of the Lippincott Foundations of Education Series, as well as Bob Richards, Martha Glenn, and Alex Fraser of Lippincott for their assistance. We particularly acknowledge the help of our wives, Emily Guttchen and Elsie Bandman.

ROBERT S. GUTTCHEN AND BERTRAM BANDMAN

New York City
November 18, 1968

Contents

Introduction

THE PURPOSE OF THIS BOOK is to bring together some philosophical studies relevant to what is generally taught in school. We have clustered materials under five main headings: the formal sciences, the physical and natural sciences, history and the social sciences, literature and the fine arts, and philosophy. These constitute the major intellectual and artistic achievements of mankind and are the main elements of school curricula. The achievements in these fields have been subjected to considerable philosophical study. In contrast, little philosophical attention has been given these achievements as subject matter in a curricular setting. Our hope is that this book of readings will stimulate philosophical study of these disciplines as subjects taught in school.

Philosophical considerations help us to appreciate and to understand important differences between logic, mathematics, the physical, natural and social sciences, the arts, literature and philosophy. In logic and mathematics, our procedures for arriving at conclusions are most settled. Moreover, the conclusions are certain, unlike conclusions in every other field. We are sure, for example, that in formal logic, A is A and that in the Euclidean system of geometry the shortest distance between two points on a plane is a straight line. We know this sort of thing as surely as we can know anything.

In the physical and natural sciences, procedures for arriving at conclusions are well established but are not as well established as

those of the formal sciences. In the formal sciences no factual
claims are made. In contrast, the purpose of the empirical sciences,
that is, the physical, natural and social sciences, is to make reliable
factual claims about the world. We are not as sure about the truth
of factual statements as we are about the truth of formal statements. The method we have for finding the shortest distance between two points is more reliable than the method for finding out
whether nails rust in damp air.

There are also differences among the empirical sciences that may
be noted. The physical sciences deal with non-living phenomena,
whereas the natural sciences deal with living things. Some living
things manifest purposive behavior, whereas non-living things do
not. The question arises as to whether life is a unique phenomenon
requiring special modes of study and explanation. (See, for example, the selections by Sommerhoff and Nagel in this volume.)

History and the social sciences present us with further difficulties. The objectivity achieved in the study of physical and biological
phenomena is difficult if not impossible to achieve in man's study
of himself. The belief is held by some social scientists, historians
and philosophers that the active participation and involvement of
human beings with their biases and the full play of their passions
makes objectivity in the social sciences an impossibility. Others believe that this obstacle to objectivity is surmountable. Value disputes play a larger role in history and the social sciences than they
do in the physical and natural sciences. And, although we have
methods for settling factual disputes, we have no comparable
methods for adjudicating value conflicts. It is accordingly more
difficult to find out what happened at the battle of Shiloh than to
find out about the properties of nails or of stars.

The arts and literature present difficulties not previously encountered. Poems and paintings are not theories about the world and
are not subject to the kind of appraisal appropriate to the various
sciences. Whereas we have a whole complex of decision-making
procedures in the sciences, there does not appear to be any comparable method of appraisal in the arts. Nor does there appear to be
any method for deciding what is worth painting or composing. Nor
do we know how to write rules for producing great works of art. If
there are not agreed upon methods for producing art works or

appraising them, this presents the teacher of the arts with serious problems regarding both what to teach and how to teach.

This is an especially unhappy state of affairs since the arts concern what is closest to our lives and can do so much to enhance the quality of life. Some claim that art makes life worth living and is also that which is most worth teaching. So despite these difficulties, there can be no question of the importance of teaching the arts.

There is finally philosophy. What has been said about the lack of established methods of appraisal applies also to philosophical disputes. Historians and social scientists observe and study human values. Artists exhibit values in their works. Philosophers, however, are concerned explicitly with the appraisal and *justification of values*. There are no set rules for this kind of enterprise, which has led some to believe that any value judgment is as good as any other. According to this view, no rational choice can be made among values; all choices are arbitrary. Other philosophers contend that there are objective grounds for deciding what is good or bad; that choices can be rational. This disagreement continues unabated.

The question remains as to whether there is any way to decide what values to teach. It would appear that any basic curriculum decision is implicated. There is then this paradox: What may ultimately be most important to teach appears to be furthest removed from a rational method for deciding between conflicting claims. Where we have the most need of a method it is least available.

Prologue

Prospects in the Arts and Sciences

J. Robert Oppenheimer

THE WORDS "prospects in the arts and sciences" mean two quite different things to me. One is prophecy: What will the scientists discover and the painters paint, what new forms will alter music, what parts of experience will newly yield to objective description? The other meaning is that of a view: What do we see when we look at the world today and compare it with the past? I am not a prophet; and I cannot very well speak to the first subject, though in many ways I should like to. I shall try to speak to the second, because there are some features of this view which seem to me so remarkable, so new and so arresting, that it may be worth turning our eyes to them; it may even help us to create and shape the future better, though we cannot foretell it.

In the arts and in the sciences, it would be good to be a prophet. It would be a delight to know the future. I had thought for a while of my own field of physics and of those nearest to it in the natural sciences. It would not be too hard to outline the questions which natural scientists today are asking themselves and trying to answer.

From *The Open Mind* by J. Robert Oppenheimer, pp. 133–146 (New York: Simon and Schuster). © 1955 by J. Robert Oppenheimer. Reprinted by permission of Simon and Schuster, Inc.

What, we ask in physics, is matter, what is it made of, how does it behave when it is more and more violently atomized, when we try to pound out of the stuff around us the ingredients which only violence creates and makes manifest? What, the chemists ask, are those special features of nucleic acids and proteins which make life possible and give it its characteristic endurance and mutability? What subtle chemistry, what arrangements, what reactions and controls make the cells of living organisms differentiate so that they may perform functions as oddly diverse as transmitting information throughout our nervous systems or covering our heads with hair? What happens in the brain to make a record of the past, to hide it from consciousness, to make it accessible to recall? What are the physical features which make consciousness possible?

All history teaches us that these questions that we think the pressing ones will be transmuted before they are answered, that they will be replaced by others, and that the very process of discovery will shatter the concepts that we today use to describe our puzzlement.

It is true that there are some who profess to see in matters of culture, in matters precisely of the arts and sciences, a certain macrohistorical pattern, a grand system of laws which determines the course of civilization and gives a kind of inevitable quality to the unfolding of the future. They would, for instance, see the radical, formal experimentation which characterized the music of the last half-century as an inevitable consequence of the immense flowering and enrichment of natural science; they would see a necessary order in the fact that innovation in music precedes that in painting and that in turn in poetry, and point to this sequence in older cultures. They would attribute the formal experimentation of the arts to the dissolution, in an industrial and technical society, of authority—of secular, political authority, and of the catholic authority of the church. They are thus armed to predict the future. But this, I fear, is not my dish.

If a prospect is not a prophecy, it is a view. What does the world of the arts and sciences look like? There are two ways of looking at it: One is the view of the traveler, going by horse or foot, from village to village to town, staying in each to talk with those who live there and to gather something of the quality of its life. This is the intimate view, partial, somewhat accidental, limited by the limited life and strength and curiosity of the traveler, but intimate and human, in a human compass. The other is the vast view, showing the earth with its fields and towns and valleys as they appear to a camera carried in a high-altitude rocket. In one sense this prospect will be more complete; one will see all branches of knowledge, one will see all the arts, one will see them as part of the vastness and complication of the whole of human life on earth. But one will miss a great deal; the beauty and warmth of human life will largely be gone from that prospect.

It is in this vast high-altitude survey that one sees the general surprising quantitative features that distinguish our time. This is where the listings of science and endowments and laboratories and books published show up; this is where we learn that more people are engaged in scientific research today than ever before, that the Soviet world and the free world are running neck and neck in the training of scientists, that more books are published per capita in England than in the United States, that the social sciences are pursued actively in America, Scandinavia, and England, that there are more people who hear the great music of the past, and more music composed and more paintings painted. This is where we learn that the arts and sciences are flourishing. This great map, showing the world from afar and almost as to a stranger, would show more: It would show the immense diversity of culture and life, diversity in place and tradition for the first time clearly manifest on a world-wide scale, diversity in technique and language, separating science from science and art from art, and all of one from all of the other. This great map, world-wide, culture-wide, remote, has some odd features. There are innumerable villages. Between the villages there appear to be almost no paths discernible from this high altitude. Here and there passing near a village, sometimes through its heart, there will be a superhighway, along which windy traffic moves at enormous speed. The superhighways seem to have little connection with villages, starting anywhere, ending anywhere, and sometimes appearing almost by design to disrupt the quiet of the village. This view gives us no sense of order or of unity. To find these we must visit the villages, the quiet, busy places, the laboratories and studies and studios. We must see the paths that are barely discernible; we must understand the superhighways and their dangers.

In the natural sciences these are and have been and are likely to continue to be heroic days. Discovery follows discovery, each both raising and answering questions, each ending a long search, and each providing the new instruments for a new search. There are radical ways of thinking unfamiliar to common sense and connected with it by decades or centuries of increasingly specialized and unfamiliar experience. There are lessons of how limited, for all its variety, the common experience of man has been with regard to natural phenomena, and hints and analogies as to how limited may be his experience with man. Every new finding is a part of the instrument kit of the sciences for further investigation and for penetrating into new fields. Discoveries of knowledge fructify technology and the practical arts, and these in turn pay back refined techniques, new possibilities of observation and experiment.

In any science there is harmony between practitioners. A man may work as an individual, learning of what his colleagues do through reading or conversation; he may be working as a member of a group on problems whose technical equipment is too massive for individual effort. But whether he is part of a team or solitary in his own study, he, as a professional, is a member of a community. His colleagues in his own branch of science will be grateful to him for the inventive or creative thoughts he has, will welcome his criticism. His world and work will be objectively communicable; and he will be quite sure that if there is error in it, that error will not long be undetected. In his own line of work he lives in a community where common understanding combines with common purpose and interest to bind men together both in freedom and in co-operation.

This experience will make him acutely aware of how limited, how inadequate, how precious is this condition of his life; for in his relations with a wider society, there will be neither the sense of community nor of objective understanding. He will sometimes find, in returning to practical undertakings, some sense of community with men who are not expert in his science, with other scientists whose work is remote from his, and with men of action and men of art. The frontiers of science are separated now by long years of study, by specialized vocabularies, arts, techniques, and knowledge from the common heritage even of a most civilized society; and anyone working at the frontier of such science is in that sense a very long way from home, a long way too from the practical arts that were its matrix and origin, as indeed they were of what we today call art.

The specialization of science is an inevitable accompaniment of progress; yet it is full of dangers, and it is cruelly wasteful, since so much that is beautiful and enlightening is cut off from most of the world. Thus it is proper to the role of the scientist that he not merely find new truth and communicate it to his fellows, but that he teach, that he try to bring the most honest and intelligible account of new knowledge to all who will try to learn. This is one reason—it is the decisive organic reason—why scientists belong in universities. It is one reason why the patronage of science by and through universities is its most proper form; for it is here, in teaching, in the association of scholars and in the friendships of teachers and taught, of men who by profession must themselves be both teachers and taught, that the narrowness of scientific life can best be moderated, and that the analogies, insights, and harmonies of scientific discovery can find their way into the wider life of man.

In the situation of the artist today there are both analogies to and differences from that of the scientist; but it is the differences which are the most striking and which raise the problems that touch most on the evil of our day. For the artist it is not enough that he communicate with others who are expert in his own art. Their fellowship, their understanding, and their appreciation may encourage him; but that is not the end of his work, nor its nature. The artist depends on a common sensibility and culture, on a common meaning of symbols, on a community of experience and common ways of describing and interpreting it. He need not write for everyone or paint or play for everyone. But his audience must be man; it must be man, and not a specialized set of experts among his fellows. Today that is very difficult. Often the artist has an aching sense of great loneliness, for the community to which he addresses himself is largely not there; the traditions and the culture, the symbols and the history, the myths and the common experience, which it is his function to illuminate, to harmonize, and to portray, have been dissolved in a changing world.

There is, it is true, an artificial audience maintained to moderate between the artist and the world for which he works: the audience of the professional critics, popularizers, and advertisers of art. But though, as does the popularizer and promoter of science, the critic fulfills a necessary present function and introduces some order and some communication between the artist and the world, he cannot add to the intimacy and the directness and the depth with which the artist addresses his fellow men.

To the artist's loneliness there is a complementary great and terrible barrenness in the lives of men. They are deprived of the illumination, the light and tenderness and insight of an intelligible interpretation, in contemporary terms, of the sorrows and wonders and gaieties and follies of man's life. This may be in part offset, and is, by the great growth of technical means for making the art of the past available. But these provide a record of past intimacies between art and life; even when they are applied to the writing and painting and composing of the day, they do not bridge the gulf between a society, too vast and too disordered, and the artist trying to give meaning and beauty to its parts.

In an important sense this world of ours is a new world, in which the unity of knowledge, the nature of human communities, the order of society, the order of ideas, the very notions of society and culture have changed and will not return to what they have been in the past. What is new is new not because it has never been there before, but because it has changed in quality. One thing that is new is the prevalence of newness, the changing scale and scope of change itself, so that the world alters as we walk in it, so that the years of man's life measure not some small growth or rearrangement or moderation of what he learned in childhood, but a great upheaval. What is new is that in one generation our knowledge of the natural world engulfs, upsets, and complements all knowledge of the natural world before. The techniques, among which and by which we live, multiply and ramify, so that the whole world is bound together by communication, blocked here and there by the immense synapses of political tyranny. The global quality of the world is new: our knowledge of and sympathy with remote and diverse peoples, our involvement with them in practical terms, and our commitment to them in terms of brotherhood. What is new in the world is the massive character of the dissolution and corruption of authority, in belief, in ritual, and in temporal order. Yet this is the world that we have come to live in. The very difficulties which it presents derive from growth in understanding, in skill, in power. To assail the changes that have unmoored us from the past is futile, and in a deep sense, I think, it is wicked. We need to recognize the change and learn what resources we have.

Again I will turn to the schools and, as their end and as their center, the universities. For the problem of the scientist is in this respect not different from that of the artist or of the historian. He needs to be a part of the community, and the community can only with loss and peril be without him. Thus it is with a sense of interest and hope that we see a growing recognition that the creative artist is a proper charge on the university, and the university a proper home for him; that a composer or a poet or a playwright or painter needs the toleration, understanding, the rather local and parochial patronage that a university can give; and that this will protect him from the tyranny of man's communication and professional promotion. For here there is an honest chance that what the artist has of insight and of beauty will take root in the community, and that some intimacy and some human bonds can mark his relations with his patrons. For a university rightly and inherently is a place where the individual man can form new syntheses, where the accidents of friendship and association can open a man's eyes to a part of science or art which he had not known before, where parts of human life, remote and perhaps superficially incompatible, can find in men their harmony and their synthesis.

These, then, in rough and far too general words, are some of the things we see as we walk through the villages of the arts and of the sciences and notice how thin are the paths that lead from one to another, and how little in terms of human understanding and pleasure the work of the villages comes to be shared outside.

The superhighways do not help. They are the mass media—from the loud-speakers in the deserts of Asia Minor and the cities of Communist China to the organized professional theater of Broadway. They are the purveyors of art and science and culture for the millions upon millions—the promoters who represent the arts and sciences to humanity and who represent humanity to the arts and sciences; they are the means by which we are reminded of the famine in remote places or of war or trouble or change; they are the means by which this great earth and its peoples have become one to one another, the means by which the news of discovery or honor and the stories and songs of today travel and resound throughout the world. But they are also the means by which the true human community, the man knowing man, the neighbor understanding neighbor, the schoolboy learning a poem, the women dancing, the individual curiosity, the individual sense of beauty are being blown dry and issueless, the means by which the passivity of the disengaged spectator presents to the man of art and science the bleak face of unhumanity.

For the truth is that this is indeed, inevitably and increasingly, an open and, inevitably and increasingly, an eclectic world. We know too much for one man to know much, we live too variously to live as one. Our histories and traditions—the very means of interpreting life—are both bonds and barriers among us. Our knowledge separates as well as it unites; our orders disintegrate as well as bind; our art brings us together and sets us apart. The artist's loneliness, the scholar despairing because no one will any longer trouble to learn what he can teach, the narrowness of the scientist—these are unnatural insignia in this great time of change.

For what is asked of us is not easy. The openness of this world derives its character from the irreversibility of learning; what is once learned is part of human life. We cannot close our minds to discovery; we cannot stop our ears so that the voices of far-off and strange people can no longer reach them. The great cultures of the East cannot be walled off from ours by impassable seas and defects of understanding based on ignorance and unfamiliarity. Neither our integrity as men of learning nor our humanity allows that. In this open world, what is there, any man may try to learn.

This is no new problem. There has always been more to know than one man could know; there have always been modes of feeling that could not move the same heart; there have always been deeply held beliefs that could not be composed into a synthetic union. Yet never before today have the diversity, the complexity, the richness so clearly defied hierarchical order and simplification; never before have we had to understand the complementary, mutually not compatible ways of life and recognize choice between them as the only course of freedom. Never before today has the integrity of the intimate, the detailed, the true art, the integrity of craftsmanship and the preservation of the familiar, of the humorous and the beautiful stood in more massive contrast to the vastness of life, the greatness of the globe, the otherness of people, the otherness of ways, and the all-encompassing dark.

This is a world in which each of us, knowing his limitations, knowing the evils of superficiality and the terrors of fatigue, will have to cling to what is close to him, to what he knows, to what he can do, to his friends and his tradition and his love, lest he be dissolved in a universal confusion and know nothing and love nothing. It is at the same time a world in which none of us can find hieratic prescription or general sanction for any ignorance, any insensitivity, any indifference. When a friend tells us of a new discovery we may not understand, we may not be able to listen without jeopardizing the work that is ours and closer to us; but we cannot find in a book or canon—and we should not seek—grounds for hallowing our ignorance. If a man tells us that he sees differently than we, or that he finds beautiful what we find ugly, we may have to leave the room, from fatigue or trouble; but that is our weakness and our default. If we must live with a perpetual sense that the world and the men in it are greater than we and too much for us, let it be the measure of our virtue that we know this and seek no comfort. Above all, let us not proclaim that the limits of our powers correspond to some special wisdom in our choice of life, of learning, or of beauty.

This balance, this perpetual, precarious, impossible balance between the infinitely open and the intimate, this time—our twentieth century—has been long in coming; but it has come. It is, I think, for us and our children, our only way.

This is for all men. For the artist and for the scientist there is a special problem and a special hope, for in their extraordinarily different ways, in their lives that have increasingly divergent character, there is still a sensed bond, a sensed analogy. Both the man of science and the man of art live always at the edge of mystery, surrounded by it; both always, as the measure of their creation, have had to do with the harmonization of what is new with what is familiar, with the balance between novelty and synthesis, with the struggle to make partial order in total chaos. They can, in their work and in their lives, help themselves, help one another, and help all men. They can make the paths that connect the villages of arts and sciences with each other and with the world at large the multiple, varied, precious bonds of a true and world-wide community.

This cannot be an easy life. We shall have a rugged time of it to keep our minds open and to keep them deep, to keep our sense of beauty and our ability to make it, and our occasional ability to see it in places remote and strange and unfamiliar; we shall have a rugged time of it, all of us, in keeping these gardens in our villages, in keeping open the manifold, intricate, casual paths, to keep these flourishing in a great, open, windy world; but this, as I see it, is the condition of man; and in this condition we can help, because we can love, one another.

PART ONE
The Formal Sciences

1. Necessary Truth

John Hospers

ANALYTIC TRUTH AND LOGICAL POSSIBILITY

Analytic Propositions

IF SOMEONE SAID, "Black cats are fierce," or "Black cats bring bad luck," one might question whether his statement was true; but probably no one would question that, whether true or false, it is a genuine proposition. However, if someone said, "Black cats are black," we might be tempted to say that he was saying nothing, or that he was saying something true but so utterly trivial as to be not worth saying.

"Black cats are black" is an example of an *analytic* proposition. The term is perhaps unfortunate, because the word "analytic" means other things as well. Nevertheless, it is now well established in common usage among philosophers, and it runs constantly through the literature of the subject. The use of this word originates in the fact that you have only to *analyze* a statement of this kind in order to know whether or not it is true. For example, you can analyze "All black cats are black" into the general form "All AB is A"—and you find that the term "black," what is called the "logical predicate" of the sentence, merely repeats what is already contained in the subject of the sentence. You would not even have to know what the word "black" means: it would be enough to know that, whatever it means in the subject, it has the same meaning in the predicate. "Black is black" would also be analytic, although it is slightly different in form: "A is A" instead of "AB is A."

Analytic propositions are of considerable interest to philosophers, since once you know that a certain proposition is analytic, you know it to be true without any further investigation—specifically, without any observation of the world, which is required before we can know the truth of most of the propositions we believe. It might seem, however, that whether or not a proposition is analytic is so obvious that

From *An Introduction to Philosophical Analysis* by John Hospers, 2nd edition, © 1967, pp. 160–174. Reprinted by permission of Prentice-Hall, Inc., Englewood Cliffs, New Jersey.

there would never be any problems about it: certainly this is true of "Black is black," which is so obvious that it would not even occur to us to utter the sentence that expresses it. But the analytic quality, or analyticity, of some propositions is by no means obvious.

"All brothers are brothers" is *explicitly* analytic: the repetition is right there before us in the words themselves. But "All brothers are males" is, as it stands, not analytic at all: one must define "brother" and substitute a specific definition for the word in order to make it so. After all, the noise "brother" could have been used to mean anything, and it is only when used to mean what we mean by it in common usage—male sibling—that is, male offspring of the same parent—that we get an analytic proposition out of it, by substituting the definition for the defined term: thus we get "All male siblings are male," which is explicitly analytic. Similarly, "A yard is three feet" becomes analytic when we substitute for the word "yard" its definition, "three feet," and thus get "Three feet is three feet." In the latter case we have a complete definition, which results in "A is A"; in the former case we have a statement of a defining characteristic, which results in "AB is A"; but in both cases the proposition is analytic.

If these examples too seem obvious, it is only because the definitions of the words are so simple and clear to us. "Bachelors are unmarried" is similarly simple and clear, for being unmarried is a defining characteristic of being a bachelor. "All matter occupies space" will doubtless not bother us very long, for we soon reflect that we wouldn't call anything matter unless it occupied space—that is, occupancy of space is a defining characteristic of matter. But in other cases it is not so simple: "The best players are the ones who win the most games" is more troublesome: whether we call it analytic or not depends on what characteristics must be possessed by those whom we call "the best players." If we define "best players" as those with the highest winning record, the resulting proposition is analytic; but if we do not—for example, if a player does not win as often as another but is counted better because of his superior skill or style—then it is not analytic. Whether it is analytic or not depends on the definitions of the terms it contains; and if we are not clear about the definitions (as often happens, for most words often have no clear-cut definition in common usage), then we cannot be clear about whether the proposition is analytic either.

Nor should we always go by the way a sentence looks. "Blackbirds are black birds" appears to be analytic but is not; it is not a defining characteristic of the class of birds we call blackbirds that they must be black: an albino blackbird would still be a blackbird. Most of the members of the species are black, hence the name "blackbird," but this should not lead us into assuming that the characteristic that gives the species its name is always a defining characteristic. Again, "Business is business" looks like a simple "A is A"; but, as used on most occasions, its meaning is something like "In business, anything goes," and the proposition expressed by *that* sentence is not at all analytic. On the other hand, "If you study this chapter long enough, you'll understand it" doesn't appear to be analytic at all, but let us look again: How long is long *enough*? Suppose you read the chapter 50 times and still don't understand it, and someone says to you, "That only shows that you haven't read it long *enough*." We now begin to suspect that he is using "long enough" to mean "till you understand it." And if this is its meaning, it *is* analytic: "If you read it till you understand it, you'll understand it." (If, after you read it 50 times, he said, "I guess I was wrong—you've read it long enough and you still don't understand it," then he would *not* be using the sentence to express an analytic proposition.)

Precisely what makes a proposition analytic? Numerous definitions of "analytic" have been advanced, of which we shall mention the two principal ones. (Each of them has variations.) The designation of the term "analytic" is different in these two definitions, though the denotation of the term is very nearly the same—that is to say, a proposition that is analytic by one definition will also be by the other, with certain exceptions, which we shall notice in due course.

1. An analytic statement is a statement whose negation is self-contradictory. If someone said, "Black is not black," he would be contradicting himself; he would be saying in effect that A is not A. If you deny a true analytic proposition, you always get a self-contradictory proposition. (A *false* analytic proposition would be a *self-contradictory* proposition. But it is usual to describe such propositions simply as "self-contradictory," leaving falsehood to characterize nonanalytic propositions, and to describe *true* analytic propositions simply as "analytic.") Similarly, "A yard is not three feet" becomes, by substitution, "Three feet is not three feet," which is self-contradictory. But if you negate "Snow is white"—assuming that whiteness is not a defining characteristic of snow—you get "Snow is not white," which, though false, is not self-contradictory.

Synthetic propositions are propositions that are not analytic. Thus we get:

Analytic propositions ("Snow is snow")	True synthetic propositions ("Snow is white")
Negative: self-contradictory propositions ("Snow is not snow")	Negative: false synthetic propositions ("Snow is not white")

2. An analytic proposition is one whose truth can be determined solely by an analysis of the meaning of the words in the sentence expressing it. You do not have to investigate anything in the world apart from language to discover whether or not the proposition is true. If you analyze the meaning of "father" (male parent), you know that "Fathers are male" is true; you know it from analyzing the sentence itself, not from observation of the way the world is. Knowing the meanings of the words is all that you need in order to determine the truth of the proposition.

The first definition describes a property of propositions themselves, and the second definition tells us how we discover them to be true. But for most purposes it will not matter which definition we choose.

.   .   .

Possibility

We have just been considering kinds of propositions; we shall now consider situations or *states-of-affairs*. But there is a close connection between them. A state-of-affairs is said to be *logically possible* whenever the *proposition* that this state-of-affairs exists is not self-contradictory, and logically *im*possible when the proposition *is* self-contradictory.

It is logically impossible for there to be a square circle. If we mean what is conventionally meant in English by the words "square" and "circle," the definitions of the two words contradict each other. A circle is, by definition, something which (among other things) is not four-sided; hence, saying that a circle is square would be saying that something not four-sided is four-sided, which of course is self-contradictory. It is logically impossible for there ever to be a square circle: if it's a circle it can't be square, and if it's square it can't be a circle. The "can't" here is a *logical* "can't," meaning that it is *logically* impossible for it to be so.

On the other hand, it is logically possible for you to jump 10,000 feet into the air by your own unaided muscular power. If you said that you had done so, you would be stating a false synthetic proposition, but not a self-contradictory one. There is nothing self-contradictory about "I jumped ten thousand feet into the air." The state of affairs described by the proposition is *logically* possible.

If this seems strange, it is because we seldom use this sense of "possibility," but another, the *empirical*. A state of affairs is empirically possible when it is not contrary to laws of nature. Thus, it is empirically, not logically, impossible for you to jump 10,000 feet in the air, or to jump out of a tenth-story window and not go downward.

As far as we know, the states-of-affairs expressed by laws of nature do not change; hence what is empirically possible at one time is empirically possible at any other time. What we *thought* a hundred years ago to be empirically impossible may have turned out to be empirically possible after all; but in that case we were simply mistaken about the laws of nature. At one time no one suspected that phenomena such as radioactivity and atomic fission were empirically possible, but they were wrong. Nature works in ways with which even now we are far from completely acquainted, which only means that more things are empirically possible than we now know.

What does change from one age to another is *technical* possibility. Technical possibility involves not merely the laws of nature but our ability to make use of these laws to produce conditions which we were unable to produce before. A hundred years ago the making of jet aircraft was not technically possible, but now it is. A spaceship landing on Mars is today not a technical possibility, but a few years hence it may be. The laws of nature themselves have not changed; what has changed is our knowledge of them, which renders technically possible many things that were not technically possible, or even imagined, a few years ago.

Relation among the types of possibility. If a state of affairs is logically impossible, then it is impossible in the other senses too. For example: it is logically impossible to fall upwards, because "fall" means to go downwards; so falling upwards would be going downwards upwards, which is a self-contradiction. It is, then, logically impossible to fall upwards, and of course empirically impossible and technically impossible as well. (The definition of "fall" may, of course, change in outer-space contexts.)

But this does not work the other way around: what is technically impossible (at any given time) need not be empirically impossible at all—for example, photographing a galaxy 500 million light-years away; and what is empirically impossible need not be logically impossible—for example, light becoming stronger with increasing distance from its source. Traveling from New York to California in three minutes is not now technically possible, but who can say that there is anything empirically impossible about it? A body not subject to gravitation is (as far as we know) empirically impossible, but it is not logically impossible because there is no contradiction in asserting it. Thus we have:

Logically possible ——————   —————— Logically impossible
Empirically possible ———————   ——————— Empirically impossible
Technically possible ———————   ——————— Technically impossible

It is for the empirical sciences, such as physics, to tell us what is empirically possible. It is for the *applied*, or practical, sciences, such as engineering, to tell us what is technically possible. Our chief concern here is what is logically possible. The others are introduced here only to distinguish them from logical possibility. The question that will confront us many times in the coming pages is, "Is or is not this or that state-of-affairs logically possible?" In doing this, we must be careful not to give a premature answer of "No" by confusing logical with other types of possibility. For example, it is *logically* possible for objects to fall faster or slower depending on their color; for you to chin yourself six million times in quick succession; for a man to live to the age of a million years; for cats to give birth to pups, and dogs to give birth to kittens. As far as we now know, none of these things is empirically possible. When we say that they are logically possible, we do *not* mean that we expect them to happen, or that we think there is the remotest *empirical* possibility that they will happen; we only mean that if we asserted that they did happen, or would happen, our assertion would *not* be self-contradictory, even though it would be false.

Another way of expressing the same idea is this: what is logically impossible could not be the case in any universe; what is only empirically impossible might be the case in *some* universe, but does not happen to be the case in ours. For example, it seems to be empirically impossible for living things to exist without oxygen, nitrogen, carbon, and hydrogen. But it is logically possible that life in some form could exist without one or more of these. It is logically possible that Newton's law of gravitation might not apply to such a universe: that whereas actually "every particle of matter attracts every other particle with a force varying inversely as the square of the distance . . ." it might vary inversely as the cube of the distance, for example. Such a law would not describe the universe we live in, but the situation it describes is just as *logically* possible as the one in our present universe. A universe in which the attraction varied inversely as the cube of the distance is logically possible; it does not happen to be actual. On the other hand, a square circle, or a male aunt, or *falling* upwards, could not occur in any universe; the states-of-affairs asserted are logically impossible, since they involve contradictions; there can be nothing for such expressions as "square circle" to refer to. We shall have abundant occasion in the coming pages to refer to states-of-affairs in (logically) possible universes which are not actual.

Conceivability. If some state-of-affairs is logically possible, is this the same as its being conceivable? It might easily seem so: "It's logically possible for you to jump out of a tenth-story window and not go downward" would then be equivalent to "It's *conceivable* that you might jump out of a tenth-story window and not go downward" (even though of course we don't expect it to happen). Of course we *can* define "conceivable" so that it means the same as "logically possible";

this is indeed one of the most common usages the word "conceivable" has in philosophy.

"Conceivable" is ambiguous, however. It may also mean "imaginable," and in this sense it is *not* equivalent to "logically possible." A thousand-sided polygon is surely logically possible; I cannot imagine one (form the image of one); what I am tempted to call my mental image of a polygon with 1,000 sides is no different from that of a polygon with 999 sides, but I would not want to deny categorically that somebody, somewhere, can form the image of a thousand-sided polygon. People's powers of imagination vary. What is imaginable depends on who is doing the imagining. You may be able to imagine things that I cannot. What is logically possible does not have this variability. Whether I can imagine it or not, a thousand-sided polygon, an animal that's a cross between walrus and a wasp, and a color different from any we have ever seen, are *all logically possible*; we need not stop to ask whether we can *imagine* them. Something can be logically possible and yet unimaginable (by you or by me, or even by everybody) because of the limitation of our powers of imagination.

On the other hand, if a state-of-affairs is really logically *im*possible, it is not imaginable by anybody: no one can imagine a tower that is both 100 and 150 feet high, or a circle that is square. If someone says he *can* form the image of a square circle, he is probably forming the image of a square, then of a circle, then of a square in rapid succession. But he can hardly imagine a figure that is both circular and not circular. (If he still says he can, let him draw one on the blackboard.)

"Conceivable" is used in other senses as well. Whether or not a certain state-of-affairs is conceivable will then depend on the sense of "conceivable" which is being employed at the time. But until the sense is clearly stated, one should not be satisfied with the simple equation "The logically possible = the conceivable."

Examples. Let us now run through a few examples of logical possibility and impossibility. There is an almost ineradicable tendency at the start to confuse logical impossibility with empirical impossibility, which only time and numerous examples can dispel; yet it is essential that it be dispelled.

1. Is it logically possible for a solid iron bar to float on water? Of course it is. There is no contradiction at all in it. It is a law of physics that objects with a greater specific gravity than water (i.e., weighing more than an equal volume of water) do not float on water (with certain exceptions such as the phenomenon of "surface tension"). There is no *logical necessity* about this—that is to say, it is logically possible for it to be otherwise. You can even imagine it now (remember, if you *can* really imagine it, it is logically possible, but if you can't, it may only mean that your powers of imagination are limited): you

take a piece of iron (a chemist has verified that it really is iron), you weigh it, then you plunge it into a vessel of water, and behold, it floats. You have also verified that it is a solid iron bar, not hollow inside with large air-filled spaces like a battleship; indeed, you have weighed it and measured it so as to make sure that its weight is really greater than that of an equal volume of water. This is a logically possible state-of-affairs; it does not actually occur, but there is nothing *logically* impossible about it.

2. Is it logically possible to remember something that never happened? As in so many cases, the answer is "Yes" in one sense and "No" in another, depending on the sense of the word "remember" that is employed. It may be used in a "weak" sense, so that you remember something whenever you have "that recollective feeling" about it, regardless of whether it really happened or not. In this sense, clearly, people often remember many events which, as it turns out, never really happened at all.

Here someone might object, "Then you didn't *really* remember it, you only thought you did!" This person is using "remember" in the "strong" sense, in which remembering involves not only "having a feeling of recollection" but also that the event about which you have this feeling really did occur. If it didn't really occur, then "you don't really remember it, you only *think* you did." In this sense, it is a defining characteristic of "(really) remembering" that the event actually occurred; therefore, in this sense it is logically impossible to remember something that never happened.

3. Is it logically possible for a cat to give birth to pups? Biologically impossible, doubtless (and hence empirically impossible), but logically possible. It is a fact of nature that like produces like, but there is no logical necessity about this.

"But isn't anything that a cat gives birth to, by definition, a cat?" You need only think this through for a moment to see that it is false. Suppose that what the cat gave birth to barked, wagged its tail, had all the contours of a dog, exhibited typical dog-behavior, and was unhesitatingly identified by everybody as a dog. Would you still call it a cat? In such a situation no one would say that the offspring was a cat —rather, they would be astounded by the unusual phenomenon that a cat had produced, not another cat, but a dog.

"But if a pup was the offspring, the mother must not have been a cat!" Not even if it looked like one, meowed, purred, and had all the other characteristics which cause us to call it a cat? Would you have hesitated to call it a cat *before* the strange birth took place? Must you wait to see what the creature's offspring look like (if it has any) before being able to identify it as a cat? Once again, cats are distinguished from dogs and other creatures . . . by their general appearance, and it is logically possible for something with all the feline appearances to give birth to something with all the canine appearances. That nature does not operate in this way, that like produces like, is fact of nature, not a logical necessity.

. . .

THE A PRIORI

We have distinguished two kinds of propositions, analytic and synthetic. We must now turn to another important way of classifying propositions, which may seem at first to be the analytic-synthetic distinction over again, but is not. Let us try to forget the distinction between analytic and synthetic, for these first few pages, and start afresh with a different way of classifying propositions, which may turn out to be even more important. There are some propositions that, when we reflect on them, seem to be *necessarily* true—they could not possibly be false—and others that seem to be *necessarily* false, and could not possibly be true. For example, "One can't be in two different places at the same time," "Whatever has shape has size," and "If one event precedes a second event and the second precedes the third, then the first precedes the third," we are tempted to say, *must* be true —we need not even bother to examine whether they are, for they are necessarily true (they would be true in all possible worlds). These we call *necessary* truths, and their negations would be necessarily false. By contrast, there are other propositions which are true, but "just happen to be true"—there is no necessity about them: "There are six people in this room," "Some dogs are white," "People can't run as fast as jackrabbits." These are only *contingently* true—their truth is contingent on what the universe happens to be like. Their negations would be contingently false. All these we call *contingent* propositions.

What is it that makes necessary truths necessary? It is that they are knowable *a priori*; indeed, the terms "necessary truth" and "truth knowable a priori" are interchangeable expressions. They are knowable a priori because they necessarily hold true for all cases—today, tomorrow, or a million years from now. If someone is in New York, we do not need to investigate further to discover whether he is also in California. If we know that something is red, we do not have to investigate further to discover whether it is colored. Any statement that we do have to test to see whether it holds for future cases is a contingent statement, knowable only *a posteriori*. (Any true statement whose truth cannot be known a priori is knowable, if at all, only a posteriori.) What makes a statement a priori—and hence necessary —is how we come to know it, not the structure of the statement itself, as with analytic statements. An a priori statement—that is, one whose truth is knowable a priori—needs no verification by further experience: we can know that it holds true, everywhere and always, without investigating all the various cases to which it applies.

What of statements such as "Water boils at 212° F. (at sea-level pressure)," "Water flows downhill," "All white tomcats with blue eyes are deaf," "All solid objects whose weight per unit of volume exceeds that of a liquid will sink in that liquid," and so on? These express uniformities of nature, which we shall examine more closely . . . when we consider laws of nature. Our present question is: Are these statements necessarily true? At first, we may be inclined to think that they are: we have become so familiar with these uniformities that we have come to take them for granted. But let us reflect: they are all statements of uniformities to be found in nature; have we any guarantee that a uniformity that held yesterday and today will continue to hold tomorrow and forever after? Don't we have to observe nature again tomorrow to see whether it behaves as it did today? Many statements have been made expressing what were thought to be uniformities of nature that on subsequent investigation turned out not to be so: the alleged uniformity had exceptions, or was true only with qualifications, etc. The test of further experience showed that it did not hold true as it was originally stated. May the same not be true of some of those we now believe to state genuine uniformities? But if we have to observe nature further to discover whether the uniformity continues to hold, then the statement in question is contingent, not necessary.

There are several common misunderstandings of the a priori against which we should guard ourselves at the outset.

1. If a man undermined the foundations of his house, wouldn't he know a priori that the house would collapse? No, not in the sense philosophers employ when they speak of a priori knowledge. At best it can be called *relatively* a priori knowledge, or knowledge *relative to* a certain body of statements *which are not themselves knowable* a priori. Relative to certain general gravitational and architectural principles—that is, assuming them to hold in all cases—a man would know that his house would collapse if he uprooted its foundations. Relative to the principle that all stones fall, he would know a priori that the stone he now holds in his hand will fall if he lets go of it. But the principles on which he rests this knowledge are not themselves knowable a priori: only by means of observation of the world around us do we know that stones fall when we let go of them, and that houses depend on what is below them for support. We are concerned here not with relatively but with absolutely a priori knowledge: that which we can know a priori, not on the basis of other pieces of knowledge which are a posteriori, but on the basis of no a posteriori knowledge whatever—prior to all experience of the world.

2. This last phrase leads us to a second distinction. It is clear that *chronologically* nobody knows anything prior to all experience. Your experience began even before you were born—a time when you can hardly be said to have *known* anything. Surely all knowledge comes posterior to experience, in the sense that if you had experienced nothing there would be nothing you could know. So how could anyone seriously suggest that anything can be known absolutely a priori?

But in calling it a priori we do not mean that a person's knowledge of it occurred prior in time to all his experiences. In calling it a priori we are not referring to the time of origin at all. We are referring not to the way of coming by the piece of knowledge in question but to the way in which it must be *verified.* For example, you can know a priori that thunder is thunder, but not that thunder follows lightning. Even in the case of "Thunder is thunder" you can hardly be said to have known this before you had any experiences, before you knew what thunder was and knew what word was used to refer to it. It was not a priori in *that* sense; but what *is* true is that in the case of "Thunder is thunder" *you do not have to await the verdict of experience to find out whether the statement always holds true.* You do not have to investigate any instance of thunder to see whether it is really thunder. (Indeed, what would it be like to do this?) On the other hand, you cannot safely say that thunder follows lightning without experiencing instances of this relationship. There lies the difference: not in the amount of experience required prior to uttering the statement but in the process required to ascertain whether it is true. When a statement is known to be true a priori, one does not need to experience any further instances of the classes of things in question in order to know that the statement always holds.

Are there synthetic necessary statements? At this point one might remark: "Of course there are necessary statements, knowable a priori —plenty of them. But they are all analytic statements or tautologies; the denial of any of them would result in a self-contradiction. In other words, none of them is *synthetic.* A is A, cats are cats, you can't be both here and not here at the same time, cats are mammals (since being a mammal is one of the defining characteristics of being a cat), and so on. I don't deny that all these statements are necessary, and it would be foolish indeed to feel that you had to verify them by observing the world. The reason that we don't have to test them by observation of the world is simply that they are empty of any factual content: they are all analytic. This is quite obvious in the examples just given, but it holds also of not-so-obvious cases like 'Everything that has shape has size.' This statement, of course, is necessarily true, and we don't have to go around testing things of various shapes to see whether they all have size. But the reason for this is that the statement is really analytic: just analyze the concepts of shape and size. Whether something is two-dimensional like a square or three-dimensional like a cube, its shape is only the total configuration of the *boundary* of its spatial extension, and its size is only the *amount* of this spatial extension. You can't have an amount of something (at least if it's of finite size) without its coming to an end somewhere, and wherever it comes to an end is its boundary. The two concepts are logically interconnected. A mathematical point, of course, has no shape, but then, it has no size either—although the little dot we write on paper to represent a point has both shape and size. So I agree that the statement is necessarily true, but only because it's analytic."

It does, indeed, seem to be true, thus far, that all the cases of necessary statements (knowable a priori) are analytic. They are, at any rate, the most obvious instances of a priori statements. But are they the only ones? Are there any a priori statements that are also synthetic—necessarily true yet not analytic?

This is one of the most controversial problems in the history of modern philosophy. Let us pause for a moment to grasp its full impact. Early in this chapter, we distinguished between analytic and synthetic statements, and later we distinguished truths knowable a priori from those knowable only a posteriori. What is the relation between these two distinctions?

A priori (necessary)	A posteriori (contingent)
Analytic	Synthetic

Most, at any rate, of the synthetic statements we hear and utter are contingent: "The desk is brown," "There are six cars in the driveway," "I feel drowsy," "1964 was a presidential election year in the United States," "Water boils at 212° F.," and so on endlessly—all of these are synthetic statements, none of them knowable a priori. Such are the vast majority of statements uttered in daily discourse. On the other hand, we have statements that we seldom have occasion to utter but that are nevertheless true, and necessarily true, such as "If you're here, you're here," "Squares are rectangles," "Quadrupeds have four legs," "Either grass is green or grass is not green," and so on—but they are all analytic. The tantalizing question is: Can we break these pairs? Are there some statements that are *not* analytic, that convey genuine information about reality, that are yet knowable a priori, so that we can know them to hold true of the world for all cases without awaiting the verdict of experience to assure us that they always hold true?

It will seem to many persons that this is like trying to eat one's cake and have it too. If a statement gives genuine information *about* the world, how can one know that it is true except by observation *of* the world? And if one doesn't have to do this, but can know a priori that it always holds true, how can it be anything other than analytic? How can one have the advantages of both sides at once? Wouldn't one be trying to run with the hare and hunt with the hounds?

Those who declare that there are no synthetic a priori truths are called *empiricists*. For every alleged instance of a synthetic a priori truth, they contend that the statement is either (1) synthetic but not a priori or (2) a priori but not synthetic: there are no truths that are both synthetic *and* a priori. On the other hand, those who declare that there are synthetic a priori truths are called *rationalists*. Rationalists may not all agree on which truths are synthetic and a priori, but anyone who holds there is even *one* synthetic a priori truth is a rationalist, for he denies the empiricist claim that there are none.

Here are some propositions that rationalists have held to be synthetic a priori truths:

> 2 plus 2 equals 4.
> Every event has a cause.
> Everything that is colored is extended. (Extended = spread out in space.)
> Everything that has volume has shape.
> All cubes have 12 edges.
> Parallel lines never meet.
> A straight line is the shortest distance between two points.
> If A precedes B and B precedes C, then A precedes C.
> A whole is the sum of its parts.
> All sounds have pitch, volume, and timbre.
> An object cannot be in two different places at the same time.
> An object cannot have two different colors at the same place at the same time.
> Time proceeds forward, never backward.
> Space is three-dimensional.

The empiricist holds that none of these propositions, nor any other alleged synthetic a priori truths, are synthetic a priori: if a priori, they turn out to be analytic, and if synthetic, they turn out not to be a priori. But the rationalist holds (in one form of rationalism—we shall come across another form shortly) that some of them—or at any rate some propositions, even if not those above—are both synthetic and a priori.

· · ·

A priori assumptions. It is, of course, a priori *knowledge* that we are here concerned with, propositions whose *truth* can be known without further recourse to experience. This is to be distinguished sharply from a priori *assumptions*, which are propositions that a person assumes to be true so staunchly that he will not admit that they can be refuted or even doubted, even though such a refutation, or grounds for doubt, may be at hand. A patient said to his physician, "Doctor, I'm dead." The doctor tried in vain to convince him otherwise and finally said, "Well, dead men don't bleed, do they?" "No." "I am now going to prick you with a pin." The doctor did so, and the patient bled. The patient said, "Doctor, I was wrong—dead men *do* bleed." The patient was so convinced that he was dead that he would accept no contrary evidence, not even the fact that he bled. That he was dead was in the case of this patient an a priori assumption.

Most people entertain many a priori assumptions. They are usually of more interest to the person's psychiatrist than to a philosopher: philosophers are concerned with the rational grounds of belief, not with whether a certain person believes this or that and why. The list of propositions that various people assume a priori to be true would be as long as the list of groundless prejudices.

An a priori assumption may, of course, be true; but it is not knowledge, because the person does not hold it on the basis of sufficient evidence. Those who refused to look through Galileo's telescope at the moons of Jupiter were assuming a priori that no such thing existed, and would accept no evidence to the contrary. In this case their assumption was false, as was the assumption of most people in ancient times that the earth was flat. But a person who today assumes that the earth is round without having evidence for it, but would refuse to accept any evidence against it even if such evidence did turn up, would be assuming "The earth is round" a priori, although in this case the assumption would be true.

Arithmetic

If we want to discover truths that are necessary yet not analytic, the most obvious candidates for this position would seem to lie in the realm of mathematics. Are not mathematical truths eternal and unchangeable? And are they not true necessarily? And do they not give us genuine information about reality? Consider a simple statement in arithmetic, such as $2 + 2 = 4$. Aren't we quite certain that this is true, that it always will be true, and that it always *must* be true? How could it be false on Mars or on the farthest star in the universe? We may not know anything about what conditions exist in these far places, but can't we be sure at any rate that if there are two things and then two more things there, then there are four things? And can't we be just as sure that this was true a million years ago or will be true a million years from now as that it is true today? Surely such a proposition is not like "All crows are black," which you couldn't really know to be true until you had examined all the crows there are. Isn't it a necessary truth, knowable a priori, and at the same time one that gives genuine information about the world, unlike "Black cats are black"?

It has sometimes been held that such statements as "2 + 2 = 4" are non-analytic (synthetic) but also non-necessary (contingent)—in short, that they are really no different from "All crows are black" or "Water boils at 212° under standard conditions." No exceptions to these last two statements have ever been found, and similarly no exceptions to the statements of arithmetic have ever been found: we have never come across any case in which two things plus two things did not equal four things. The mathematical laws are more general than are the laws of physics and chemistry and biology, for they apply to everything—not only to physical things but to thoughts, images, feelings, and to everything one could possibly think of: it is true of absolutely everything that two of it and two more of it make four of it. The mathematical laws are also better established than even the laws of the physical sciences. For thousands of years before anything was known of the laws of physical science, people had found that statements such as "2 and 2 makes 4" always hold true; it had been found to be true countless times, without one single negative instance. Nevertheless, according to this view, the laws of the physical sciences and those of arithmetic are of the same fundamental kind: they are both synthetic and contingent. Both can be known to be true only by observation of the world, and both can be falsified by observation of the world. Just as it is logically possible that we might find exceptions to well-established laws of physical science (it is logically possible that we might find water when heated turning into ice instead of boiling), so it is also logically possible that we might find exceptions to the laws of arithmetic (2 plus 2 equaling 5, for example). We never have, of course, in spite of countless observed cases throughout human history, and that is why we are so sure that these laws always hold true. But if we are more certain of "2 plus 2 equals 4" than we are of the proposition about water and crows, it is only because human beings have had evidence to support the arithmetical propositions many times a day for thousands of years, while our experience of crows is more limited and intermittent.

Virtually no one today holds this interpretation of arithmetical statements. In whatever ways people may differ about arithmetical statements, they all agree that they are necessary (necessarily true) and knowable a priori, unlike the statements in the physical sciences. There might be white crows on Mars, or even on the earth; there might be vast reaches of the universe in which physical laws we believe in now do not hold; but always and everywhere and forever, 2 plus 2 equals 4. There may somewhere exist creatures so different from ourselves that we cannot even imagine them; the biological laws that would describe their function and operation might be far different from those in our biology textbooks; but this much is sure, if there are two of such organisms, and then two more, then there are four. Could anything be more certain than this? And do we not know it a priori? Do we really have to wait for further observation to decide the matter for future instances? Is there any danger whatsoever that the next time we have two and then two more we may *not* have four? As we shall see in the coming pages, there is no such danger, since there is no way this arithmetical proposition can be refuted.

But whether or not such propositions are necessary, let us ask whether they are analytic or synthetic. They seem at first glance to be synthetic: "2 plus 2 equals 4" does not seem to be at all like "Black cats are black" or "Tigers are tigers" or even like "Either snow is white or snow is not white." Arithmetical statements seem to give us knowledge of things in a way that these other statements do not. We can figure out sums in arithmetic, for example: we add, subtract, multiply, and divide large numbers, and the outcome gives us new information; we know something we didn't know before. And we can certainly think of the numbers involved in an addition without knowing what their sum is: if we did know, we wouldn't have to figure it out.

In spite of all this, it is customary today to hold that arithmetical propositions are analytic. What does "4" mean, we might ask, but "2 + 2"? And what does "2" mean but "1 and 1"? When we say "2 + 2 = 4," we are saying merely that "1 + 1 + 1 + 1" equals "1 + 1 + 1 + 1, which is just as analytic as "Black is black." The reason we can be so sure— and are *entitled* to be so sure—that these propositions necessarily hold true and always will, is simply that they are analytic.

But how can this possibly be true, in virtue of the fact that we do get new information from these propositions? Let us consider several objections to the view that arithmetical propositions are synthetic, and then see how the proponents of the objections would try to answer them:

1. "I can think of 2 and 2 without thinking of 4." Probably I can, or at any rate I could in childhood before I learned that 2 and 2 makes 4. So can I think of the sum of 7 and 5 without thinking of 12, as Kant pointed out. But the statement that 7 and 5 makes 12 is not a law of psychology: it does not state that when I think of this I also think of that; it states that this *is* that, whether I think of the two together or not. I can think "He is my brother" without thinking "He is my male sibling," but the two have the same meaning anyway, and "He is my brother but not my male sibling" is self-contradictory whether I know it or not. It is the equivalence of one number with another set of numbers that we are talking about, not what our psychological processes are like.

2. "But even if I grant that '2 + 2 = 4' is analytic, what about more

complex calculations like '40694 plus 27593 equals 68287'? Surely the
principle of the two is the same, and if the first is analytic, so is the
second. Yet how can the second be analytic, when it requires us to
figure out whether it is even true, and when we can make mistakes in
addition besides?"

The principle of the two *is* the same (it would be replied): they are
both analytic. It would take a long time to write out the second into a
series of 1 + 1 + 1's, but if we did so we would find that it is the
"2 + 2 = 4" story all over again, only with more 1's. And if we made
a mistake in addition, our statement that the two figures added together equals that sum would be self-contradictory: we would be
stating that 1 + 1 + 1 . . . does not equal 1 + 1 + 1 . . . .

The sum in the second case is, of course, not so obvious as it is in
the case of 2 plus 2. But again, this makes no difference. To be analytic it is not required that it be obvious. What is obvious to one person
is not obvious to another, and what is obvious to a person at one time
may not be at another time. What may not be obvious to you and me
may well be obvious to a mathematical genius. Obviousness is a psychological characteristic that is in no way involved in the conception
of being analytic. Propositions of arithmetic are analytic because their
denial is self-contradictory, whether the self-contradictoriness is immediately obvious or not. To a being with very great mathematical
powers the sum of very large numbers would be as obvious as
"2 + 2 = 4" is to us.

3. "But the *meaning* of the two is not the same: 40694 and 27593
are not a part of the meaning of '68287.' When you ask me what I
mean by this number, I don't give the other two—or any of the other
sets of numbers that when added together would yield it. So how
can the statement be analytic if the one is not all or even a part of the
meaning of the other?"

But it doesn't need to be a part of the meaning, in the sense of
what we mean when we say it. A may be B although "B" may not be
what we mean when we say "A." 68287 may not be what we mean by
40694 and 27493, but it is the sum of those two numbers just the same.
It is still a necessary truth, and the denial of it would still be self-
contradictory.

4. "But isn't even such a simple statement as '2 plus 2 equals 4' a
generalization from experience? Don't we *learn* its truth from experience? And isn't it based on instances? I first learn about 2 and 2
houses, then about 2 and 2 apples, and so on. How is its being learned
from experience compatible with its being analytic?"

Of course I learn that 2 and 2 makes 4, and probably we all learned
it as children, using examples such as houses and apples. But what is it
that we learned? Is it anything about apples and houses? No, it is

simply that 2 and 2 when added together makes 4; all the business about houses and apples was just window-dressing. What we learned was that the symbol "4" is equivalent in meaning to the symbol "2 and 2"—that *these two expressions can be used interchangeably*.

We do indeed learn the meanings of words through experience—how else? But this does not have anything to do with whether the propositions in which they occur are analytic. What makes them analytic is whether or not their negation is self-contradictory. To say that 2 and 2 does *not* make 4 would be to say that 1 and 1 and 1 and 1 does not make 1 and 1 and 1 and 1, which is self-contradictory.

When we put two pennies into our new piggy bank, and later two more pennies, we learned to say that we had put in four pennies, simply because "putting 4 pennies in" means the same as "putting 2 pennies and 2 pennies in." We learned to say it as a result of our experience—our experience of learning language—but *what* we said was a necessary truth, and analytic. But we *also* learned to predict that if we should open the bank later we would find four pennies in it. In this case what we learned was not an arithmetical truth but a truth about the world that we might call the *conservation of pennies*; and, unlike "2 plus 2 equals 4," this proposition might have turned out to be false without contradiction. If it had turned out to be false, we could still agree that "2 and 2 makes 4" is an analytic truth following from the definition of what we mean by "2," "4," "plus," and "equals."

This leads us directly into the next, and very important, objection.

5. "Far from being analytic, the propositions of arithmetic are not even true—at least not in all cases. Two and two doesn't always make four. For example, if you add two quarts of water to two quarts of alcohol, you ought (if the arithmetical proposition is true) to get four quarts—but you don't; you get a little less, owing to the inter-penetration of molecules of the two substances. If you put together two lions and two lambs, and turn your back for a moment, you will have not four things, but only two—two lions. When two amoebas subdivide, they become four—what was two is now four! How can arithmetical propositions be necessary at all, much less analytic, if they aren't even true in all cases—when reality often shows them to be false?"

But this objection is the result of a total misunderstanding. When we say that 2 plus 2 equals 4, we do not deny for a moment that what *was* two can *become* four (the amoebas), or that you can have four things at one time and have only two things at a later time (the lions and the lambs). It says only that *if* you have two and two, then at that moment you have four. Arithmetic does not tell you anything about natural processes—how two things can become four things, or how four things can be reduced to two things. Arithmetic doesn't even tell you that there are four of anything in the world at all, or even that there *is* a world in which such distinctions can be made. It says only that *if* there are two, and then two more, *then* there must be four: that *to say there are two plus two and to say that there are four is to say the same thing.* When there are two lions and two lambs, then there are four things; when there are only two lions, then there are only two—that is, one plus one—things. If two things gave rise to a million things, this would not violate "2 and 2 equals 4" or any other proposition of arithmetic. Two rabbits soon become a million rabbits; and if two things exploded into a million things, or into nothing at all, this would not refute any law of arithmetic. What turns into what, what becomes what, how one thing changes into another—all these are matters for the physical sciences to investigate; these are all a part of what happens in the world, and propositions about these things are all synthetic and contingent. But the propositions of arithmetic say nothing whatever about the changes that go on in nature; they say nothing at all about the kind of a world we live in, nor would they be changed in the slightest if the world were quite different from what it is, for the laws of arithmetic do not describe what the world is like. Arithmetic doesn't even tell you that the number 4 applies to anything in the world, but only that *if* it applies, then "2 plus 2" also applies, because the two symbols mean the same thing.

Now consider the example of the water and the alcohol. It is a proposition in chemistry, not in arithmetic: it tells you what happens when you do something to something else. The formulation of the example, in fact, is quite misleading: we speak of "adding" water to alcohol. But adding is an arithmetical process: it is an operation we perform with numbers, not with physical things. Strictly speaking, we do not *add* water to alcohol; we *pour* some water into a vessel of alcohol. (Or if you do want to call it adding, it is adding in a very different sense from the one we use in arithmetic.) You have to discover what happens when you pour something into something else by observation of the world. If you pour water into gasoline, you get no mixture at all. If you pour water onto pure sodium, you get an explosion, with neither water nor sodium left at the end of it. What happens when you do something to something else is a matter for the physical sciences to investigate, but nothing thus discovered can refute any law of arithmetic, since they have nothing whatever to do with arithmetic.

"But arithmetical laws are not just about combinations of symbols: they are very general statements about reality. How else could the laws of arithmetic *apply to the world?* Yet they do. It is not merely true that 2 and 2 is 4; it is also true that 2 trees and 2 trees makes 4 trees. Laws of arithmetic have to do with quantities, but quantities of anything—trees and everything else. It is because they are so general that they seem to be about nothing—but they are about things, only *all* things."

Suppose you are counting trees: 2 trees to your left, 2 trees to your right, but every time you tried to count them all together you got 5 as your result instead of 4. What would we say if this kept on happening? Would it refute any of the laws of arithmetic? Would textbooks of arithmetic have to be revised, saying "Sometimes 2 and 2 makes 5"? Not at all; "2 and 2 makes 4" would remain true *no matter what happened in the counting process.* If you kept on getting 5 trees as a result, you might decide that you were systematically miscounting; more probably you would decide that in the very act of counting, another tree was created, or just popped into existence. But the one thing you would *not* say is that 2 and 2 sometimes makes 5. If you found an additional tree every time you tried to count them all together, you would say that 2 trees plus 2 trees plus the 1 tree that seems to pop into existence when you count, together makes 5 trees. So the arithmetical law would not be refuted after all.

"Granted that it wouldn't, I still insist that it's a necessary truth. Not merely '2 plus 2 equals 4'—that is only a generalization of '2 trees and 2 trees makes 4 trees,' '2 apples and 2 apples makes 4 apples,' etc. The arithmetical law says that two of *anything* and two more *of anything* makes four, and this is a law about reality, not about the manipulation of symbols. The law that 2 and 2 makes 4 *does* hold true of apples, as of everything else; it holds true *of reality*."

"I think you are confusing two different things. It's easy to see that '2 plus 2 equals 4' as a proposition of pure arithmetic simply entitles you to use '4' equivalently with '2 plus 2.' It's easy to see that 'If you add 2 quarts to 2 quarts (pour into, that is), you get almost 4 quarts' is not a proposition of arithmetic at all. But if you say '2 apples and 2 apples makes 4 apples,' it isn't clear which side of the fence this statement is on. It sounds *both* like a statement of pure mathematics *and* like a statement about physical objects, apples. But no wonder, for the statement is ambiguous, and that is what I now must expose: '2 apples makes 4 apples' is a 'straddling' statement. To find out how the speaker means it, one has to ask, 'Is it of importance whether it's *apples* that are being talked about?' Suppose it were 2 cc.'s of sodium being poured into 2 cc.'s of water, would that make a difference? (1) If it's a statement of pure (unapplied) arithmetic, then it doesn't matter whether it's apples, elephants, grains of sand, thoughts about Thursday—what the statement is about is numerical quantities, and the rest is merely illustrative. Such statements are all a priori and analytic. (2) But if it *does* matter that it's apples that you're talking about, then the statement is not about arithmetic at all, and may not even be true. We are easily misled about this, because apples, unlike water and sodium, normally sit quietly side by side and don't interact with each other. So if that's what it means—that apples when put together remain apples as they were before—then it is true, but a synthetic truth about physical reality, not a truth of mathematics. It is logically possible that when they are placed together the four apples would all coalesce into one huge apple, or spawn a thousand little apples, or explode in one another's presence. What happens when you put apples together is a matter for observation of nature, not for a priori pronouncements. Any statement that is about apples in which it matters that it's apples *and not something else* is a synthetic statement, but it is also contingent. It all depends on which of these you mean. But if you just say '2 apples and 2 apples makes 4 apples' and squint a bit, forgetting about these distinctions, you may think that you have achieved the necessity of the first statement together with the synthetic character of the second, and that then, presto, you have a synthetic a priori statement on your hands. But you haven't. You have the same sentence expressing two different propositions—the one necessary and analytic, the other synthetic and contingent."

There is still another point, which would require a long and technical discussion once it was introduced, without substantially changing the outcome. Speaking of pure (not applied) mathematics, one might say:

6. "Arithmetical propositions are not analytic by themselves: they are analytic only in the context of an arithmetical *system*. If you accept Peano's postulates, you can generate all of arithmetic as a logical consequence of these postulates; but you must first accept the postulates."

Peano's postulates are as follows:

1. O is a number.
2. The successor of any number is a number.
3. No two numbers have the same successor.
4. O is not the successor of any number.
5. If P is a property such that (a) O has the property P, and (b) if a number n has P, then the successor of n has P, then every number has P.

Using three undefined terms—"number," "O," and "successor"—he was able to generate an infinite series of numbers from these axioms. The axioms yield the entire system of integers. Are the axioms themselves analytic? If they are taken as definitions and statements of defining characteristics, they are; and since any propositions deduced from analytic propositions are also analytic, the propositions of arithmetic are as analytic as before.

For the sake of accuracy, however, we must remind ourselves that the postulates can be construed (and were intended to be construed) not as propositions but as propositional forms, like the *p, q,* and *r* of our tautologies. Peano left the terms "number," "O," and "successor" uninterpreted. We might give the postulates an entirely non-arithmetical interpretation: for example, we could take "successor" to mean offspring, and "number" to mean chicken, and then by Axiom 2 we could derive the conclusion that the offspring of a chicken is a chicken—which is a synthetic statement about the world, and although it happens to be true, it is a contingent truth, not a necessary truth. The axioms become arithmetical only when the terms "number," "O," and "successor" are interpreted in accordance with customary arithmetical usage (as is done for example in Bertrand Russell and Alfred Whitehead's *Principia Mathematica* and Gottlob Frege's *Foundations of Arithmetic*). The only point that concerns us here is that when this is done, the axioms become analytic, and in consequence all arithmetical propositions deducible from these axioms are also analytic.

Geometry

But now what of geometry? When we study geometry, we find numerous propositions that strike us as being necessarily true and also synthetic. "The sum of the angles of a triangle is equal to 180°." "Two parallel lines cannot be drawn through a given point." "A straight line is the shortest distance between two points." "A cube has twelve edges." "A circle encloses the largest possible area for a given perimeter." And so on.

Not all these propositions have the same status, and we shall be able to discuss only a few of them, and only very briefly. Consider, for example, the statement about the sum of the angles of a triangle. One might well ask: "Don't you *know* that this statement is true? It may not seem obvious, but any high-school geometry student who has just studied the proof can prove it for you. And once you have the proof before you, you can no longer deny that it holds true for all cases—in other words, you can know it a priori, and you don't have to go through a separate process of measurement or observation for every triangle, the way you do for every crow that comes along to see whether it is black. But the statement is also synthetic: there is nothing in the definition of 'triangle' about 180°. So here we have a statement that is both necessary (a priori) and synthetic. Thus the rationalist is right: there is at least one synthetic necessary proposition."

What shall we say of this contention? In dealing with it we must first make some distinctions.

The statement about the sum of the angles is a *theorem* in geometry. You doubtless remember from high-school geometry that you begin with certain *axioms*, or unproved statements, together with certain *definitions* of important terms to be used in the study, and from these you begin proving various theorems by showing that they can be deduced from certain of the axioms and definitions. Once you have proved the first theorem, you can get the second by means of it plus previous axioms and definitions. We do not use all of them all of the time: we may get Theorem 50 from Axioms 1 and 3 plus Theorems 3, 13, and 42, for example.

Though you may not have known it when you studied geometry, one thing more is needed: *rules of inference.* You need some way of getting from the axioms and earlier theorems to later ones, to be sure that your deductions are valid. These are rules of logical inference, of which simple examples are "If p is true and p implies q, then q is true"; "If p implies q and q implies r, then p implies r"; "If p implies q and r implies s, and either q or s is false, then either p or r is false," and so on. These rules are used and analyzed in courses in logic, and we shall have more to say about them later in this chapter. Without rules of inference we could not get from the axioms even to the first theorem.

The theorems, including the one about the sum of the angles of a triangle, do follow logically from the other propositions prior to it in the geometrical system; that is, they are logically deducible from those earlier propositions. The actual deductions often become quite complex, but in principle they are no different from simple ones we are accustomed to making every day; for example, given "All members of the crew were drowned," and "Smith was a member of the crew," we are entitled to assert that "Smith was drowned" (if p then q, and p, therefore q). In both cases, if the premises are true then the conclusion must be true. Thus if the premises from which the theorem about the angles is deduced are true, then (assuming the deduction is valid) the theorem is true.

But are the premises true? Here, as in the case of arithmetic, we must make an important distinction, between *pure* and *applied* geometry. The geometrical system of Euclid (fl. ca. 300 B.C.), which is the one you learned in high school, does not make this distinction: the tacit assumption is that the premises are true, and if this is so and the deductions are valid, the theorems of the Euclidean system must be true. But how does one know that the axioms are true? The pure geometer does not care. He is concerned only in making sure that the complex deductions are correct, the reasoning valid. He does not care what kind of meat goes into the grinder, but only that it is thoroughly ground. He is like the accountant who checks the addition on all your bills but does not check into the correctness of the entries. Like the logician, the geometer is concerned with valid reasoning, not with the truth of propositions. It does not even matter to him whether the axioms are interpreted as statements about space, which is what they seem to be. Instead of talking about points, lines, and planes, he would just as soon talk about x, y, and z, leaving it open what the terms "x," "y," and "z" mean, so long as the system of relations between the terms remains the same. In short, he is interested in *uninterpreted* geometry, not in *interpreted* or applied geometry.

For many centuries, Euclid's was the only geometrical system that had been developed. But other geometrical systems were developed during the nineteenth century, notably those of Lobachevski and Riemann. One of the axioms of Euclid's system is that given a straight line and any point outside the line, there is only one straight line that can be drawn through that point (in the same plane as the line) that does not intersect the line; that line will be parallel to the other line, and the axiom is known as the "axiom of parallels." Once we understand this axiom, it seems to be obviously true. But no attempt to prove this axiom by means of the other ones has succeeded. (Indeed, geometers have proved it is *not* derivable from them.) In a system of geometry designed by Lobachevski, it is assumed that *more than one* straight line can be drawn through a given point yet fail to intersect the other line. And in the geometry of Riemann, it is assumed that *no* such lines can be drawn. Each of these three systems of geometry is perfectly consistent. As deductive systems, there is nothing to choose among them. The difference among them is that each begins with a somewhat different set of axioms, and for that reason they each yield somewhat different conclusions. If you start with a different set of premises, you will naturally get different conclusions, all reached by perfectly valid reasoning.

"But they can't all be true!" This objection takes us out of the realm of pure or uninterpreted geometry into that of applied or interpreted geometry. You could doubtless build a whole deductive system with such propositions as "All people are over ten feet tall" and "No one over ten feet tall is green," and arrive at utterly false conclusions by means of valid reasoning. But aren't we interested in whether the initial premises are true? Certainly the person who wants to apply geometry to the world is interested in truth—for example, surveyors, whether in America in the 20th century A.D. or in Egypt in the 20th century B.C. They were attempting, surely, to begin with true propositions, and by means of these to arrive deductively at other ones.

For example, isn't it true that the angles of a triangle equal 180°, quite apart from the fact that this proposition can be deduced from other ones in the Euclidean geometry? Isn't it true that on measuring the angles you always get 180°? So isn't the proposition, regardless of its place in a deductive system, true of the world?

"I hold that it is a necessary synthetic statement about the world. Everything that is a triangle necessarily has this property."

"As a part of a deductive system (if . . . [premises], then . . . [theorem]) it is a priori, but only because it is analytic. As a description of the world, it is synthetic all right, but not a priori."

"What? You mean we don't know a priori that the angles of a triangle will be 180°? that we have to measure it for every separate case?"

"I agree that we seem to know it in a way we don't know that all crows are black, which is always in danger of being refuted by the next case. Still, are you quite sure that we do? What would you say if you were measuring a triangular field and found that the angles always added up to 181°?"

"I would say either that there was an observational error or that the field was not really triangular."

"If you and others always got the same results, you would finally have to discount the possibility that it was an observational error. So you would say the field was not really triangular. You would not admit even the logical possibility that a triangular field could be other than 180°. So it's analytic after all, isn't it? You won't call it triangular unless it does add up to 180°."

"Well, how could it be triangular if it didn't add up to 180°?"

"It couldn't, by the Euclidean definition of 'triangle.' Adding up to 180° is not a part of the explicit *definition* of 'triangle' in Euclid's system, but it *is* logically deducible from that definition, together with other propositions in the system. We are justified, then, in saying 'if not 180°, then not triangle'; this is analytic *within the Euclidean system*. But what about the actual field out there? Suppose you kept getting this peculiar result that you could no longer put down to observational error. Then you would have to say, puzzling as it might seem at first, that Euclidean geometry does not describe our actual space—that actual space is *not Euclidean*. The deductive system is one thing, actual physical space another. Whether physical space is obliging enough to follow the simple Euclidean system, only careful observation can tell."

"But if the premises are true, and the deduction valid, the conclusion must be true. Now if the conclusion is false, and yet the deduction is valid, then . . . ."

"Then one or more of the Euclidean *premises* is false, if interpreted as description of physical reality."

Let us turn, then, to the premises of the system.

Are the premises true? We cannot answer in general, for not all of them are of the same nature. Some are definitions; for example, "A circle is a plane closed figure all the points on whose circumference are equidistant from the center" is not a true proposition about the world but a definition of "circle": it tells us under what conditions a given figure is to be called a circle. But others *seem*, at any rate, to make statements about the world. Consider, for example, "A straight line is the shortest distance between two points."

It seems intuitively obvious that a straight line must be the shortest distance between two points. Surely we know it a priori, and don't have to measure every straight line to see whether it really is the shortest distance between the two points it connects. "Obviously it's true," someone may say, "but equally obviously, it's analytic. What do we mean by the phrase 'straight line' *except* 'the shortest distance between two points'? That's what a straight line is, by definition."

But this is too easy a way with the problem. As Kant remarked, straightness is a qualitative concept and shortness a quantitative concept, and they are not identical. To have the idea of a straight line is one thing, to have the idea of the shortest distance is another; indeed, one might have the one concept without having the other. One *learns* that a straight line is the shortest distance between two points; this fact isn't already contained in the concept of what it is to be the shortest distance. The definition of "straight" contains no reference to its being the shortest distance between two points that it connects.

What, then, *is* the definition of "straight"? That is the crux of the whole problem. As with "colored," we seem to know what it means yet are unable to define it. "A straight line is a line no part of which is curved" will not help us, for, asking what a curved line is, we are told, "A curved line is a line not all of which is straight." Nor will it do to identify the quality of straightness with some physical entity, such as "A straight line is the path of a ray of light." Is this really what is meant by "straight"? Don't we understand what a straight line is before we know anything about rays of light? If rays of light travel in straight lines, isn't that a synthetic proposition rather than a definition? Isn't it logically possible that rays of light might travel in curved or jagged lines, so that one might see around corners, for example? If the world were like this, the statement would be false. In this case, however, it can hardly be a definition. It would seem that straightness is a quality we can recognize but not define; and in that case, all the statements we make about it will be synthetic, not analytic.

What alternatives, then, are open to us? We can hold that the statement is a synthetic a priori truth, with all the discomforts involved in attempting to justify it. Or we can hold that it is a contingent truth: that all straight lines are the shortest distance between two points, but that there is no logical necessity about this—that it would be logically possible for it to be otherwise. Or we can hold— and this may be somewhat surprising—that not only is it not a necessary truth, it is not even a truth at all. It is an axiom in Euclid's geometry, but it has been questioned whether space is Euclidean, the point being that Euclidean geometry gives us only an *approximate* description of actual space, which suffices for terrestrial distances but will not suffice in our measurements of the millions of light-years in vast interstellar spaces. The shortest distance on the surface of a sphere is the arc of a great circle; and perhaps owing to the "curvature" of space, the shortest distance from one place to another in space is not a straight line at all. The physics of the matter would be far too complex to enter into here, but the moral of the tale should be clear enough: applied geometry has to do with the structure and properties of actual space, and one cannot know a priori what they will be. For this, one requires empirical investigation (observation and measurement). As the starting point of a deductive system, Euclid's axiom is unexceptionable; but as a true description of the universe, it is subject to all the qualifications and all the uncertainty that attends any proposition purporting to describe the universe: it can always be upset by discoveries (embodied in a posteriori propositions) about the way the universe actually is.

Thus far, it would seem, geometry presents no satisfactory recruiting-ground for synthetic a priori propositions. A given proposition within a deductive system (including a system of geometry) is analytic in relation to the premises $p, q, r \ldots$ from which it is deduced: that is, "If $p, q, r \ldots$ then x" is analytic, and it would be self-contradictory to deny it if the reasoning is valid. But as propositions *about reality* (applied geometry), they are synthetic all right, but thus far, at any rate, they do not seem to be knowable a priori. The statements of applied Euclidean geometry, which seemed a priori, turn out to be a posteriori, and many of them not even true.

The distinction between pure and applied geometry appears to have put an end to the search for synthetic a priori propositions in geometry: the sense in which such a proposition is a priori is not the sense in which it is synthetic, and in the sense in which it is synthetic it is not a priori.

This, however, is not the end of the matter. The rationalist may still have a case, for there may be certain propositions about space that are necessarily true. If so, and if they are also synthetic, then we may still be able to arrive at some synthetic a priori propositions. . . .

2.   Fundamental Concepts of Algebra and Geometry

John W. Young

EUCLID'S ELEMENTS

TWO ASPECTS OF MATHEMATICS. Mathematics may be considered
from two aspects. The first, or utilitarian, regards mathematics
as presenting in serviceable form a body of useful information. The
second and educationally more important aspect, the one with which
we shall chiefly concern ourselves in these lectures, relates to the fact
that mathematics, in particular algebra and geometry, consists of a
body of propositions that are *logically connected*. It is proposed to
consider the more important fundamental concepts of algebra and
geometry with regard to their logical significance and their logical
interrelations. Let it be said at the outset that we shall not be primarily concerned with the psychological genesis of these concepts, nor
with the manifold and interesting philosophical questions to which
they give rise.

"**Mathematical Science**" **defined.** We are at once confronted with
the question: What is mathematics? To give a satisfactory definition
is difficult, if not impossible. We shall be in a better position to
appreciate the difficulties attaching to this question at the close of the
lectures. We may, however, define what we shall understand by a
mathematical science. A *mathematical science,* as we shall use the
term, is any body of propositions arranged according to a sequence of
logical deductions; *i.e.* arranged so that every proposition of the set
after a certain one is a formal logical consequence of some or all of the
propositions that precede it.[1] This definition is open to the criticism
that it is too broad; it contains more than is usually understood by the
term it professes to define. The idea, however, is simply that whenever
a body of propositions is arranged or can be arranged in a strictly
logical sequence, then by virtue of that fact we may call it mathematical. It will do no harm, if the meaning we attribute to this term in the
present connection is broader than that usually attributed to it; the
considerations that follow merely have a wider field of application.

Reprinted with permission of The Macmillan Company from *Lectures on the Fundamental Concepts of Algebra and Geometry* by J. W. Young, pp. 1–13. Copyright 1911
by The Macmillan Company. Renewed 1939 by Mary A. Young and William Wells
Denton.

[1] This definition is closely related to a definition given by Benjamin Peirce, when he
said that "mathematics is the science which draws necessary conclusions."

Unproved Propositions and Undefined Terms. Let us suppose that we have before us a body of propositions satisfying this definition, and let us inquire what it must have for a point of departure. The first proposition cannot, of course, be a logical consequence of a preceding proposition of the set. The second, if the body of propositions is at all extensive, is probably not deducible from the first; for the logical implications of a single proposition are not many. If we consider the nature of a deductive proof, we recognize at once that there must be a hypothesis. It is clear, then, that *the starting point of any mathematical science must be a set of one or more propositions which remain entirely unproved.* This is essential; without it a vicious circle is unavoidable.

Similarly we may see that there must be some *undefined terms.* In order to define a term we must define it in terms of some other term or terms, the meaning of which is assumed known. In order to be strictly logical, therefore, a set of one or more terms must be left entirely undefined. One of the questions to be considered relates to the logical significance of the undefined terms and the unproved propositions. The latter are usually called axioms or postulates. Are these to be regarded as self-evident truths? Are they imposed on our minds *a priori*, and is it impossible to think logically without granting them? Or are they of experimental origin? Are the undefined terms primitive notions, the meaning of which is perfectly clear without definition? Closely connected with these questions are others relating to the validity of the propositions derived from the unproved propositions involving these undefined terms. We often hear the opinion expressed that a mathematical proposition is certain beyond any possibility of doubt by a reasonable being. Will a critical inspection bear out this opinion? We shall soon see that it will not. As an illustration of an extreme view, we may cite a definition of mathematics recently given by Bertrand Russell, one of the most eminent mathematical logicians of the present time. "Mathematics," he said, "is the science in which we never know what we are talking about, nor whether what we say is true." [2] It is probable that many of our pupils will heartily concur in this definition. We shall see later that there is a sense in which this more or less humorous dictum of Russell is correct.

The Teaching of Mathematics. There should be no need of emphasizing the importance of the questions just referred to. They lie at the basis of all science; every one interested in the logical side of scientific development is vitally concerned with them. Moreover, the

---

[2] B. Russell, "Recent Work on the Principles of Mathematics," *The International Monthly*, vol. 4 (1901), p. 84.

general educated public shows signs of interest. The articles appearing from time to time in our popular magazines on the subjects of non-euclidean geometry and four-dimensional space give evidence hereof. It is merely one of the manifestations of the awakened popular interest in scientific progress.

These questions are, however, of particular interest to teachers of mathematics in our schools and colleges. Whether we regard mathematics from the utilitarian point of view, according to which the pupil is to gain facility in using a powerful tool, or from the purely logical aspect, according to which he is to gain the power of logical inference, it is clear that the chief end of mathematical study must be to make the pupil *think*. If mathematical teaching fails to do this, it fails altogether. The mere memorizing of a demonstration in geometry has about the same educational value as the memorizing of a page from the city directory. And yet it must be admitted that a very large number of our pupils do study mathematics in just this way. There can be no doubt that the fault lies with the teaching. This does not necessarily mean that the fault is with the individual teacher, however. Mathematical instruction, in this as well as in other countries, is laboring under a burden of century-old tradition. Especially is this so with reference to the teaching of geometry. Our texts in this subject are still patterned more or less closely after the model of Euclid, who wrote over two thousand years ago, and whose text, moreover, was not intended for the use of boys and girls, but for mature men.

The trouble in brief is that the authors of practically all of our current textbooks lay all the emphasis on the formal logical side, to the almost complete exclusion of the psychological, which latter is without doubt far more important at the beginning of a first course in algebra or geometry. They fail to recognize the fact that the pupil has reasoned, and reasoned accurately, on a variety of subjects before he takes up the subject of mathematics, though this reasoning has not perhaps been formal. In order to induce a pupil to think about geometry, it is necessary first to arouse his interest and then to let him think about the subject *in his own way*. This first and difficult step once taken, it should be a comparatively easy matter gradually to mold his method of reasoning into a more formal type. The textbook which takes due account of this psychological element is apparently still unwritten, and as the teacher is to a large extent governed by the text he uses, the failure of mathematical teaching is not altogether the fault of the teacher.

The latter must be prepared, however, to make the best of existing conditions. Much can be accomplished, even with a pedagogically inadequate text, if the teacher succeeds in awakening and holding his pupils' interest. It is well known that interest is contagious. Let the teacher be vitally, enthusiastically interested in what he is teaching, and it will be a dull pupil who does not catch the infection. It is hoped that these lectures may tend to give a new impetus to the enthusiasm of those teachers who have not as yet seriously considered the logical foundations of mathematics. Every thoughtful teacher has doubtless been confronted with certain logical difficulties in the treatment of topics in algebra and geometry. Even on the assumption that he has not had the hardihood of questioning the axioms and postulates which he finds placed at the basis of his science,—and it is hardly to be expected that he should thus question the validity of propositions which stood unchallenged for over two thousand years,—many serious difficulties attach to such topics as irrational numbers and ratios, complex numbers, limits, the notion of infinity, etc. How serious some of these difficulties are is made evident by the fact that in spite of the attention they received during several centuries, a satisfactory treatment has been found only within the last hundred years. Indeed, the present abstract point of view, which is to be described in these lectures, has been developed only within the last three or four decades.

Historical Development to be Emphasized. It is proposed throughout to emphasize the historical development of the conceptions and points of view considered. It is hoped hereby to give a comprehensive view of mathematical progress in so far as it relates to fundamental principles. This should tend to eradicate the all too common feeling that the fundamental conceptions of mathematics are fixed and unalterable for all time. Quite the contrary is the case. Mathematics is growing at the bottom as well as at the top; indeed, not the least remarkable results of mathematical investigation of recent years and of the present time relate to the foundations. Let the teacher once fully realize that his science, even in its most elementary portions, is alive and growing, let him take note of the manifold changes in point of view and the new and unexpected relations which these changes disclose, let him further take an active interest in the new developments, and indeed react independently on the conceptions involved, —for an enormous amount of work still remains to be done in adapting the results of these developments to the requirements of elementary instruction,—let him do these things, and he will bring to his daily teaching a new enthusiasm which will greatly enhance the pleasure of his labors and prove an inspiration to his pupils.

Results not of Direct Use in Teaching. Reference has just been made to the need of *adapting* the results of the recent work on fundamental principles to the needs of the classroom. It should here be emphasized, perhaps, that the points of view to be developed in these lectures and the results reached are not directly of use in elementary teaching. They are extremely abstract, and will be of interest only to mature minds. They should serve to clarify the teacher's ideas, and thus indirectly to clarify the pupil's. The latter's ideas will, however, differ considerably from the former's. The results referred to do, nevertheless, have a direct bearing on some of the pedagogical problems confronting the teacher. This will be discussed briefly as occasion arises.

Euclid's Elements of Geometry. We propose in the first five lectures to consider rather informally our conceptions of space, and to illustrate in a general way the point of view to be followed in the later, more formal discussion. True to our purpose of taking into account the historical development of the conceptions involved, we can do no better than consider briefly at this point the fundamental notions that are found at the beginning of the earliest work in which mathematics is exhibited as a logically arranged sequence of propositions. I refer, of course, to Euclid's *Elements of Geometry*. This is the first attempt of which we have any record to establish a mathematical science as we have defined the term. Euclid lived about the year 300 B.C., and his greatest claim to fame is the fact that he furnished the succeeding centuries with the ideal of such a mathematical science. There is no doubt that it was his purpose to derive the properties of space from explicitly stated definitions, axioms, and postulates, without the use of any further assumptions, in particular without any further appeal to geometric intuition. It is true that he made use of many propositions which he did not prove and which he did not explicitly state as unproved. But there is much evidence to show that his ideal was in accordance with our definition of a mathematical science. We may use Euclid's Elements as a convenient starting point to introduce the order of ideas which is to engage our attention. Any attempt to criticize Euclid's treatment of geometry is rendered peculiarly difficult at the outset on account of the great uncertainty that exists as to the real content of Euclid's text. Although he lived, as has been stated, about the year 300 B.C., the oldest manuscripts which purport to give Euclid's Elements date from about the year 900 A.D.[3] An interval of twelve hundred years intervenes between the time at which Euclid wrote and any record we have of his work. Moreover, there are several manuscripts dating from that time, and they differ considerably from one another.

Definitions. How, then, did Euclid begin his treatment of geometry? We have seen what the starting point ought to be. It ought to be

---

[3] Klein, *Elementarmathematik vom höheren Standpunkte aus*, vol. II, p. 404.

a set of undefined terms and a set of unproved propositions such that every other term can be defined in terms of the former and every other proposition derived from the latter by the methods of formal logic. Euclid does indeed begin with a series of definitions, of which we will give a few examples:

A *point* is that which has no parts.

A *line* is length without breadth.[4]

A *straight line* is a line which lies evenly between two of its points.

These definitions serve to illustrate how it is necessary to define a term in terms of something else, the meaning of which is assumed known. The terms "part," "length," "breadth," "lies evenly" are undefined. These definitions are entirely superfluous, in so far as they do not enable us to understand the terms defined, unless we are already familiar with the ideas they are intended to convey. It is probable that Euclid himself did not regard these as real definitions. He probably regarded the notions of "point," "line," "straight line," etc., as primitive notions the meaning of which was clear to every one. The definitions then merely serve to call attention to some of the most important intuitional properties of the notions in question. We will so regard them for the time being. We shall have more to say of them presently.

Postulates. Euclid gives us next a set of *postulates*. On account of their historical importance we will give them in full as they appear in the text of Heiberg: [5]

1. *It shall be possible to draw a straight line joining any two points.*
2. *A terminated straight line may be extended without limit in either direction.*
3. *It shall be possible to draw a circle with given center and through a given point.*
4. *All right angles are equal.*
5. *If two straight lines in a plane meet another straight line in the plane so that the sum of the interior angles on the same side of the latter straight line is less than two right angles, then the two straight lines will meet on that side of the latter straight line.*[6]

This fifth postulate is the famous so-called *parallel postulate*. On it is made to depend the theorem that through a point not on a given straight line there is only one parallel to the given line.

---

[4] Some Mss. add: The extremities of a line are points.

[5] *Euclidis oper omnia*, edited by Heiberg (Leipzig, 1883–1895). An excellent English edition based on Heiberg's text with critical notes has recently appeared; vis. T. L. Heath, *The Thirteen Books of Euclid's Elements, translated from the Text of Heiberg*, with Introduction and Commentary, 3 vols. (Cambridge, 1908).

[6] Another discrepancy between the old manuscripts may here be noted. The fifth postulate, as just given, is in some texts given as the eleventh or twelfth axiom.

Axioms. Euclid now gives a set of *axioms*, "common conceptions of thought," to translate approximately the meaning of the Greek. There are also five of these:

1. *Things equal to the same thing are equal to each other.*
2. *If equals be added to equals, the results are equal.*
3. *If equals be subtracted from equals, the remainders are equal.*
4. *The whole is greater than any one of its parts.*
5. *Things that coincide are equal.*

These definitions, axioms, and postulates form the starting point of Euclid's Elements. We may note in passing a very plausible distinction between the axioms and the postulates, which is suggested by this arrangement into sets of five. It appears that the axioms are intended to state fundamental notions of logic in general, which may be regarded as valid in any science. The postulates, on the other hand, seem to be intended as primitive propositions concerning space; they are all geometrical.

Criticism of Euclid's Treatment. We have seen what from a purely logical point of view the starting point of a mathematical science should be. Does this set of axioms and postulates satisfy the requirements? We may at this point dismiss the axioms with the statement that modern criticism is chiefly to the effect that they are too general to be valid in the sense in which the terms involved are now used. As an example, we may call attention to the fact that Axiom 4 (the whole is greater than any of its parts) is not always true in the sense in which the words "whole," "part," and "greater than" are used to-day. We shall return more fully to this on a later occasion.

As to the postulates relating to the fundamental conceptions of space, we must note first that Euclid fails to specify with the necessary precision what terms are to be regarded as undefined. We have already ventured the opinion that he probably regarded such notions as "point," "line," "straight," "length," etc., as primitive notions, the meaning of which is to be regarded as sufficiently clear without any more formal characterization. Is this conception of these notions justifiable? Waiving this question for the moment, we are confronted with the other: Do the postulates satisfy the requirement of a set of unproved propositions; *i.e.* can all the theorems of geometry be derived from them by the methods of formal logic without any further appeal to geometric intuition? We have already stated that Euclid made many tacit assumptions in his derivation of these theorems. He assumes for example without explicit statement that the shortest distance between two points is measured along the straight line joining them. The answer to the last question must then be negative. There remains still another question: What is the logical significance of the postulates? Are they to be regarded as self-evident, necessary truths? This question is at once seen to be closely connected with the first: Are the fundamental notions of "point," "line," "distance," etc., so simple as to have a perfectly clear, precise meaning? . . .

---

3. On the Foundations of Mathematics

Eliakim Hastings Moore

Abstract Mathematics

THE NOTION within a given domain of defining the objects of consideration rather by a body of properties than by particular expressions or intuitions is as old as mathematics itself. And yet the central importance of the notion appeared only during the last century—in a host of researches on special theories and on the foundations of geometry and analysis. Thus has arisen the general point of view of what may be called *abstract mathematics*. One comes in touch with the literature very conveniently by the mediation of Peano's *Revue des Mathématiques*. The Italian school of Peano and the *Formulaire Mathématique*, published in connection with the *Revue*, are devoted to the codification in Peano's symbolic language of the principal mathematical theories, and to researches on abstract mathematics. General interest in abstract mathematics was aroused by Hilbert's Gauss-Weber Festschrift of 1899: "Ueber die Grundlagen der Geometrie," a memoir rich in results and suggestive in methods; I refer to the reviews by Sommer,[1] Poincaré,[2] Halsted,[3] Hedrick,[4] and Veblen.[5]

We have as a basal science, logic, and as depending upon it the special deductive sciences which involve undefined symbols and whose

Reprinted by permission from *The Mathematics Teacher*, LX:4 (April 1967), 360–374. Copyright © 1967 by the University of Chicago Press.

[1] *Bulletin of the American Mathematical Society* (2), vol. 6 (1900), p. 287.
[2] *Bull. Sciences Mathém.*, vol. 26 (1902), p. 249.
[3] *The Open Court*, September, 1902.
[4] *Bull. Amer, Math. Soc.* (2), vol. 9 (1902), p. 158.
[5] *The Monist*, January, 1903.

propositions are not all capable of proof. The symbols denote either classes of elements or relations amongst elements. In any such science one may choose in various ways the system of undefined symbols and the system of undemonstrated or primitive propositions, or postulates. Every proposition follows from the postulates by a finite number of logical steps. A careful statement of the fundamental generalities is given by Padoa in a paper [6] before the Paris Congress of Philosophy, 1900.

Having in mind a definite system of undefined symbols and a definite system of postulates, we have first of all the notion of the compatibility of these postulates; that is, that it is impossible to prove by a finite number of logical steps the simultaneous validity of a statement and its contradictory statement; in the next place, the question of the independence of the postulate or the irreducibility of the system of postulates; that is, that no postulate is provable from the remaining postulates. Padoa introduces the notion of the irreducibility of the system of undefined symbols. A system of undefined symbols is said to be reducible if for one of the symbols, X, it is possible to establish, as a logical consequence of the assumption of the validity of the postulates, a nominal or symbolic definition of the form $X = A$, where in the expression A there enter only the undefined symbols distinct from X. For the purpose of practical application, it seems to be desirable to modify the definition so as to call the system of undefined symbols reducible if there is a nominal definition $X = A$ of one of them X in terms of the others such that in any interpretation of the science the postulates retain their validity when instead of the initial interpretation of the symbol X there is placed the interpretation of the symbol A of that symbol. If the system of symbols is reducible in the sense of the original definition it is in the sense of the new definition, but not necessarily conversely, as appears for instance from the following example, occurring in the foundations of geometry.

Hilbert uses the following undefined symbols: "point," "line," "plane," "incidence" of point and line, "incidence" of point and plane, "between," and "congruent." Now it is possible to give for the symbol "plane" a symbolic definition in terms of the other undefined symbols—for instance, a plane is a certain class of points (as Peano showed in 1892), or again, a plane is a certain class of lines; while the notion "incidence" of point and plane receives convenient definition. It is apparent from the fact that these definitions may be given in these two ways that Hilbert's system of undefined symbols is not in Padoa's sense irreducible, at least, in so far as the symbols "plane," "incidence"

[6] Essai d'une théorie algébrique des nombres entiers, précédé d'une introduction logique à une théorie déductive quelconque," *Bibliothèque du Congrès International de Philosophie*, vol. 3, p. 309.

of point and plane are concerned—while it is equally clear that these symbols are in the abstract geometry superfluous.

In his dissertation on Euclidean geometry, Mr. Veblen, following the example of Pasch and Peano, takes as undefined symbols "point" and "between," or "point" and "segment." In terms of these two symbols alone he expresses a set of independent fundamental postulates of Euclidean geometry, in the first place developing the projective geometry, and then as to congruence relating himself to the point of view of Klein in his "Erlangen Programm," whereby the group of movements of Euclidean geometry enters as a certain subgroup of the group of collineations of projective geometry. Here arises an interesting question as to the sense in which the undefined symbol "congruence" is superfluous in the Euclidean geometry based upon the symbols "point," "between." One sees at once that a definition of "congruence" involves parametric points in its expression, while on the other hand a definition of the system of all "planes," that is, of the general concept "plane," involves no such parametric elements. But, again, just as there exist distinct definitions of "congruence," owing to a variation of the parametric points, so there exist distinct definitions of the general concept "plane," as was indicated a moment ago. One has the feeling that the state of affairs must be as follows: In any interpretation of, say, Hilbert's symbols, wherein the postulates of Hilbert are valid, every valid statement which does not involve the symbol "plane" in direct connection with the general logical symbol $(=)$ of symbolic definition, remains valid when we modify it in accordance with either of the definitions of "plane" previously referred to. On the other hand, this state of affairs does not hold for the symbol "congruence." The proof of the former statement would seem to involve fundamental logical niceties.

The compatibility and the independence of the postulates of a system of postulates of a special deductive science have been up to this time always made to depend upon the self-consistency of some other deductive science; for instance, geometry depends thus upon analysis, or analysis upon geometry. The fundamental and still unsolved problem in this direction is that of the direct proof of the compatibility of the postulates of arithmetic, or of the real number system of analysis. (To the society this morning Dr. Huntington exhibited two sets of independent postulates for this real number system.) This is the second of the twenty-three problems listed by Hilbert in his address before the Paris Mathematical Congress of 1900.

The Italian writers on abstract mathematics for the most part make use of Peano's symbolism. One may be tempted to feel that this symbolism is not an essential part of their work. It is only right to state, however, that the symbolism is not difficult to learn, and that there is testimony to the effect that the symbolism is actually of great value to the investigator in removing from attention the concrete connotations of the ordinary terms of general and mathematical language. But of course the essential difficulties are not to be obviated by the use of any symbolism, however delicate.

Indeed the question arises whether the abstract mathematicians in making precise the metes and bounds of logic and the special deductive sciences are not losing sight of the evolutionary character of all life-processes, whether in the individual or in the race. Certainly the logicians do not consider their science as something now fixed. All science, logic and mathematics included, is a function of the epoch— all science, in its ideals as well as in its achievements. Thus with Hilbert let a special deductive or mathematical science be based upon a finite number of symbols related by a finite number of compatible postulates, every proposition of the science being deducible by a finite number of logical steps from the postulates. The content of this conception is far from absolute. It involves what presuppositions as to general logic? What is a finite number? In what sense is a postulate— for example, that any two distinct points determine a line—a single postulate? What are the permissible logical steps of deduction? Would the usual syllogistic steps of formal logic suffice? Would they suffice even with the aid of the principle of mathematical induction, in which Poincaré finds [7] the essential synthetic element of mathematical argumentation the basis of that generality without which there would be no science? In what sense is mathematical induction a single logical step of deduction?

One has then the feeling that the carrying out in an absolute sense of the program of the abstract mathematicians will be found impossible. At the same time, one recognizes the importance attaching to the effort to do precisely this thing. The requirement of rigor tends toward essential simplicity of procedure, as Hilbert has insisted in his Paris address, and the remark applies to this question of mathematical logic and its abstract expression.

Pure and Applied Mathematics

In the ultimate analysis for any epoch, we have general logic, the mathematical sciences,[8] that is, all special formally and abstractly deductive self-consistent sciences, and the natural sciences, which are inductive and informally deductive. While this classification may be satisfactory as an ideal one, it fails to recognize the fact that in mathe-

---

[7] "Sur la nature du raisonnement mathématique," *Revue de Métaphysique et de Morale*, vol. 2 (1894), pp. 371–384.
[8] Of which none is at present known to exist.

matical research one by no means confines himself to processes which are mathematical according to this definition; and if this is true with respect to the research of professional mathematicians, how much more is it true with respect to this study, which should throughout be conducted in the spirit of research, on the part of students of mathematics in the elementary schools and colleges and universities. I refer to the articles [9] of Poincaré on the role of intuition and logic in mathematical research and education.

It is apparent that this ideal classification can be made by the devotee of science only when he has reached a considerable degree of scientific maturity, that perhaps it would fail to appeal to nonmathematical experts, and that it does not accord with the definitions given by practical work in mathematicians. Indeed, the attitude of practical mathematicians toward this whole subject of abstract mathematics, and especially the symbolic form of abstract mathematics, is not unlike that of the practical physicist toward the whole subject of theoretic mathematics, and in turn not unlike that of the practical engineer toward the whole subject of theoretical physics and mathematics. Furthermore, every one understands that many of the most important advances of pure mathematics have arisen in connection with investigations originating in the domain of natural phenomena.

Practically then it would seem desirable for the interests of science in general that there should be a strong body of men thoroughly possessed of the scientific method in both its inductive and its deductive forms. We are confronted with the questions: What is science? What is the scientific method? What are the relations between the mathematical and the natural scientific processes of thought? As to these questions, I refer to articles and addresses of Poincaré,[10] Boltzmann,[11] and Burkhardt,[12] and to Mach's *Science of Mechanics* and Pearson's *Grammar of Science*.

Without elaboration of metaphysical or psychological details, it is sufficient to refer to the thought that the individual, as confronted with the world of phenomena in his effort to obtain control over this

---

[9] "La logique et l'intuition dans la science mathématique et dans l'enseignement," *L'Enseignement Mathématique*, vol. 1 (1899), pp. 157–161. "Du role de l'intuition et de la logique en mathématiques," *Compte Rendu de Deuxième Congrès International des Mathématiciens, Paris* (1900), 1902, pp. 115–130. "Sur les rapports de l'analyse pure et de la physique mathématique," Conference, Zurich, 1897; *Acta Mathematica*, vol. 21, p. 238.

[10] In addition to those already cited: "On the Foundations of Geometry," *The Monist*, vol. 9, October, 1898, pp. 1–43. "Sur les principes de la mécanique," *Bibliothèque du Congrès International de Philosophie*, vol. 3, pp. 457–494.

[11] "Ueber die Methoden der theoretischen Physik," *Dyck's Katalog mathematischer und mathematisch-physikalischer Modelle, Apparate und Instrumente*, pp. 89–98, Munich, 1892.

[12] "Mathematisches und Naturwissenschaftliches Denken," *Jahresbericht der Deutschen Math.-Ver.*, vol. 11 (1902), pp. 49–57.

world, is gradually forced to appreciate a knowledge of the usual coexistences and sequences of phenomena, and that science arises as the
body of formulas serving to epitomize or summarize conveniently
these usual coexistences and sequences. These formulas are of the
nature of more or less exact descriptions of phenomena; they are not
of the nature of explanations. Of all the relations entering into the
formulas of science, the fundamental mathematical notions of number and measure and form were among the earliest, and pure mathematics in its ordinary acceptation may be understood to be the systematic development of the properties of these notions, in accordance
with conditions prescribed by physical phenomena. Arithmetic and
geometry, closely united in mensuration and trigonometry, early
reached a high degree of advancement. But after the development of
the generalizing literal notation of algebra, and largely in response to
the insistent demands of mechanics, astronomy and physics, the
seventeenth century, binding together arithmetic and geometry infinitely more closely, created analytic geometry and the infinitesimal
calculus, those mighty methods of research whose application to all
branches of the theoretical and practical physical sciences so fundamentally characterizes the civilization of today.

The eighteenth century was devoted to the development of the
powers of these new instruments in all directions. While this development continued during the nineteenth century, the dominant note of
the nineteenth century was that of critical reorganization of the foundations of pure mathematics, so that, for instance, the majestic edifice
of analysis was seen to rest upon the arithmetic of positive integers
alone. This reorganization and the consequent course of development
of pure mathematics were independent of the question of the application of mathematics to the sister sciences. There has thus arisen a
chasm between pure mathematics and applied mathematics. There
have not been lacking, however, influences making toward the bridg-
ing of this chasm; one thinks especially of the whole influence of
Klein in Germany and of the École Polytechnic in France. As a basis
of union of the pure mathematicians and the applied mathematicians,
Klein has throughout emphasized the importance of a clear understanding of the relations between those two parts of mathematics
which are conveniently called "mathematics of precision" and "mathematics of approximation," and I refer especially to his latest work of
this character, *Anwendung der Differential und Integral-Rechnung
auf Geometrie: Eine Revision der Principien* (Göttingen, summer
semester, 1901, Teubner, 1902). This course of lectures is designed to
present particular applications of the general notions of Klein, and
furthermore, it is in continuation of the discussion between Pring-
sheim and Klein and others, as to the desirable character of lectures
on mathematics in the universities of Germany.

Elementary Mathematics

This separation between pure mathematics and applied mathematics is grievous even in the domain of elementary mathematics. In witness, in the first place: The workers in physics, chemistry, and engineering need more practical mathematics; and numerous textbooks, in particular on calculus, have recently been written from the point of view of these allied subjects, I refer to the works by Nernst and Schoenflies,[13] Lorentz,[14] Perry,[15] and Mellor,[16] and to a book of the very elements of mathematics now in preparation by Oliver Lodge.

In the second place, I dare say you are all familiar with the surprisingly vigorous and effective agitation with respect to the teaching of elementary mathematics which is at present in progress in England, largely under the direction of John Perry, professor of mechanics and mathematics of the Royal College of Science, London, and chairman of the Board of Examiners of the Board of Education in the subjects of engineering, including practical plane and solid geometry, applied mechanics, practical mathematics, in addition to more technical subjects, and in this capacity in charge of the education of some hundred thousand apprentices in English night schools. The section on Education of the British Association had its first session at the Glasgow meeting, 1901, and the session was devoted to the consideration, in connection with the section on Mathematics and Physics, of the question of the pedagogy of mathematics, and Perry opened the discussion by a paper on "The Teaching of Mathematics." A strong committee under the chairmanship of Professor Forsyth, of Cambridge, was appointed "to report upon improvements that might be effected in the teaching of mathematics, in the first instance, in the teaching of elementary mathematics, and upon such means as they think likely to effect improvements." The paper of Perry, with the discussion of the subject at Glasgow, and additions including the report of the committee as presented to the British Association at its Belfast meeting, September, 1902, are collected in a small volume, *Discussion on the Teaching of Mathematics*, edited by Professor Perry (Macmillan, second edition, 1902).[17]

[13] Nernst und Schoenflies, *Einführung in die mathematische Behandlung der Naturwissenschaften* (Munich and Leipsic, 1895); the basis of Young and Linebarger's *Elements of Differential and Integral Calculus*, New York, 1900.

[14] Lorentz, *Lehrbuch der Differential- und Integralrechnung*, Leipsic, 1900.

[15] Perry, *Calculus for Engineers* (second edition, London, E. Arnold, 1897); German translation by Fricke (Teubner, 1902). Cf. also the citations given later on.

[16] Mellor, *Higher Mathematics for Students of Chemistry and Physics, with special reference to Practical Work*, Longmans, Green & Co., 1902, pp. xxi+543.

[17] Cf. also *Report on the Teaching of Elementary Mathematics issued by the Mathematical Association*, G. Bell & Sons, London, 1902.

One should consult the books of Perry, *Practical Mathematics*,[18] *Applied Mechanics*,[19] *Calculus for Engineers* [20] and *England's Neglect of Science,* [21] and his address [22] on "The Education of Engineers"— and furthermore the files from 1899 on of the English journals, *Nature, School World, Journal of Education* and *Mathematical Gazette.*

One important purpose of the English agitation is to relieve the English secondary school teachers from the burden of a too precise examination system, imposed by the great examining bodies; in particular, to relieve them from the need of retaining Euclid as the sole authority in geometry, at any rate with respect to the sequence of propositions. Similar efforts made in England about thirty years ago were unsuccessful. Apparently the forces operating since that time have just now broken forth into successful activity; for the report of the British Association committee was distinctly favorable, in a conservative sense, to the idea of reform, and already noteworthy initial changes have been made in the regulations for the secondary examinations by the examination syndicates of the universities of Oxford, Cambridge, and London.

The reader will find the literature of this English movement very interesting and suggestive. For instance, in a letter to *Nature* (vol. 65, p. 484, March 27, 1902) Perry mildly apologizes for having to do with the movement whose immediate results are likely to be merely slight reforms, instead of thoroughgoing reforms called for in his pronouncements and justified by his marked success during over twenty years as a teacher of practical mathematics. He asserts that the orthodox logical sequence in mathematics is not the only possible one; that, on the contrary, a more logical sequence than the orthodox one (because one more possible of comprehension by students) is based upon the notions underlying the infinitesimal calculus taken as axioms; for instance, that a map may be drawn to scale; the notions underlying the many uses of squared paper; that decimals may be dealt with as ordinary numbers. He asserts as essential that the boy should be *familiar* (by way of experiment, illustration, measurement, and by every possible means) with the ideas to which he applies his logic; and moreover that he should be thoroughly *interested* in the subject studied; and he closes with the following peroration:

[18] Published for the Board of Education by Eyre and Spottiswoode, London, 1899.
[19] D. Van Nostrand Co., New York, 1898.
[20] Second edition, London, E. Arnold, 1897.
[21] T. Fisher Unwin, London, 1900.
[22] In opening the discussion of the sections on Engineering and on Education at the Belfast, 1902, meeting of the British Association; published in Science, November 14, 1902.

"Great God! I'd rather be
A pagan, suckled in a creed outworn."
I would rather be utterly ignorant of all the wonderful literature
and science of the last twenty-four centuries, even of the wonderful achievements of the last fifty years, than not to have the sense
that our whole system of so-called education is as degrading to
literature and philosophy as it is to English boys and men.

As a pure mathematician, I hold as the most important suggestion
of the English movement the suggestion of Perry's, just cited, that by
emphasizing steadily the practical sides of mathematics, that is, arithmetic computations, mechanical drawing and graphical methods generally, in continuous relation with problems of physics and chemistry
and engineering, it would be possible to give very young students a
great body of the essential notions of trigonometry, analytic geometry, and the calculus. This is accomplished, on the one hand, by the
increase of attention and comprehension obtained by connecting the
abstract mathematics with subjects which are naturally of interest to
the boy, so that, for instance, all the results obtained by theoretic
process are capable of check by laboratory process, and, on the other
hand, a diminution of emphasis on the systematic and formal sides of
instruction in mathematics. Undoubtedly many mathematicians will
feel that this decrease of emphasis will result in much, if not irrepara-
ble, injury to the interests of mathematics. But I am inclined to think
that the mathematician with the catholic attitude of an adherent of
science, in general (and at any rate with respect to the problems of
the pedagogy of elementary mathematics there would seem to be no
other rational attitude) will see that the boy will be learning to make
practical use in his scientific investigations—to be sure, in a naïve and
elementary way—of the finest mathematical tools which the centuries
have forged; that under skillful guidance he will learn to be interested
not merely in the achievements of the tools, but in the theory of the
tools themselves, and that thus he will ultimately have a feeling
toward his mathematics extremely different from that which is now
met with only too frequently—a feeling that mathematics is indeed
itself a fundamental reality of the domain of thought, and not merely
a matter of symbols and arbitrary rules and conventions.

The American Mathematical Society

The American Mathematical Society has, naturally, interested itself
chiefly in promoting the interests of research in mathematics. It has,
however, recognized that those interests are closely bound up with the
interests of education in mathematics. I refer in particular to the
valuable work done by the committee appointed, with the authoriza-
tion of the Council, by the Chicago section of the society, to represent

mathematics in connection with Dr. Nightingale's committee of 1899 of the National Educational Association in the formulation of standard curricula for high schools and academies, and to the fact that two committees are now at work, one appointed in December, 1901, by the Chicago Section, to formulate the desirable conditions for the granting, by institutions of the Mississippi valley, of the degree of Master of Arts for work in mathematics, and the other appointed by the society at its last summer meeting to cooperate with similar committees of the National Educational Association and of the Society for the Promotion of Engineering Education, in formulating standard definitions of requirements in mathematical subjects for admission to colleges and technological schools; and furthermore I refer to the fact that (although not formally) the society has made a valuable contribution to the interests of secondary education in that the College Entrance Examination Board has as its secretary the principal founder of the society. I have accordingly felt at liberty to bring to the attention of the society these matters of pedagogy of elementary mathematics, and I do so with the firm conviction that it would be possible for the society, by giving still more attention to these matters, to further most effectively the highest interests of mathematics in this country.

A VISION

An Invitation

The pure mathematicians are invited to determine how mathematics is regarded by the world at large, including their colleagues of other science departments and the students of elementary mathematics, and to ask themselves whether by modification of method and attitude they may not win for it the very high position in general esteem and appreciative interest which it assuredly deserves.

This general invitation and the preceding summary view invoke this vision of the future of elementary mathematics in this country.

The Pedagogy of Elementary Mathematics

We survey the pedagogy of elementary mathematics in the primary schools, in the secondary schools and in the junior colleges (the lower collegiate years). It is, however, understood that there is a movement for the enlargement of the strong secondary schools, by the addition of the two years of junior college work and by the absorption of the last two or three grades of the primary schools, into institutions more

of the type of the German gymnasia and the French lycée; [23] in favor
of this movement there are strong arguments, and among them this,
that in such institutions, especially if closely related to strong colleges
or universities, the mathematical reforms may the more easily be
carried out.

The fundamental problem is that of *the unification of pure and
applied mathematics.* If we recognize the branching implied by the
very terms "pure," "applied," we have to do with a special case of *the
correlation of different subjects* of the curriculum, a central problem
in the domain of pedagogy from the time of Herbart on. In this case,
however, the fundamental solution is to be found rather by way of
indirection—by arranging the curriculum so that throughout the
domain of elementary mathematics the branching be not recognized.

The Primary Schools

Would it not be possible for the children in the grades to be trained
in power of observation and experiment and reflection and deduction
so that always their mathematics should be directly connected with
matters of thoroughly concrete character? The response is immediate
that this is being done today in the kindergartens and in the better
elementary schools. I understand that serious difficulties arise with
children of from nine to twelve years of age, who are no longer con-
tented with the simple, concrete methods of earlier years and who,
nevertheless, are unable to appreciate the more abstract methods of
the later years. These difficulties, some say, are to be met by allowing
the mathematics to enter only implicitly in connection with the other
subjects of the curriculum. But rather the material and methods of
the mathematics should be enriched and vitalized. In particular, the
grade teachers must make wiser use of the foundations furnished by
the kindergarten. The drawing and the paper folding must lead on
directly to systematic study of intuitional geometry,[24] including the
construction of models and the elements of mechanical drawing, with
simple exercises in geometrical reasoning. The geometry must be
closely connected with the numerical and literal arithmetic. The
cross-grooved tables of the kindergarten furnish an especially important type of connection, viz., a conventional graphical depiction of

[23] As to the mathematics of these institutions, one may consult the book on *The
Teaching of Mathematics in the Higher School of Prussia* (New York, Longmans, Green
& Co., 1900) by Professor Young and the article (*Bulletin Amer. Math. Soc.* (2), vol. 6,
p.225) by Professor Pierpont.
[24] Here I refer to the very suggestive paper of Benchara Branford, entitled, "Measurement and Simple Surveying. An Experiment in the Teaching of Elementary Geometry"
to a small class of beginners of about ten years of age (*Journal of Education*, London,
the first part appearing in the number for August, 1899).

any phenomenon in which one magnitude depends upon another. These tables and the similar cross-section blackboards and paper must enter largely into all the mathematics of the grades. The children are to be taught to represent, according to the usual conventions, various familiar and interesting phenomena and to study the properties of the phenomena in the pictures: to know, for example, what concrete meaning attaches to the fact that a graph curve at a certain point is going down or going up or is horizontal. Thus the problems of percentage—interest, etc.—have their depiction in straight or broken line graphs.

The Secondary Schools

Pending the reform of the primary schools, the secondary schools must advance independently. In these schools at present, according to one type of arrangement, we find algebra in the first year, plane geometry in the second, physics in the third, and the more difficult parts of algebra and solid geometry, with review of all the mathematics in the fourth.

Engineers tell us that in the schools algebra is taught in one watertight compartment, geometry in another, and physics in another, and that the student learns to appreciate (if ever) only very late the absolutely close connection between these different subjects, and then, if he credits the fraternity of teachers with knowing the closeness of this relation, he blames them most heartily for their unaccountably stupid way of teaching him.[25] If we contrast this state of affairs with the state of affairs in the solid four years' course in Latin, I think we are forced to the conclusion that the organization of instruction in Latin is much more [nearly] perfect than that of the instruction in mathematics.

The following question arises: *Would it not be possible to organize the algebra, geometry and physics of the secondary school into a thoroughly coherent four years' course,* comparable in strength and closeness of structure with the four years' course in Latin? (Here

[25] Why is it that one of the sanest and best-informed scientific men living, a man not himself an engineer, can charge mathematicians with killing off every engineering school on which they can lay hands? Why do engineers so strongly urge that the mathematical courses in engineering schools be given by practical engineers.

And why can a reviewer of "Some Recent Books of Mechanics" write the truth: "The students' previous training in algebra, geometry, trigonometry, analytic geometry, and calculus as it is generally taught has been necessarily quite formal. These mighty algorithms of formal mathematics must be learned so that they can be applied with readiness and precision. But with mechanics comes the application of these algorithms, and formal, do-by-rote methods, though often possible, yield no results of permanent value. How to elicit and cultivate thought is now of primary importance?" (E. B. Wilson, *Bulletin Amer. Math. Soc.,* October 1902). But is it conceivable that in any part of the education of the student the problem of eliciting and cultivating thought should not be of primary importance?

under physics I include astronomy, and the more mathematical and physical parts of physiography.) It would seem desirable that, just as the systematic development of theoretical mathematics is deferred to a later period, likewise much of theoretical physics might well be deferred. Let the physics also be made thoroughly practical. At any rate, so far as the instruction of boys is concerned, the course should certainly have its character largely determined by the conditions which would be imposed by engineers. What kind of two or three years' course in mathematics and physics would a thoroughly trained engineer give to boys in the secondary school? Let this body of material postulated by the engineer serve as the basis of the four years' course. Let the instruction in the course, however, be given by men who have received expert training in mathematics and physics as well as in engineering and let the instruction be so organized that with the development of the boy, in appreciation of the practical relations, shall come simultaneously his development in the direction of theoretical physics and theoretical mathematics.

Perry is quite right in insisting that it is scientifically legitimate in the pedagogy of elementary mathematics to take a large body of basal principles instead of a small body and to build the edifice upon the larger body for the earlier years, reserving for the later years the philosophic criticism of the basis itself and the reduction of the basal system.

To consider the subject of geometery in all briefness: with the understanding that proper emphasis is laid upon all the concrete sides of the subject, and that furthermore from the beginning exercises in informal deduction [26] are introduced increasingly frequently, when it comes to the beginning of the more formal deductive geometry why should not the students be directed each for himself to set forth a body of geometric fundamental principles, on which he would proceed to erect his geometric edifice? This method would be thoroughly practical and at the same time thoroughly scientific. The various students would have different systems of axioms, and the discussions thus arising naturally would make clearer in the minds of all precisely what are the functions of the axioms in the theory of geometry. The students would omit very many of the axioms, which to them would go without saying. The teacher would do well not to undertake to make the system of axioms thoroughly complete in the abstract sense. "Sufficient unto the day is the precision thereof." The student would

---

[26] In an article shortly to appear in the *Educational Review*, on "The Psychological and the Logical in the Teaching of Geometry," Professor John Dewey, calling attention to the evolutionary character of the education of an individual, insists that there should be no abrupt transition from the introductory, intuitional geometry to the systematic, demonstrative geometry.

very probably wish to take for granted all the ordinary properties of measurement and of motion, and would be ready at once to accept the geometrical implications of coordinate geometry. He could then be brought with extreme ease to the consideration of fundamental notions of the calculus as treated concretely, and he would find those notions delightfully real and powerful, whether in the domain of mathematics or of physics or of chemistry.

To be sure, as Study has well insisted, for a thorough comprehension of even the elementary parts of Euclidean geometry the non-Euclidean geometries are absolutely essential. But the teacher is teaching the subject for the benefit of the students, and it must be admitted that beginners in the study of demonstrative geometry can not appreciate the very delicate considerations involved in the thoroughly abstract science. Indeed, one may conjecture that, had it not been for the brilliant success of Euclid in his effort to organize into a formally deductive system the geometric treasures of his times, the advent of the reign of science in the modern sense might not have been so long deferred. Shall we then hold that in the schools the teaching of demonstrative geometry should be reformed in such a way as to take account of all the wonderful discoveries which have been made—many even recently—in the domain of abstract geometry? And should similar reforms be made in the treatment of arithmetic and algebra? To make reforms of this kind, would it not be to repeat more gloriously the error of those followers of Euclid who fixed his *Elements* as a textbook for elementary instruction in geometry for over two thousand years? Every one agrees that professional mathematicians should certainly take account of these great developments in the technical foundations of mathematics, and that ample provision should be made for instruction in these matters; and on reflection, everyone agrees further that this provision should be reserved for the later collegiate and university years.

The Laboratory Method

This program of reform calls for the development of a thoroughgoing laboratory system of instruction in mathematics and physics, a principal purpose being as far as possible to develop on the part of every student the true spirit of research, and an appreciation, practical as well as theoretic, of the fundamental methods of science.

In connection with what has already been said, the general suggestions I now add will, I hope, be found of use when one enters upon the questions of detail involved in the organization of the course.

As the world of phenomena receives attention by the individual, the phenomena are described both graphically and in terms of number and measure; the number and measure relations of the phenomena enter fundamentally into the graphical depiction, and furthermore the graphical depiction of the phenomena serves powerfully to illuminate the relations of number and measure. This is the fundamental scientific point of view. Here under the term graphical depiction I include representation by models.

To provide for the needs of laboratory instruction, there should be regularly assigned to the subject two periods, counting as one period in the curriculum.

As to the possibility of effecting this unification of mathematics and physics in the secondary schools, objection will be made by some teachers that it is impossible to do well more than one thing at a time. This pedagogic principle of concentration is undoubtedly sound. One must, however, learn how to apply it wisely. For instance, in the physical laboratory it is undesirable to introduce experiments which teach the use of the calipers or of the vernier or of the slide rule. Instead of such uninteresting experiments of limited purpose, the students should be directed to extremely interesting problems which involve the use of these instruments, and thus be led to learn to use the instruments as a matter of course, and not as a matter of difficulty. Just so the smaller elements of mathematical routine can be made to attach themselves to laboratory problems, arousing and retaining the interest of the students. Again, everything exists in its relations to other things, and in teaching the one thing the teacher must illuminate these relations.

Every result of importance should be obtained by at least two distinct methods, and every result of especial importance by two essentially distinct methods. This is possible in mathematics and the physical sciences, and thus the student is made thoroughly independent of all authority.

All results should be checked, if only qualitatively or if only "to the first significant figure." In setting problems in practical mathematics (arithmetical computation or geometrical construction) the teacher should indicate the amount or percentage of error permitted in the final result. If this amount of percentage is chosen conveniently in the different examples, the student will be led to the general notion of closer and closer approximation to a perfectly definite result, and thus in a practical way to the fundamental notions of the theory of limits and of irrational numbers. Thus, for instance, uniformity of convergence can be taught beautifully in connection with the concrete notion of area under a monotonic curve between two ordinates, by a figure due to Newton, while the interest will be still greater if "in the diagram and area" stands for "work done by an engine."

The teacher should lead up to an important theorem gradually in such a way that the precise meaning of the statement in question, and

further, the practical—*i.e.*, computational or graphical or experimental
—truth of the theorem is fully appreciated; and, furthermore, the
importance of the theorem is understood, and, indeed, the desire for
the formal proof of the proposition is awakened, before the formal
proof itself is developed. Indeed, in most cases, much of the proof
should be secured by the research work of the students themselves.

Some hold that absolutely individual instruction is the ideal, and a
laboratory method has sometimes been used for the purpose of attaining this ideal. The laboratory method has as one of its elements of
great value the flexibility which permits students to be handled as
individuals or in groups. The instructor utilizes all the experience
and insight of the whole body of students. He arranges it so that the
students consider that they are studying the subject itself, and not
the words, either printed or oral, of any authority on the subject. And
in this study they should be in the closest cooperation with one another and with their instructor, who is in a desirable sense one of them
and their leader. Instructors may fear that the brighter students will
suffer if encouraged to spend time in cooperation with those not so
bright. But experience shows that just as every teacher learns by teaching, so even the brightest students will find themselves much the
gainers for this cooperation with their colleagues.

In agreement with Perry, it would seem possible that the student
might be brought into vital relation with the fundamental elements
of trigonometry, analytic geometry and the calculus, on condition
that the whole treatment in its origin is and in its development remains closely associated with thoroughly concrete phenomena. With
the momentum of such practical education in the methods of research
in the secondary school, the college students would be ready to
proceed rapidly and deeply in any direction in which their personal
interests might lead them. In particular, for instance, one might expect to find effective interest on the part of college students in the
most formal abstract mathematics.

For all students who are intending to take a full secondary school
course in preparation for colleges or technological schools, I am convinced that the laboratory method of instruction in mathematics and
physics, which has been briefly suggested, is the best method of instruction—for students in general, and for students expecting to spe-
cialize in pure mathematics, in pure physics, in mathematical physics
or astronomy, or in any branch of engineering.

Evolution, Not Revolution

In contemplating this reform of secondary school instruction we
must be careful to remember that it is to be accomplished as an evolution from the present system, and not as a revolution of that system.

Even under the present organization of the curriculum the teachers will find that much improvement can be made by closer cooperation one with another; by the introduction, so far as possible, of the laboratory two-period plan; and in any event by the introduction of laboratory methods; laboratory record books, cross-section paper, computational and graphical methods in general, including the use of colored inks and chalks; the cooperation of students; and by laying emphasis upon the comprehension of propositions rather than upon the exhibition of comprehension.

The Junior Colleges

Just as secondary schools should begin to reform without waiting for the improvement of the primary schools, so the elementary collegiate courses should be modified at once without waiting for the reform of the secondary schools. And naturally, in the initial period of reform, the education in each higher domain will involve many elements which later on will be transferred to a lower domain.

Further, by the introduction into the junior colleges of the laboratory method of instruction it will be possible for the colleges and universities to take up a duty which for the most part has been neglected in this country. For, although we have normal schools and other training schools for those who expect to teach in the grades, little attention has as yet been given to the training of those who will become secondary school teachers. The better secondary schools of today are securing the services of college graduates who have devoted special attention to the subjects which they intend to teach, and as time goes on the positions in these schools will as a rule be filled (as in France and Germany) by those who have supplemented their college course by several years of university work. Here these college and university graduates proceed at once to their work in the secondary schools. Now in the laboratory courses of the junior college, let those students of the senior college and graduate school who are to go into the teaching career be given training in the pedagogy of mathematics according to the laboratory system; for such a student the laboratory would be a laboratory in the pedagogy of mathematics; that is, he would be a colleague-assistant of the instructor. By this arrangement, the laboratory instruction of the colleges would be strengthened at the same time that well equipped teachers would be prepared for work in the secondary schools.

The Freedom of the Secondary Schools

The secondary schools are everywhere preparing students for colleges and technological schools, and whether the requirements of those institutions are expressed by way of examination of students or by way of the conditions for the accrediting of schools or teachers, the requirements must be met by the secondary schools. The stronger secondary school teachers too often find themselves shackled by the specific requirements imposed by local or college authorities. Teaching must become more of a profession. And this implies not only that the teacher must be better trained for his career, but also in his career he be given with greater freedom greater responsibility. To this end closer relations should be established between the teachers of the colleges and those of the secondary schools; standing provisions should be made for conferences as to improvement of the secondary school curricula and in the collegiate admission requirements; and the leading secondary school teachers should be steadily encouraged to devise and try out plans looking in any way toward improvement.

Thus the proposed four years' laboratory course in mathematics and physics will come into existence by way of evolution. In a large secondary school, the strongest teachers, finding the project desirable and feasible, will establish such a course alongside the present series of disconnected courses—and as time goes on their success will in the first place stimulate their colleagues to radical improvements of method under the present organization and finally to a complete reorganization of the courses in mathematics and physics.

The American Mathematical Society

Do you not feel with me that the American Mathematical Society, as the organic representative of the highest interests of mathematics in this country, should be directly related with the movement of reform? And, to this end, that the society, enlarging its membership by the introduction of a large body of the strongest teachers of mathematics in the secondary schools, should give continuous attention to the question of improvement of education in mathematics, in institutions of all grades? That there is need for the careful consideration of such questions by the united body of experts, there is no doubt whatever, whether or not the general suggestions which we have been considering this afternoon turn out to be desirable and practicable. In case the question of pedagogy does come to be an active one, the society might readily hold its meetings in two divisions—a division of research and a division of pedagogy.

Furthermore, there is evident need of a national organization having its center of gravity in the whole body of science instructors in the secondary schools; and those of us interested in these questions will naturally relate ourselves also to this organization. It is possible that the newly formed Central Association of Physics Teachers may be the nucleus of such an organization.

CONCLUSION

The successful execution of the reforms proposed would seem to be of fundamental importance to the development of mathematics in this country. I urge that individuals and organizations proceed to the consideration of the general question of reform with all the related questions of detail. Undoubtedly in many parts of the country improvements in organization and methods of instruction in mathematics have been made these last years. All persons who are, or may become, actively interested in this movement of reform should in some way unite themselves, in order that the plans and the experience, whether of success or failure, of one may be immediately made available in the guidance of his colleagues.

I may refer to the centers of activity with which I am acquainted. Miss Edith Long, in charge of the Department of Mathematics in the Lincoln (Neb.) High School, reports upon the experience of several years in the correlation of algebra, geometry, and physics, in the October, 1902, number of the *Educational Review*. In the Lewis Institute of Chicago, Professor P. B. Woodworth, of the Department of Electrical Engineering, has organized courses in engineering principles and electrical engineering in which are developed the fundamentals of practical mathematics. The general question came up at the first meeting [27] (Chicago, November, 1902) of the Central Association of Physics Teachers, and it is to be expected that this association will enlarge its functions in such a way as to include teachers of mathematics and of all sciences, and that the question will be considered in its various bearings by the enlarged association. At this meeting informal reports were made from the Bradley Polytechnic Institute of Peoria, the Armour Institute of Technology of Chicago, and the University of Chicago. The question is evoking much interest in the neighborhood of Chicago.

I might explain how I came to be attracted to this question of pedagogy of elementary mathematics. I wish, however, merely to express my gratitude to many mathematical and scientific friends, in particular, to my Chicago colleagues, Mr. A. C. Lunn and Professor C. R. Mann, for their cooperation with me in the consideration of these matters, and further to express the hope that we may secure the active cooperation of many colleagues in the domains of science and of administration, so that the first carefully chosen steps of a

---

[27] Subsequent to the meeting of organization in the spring of 1902. Mr. Chas. H. Smith of the Hyde Park High School, Chicago, is president of the Association. Reports of the meetings are given in *School Science* (Ravenswood, Chicago).

really important advance movement may be taken in the near future.

I close by repeating the questions which have been engaging our attention this afternoon.

In the development of the individual in his relations to the world, there is no initial separation of science into constituent parts, while there is ultimately a branching into the many distinct sciences. The troublesome problem of the closer relation of pure mathematics to its applications: can it not be solved by indirection, in that through the whole course of elementary mathematics, including the introduction to the calculus, there be recognized in the organization of the curriculum no distinction between the various branches of pure mathematics, and likewise no distinction between pure mathematics and its principal applications? Further, from the standpoint of pure mathematics: will not the twentieth century find it possible to give to young students during their impressionable years, in thoroughly concrete and captivating form, the wonderful new notions of the seventeenth century?

By way of suggestion these questions have been answered in the affirmative, on condition that there be established a thoroughgoing laboratory system of instruction in primary schools, secondary schools, and junior colleges—a laboratory system involving a synthesis and development of the best pedagogic methods at present in use in mathematics and the physical sciences.

---

4. Insight into Arithmetical Processes

Zoltan P. Dienes

INTRODUCTION

INSIGHT IS A VERY DIFFICULT TERM to define. When we say we have had an insight, we probably mostly mean that somehow things have fallen into place in a way in which they have not done so before, thereby making the whole field under consideration a great deal

Reprinted by permission of the author and publisher from *The School Review*, LXXII:2 (Summer, 1964), 183–200. Copyright © 1964 by the University of Chicago Press.

clearer. According to this "definition," insight is a relative affair. We can have progressively clearer and clearer ideas on how certain things fit together. Arithmetical insight can vary from the appreciation of the cardinal values of the numerals as permanent attributes of a class of sets, to the appreciation of Peano's axioms or Gödel's theorem on non-contradiction within arithmetic. In a rational approach to the learning of arithmetic it might be stipulated that the aims of such learning are the eventual deepening of insights through progressively more and more complex experiences in the various areas of arithmetic.

Through considerable experience with children and with teachers during the past five years, I have become aware of the great paucity of mathematical insights acquired by the population, and of the lack of depth of the insights that have been acquired. I should like to list the kinds of lack which I have found surprising, particularly in teachers who are engaged actively in teaching arithmetical processes to children.

The first example on the list is the basic idea of natural number. Briefly, the objects and events we see around us are classified into classes or sets, usually according to whether they do or do not possess certain properties. Often, however, we put objects or events into classes by the process of enumeration. We can talk about all the brown-haired children in a second grade in a certain school, or we can talk about Mary, John, and Susan, who happen to be just the brown-haired children in that particular second grade. In these and other ways we form *sets* or *classes* of objects, of people or of events. Then we proceed to classify these sets. For example, we might be thinking about all possible sets of things that have two objects in them. The common property of all these sets is their property of "two-ness," that of containing two elements and no more. It is just this property that we call the number two. As long as we have not stripped this "two-ness" of all irrelevant properties (such as the color or the shape or other properties of the elements, or the way or the order in which the elements are arranged), the property of "two" has not been abstracted from all possible pairs of objects or events. When this *has* happened, then a *symbol* may be used to indicate this abstract property of two-ness. This could be the symbol "2," or "II," or any other symbol on which we agree. The symbol "2" is often confused with the number "two," although the word "chair" is seldom confused with the article of furniture on which I am sitting while typing these lines. The word "numeral" has come to be used to mean the symbol, and the word "number," the abstract property of collections or sets of things which single out all sets with that particular number of things in them. To tell children that the squiggles "2," "1," "3," etc., *are* the *numbers* "two," "one," "three," etc., is to tell them an untruth, just as if we told children that the word "green" was itself necessarily green, or any such nonsense. I suggest that this fundamental idea of natural number, built on properties of sets, and the corresponding numerational notation are little appreciated by teachers in elementary schools. While the role of number itself is unclear, to tell children that two and one make three is of doubtful value. Even the introduction of physical aids could be retrogressive in the hands of a teacher unaware of the foundations of number, as the *representation* might well be confused with that which is being represented.

Another example, following from the last, would be the concept of multiplication. What do we mean by a multiplication such as

$$2 \times 3 ? \quad (\text{i.e., "two times three"}).$$

One of the factors describes a number property of sets, in which the elements are, let us say, *objects*. The other factor describes a number property of sets, in which the elements are not objects but *sets of objects*. The numeral 3 is the property of a set of sets containing three elements, these elements in this case being *objects*. Let us typify these by circles

The numeral 2 is the property of a set of sets containing two elements, these elements in this case being themselves *sets of three objects each*. The total number of objects may now be considered as belonging to yet a third set; the act of computing the number of elements, that is, the total number of objects contained in this final set, is what we term the operation of multiplication; the term "multiplicand" is given to the number of elements in the set of objects, and the term "multiplier" to the number of elements in the set of sets, numbering as many objects each as indicated by the multiplicand. It must be remembered that the multiplier and the multiplicand are *not* the sets we have considered, but the number of elements in these sets. The product is not the final set of objects obtained; it is the number of objects in this final set of objects.

This somewhat complex structure of the multiplication concept is seldom appreciated, and, it can fairly be said, it is ignored for the most part in our teaching. It would seem fairly evident that careful distinctions must be drawn between sets of objects, sets of sets of objects, and the corresponding number properties, before it can be expected that the confusions surrounding multiplication are cleared up. These confusions only become embarrassingly apparent when *properties* of multiplication are taught; until then children will be only too willing to learn by rote the "multiplication facts" and some simple mechanical procedures related to the process of multiplication with notation. The use of the laws of exponents in "long" multiplication is practically never attempted, and so the large majority of children simply learn by rote all the arithmetical processes, as the concepts involved are considered "too difficult" for them. I should like to suggest that this is so mainly because the basic idea of multiplication is unclear to most of those children who are at the moment having to learn these processes. And this state of affairs *can be* altered.

This brings me to the third example, namely, to that of the four arithmetical operations, but mainly multiplication and division. It is quite certain that only a negligible portion of the children learning "long" multiplication could possibly justify the methods used by them to obtain the products. In my experience, even the very bright children in school simply do not have any idea on this point, and if they are asked to explain, they simply say that they were taught to do it that way. What a travesty of mathematical education!

Such examples could be multiplied indefinitely. The accent is on getting the right answer, and the task of the teacher of mathematics is more often than not conceived as the business of providing children with the most effective methods of finding correct answers, irrespective of any understanding of the processes whose formal equivalents are carried out by the children. Those readers who are satisfied with this conception of the teaching of mathematics need not trouble to read any further, as the assumption will be made from now on that at least one of the principal reasons for teaching children mathematics is to get them accustomed to thinking in terms of mathematical structures. The perception and the handling of relationships within and between structures will be assumed both as a principal *aim* and a principal *payoff* in the learning of mathematics.

How can we increase and deepen mathematical insights? There are essentially two approaches: One is to go to the children in the classrooms and show them that mathematical thinking is fun, in the hope that the children's enthusiasm will infect the teachers. The other is to go to the teachers and attempt to induce mathematical insights at depth in their minds by persuading *them* that it is fun. And of course it is possible to do both at the same time.

A PRACTICAL OPPORTUNITY FOR THE DEEPENING OF INSIGHTS

It is sometimes difficult to find an opportunity to use either of these approaches—approaches necessary before any deepening of insights can be attempted. It is people who have insights, and so first and foremost, it is necessary to get hold of people so that the process of generating insights can be demonstrated. A very good opportunity came when I was asked to be mathematical consultant during a recent Peace Corps training program, whose purpose was to train teachers' aides bound for Southeast Asia. It happened that I was passing through the area where the program was being operated, and I was asked to visit for a few days. To encourage more extensive and intensive work, it was necessary to show that mathematical insights could be generated in a relatively short time. A demonstration class was arranged with a mixture of fourth and fifth graders, the trainees and some local teachers forming the audience. I adopted the "image manipulation technique," which is one of telling the class a story, in which a certain rule structure was governing events. This rule structure would of course be the one that was identical with the mathematics that was going to be learned. The children soon started manipulating the stories "to see what would happen if . . ." under various circumstances. Two sessions were held on two successive days (both out of school hours); all the children thoroughly enjoyed the lessons, and they learned a great deal about vector spaces, the construction of algebras, the formation of isomorphisms, etc.[1]

The classes had the result of arousing interest both among the organizers of the training center and among the teachers, not to mention the children, who extracted a firm promise from me of an eventual return "for more stories." It was tentatively arranged that the next program would make use of my services full time, and the stage was set for some very interesting work.

There were about six weeks in which to operate. Material was quickly ordered from some of the mathematics projects in the United States and some from England, notes were prepared, and all was ready when the new batch of trainees arrived. I decided to use both methods suggested in the introduction: generation of insights in the minds of the trainees, and observation of generation of insights in classrooms by the trainees. The ease with which children take to abstractions has to be seen to be believed, and so I considered it just as important for the trainees to see the children abstract as to induce them to abstract themselves.

During the whole training period the trainees only had three full lectures. The rest of the time they were organized into mathematical laboratories, observation of demonstration classes, and teaching

---

[1] For details see my *The Power of Mathematics* (London, 1963) and *An Experimental Study of Mathematics Learning* (London, 1963).

practice. In laboratory periods trainees handled mathematically structured materials with the aid of which they were asked to solve certain mathematical problems. There was arithmetical as well as algebraical material, but the stress was on the arithmetical materials. In the demonstration classes trainees were able to observe children making progress with problems similar to the ones they themselves were coping with. Some were discouraged when they realized that the children were making much more rapid headway than they themselves, but all were struck by the high level of motivation present in the classes, and the obvious pleasure the children were deriving from their learning. This acted as a spur at any rate for those of the trainees who were determined to do the best they could for their future charges, and such trainees got down to their problems all the more seriously during the succeeding laboratory periods. A small percentage of the trainees had sufficient confidence toward the end of the training period to put into practice during their teaching practice period some of the laboratory work they had experienced and observed. In the notes suggestions were made as to the adaptation of the mathematical materials to local conditions. One arithmetic set was in fact constructed out of bamboo and was a great success in the classroom.

For the demonstration classes a third grade was chosen for arithmetic and a fifth grade for algebra. The third grade worked with the arithmetic materials, learning to add and subtract in an arbitrary base of numeration. They also did much practical work, such as measuring lengths, areas, capacity, etc. The purpose of this, as far as the trainees were concerned, was to show them that it was possible to decentralize a classroom, with all the children working and yet with every small group possibly doing something different. This enables children to proceed at their own pace, as well as providing a higher level of motivation through effective choice of activity. The class was not "taught" at all; there were no class lessons, with the exception of an occasional short discussion, and even in these not all the children would necessarily participate.

Similar organization was introduced into the fifth grade, where algebraical experiences made up the bulk of the time of the lessons. Children worked from individual instruction cards, much as the trainees had worked in their laboratory periods. The laws of addition and multiplication (commutative, associative, and distributive laws) were introduced through physical experiences, followed by experiences leading to the square of the binome. Some children very quickly went through these instruction cards, and another set of experiences, leading to the properties of positive and negative numbers, was introduced. Balance beams, pegboards, squares, triangles, rhombi, number tracks, and the like were the materials for much of this work, with a few mathematical stories thrown in to encourage "image manipulation." Some of the children in this class had been in the original two pilot demonstration classes, and proudly considered themselves old hands.

Before the training program was over, the teaching of mathematics through the generation of insights had spread to a large number of other classes. There were several first, second, third, and fourth grades doing arithmetic in different bases, logical sorting of attributes, fractions, practical measuring, etc., and the algebra spread to one of the sixth grades, where a few children were able to construct algebras and handle matrices. It became necessary to co-ordinate a miniature teacher-training program, and there were the makings of a new mathematics project in which children, faculty, and administrators had become keenly interested. The Peace Corps trainees were able to observe the birth and subsequent development of this project, and could possibly conclude that it was the children's own keen interest in passing to the abstract from the concrete that persuaded teachers and administrators that it was a worthwhile method of teaching mathematics.

All the trainees did not take to the insightful method equally rapidly. It took some of them a considerable time to realize that there was any difference between carrying out a mechanical arithmetical task and being aware of what the motions signified in terms of groupings. Multiplications and divisions in different bases were introduced in order to compel trainees to think about what they were doing, so as to make them aware of the extent of the complexity of these processes. Such awareness would stand them in good stead when confronting children called upon to learn these processes for the first time. Even so, some complained that they were able after a while to carry out quite complex operations in any base *on paper*, but that they could not do them if they had to be carried out with physical material embodying the various powers of the bases. I suggested to such trainees that they had simply transferred their mechanical knowledge of multiplication in base 10 to some other base, say, base 6, by always arranging to "carry" 6 instead of 10.

If they could not handle a physical embodiment, the insight was not complete. There appeared to be several stumbling blocks in the way of understanding. One was that some had only a somewhat hazy notion about multiplication. They were not explicitly aware that they had physically to make "equal" piles, and that they had to make as many of these "equal" piles as there were unit pieces in some other pile. The multiplicand counted the units in "the pile," the multiplier counted the piles. The next difficulty to overcome was the multiplication by the base number. To make a pile just six times, in which the pieces are "tailored" to the base 6, will result in a final pile in which each piece is replaced by a piece six times as big, that is, by the *next* piece up in the series of pieces. Multiplying by a multiple of the base number introduces the additional difficulty of the use of the associative law of multiplication. Practical illustrations of these will be given in the next section.

It was also not clear just how many trainees had realized the fundamental logical structure of number itself. Children's booklets and teachers' manuals on "Sets and Numbers," devised by Patrick Suppes, were made available to the trainees, so that they could see through to this logical structure at the children's level. Not many trainees availed themselves of this information, although it was emphasized in each of the three lectures. It must be said that the schedules were extremely full, mathematics forming only a small part of the total program, and there was very little time for the carrying out of a complete metamorphosis of mathematical ideas from the logical foundations upward. I thought that the concepts of set and number should be clarified in the context of the arithmetical operations; sets were in fact handled by the trainees in the form of physical sets of objects; these *represented* the successive powers of various bases. Consistent attempts at reminding trainees of the difference between a set of blocks and the number of units that the set of blocks was made up of succeeded in making this important distinction clear only to some of them.

There were several indications that in a large number of cases some mathematical metamorphosis did take place. One such indication was the difference between the mid-term and the final test scores. In each case the test consisted of two parts, one part in which the "answer" could be obtained by just thinking about the problem from first principles, and another in which arithmetical operations in bases different from the base 10 had to be carried out. The mid-term scores were distributed normally, some doing very badly, some very well, but the vast majority clustering around the mean. In the final test about six obtained 100 percent, more than half obtained over 80 per cent, and only four trainees obtained less than 45 per cent. Although it is possible to do the multibase arithmetic by a transfer of rote methods, it is fair to assume that the changed scores represent a considerable amount of thinking at the final test that was not possible at mid-term. This conclusion is supported by the fact that a great number of trainees declared that it was the first time they had really understood multiplication and division, the idea of a power, and that of an exponent, and that they were very thrilled that they had been able to achieve these insights. Many had been through "work with bases" in one or the other of the new mathematics projects, and a number of these declared that they had clearly done the "bases" work by mechanical transfer as suggested earlier and that they had only been enabled to see what it was all about through work with physical embodiments.

The vast majority of mathematical learning situations that are created in the United States are based on one assumption, which I believe to be false, and it is this: That the connection between mathematical symbols and the structures symbolized by them is as firm as the connection between other symbols, such as words, and that which is symbolized by them.

Even the "modern" mathematics, which appears to have become the vogue over the past few years, is done almost exclusively on the symbolic level. Lip-service is paid to experience by including some diagrams and pictures, and warnings are uttered, somewhat ineffectually, about the value of the inductive method. It is not made clear that induction has to take place out of something, and as far as I can see, this something is very seldom effectively provided. The work here reported with Peace Corps trainees has convinced me of the existence of a very dangerous lack in the mathematical build-up of our future teachers, and of the efficacy of using a truly inductive, experiential method, leading to the possibility of filling in these gaps in at least some cases. The mathematics laboratory is an effective, exciting way of learning mathematics, both for children and for adults, and I hope that it will be adopted in pilot schools and pilot teachers colleges at the earliest opportunity, as it is already being done in Great Britain in a rapidly increasing number of areas.[2]

EXAMPLES OF ARITHMETICAL TASKS

Physical materials embodying bases of numeration to the bases 2, 3, 4, 5, 6, and 10 were provided. Some of these were rectangular blocks, some were cut in the shapes of triangles, trapezoids, or hexagons. For example, in one of the base 3 sets the pieces were all of equal thickness, so that only two dimensions were being used. The "unit" piece was an equilateral triangle the length of whose sides we might call 1 unit length. The other pieces were as shown in Figure 1.

[2] See the report on the starting of these operations in my *Building Up Mathematics* (New York: Humanities Press, 1960).

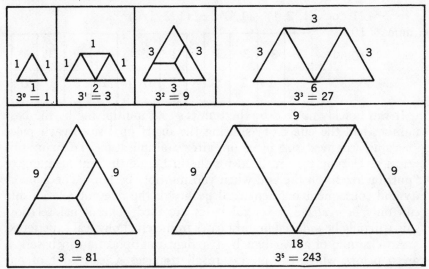

Fig. 1.—The numerals in base 10 express in this usual base the number of unit triangles in each piece. The corresponding base 3 numerals would be

1, 1 0, 1 0 0, 1 0 0 0, 1 0 0 0 0, 1 0 0 0 0 0, ...

A multiplication by the base number (i.e., by 3 here) would look like this:

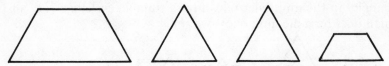

Example: Make this pile →

as many times as there are unit triangles in this pile →

The given pile must be made three times. After exchanging for equal amounts of material but larger pieces, the resulting set of blocks will be:

The *number* of unit triangles in the original pile can be symbolized by the 3-base numeral 1 2 1. The *number* of triangles in the second pile (the one that told us how many times to build the first pile) can be symbolized by the 3-base numeral 1 0. The *number* of triangles (of the original unit size) in the final pile can be symbolized by the 3-base numeral 1 2 1 0. The multiplication that has been carried out may be symbolized in some such way as

121 or $(1, 2, 1) \times (1, 0) = (1, 2, 1, 0)$

times   10

=   1210 or

3^3	3^2	3^1	3^0		3^1	3^0		3^3	3^2	3^1	3^0
1	2	1		$\times$	1	0	$=$	1	2	1	0

It was quickly noticed by the trainees that multiplying by the base number had the effect of "shifting the digits up," since each piece "became" the next size piece up, after multiplication. To many this was a revelation; they realized for the first time the real meaning of "putting a zero on the end when you multiply by ten." The *generality* and consequent mathematical beauty of the relevant relationship can only be realized if several bases are used. The actual relationship can only be *induced* in most cases from actual physical experience.

An example of a two-digit by two-digit multiplication in base 4 is given below, where the pieces are all triangles. Clearly out of any four triangles it is possible to build another triangle. So the successive powers of 4 can be represented by triangles of increasing size, the lengths of the sides of neighboring triangles being in the ratio of 1 to 2. The different-sized triangles came to be known as unit, small, medium, and large triangles. The first pile became the multiplicand pile (but not the multiplicand!); the second pile, the multiplier pile (but not the multiplier!).

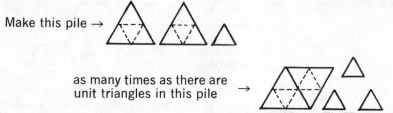

Make this pile →

as many times as there are
unit triangles in this pile →

If we make three multiplicand piles, as indicated by the three unit triangles in the multiplier pile, after a suitable exchange (i.e., of four small ones for a medium one), we get:

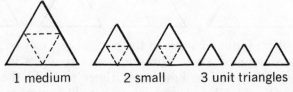

1 medium   2 small   3 unit triangles

Making the multiplicand pile the base number times, that is, four times, would yield 2 medium and 1 small, so twice this will yield 4 medium and 2 small triangles, which is equivalent in size to 1 large and 2 small triangles. Putting these together with 1 medium, 2 small, and 3 unit triangles, we obtain 1 large, 2 medium, 4 small, and 3 unit triangles. The 4 small are exchanged for 1 medium and the result is

{1 large, 3 medium, no small, 3 unit triangles,}

which is the product pile or set. The number of unit triangles in this pile is expressed by means of the four-base numeral (1, 3, 0, 3).

Here is an example of long division in base 4.

EXAMPLES: How many piles like

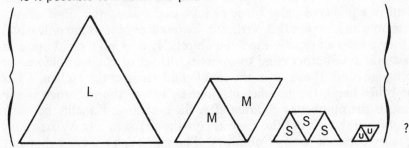

is it possible to find in the pile

Each pile is separated off into parts, each part containing only the same size pieces; let us call the pile

the A pile, and the other, larger pile, the B pile. The problem is to find out how many piles like the A pile it is possible to find in the B pile.

In the first two parts of the B pile there are exactly as many A piles as there are units in a medium triangle. So a medium triangle is the first part of the quotient pile. There remain 3 small and 2 unit triangles of the B pile to examine. In this there are 2 A piles, with 2 unit triangles left over. So there are

as many A piles in a B pile as there are unit triangles
in 1 medium triangle and 2 unit triangles,

with 2 unit triangles left over. The division of the corresponding *numbers* (i.e., not of the piles) would be symbolized in 4-base numerals as follows:

(1, 2, 3, 2)   ÷ (1, 2) = (1, 0, 2).
(1, 2, 0, 0)   being the number of units in the B pile "used up"
             by taking (1, 0, 0) number of A piles.

(3, 2)   number of units in section of the B pile in which
         further A piles must be looked for.
(3, 0)   being the number of units in the B pile "used up" by
         taking two A piles.

2   being number of units in section of the B pile in
         which no more A piles can be found.
         This is therefore the *remainder*.

EXAMPLES OF ALGEBRAICAL TASKS

The predicate "equal" applies to two subjects. Whether the statement of equality is judged true or false depends on the kinds of subjects on which we use this predicate. Two sets of objects are only equal
if they consist of exactly the same objects. If we send a child out of a
class and ask another child to come in, the set of children before the
exchange is not the same as the set of children after the exchange. On
the other hand, the number of children before the exchange is the
same as the number of children after the exchange. Equality between
natural numbers is not the same as equality between sets. What about
equality between pairs of numbers? The pair (2, 3) may or may not
be judged equal to the pair (3, 2). If these two pairs are not judged
equal, then we are taking account of the order; for example, if Mrs.
Brown has 3 dollars and Mrs. Smith has 2 dollars, this is not the same
situation as Mrs. Brown having 2 dollars and Mrs. Smith having 3
dollars. But if Mrs. Brown receives 2 dollars from one source and 3 dollars from another source, she is unlikely to be disturbed if the amounts
coming from the two sources are exchanged. In other situations (2, 3)
may be judged to be equal to (4, 6) or to (6, 9); this will be so if we
are only interested in the ratio of the two numbers. For example, in
a 50 per cent profit the first number would represent the initial outlay,
the second the final amount to hand. If we are only interested in the
percentage profit, the above pairs will be judged equal from that point
of view. On the other hand, (2, 3) might be judged equal to (7, 8)
or to (17, 18), if what we were concerned about was that the second
amount should be 1 more than the first amount. It is salutary to remind ourselves that "equal" is a very changeable kind of predicate,
and that whether we judge two situations as "equal" depends very
much on the point of view we happen to be adopting. To illustrate
this point, "directed numbers" exercises were introduced both for the
trainees and for the children in the fifth- and sixth-grade demonstration classes.

Some squares were painted red and others were left their natural
brown color. Piles of squares were classified into classes according to
whether they had a certain number more red than brown squares, or

more brown than red squares. All piles of squares in which, for example, "there were three more red than brown squares" were classified as equivalent and were described as *three-red* and symbolized $3r$. Similarly for all other numbers. Such a class of piles of squares provided an *embodiment* of the class of *pairs of natural numbers* of which

$$(1, 4), (5, 8), (100, 103), (49, 52), \ldots, \text{etc.},$$

are exemplars.

The interesting thing about such a classification is that, if you united two piles, say, one belonging to the *two-red* class and the other belonging to the *five-brown* class, you invariably came out with a pile belonging to the *three-brown* class. It did not matter what exemplars of these classes were chosen; the resulting pile always belonged to the *three-brown* class. From these experiences it was natural to *induce* that

$$2r + 5b = 3r,$$

where the result of the "adding" indicated the computation of the class name of the united pile from the class names of the separate piles. It is easy to see how "subtraction situations" can be created by removal.

Equality of two number pairs was defined by the excess number of one kind over the other kind being the same in the two number pairs. This led to experiences on which addition of directed numbers could be based. The equality of natural numbers is based on the equal numerosity of two sets of objects. The equality of directed numbers is (or, at any rate, can be) based on the equal difference between members of pairs of natural numbers. Unless some such difference in the meaning of equality is established in the different situations in which "equal" is used, it is hard to imagine how the appreciation of the relationships to each other of the corresponding mathematical structures becomes possible. The greater part of the headaches resulting from "pluses and minuses" could be avoided if a rational approach were employed as regards the nature of the extension made from natural to directed numbers. This is a similar distinction, but on a higher level, to the distinction between sets of things and the number of things in sets of things. On the understanding of the latter distinction depends the rational build-up of the arithmetic of natural number, that is, the greater part of the arithmetic learned by children in elementary schools. On the understanding of the former depend the rational build-up of the arithmetic of directed number and the understanding of the algebraical properties arising out of such arithmetic.

It must be said that the Peace Corps trainees made heavy weather of such considerations as the above, whereas the children seemed much more able to become familiar with the new, and to them exciting, situations, that were created through each extension. The children did not stop at the arithmetic of real numbers; they were able to proceed, through the playing of suitably structured games, to the unravelling of complex numbers and other creations of the mind, which they themselves created as acts of generalization from previously established simpler situations.

CONCLUDING REMARKS

It is not possible in a short space to indicate all the varieties of ways in which mathematical insights may be generated in adults and/or in children. In the work here described, three somewhat different ways were tried, some with the children, some with the trainees, and some with both.

(a) The use of physical embodiments, tailored to the mathematical structure required to be learned.

(b) The use of games, the rules of which coincided with the rules of the mathematics to be learned.

(c) The use of stories, in which events followed a pattern prescribed by the mathematical structure to be learned.

In order to achieve abstraction, and not mere association, it is essential to vary the embodiments, the games, the stories, while keeping the structure constant. The mathematical similarity between the embodiments, or between the games, or between the stories, while other details are totally different, will pinpoint the mathematical aspect of the experiences which have been provided. The technique of bringing out the mathematical similarity in two different versions of the same mathematics is to ask children to construct "dictionaries," by means of which true statements from one version are translated into true statements in the other version. If two situations are such that any dictionary that it is possible to construct will always translate some true statements into false statements, then the two situations do not represent the same mathematics. Conversely, if such a dictionary is constructed, then the two situations are merely different ways of talking about the same mathematical structure; we have put different clothes on the same piece of mathematics. When children have acquired agility in judging aright on the structural similarity or dissimilarity of situations from the mathematical point of view, then they have truly been initiated into the mysteries of the mathematical workshop. Nothing less than this is worth aiming at; it can be said that, from the experience of many mathematics projects in different parts of the world, tackling the problems in a great variety of ways, *this aim is not utopian;* children can and do acquire the mathematical skill required to handle complex structures; they enjoy both the acquisition and the subsequent wielding of such skill. Let us hope that teachers will rise to this challenge and become instrumental, on a large scale, in helping children acquire these exciting skills.

PART TWO
The Physical and Natural Sciences

5. On the Structure of Physical Knowledge

Norwood Russell Hanson

I

UNDER WHAT CIRCUMSTANCES would a person try to find some structural principles underlying all the physical sciences? Well, being *asked* to do so, for an occasion such as this, might be one such set of circumstances. But why should professional educators ask a mere philosopher of science to try? Presumably because if what I say is both true and new it might have constructive implications for the design of curricula in schools; let me at least hope that what I say will be true, even if not new. Whereas, if what I say is false, it may even then stimulate discussion which could, perhaps negatively, and certainly indirectly, affect the reflections of you pedagogical theorists; in that case I must hope that my views will be new, even if not true. With this much I am asking for it: "what Hanson says that is true, is not new—what is new is not true—and the rest is neither new nor true."

For reasons analogous to this "discussion-stimulating" function (of a structural analysis of physical knowledge) the chairman of a college's physics department might seek to order, classify, and systematize his own discipline—now in order to facilitate its consumption by undergraduates. The writer of a textbook in physics might be similarly motivated; here, too, what will constitute the best introduction to the subject will be determined by the author's conceptions of just what comprise the more elementary and fundamental problems; from these he will guide his readers to the advanced features of physical science.

But these all seem very practical reasons for undertaking such a study. One can imagine undertaking reflections on the conceptual structure of physical science *not* because of having been invited to so reflect, nor because of having to design a college science program, or a textbook's table of contents; one can imagine engaging in such an inquiry "for its own sake." Plato's discussions (in *The Republic*) of his Divided Line, Auguste Comte's "Classification of the Sciences" as

Reprinted by permission from *Education and the Structure of Knowledge* edited by Stanley Elam, pp. 148–187 (Chicago: Rand McNally and Company, 1964).

well as those of J. A. Thomson and Hügo Munsterberg—these were studies of the conceptual interrelations of the physical sciences (amongst others), studies made for no reason beyond achieving clarity and understanding about how mathematics and the several physical sciences are related and hang together, and where they differ and should never be fused or confused. Knowing this much about the physical sciences is thus to understand each of them a little better— optics, particle dynamics, celestial mechanics, electro-dynamics, microphysics, etc.—just as being able to distinguish, in general, pure mathematics from mathematical physics is to have a more reliable comprehension of each. And, indeed, that is just where my analysis will begin today, for perceiving where to cleave the study of numbers from the study of matter-and-motion already invokes those principles operative in ordering the several physical sciences themselves.

II

A proposition of pure mathematics—one such as the Binomial Theorem—is often characterized as being "purely formal." Its validity is in no way contingent on observation or experiment, on measurement or microscopes. Indeed, the Binomial Theorem is something "merely unpacked" from the number-theoretic commitments one must make when playing the mathematics game at all. Follow the Rules Consistently—constitutes the *sine qua non* of pure mathematics. Of course, there can be endless discussions at the foundations; e.g., whether, for certain purposes, to accept Peano's Postulates, or Huntington's, or Zermelo's—Russell's or Hilbert's, Quine's or Kleene's, or Heyting's. But such inquiries turn on different considerations. Once one *has* decided to play the numbers game *à la* Hilbert, or *à la* Heyting, then the validity of all derivations generable therefrom is determined. Thus within either of these last-mentioned formulations the Binomial Theorem is quickly constructed.

Despite the indispensable role played by mathematical techniques in the articulation of physical statements, there must always remain a profound and indissoluble difference between, e.g., the "pure Binomial Theorem" and a description of physical phenomena in binomial form. In physics, following the rules is not enough. For the physicist's subject-matter is not exclusively determined for him by the postulates and principles of inference he accepts—as is the case in the formal disciplines like mathematics and logic. *Nature* has written the physicist's script—in invisible ink. The task is then subtly to devise techniques, theoretical and experimental, by which to render more and more of that script visible and intelligible. For in physics the inferential techniques are created in order to decipher the script, whereas in pure mathematics the inferential techniques *are* the script. Similarly, at war colleges generals play board games to sharpen their strategies and tactics for future campaigns. But those same games might be sold later to tired businessmen seeking diversion—sold under names like "Battleground," "Cavalry Tactics," or "Air War." Construed in this way the games are self-contained, closed, rule-governed, and impervious to questions of use—much as with the game now called "Monopoly." But for generals and physicists (as against tired businessmen and mathematicians) it is the degree to which such formal games can help them to "tell the truth" and "predict the future" which constitutes the rationale behind playing them at all.

This contrast demarcates the deep logical difference between physics and mathematics. Any well-made claim of mathematics, e.g., that $(x + y)^3 = x^3 + 3x^2y + 3xy^2 + y^3$, is such that its negation is not even false—it is self-contradictory. Similarly, to be playing chess and yet moving the rook diagonally is simply to have made an error (as when one assigns the wrong melting point to phosphorous); it is to have broken the rules altogether! Game-like disciplines, chess and mathematics, are such that inferences, moves and theorems permissible within them are *necessarily* permissible. Their negations don't even make sense—given the game's rules. Whereas in the physical sciences, despite their degree of mathematical sophistication, the observation-statements which form at the bottom of a page of calculation are not necessary, as are theorems of mathematics. The physicist may indeed reason that P will melt at $44°C$. (ptc); but since this is not just a formal theorem, but an observation statement, it is not senseless to suppose that P might melt at some temperature other than $44°C$.—at most it is false, not absurd. What temperature phosphorous does in fact melt at has been determined by nature, not by our rules. Well-made claims in mathematics, therefore, are either necessarily valid or necessarily inconsistent—depending on the local rules of the algorithm-game one is playing. Well-made claims within physics, however, are quite otherwise; that they are well-made may mean that they are legitimately inferred from initial conditions in accordance with certain laws and principles. But that they are *true*, or *false*, this cannot be ascertained simply from scrutiny of the physicist's inference. The best celestial mechanicians of the last century certified that, according to Newtonian theory, the perihelial point of Mercury's orbit should advance $528''$ of celestial arc per century. But that observational conclusion is in fact false, however consistent with the theory. For Mercury's perihelion insists on advancing $528'' + 38''$ of arc each century (these are Leverrier's figures of 1859). This intractable fact forced physicists continually to amend Newtonian theory, and ultimately to abandon it altogether in determinations of near-solar perturbations. Is there anything comparable which, if it did occur in physical nature, would force our abandonment of chess, or of the number theories within which we generate the Binomial Theorem? No, nothing!

This logical ravine between the rule-governed sign-designs of higher mathematics and the mountains of observation statements articulated in physics is *the* major landmark in any charting of the structure of physical knowledge. On the one hand the stark simplicity of the distinction makes it fit for consumption by high school students, and even children in grammar school. Yet it is arresting to remark how late in the history of science this clear cleavage was effected. Galileo was not fully aware of the distinction, and many passages in Newton, Laplace, Lagrange, Maxwell, Whewell, and Thomson reflect considerable uncertainty over the matter. Even fairly recent works by physicists, like Kolin's *Physics* (New York, 1950) and Pieirl's *Laws of Nature* (London, 1955), decompose over this point. And it is easy to see why the glass darkens. Ask a student the following:

Q. Does $2 + 2 = 4$?
A. Of course!
Q. Does 2 quarts of mercury added to another 2 quarts equal 4 quarts of mercury?
A. Of course (really!).

Then, before his eyes you pour quarts of *Hg* into a precisely graduated beaker. The meniscus, of course, fails to reach up to the "4 quarts" line. Sometimes an astonished student will conclude that $2 + 2 = 4$ is not true! Sometimes the accuracy of the beaker is doubted. But more often, thankfully, the student will construe all this as marking something unusual about *Hg* itself. The moral? *No statement of pure mathematics can be presumed necessarily true when adapted to physical inquiry.*

A variation of this "philosophical quiz" consists in asking the student if substance A will be harder than substance C, given that A is harder than B and B is harder than C. Again the ready reply: "of course." Thence to the famous demonstration involving deformations —wherein three substances are chosen such that A deforms B (as, e.g., by scratching it) but not vice versa and B deforms C, yet A cannot deform C.

The point can be made to the student in an even more obvious way by asking him whether it is true that the sun rises in the east.

A. Of course!
Q. But what if, tomorrow, the sky lightens first in the direction of Monticello, and up comes the sun at 260° (instead of "where it belongs"—90°, in the direction of Danville).

I have encountered two responses to this serio-comic query.

A₁. The sun would still be rising in "the east" since that is what we *call* the direction (*any* direction) in which the sun rises.

A₂. We would have to deny that the sun rises in the east, since that is a direction fixed by the North Star and the stellar constellations.

These two answers illuminate the distinction we have been delineating. For the student who answered as in A₁, "The sun rises in the east" is an *analytic* or a *necessary* claim—invulnerable just like the Binomial Theorem. It could not be false since all it does is to unpack what was built into his semantical rule box. For our A₂ student, however, "The sun rises in the east" is a *synthetic* or a *contingent* claim—vulnerable, just like saying that phosphorous melts at 44°C., a claim which *could* be false, but just happens not to be.

III

Some perplexing statements in physics have the same need for analysis, in the absence of which students often reach the Ph.D. level and remain unclear as to the essential differences between physics and mathematics. Consider these claims:

"No perpetual motion machine is constructible."

"An infinite amount of energy would be required to accelerate a body faster than c."

"Electrons must be described only in terms of partially defined states."

It is sometimes difficult to know whether such claims are only succinct restatements of the rules of an algorithm, or whether they are genuine empirical descriptions—whether they are like "No rook can move diagonally" or more like "Phosphorous melts at 44°C." Or sometimes they can be supposed to oscillate, as does "The sun rises in the east"—the real meaning of which is clear only in a careful description of the context of utterance. Professor Pieirls describes the Law of Universal Gravitation as being a mixture of empirical and mathematical elements (in his book *The Laws of Nature*). The valuable insight behind his remark is quite destroyed in his exposition, since (like oil and water) physics and mathematics don't mix, logically, however true it is that contemporary physics must be well lubricated mathematically at every turn.

In all the formidable jungles of pedagogy faced by physics teachers there seems to be no more troublesome pitfall than this one. And, as the mathematical sophistication expected of a physics student increases, the likelihood of perplexity on this issue likewise increases. Yet, the distinction is quite comprehensible even for youngsters. My eight-year-old son has understood the simple example I've tendered

here. The trick is to keep the student alert to the distinction as he
ascends higher into the more rarified structures of physical knowledge. Accomplishing this, however, will be inestimably easier when
one's students have teethed on the contrast between the sign-design
game of pure mathematics and the informative (hence vulnerable)
claims at the bottom of every page of physical calculation.

IV

Once having located the edifice of physics on one side of this logical
canyon, the local *intraphysical* geography becomes somewhat more
tractable—although, again, intellectual wind currents caused by the
canyon are continually felt at the upper levels of physical science. This
is because our claims about the physical world *must* be embodied in
the language of mathematical transformations and functions. This
practical advantage constitutes a logical disadvantage and a pedagogic
problem—one rarely known to biology teachers or to historians and
philosophers of biology (e.g., Nordenskiöld, Woodger, Arber, Singer,
Beckner, Gregg, Pirie, Fulton, Stannard, or Greene).

Very early in one's study of matter it becomes necessary to address
the structure and properties of the subject matter, i.e., matter itself.
The question "What is matter?" however, is too rarely faced *as such*
in physics teaching; and, granted, it does seem a disconcertingly
philosophical query—such as might trigger a symposium at Notre
Dame. But in the context of physics teaching the question quickly
transforms into a mosaic of constituent queries like "What is a body?"
"What is inertia?" "What is mass?" "What is weight?" "What is a
c. of *g*.?" "What is density?" "What is specific gravity?" Quite quickly
the student learns a list of little rules by the use of which these properties of objects can be determined. Even here the exposition could be
spiced up with puzzlers like "Could a physical object be intangible?"
"Could a body be in two places at once?" or "Could two objects be in
the same place at one time?" or "Could an event or an experiment be
exactly duplicated at two different times?" and so on. Grappling with
these would relieve the rigors of rote repetition somewhat; and let's
face it, really rehearsing the formulae will always require some rote
repetition. Furthermore, such examples would also test the strength of
our earlier distinction, for more than one physicist has laid it down as
"mathematically necessary" that bodies cannot be in two places at
once—or more exactly, that distinct masses cannot be mathematically
described by more than one set of coordinate values for any given
value of *t*. (This must remind one of Phillip Frank's justifiable attack
on a colleague who purported to "prove mathematically" that no
body's velocity could surpass *c* [in *Philosophy of Science*].)

Talking about the static properties of physical objects—their equilibria, centers, stability, relative impenetrability, etc.—this comes seductively near to representing physics as "almost-pure" mathematics; indeed the history of analytical mechanics appears thus, and most of what one would master in that discipline figures within Part III of the *Mathematical Tripos*. For the extra-formal "physical" interpretations required at this level of natural science are minimal. It is as if we began with pure geometry, arithmetic, and algebra and added the fewest possible physical concepts (i.e., parameters pertaining to the properties of objects), their divisibility, their measurability, their ponderosity, their "balance," etc. Even here our earlier "mathematics *versus* physics" distinction obtains; but here it can appear that physics is simply geometry-plus-mass. Reflect for a moment on Galileo's references to the physical world as a book written entirely in geometrical figures, such that the nongeometer struck him as an utter illiterate among natural philosophers. Newton's use of the idea of punctiform masses—geometrical points which behaved on paper as do physical masses in our world; this is another example of the historical intimacy between physics and mathematics which obtained at the level of statics and the properties of bodies.

Once one brings in motions—in kinematics—the simplicity of a purely mathematical model for physics begins to get ornate. For it is not a *mathematical* truth that a body will either remain at rest or else move uniformly and rectilinearly to infinity (in the absence of impressed forces, the standard assumption in kinematics). Alternatives to this state of affairs can consistently be imagined. Our students should know that Aristotle and two millennia of Aristotelians would have denied such a kinematical claim. It was only three hundred years ago that this commitment was nailed to the top of the physicists' theoretical pages. As for the "Law" that the magnitude of a force is a function of the accelerations to which a mass is subjected—the status of this vis-à-vis our earlier distinction is markedly difficult to determine. Ernst Mach and C. D. Broad would cite this "Second Law of Motion" as an unqualifiedly empirical claim, a generalization of what we encounter when pushing pianos and catching medicine balls. But opponents of no less stature, e.g., Henri Poincaré and Victor Lenzen, would stress the conventional (or definitional) function of $F = ma$. They would argue that these symbols instruct us as to what we *mean* by "force," and that hence no mere empirical finding could upset it. For should an acorn kicked over smooth ice describe a "figure eight" we would not count the Second Law thus disconfirmed. Rather, we would hunt for the hidden forces, strings, air currents, or effluvia responsible for such a queer, noninertial, and force-bound motion. Indeed, we would be virtually certain a priori that *something* must have deflected the acorn into its lemniscoid path.

Again, here is an occasion for a student's speculative inquiry—

inquiry of a type with the questions he will certainly encounter when he one day finds himself stranded and alone on the frontiers of quantum mechanics or astrophysics. Just as Florence Nightingale urged that hospitals should not spread disease, so also educators should insure that schools do not stifle inquiry. But how often all of us smother such searching questions in the interests of rehearsing the algebraic recipes needed right now to describe uniform motion in a straight line, or accelerated motion, or gravitationally induced motions, or rectorial analysis. It is sometimes too easy to carp on the cruel cutoffs we impose on students' conversations—in the business of "getting on with" the curricula. I've done it too often myself (cf. *Physics Today*, 1955). But when my own son asked me (just as I was starting the car), "Daddy, what *causes* gravity?" I felt the knife all teachers feel sometimes. Should I have missed my morning class and discussed the rudiments of general field theory with the boy? (He was also late for school!) We agreed to discuss the matter later. So I can well understand the teacher who opts for discussing the conceptual foundations of physics "later." A practical conscience makes intellectual cowards of us all. But in an ideal world of ideal schools composed of ideal students—we could there discuss the philosophical status of Newton's Laws of Motion to our hearts' content—without fear of falling behind the syllabus (or behind Canaveral's orders for more "slide-rule soldiers"). And our understanding of all the physics to follow would be broadened and deepened thereby.

Thus from statics (= the properties of bodies at rest), where we add but a physical minimum to our mathematical structures, to kinematics (= the descriptive aspects of bodies in motion)—where we add more. Thence to dynamics where we add much more still. For here we do not simply describe the motions of bodies; it is the *causes* of those motions—the pushes, pulls, rubs, attractions, and repulsions which set things off, keep them moving, or halt them—which hold us now. Classical particle dynamics is really a Pandora's box of philosophical perplexities, the box out of which spilled some of the greatest glories of modern science. For when Newton opened the lid he dimly perceived the key for understanding *all* motions in our universe—from the majestic circlings of planets, to the insignificant fall of a Lincolnshire apple. That key lay in $F \propto \gamma (Mm)/r^2$—The Principle of Universal Gravitation. This mighty pronouncement at once fused ballistics with kinematics, celestial mechanics with tidal theory, hydrodynamics with particle theory. But, despite the dramatic unification effected within physics by the Newtonian synthesis, the box of Pandora dumped many further perplexities into the Natural Philosopher's broad lap. For gravity was apparently a universal *attraction* of all objects for all other objects, an attraction varying directly as the masses of the objects and inversely as the distances between them. But what a remarkable *kind* of attraction! The earth attracts the moon, and the moon the earth—but no ordinary knife can cut the tie that binds them. No leaden wall (laid Van Allen-wise) can affect gravitational attraction—as one might break up a comparable electromagnetic attraction with sheet copper reflections. No generator could increase such a gravitational attraction—only increasing the masses of earth and moon or decreasing the distance between them will do that. No wonder my boy asked, "What causes gravity?"

No wonder my best student ever urged rewriting the classical Law of Inertia to make it read "every two bodies in the universe are such that they move toward each other directly as their masses and inversely as the distance between them." This is a kinematical pronouncement *merely*, one which slices all the specious causality right out of classical physics. That is, it lays down $F \propto \gamma (Mm)/r^2$ as a descriptive fact about the motion of bodies, similar to the Law of Inertia as usually construed. So attraction need not serve as a ghostly explanation of, e.g., planetary motion, since this latter just *is* as $(Mm)/r^2$! Similarly, one doesn't explain the tangibility of physical objects, since that is what physical objects are.

V

Now, such an intellectual encounter *must* reveal elementary physics as an inviting path to contemporary natural philosophy, and not (as it so often is now) a rather boring, rote rehearsal of recipes preparatory to the "exciting, modern stuff." Once the student sees the *rationale* behind the controversy which rages over gravitational attraction, he can more fully understand other attempts to avoid animistic explanations in physics, explanations in terms of pushes and pulls. Thus a youngster *could* see the point of having planets move along geodesics within "space-time envelopes" whose geometrical properties are altered by the presence of large masses. General relativity, indeed, is the physical theory that treats planetary orbital motion not as a resultant deflection from "natural" inertial motion; rather Mercury's path is the most "natural" line (of least resistance) through spaces whose formal properties have been affected by the presence of other enormous bodies.

The relationship between classical optics and quantum field theory also reveals that a student's first questions are not about *elementary* physics, but about *fundamental* physics. For on reconsidering the vexatious debate over whether light was undulatory or corpuscular, the alert youngster *must* have questions concerning how such things as the findings of Young, Fresnel, Foucault, and Fizeau—while they *did* reveal light as wave-like—could also have proved that light lacked particularity. This latter was a massive inference made in nineteenth-century physics; all the more difficult then to move men's minds to where they could appreciate the findings of Hertz, Planck, Einstein, Compton, Raman, Thompson, Davisson and Germer, Stern and Gerlach—findings which established the "fine structure of light" as granular, in addition to its grosser undulatory manifestations.

In short, the departmental structures within physical science soon melt under the student's sizzling, searching questions—*if* he is encouraged to ask them. Quantum electrodynamics and classical optics emerge for him as two different attempts to comprehend the one subject matter, LIGHT. And General Relativity and Classical Celestial Mechanics also appear as different attempts to comprehend planetary perturbations. In this way physical science is a conceptual mosaic reflecting the natural phenomena of our world first this way, then that way—sometimes with quite different objectives. And *that's* the point: physics' objectives at different times may be quite distinct from what they are at other times. For a man building a radio telescope will not, and should not, get cramps over nuclear shell theory. And a man theorizing about theodolites need not wax neurotic about advances in the perihelion of Mercury. So specific tasks easily fall into compartments—but the content of physical science as a whole does not. In an engineering class on internal combustion engines the student who asks about solid state configurations of hot metal crystal lattices is just "changing the subject" and should be kept in line for the good of all. But physics is natural philosophy: the boy who asks "What causes gravity?" or "Why do planets move in conic sections?" or "Why does Mercury's perihelion show a secular advance?" is not changing the subject dealt with in "Physics I." Rather, he is deepening it for everyone around him. The student who *must* ask how physical laws came to be known at all *before* he can use them in churning out answers like a slot machine—such a student should be wreathed in gold stars, for he is showing his fellows, and his seniors, what kinds of questions will one day grip the man who fights to the frontiers of physics. Questions like "What is a measurement, really?" "What is an observation in physics?" "What should a theory do?" "How should a conservation principle be employed?" and "What is the relationship between a physical phenomenon and its mathematical description?"—these are the deep, exciting queries of contemporary physics, in response to which the slide-rule slickers fade in stature. "Getting the numbers right" and "Working the transformations well" are matters more for answer-giving machines, like the IBM 7090. But for those problems that make physics into natural philosophy, it will take a question-asking man every time.

VI

My thesis is now in danger of collapsing. Am I saying (the kind of thing sometimes said in pure analytic philosophy) that all questions are, ultimately, the same question—and that therefore the subject cannot be structured, save by second-rate textbook writers for second-rate students at second-rate colleges? No—that would be too much. Let me concede that there *is* such a thing as "changing the subject" in natural science—as when a discussion of semi-permeable membranes is halted by queries concerning interpretations of Quantum Mechanics. However, in physical science it is risky to draw any hard and fast lines. One should certainly not try to do so in the presence of students who cannot yet respond as the subject may later permit. The student who probes with "What is gravity?" or "What is space?" or "What is energy?"—he *may* be just a brat bent on battering the busy teacher. But he may also be tenacious enough to resist all pedagogic deflections and balm, in which case all around him may profit from seeing the paper walls set up in textbooks torn to shreds.

Let me conclude by saying again that physics, at its best, is natural philosophy. When any philosophy is too hastily restructured in "architectonic" terms the result can be dreary in its details and degenerate in its design. An architectonic of physical science, then, should never be more than loose guidelines for the guidance of syllabus drafters and textbook writers. But an architectonic ought never to crystallize into a set of *rigid* criteria for determining relevance or significance. Anyone who seeks to break down a wall rather than go through a door should be encouraged whenever possible. Physics today is a powerful instrument of mind and matter because of the irreverent wall-breakers of the seventeenth and twentieth centuries. A purported "Structure of Physical Knowledge" can never be more than a pedagogically heuristic blueprint. When conceived of as more—as an hierarchical series of disciplines, trials, and achievements—it must fail, even for the youngest students. For they will, after all, only ask the questions which a subject matter naturally presents to them. Their *genuinely* unsettling juvenile perversities are usually manifested in other ways.

DISCUSSION OF DR. HANSON'S PAPER

DR. SCHWAB: No one would deny that physics belongs on the side of the ravine that you put it on. However, I do want to raise a question as to whether you are quite right in your metaphor about mathematics and physics not mixing. To raise the question by noting a slip: at one point you said, "For it is not a mathematical truth that a body will either remain at rest or else move uniformly and rectilinearly to infinity in the absence of impressed . . ." what?

Dr. HANSON: "Forces," I said quite clearly.

Dr. SCHWAB: Yes, yes, I know, but is it not the case that at the moment you mention force you are no longer in kinematics but in dynamics?

DR. HANSON: Actually I want to do two things which are slightly inconsistent. I will grant that there is a real thrust to your question: in any discipline one must set up boundary conditions. One determines which set of unquestioned considerations is going to be fully operative in the discipline in question and then addresses an ideal case. The kind of kinematics we are discussing here resides strictly within analytical mechanics. There never has been a physical context free of impressed forces nor could there be. In other words, the physical discipline we have addressed is conditional, and unfilled; it is hypothetical all the way through. The theoretician here is simply telling us *what it would be like* to realize a physical state of affairs within which an ideal kinematics might be fully realized. What you are pointing out is that there is in fact no such state of affairs to be encountered, observationally or experimentally.

DR. SCHWAB: Yes.

DR. HANSON: And that much constitutes a dynamical statement. It's a statement of physics that there can be no such state of affairs as force-free motion. However, once one grants this the formal properties of a theory of motion which granted such a theoretical springboard might still be studied.

DR. SCHWAB: In a way this is more complex than I had hoped to deal with. You have spoken to my point not as an answer to the question but as an agreement with a peculiarity which exists. I want to state it more simply.

DR. HANSON: I won't deny the peculiarity.

DR. SCHWAB: I know, but let me indicate the full range of what I think is peculiar and invite your response. You will recall that Karl Pearson, speaking in the voice of Clifford, says, roughly, "As for me, I would wish that the conception of force be barred eternally from physics and thus return dynamics to the pure science of kinematics." Now the fact that he could say this and that nobody listened indicates how far there is something about physics in which notions like force are so vexed that it is hard to know whether they are mathematical or physical.

At another point you did something which may have been tongue-in-cheek. You have a list of names, all of whom but one are physicists. That one is a logician, Whewell.

DR. HANSON: Sorry, Whewell was a *geophysicist,* and also the

Master of Trinity College at Cambridge University. He was a professional scientist. He wrote an influential book called *Astronomy and General Physics*. The fact that his works on the philosophy of discovery and the history of science got more reputation for him than his works in science was for him a disappointment.

Dr. Schwab: An interesting biography, which makes more interesting the fact that he expressed an idea developed by Einstein that the greatest mistake that we make about physics is to suppose that it is an "inductive" science. Einstein and Whewell suggest that physics, quite the contrary, is the imaginative invention of an essentially mathematical construction adequate to subsume the data which one is concerned to organize and account for. Now this in no way denies that physics is on the physical side of the physics-mathematics ravine, but it does suggest—and this is what I want to invite your attention to and your comments on—that the physics and the mathematics do mix in the sense that the set of what Einstein called primary propositions (from which one deduces propositions which are empirical) are *freely chosen*, and, therefore, have the quality of mathematics.

Dr. Hanson: What you say is false.

Dr. Schwab: Wait a minute. And consequently when the empirical test is made, as you are insisting that it must be made, it is made not of an isolated proposition alone but on the entire corpus.

Dr. Hanson: That's all right.

Dr. Schwab: That's all I am asking you to clarify.

Dr. Hanson: Yes, that is true. But if I were to cast about for a mathematical paradigm within physics, Lagrange's analytical mechanics might serve well. There, from terse statements of abstract principles, even from "philosophical" principles, he's able to unpack a multiformity of observational claims, and to do so in a quite rigorous manner. The only test of the whole game is whether or not the stuff that comes out at the bottom of a page of calculation does truly square with the facts.

Dr. Schwab: And all I am suggesting is that insofar as the whole big corpus of theory can be treated algorithmically then there is a funny way in which physics and mathematics do mix to such an extent that physics is, as you yourself were saying, peculiar among the sciences. Biologists don't have the problem.

Dr. Hanson: That's what you are suggesting and that's what I am denying—that what comes out of the bottom of the page is invulnerable. The entire semantical structure of the rest of the system is affected in this because it is connected logically to the observation statements in the most intimate way. What this means, if I may just continue, is that even the most "transparent" principle, like the Principle of Conservation of Energy (which might well figure at the top of any page of calculation), looks like little more than a decision on the part of the theoretician to "balance" his equations in one way or another—even so, such as these remain empirically vulnerable claims. If one can make this point all the other jazz about the algorithmic similarities between doing pure mathematics and doing theoretical physics can be granted —because these are, after all, concerning one's self only with chains of inference and axiomatically designed systems. I can grant all that and still say nonetheless that, semantically, the pure physics and the pure mathematics are on opposite sides of the logical ravine; this goes for every single statement within the entire deductive unpacking.

DR. SCHWAB: We don't have any argument, so somehow or other you and I have not come to grips with the issue that I was trying to clarify. I will agree with every word you said. . . .

DR. HANSON: Say it again. I. . . .

DR. SCHWAB: Nobody in his right mind could argue against your thesis as to which side of the ravine physics is on.

DR. HANSON: Then I don't understand what *you* are arguing about.

DR. SCHWAB: I am not arguing. I am inviting clarification of the fact that as you do your algorithmic job down toward but not quite to the empirical level, the terms involved in the propositions are not terms that point to a physical, e.g., the conservation, law. The propositions are not talking about point-at-able things if one looks at them carefully. For example, you know very well that one of the particles that Pauli invented was invented precisely for the convenience of preserving one of the conservation laws as a convenient first gimmick at the top.

DR. HANSON: You are really answering my question for me, because it was the nature of that "invention" of the *neutrino* (in 1929 and 1930), an invention generated solely in order to save the conservation principle, which threw a shadow of dubiety on that particular discovery. It wasn't until the empirical work of Cowan and Reines in 1956 and 1957 (at Savannah River) that the neutrino became fully respectable; *there* was an observable effect that showed the physicist not only to be *inventing* entities to save a theory, but also to be discovering empirical evidence for this invention.

DR. SCHWAB: I agree.

DR. HANSON: This is what happened. I can give you scores of examples like this—Leverrier and Adams, for example. They were also concerned with a similar problem. They said, "Look here, the planet Uranus is not keeping time properly; the only way we can both acknowledge that fact and also save celestial mechanics is to suppose that there is another object, some 'dark body,' which has the following properties, a, b, c . . . etc." And they worked out the properties of this "in reverse," as it were. What would have to be the properties of a planet in order to perturb Uranus as it is perturbed?

Dr. Schwab: And then you go and look and there it is.

Dr. Hanson: Adams had entertained this hypothesis two years before Leverrier himself had. He argued that there might well be a body of this required sort—but he wasn't taken too seriously, for a number of reasons. This makes a long story, but certainly no one paid much attention to this early conjecture and it would have been a lot better for Adams if, in addition to generating the claim that would have saved celestial mechanics, he could also have located an observation then and there. Of course, there *was* material available in his manuscripts which, had observers then been more steadfast and careful, probably would have established Neptune's existence. But it wasn't until the insight which was precipitated by Leverrier's work, and the telescopic discovery by Galle in Berlin, that this actually became a vital hypothesis.

So you see, Joe, this is all still wide open vis-à-vis the question of what is the logical status of the claims. I want to argue that if there is an issue between Professor Schwab and myself, it is this: he's calling attention to the similarities between the inferential techniques that go into the doing of mathematics on the one hand, and those in physical theory on the other; this seems to be no more than the recognition that when you get a cluster of premises you unpack them by the logically most acceptable and direct techniques. Of course, it turns out that when the premises are expressed mathematically one unpacks them according to the techniques of *mathematical* unpacking. This, whether they be inferences in mathematics or in physics.

Dr. Schwab: I thought I was adding one other thing: the question of the purport of the terms in the premises. They do not refer directly to empiricals and consequently suggest something strangely mathematical about physics.

Dr. Hanson: You are calling attention to something, but I think you are doing it in the wrong way. If you say that there is something strangely mathematical about physics this is like injecting the mistaken suggestion that after all when you are concerned with axioms as in physics the best people to have around are professors of mathematics.

Dr. Schwab: No, no, I am not suggesting that.

Dr. Hanson: Well, in any event let's *suppose* that you were. If you *had* suggested that, it would have been false. (It's sometimes difficult to know *what* you are suggesting!) I think you are calling attention to the fact that at the level of the highest order premises in advanced physical theory one can't always tie the constituent terms to observables. Take thermo-dynamics: you find a term like "$\sqrt{-1}$." What the hell does this tie up with?

Dr. Schwab: Well, then, what the hell does force tie in within classical mechanics?

DR. HANSON: If there are problems about *force* and problems about $\sqrt{-1}$, what you have got to do at the top of the page is to make the machinery go well enough so that you can get observations at the bottom. Given this, one can tolerate some queer things topside.

DR. SCHWAB: That's what I am suggesting. And this queerness is very strangely mathematical.

DR. HANSON: No, the queerness is very strangely physical. This is what one must put up with in physics to get observation-statements at the bottom of the page.

DR. SCHWAB: Okay.

DR. HANSON: You don't have to do the same thing as that in mathematics at all.

DR. SCHWAB: Go back to the Mendel case that you were kind enough to refer to earlier. When Mendel invents his hypothetical expansion of the binomial it turns out, by the kind of empirical test you have emphasized, to take very good account of what kind of babies we have, depending on what kind of papas and mamas they have. The biologist nods and says, "how interesting," but always somebody has got to show me a gene under the microscope. Physicists don't do that.

DR. HANSON: Now, it depends. It depends on the physicist, you know. . . .

DR. SCHWAB: No, no, not about the terms at those high-level premises.

DR. HANSON: Well, I will make one reference to a remark made to me by the discoverer of the positron—by Carl D. Anderson. At the High Energy Conference in Rochester in 1957 we were discussing the evidence for the existence of the neutrino; the remark he made was significant for an experimental physicist. He said, "I don't believe there is any such thing. All they (Cowan and Reines) show are some numbers, and not all of the numbers. I can just barely believe there is a genuine effect." Now, of course, these doubts have been laid to rest; but what Anderson was saying then was this: "If you really want me to entertain the neutrino as a physical entity capable of all the explanatory tricks the theoreticians want, then show me something, in a cloud chamber or somewhere, something that is really going to make a difference. I want to see what the *difference* is that answers to the name 'neutrino.'" Now you are quite right to point out that, to theoreticians, this kind of complaint doesn't mean much—or not very much.

DR. SCHWAB: Well, this is all—I think I'll put it since you have gone back to those chaps that you wouldn't let Phenix have. For every ten Carl Andersons, there is also a physicist who postulates the existence of a particle which by definition was virtually detectable. You will agree that's why it took so long. . . .

DR. HANSON: Well, it was detectable but the whole occasion was just. . . .

DR. SCHWAB: You interrupted that time. . . .

DR. HANSON: Because I think you are going to make a mistake and I want to prevent that, for you, and for us; for the sake of the discussion, you know. Consider a radioactive source, a homogeneous source, and shield it against the beta and gamma rays. The alpha rays then emitted will trace out a star: spokes of a rimless wheel. Let us say then that all of these particles will be of roughly the same range; this we will call an "alpha star," it being quite compatible with the expected conservation of energy. But now change the shielding: shield the source against the alpha rays and the gamma rays. Then we get the beta *spectrum*, not a star. One little beta ray comes out there and another long one goes way over there, and every which way. It looks as if, since by the available theory all these particles had to be identical each to each, an energy loss is occurring. There is no way of setting out in the wave-equation appropriate to the beta particles any difference which could account for this. They are all supposed to have the same energy. What the heck is happening to the surplus energy? Now (here it seems to me) you can put it as you do. But it was necessary to *invent* a hypothetical particle which in each of these cases took up just what one needed in order to make an imaginary star out of neutrino-plus-beta-particle tracks; but you can't say there was no experimental occasion for this. The phenomenon is that the beta rays describe a spectrum of ranges, hence energies. They are all over the bloody map here.

DR. SCHWAB: There was an empirical *occasion* for the inquiry. One *can* say that if it weren't for the defect of the beta ray spectrum we would have no good evidence for the existence of the neutrino. This is the evidence—this is the way the neutrino shows its footprints and so there is nothing, as it were. However, there is another way to tell the story, namely, that the reason one invented the neutrino was to account for . . . .

DR. AGASSI: Perhaps what you are saying is this, that the physicist's problems are different from the mathematician's problem.

DR. HANSON: I am saying at least that, yes.

DR. SCHWAB: I do not suggest that physicists are lyric poets. Of course, there are empirical occasions for the invention of each of these things. I was only suggesting that contrary to the sorts of hypotheses constructed in biology for which verification is always defined as "show me," it is often the case in physics that high order concepts are considered verified when they take care of the problem.

DR. HANSON: Quite often indirect confirmation.

DR. BROUDY: Very indirect. They are blocked sometimes by definition. The finished article was ultimately possibly verifiable, but you must agree that the properties assigned to it were such that the quantity of mass to which they would have to move and the number of them which would have to move before you had a chance of getting assigned to their existence was exceedingly large.

DR. HANSON: Well, this was the first formulation of the hypothesis. It wasn't well made in 1929 and 1930. Now people know quite well what they are looking for in neutrino-work.

DR. SCHWAB: When you say not "well formulated" this is part of my earlier remark which you interrupted. I was going to say that for every ten Andersons there is one Fermi, who said it would be nice if neutrinos were verified in the way which neutrons, protons, and electrons were, but I think it would be helpful to adopt it now.

DR. HANSON: Well, that is a nice statement about *you*, Joe. I am glad to know that you think that. All I am trying to call attention to is what you are obscuring (and in so doing you are being "nasty, brutish, and short"). If one stresses what you are stressing, namely, that in physics you . . . .

DR. SCHWAB: Well, you . . . .

DR. HANSON: If I may just finish, *please*. If one stresses what you have been stressing, that in mathematical physics one uses the techniques of mathematical deduction—hence many of the moves made by theoretical physicists and by pure mathematicians look like the same kind of thing—this naturally stresses the similarities, all of which are important to note. It is obvious that the best microphysicists are good mathematicians. No doubt about it; but if one is carried away with this, one fails to perceive the fundamental logical difference between every single proposition of physical theory and every single proposition in a purely mathematical algorithm. I say this despite the fact that many of the things that get set out at the top of a page in physical theory may indeed come from the back of some mathematician's head. It can hardly matter if, e.g., one looks at the Heisenberg (1956) "stuff" concerning "the propertyless wave equation for all matter." This certainly was designed as a pure form of physical science. The question is: what semantical and physical *content* does it pick up after actually having been exposed to the facts; when did it turn out that that particular suggestion was false, and *factually* false? There's a question one should never ask of any proposition at the top of the page in pure mathematics. So I agree that many of the inferential techniques are the same in physics and mathematics; and I want to agree that, genetically, many things in theoretical physics *get* to "the top of the page" much as they do in mathematics. But once one is in a position to say, "This theory is true and that high-order theoretical premise is acceptable," then one is playing the game on the vulnerable side of this dichotomy I am focusing upon. This makes a profound difference to our understanding of physical theory.

DR. SCHWAB: I shall withdraw here because we haven't really joined the issue and I don't think we can.

(RECESS)

CHAIRMAN CLARK: We have a lineup of people with comments and questions. We will begin with Professor Smith.

DR. PHIL SMITH: Professor Hanson, I would like to enlarge the context of the same point that was under discussion here, if I may. We, of course, recognize that the distinction between necessary and contingent statements is essential for understanding mathematics or physics. I wonder if it is not also essential for understanding a number of other things that we get concerned with in education. It seems to me that when you looked at the assertion, "The sun rises in the east," you correctly pointed out that only a careful description of the context of utterance enables one to determine what function such an assertion is performing. Is it acting as a necessary statement or is it acting as a contingent statement? At this point I am reminded of Quine, who said that if a person were obdurate enough, he could allow almost any assertion to perform this sort of analytic function. I invite your comments on this point.

Perhaps the problem, say in the case of students thinking in stereotypes, is that they are allowing empirical generalizations to function as if they were necessary statements in their lives—that is, in the way they are structuring their experiences. I submit that this point is crucial in a much larger context than you put it. I wonder if you would care to comment.

DR. HANSON: Well, only to agree. I believe that yours is a general recognition of what it takes to understand what another person means when he says anything at all. One must place the claim in a context of utterance. Let's imagine a bit of paper floats through the window and into this room. On it is written, "It is *close* in here." It's difficult to know what this could mean; but think of the impact of that message in a very smoky room. Or, its impact in a very small room, or in a closet. In a very large, airy room full of university provosts and vice-presidents the message would have quite a different force. Yet, to get the thrust of each of these claims is really to have placed it within a semantical interchange in a specified context. Now as to the other point you are making, namely, that students treat lawlike claims which have this unrestricted universal form in remarkable ways: I agree they use them almost as principles in inference; what it takes on the part of a teacher is a fairly sinewy attempt to show that *every* one of these claims looks as if *something* could count as evidence for, or against, them. They are not just definitions. Especially is this so if the claims have an empirical genesis and verification. But my point was that, concerning the claim "The sun rises in the east," although the context of utterance makes it clear *which* assertion a person is actually making, the two assertions are at opposite logical poles. You mentioned Quine and you also used the expression "obdurate." I think he *is* obdurate with respect to many of the things that "right-thinking" philosophers call attention to. (Smile!) He virtually plays on words in some of his writings. He would melt this "analytic-synthetic," or "necessary-contingent," distinction away on the grounds that it is awfully difficult in real life to find a genuinely invulnerable claim. Well, it may even be impossible, for all I care, but *that* doesn't obliterate the distinction. There *is* a distinction even though one may have to invent an almost ideal case as candidate for the title "invulnerable claim." If I say "All bachelors are male," that won't satisfy Quine as being invulnerable, and for a number of reasons. If I say "A equals A," that won't satisfy him either because he has problems about "equals." (He has problems.) That is what it comes to. But all these perplexities could be set to one side as a sort of professional skirmish. There is still a clear-cut contrast in principle between claims of the totally invulnerable kind and those which are quite vulnerable. Another way of getting "into" your comment is to point out that were the student apprised of this distinction earlier in life he might be much more receptive to your remark, namely, that many claims which are in unrestricted universal form—e.g., "All white, male, blue-eyed cats are deaf" (true so far as I know)—the student too often wants to treat these like the binomial theorem. I have seen this happen: if a pussycat walked into this room, white, male, blue-eyed and yet hearing perfectly well, will the student's whole concept of "cat" have changed? No! But if I let go of this pencil here in my hand and it levitates (and it's *genuine* levitation), then, in a way, our concepts of "physical object" and of "terrestrial space" are put in jeopardy. That's what makes the difference here.

To really generalize this for educational theory would be admirable. For, as soon as kids get into college and face their first philosophy course, if "the old man" up front knows what he is doing and makes this distinction well for them they'll keep using it back and forth, forever after. It's a very sophisticated thing to come up with Quine's doubts. It sometimes *is* difficult (as Quine perceived) to make this distinction *stick* all the way. That's something that one could learn later on, though. If students could begin making this distinction in high school when doing physics—if they could sharply distinguish the mathematics within the ordinary dynamical computations from the strictly physical content—they would be a lot better off.

DR. PHIL SMITH: Well, one of the difficulties is that when an assertion performs this kind of analytic function then the teacher is, in some sense, being irrelevant if he tries to introduce a negative instance. I mean, if a first-grade child thinks that all policemen are mean, you don't destroy this stereotype by showing him a nice policeman.

DR. HANSON: No, because if he is nice he cannot be a policeman—not really.

DR. PHIL SMITH: I take it that some of the questions that you have given examples of later in the paper are related perhaps to the little circles of professors that straddle the dotted lines and those circles and your questions and especially your remarks at the end of your paper about paper walls that were set up in textbooks and possibly set up by administrators. All of these things have reference to this way of teaching the physical sciences that may either help or hinder learning in that field. I want to ask a question which isn't really on your paper because I don't know enough about it to disagree. It seems clear enough to me, so let me ask you a question not on your paper but which is suggested by your paper. Toward the end you mention structures of knowledge as being possible only in terms of a pedagogically heuristic blueprint. I would like to know whether or not you think that the current way of reaching the physical sciences, which presents areas within the sciences as separate and discrete, hinders or helps learning in the physical sciences.

DR. HANSON: There is first, if I may bifurcate that question, the issue of whether or not such departmentalization will help the student focus on particular problems without the encumbrances of other disciplines. And then, secondly, there is the auxiliary question of whether this will blind him to certain problems coming up again, intricacies within which make them important for newer disciplines like biophysics and biochemistry, etc. There can be little doubt but that teaching any of the natural sciences in this compartment-like way tends to make it difficult for researchers to branch out into these interim areas. The whole history of DNA lies in the middle of one of these interim areas; these turn out quite often to be the most exciting. One of the things that I am most interested in now is the history of theoretical aerodynamics. Chaps had an awful time getting off the ground on this "idea-side" of flight; they were too concerned with the tradition founded by Euler and Bernoulli in theoretical hydrodynamics—a thoroughly classical discipline built upon the notion of an *ideal* fluid—inviscid and irrotational. For practical purposes, however, early aerodynamicists were concerned with the moving of a solid object through a thin, viscous medium, one not at all "ideal." *This* is the theoretical problem of flight and, of course, it all got confounded with the First World War and with stiff upperlips hurtling down the runway, hot-rods, parachutists, wing-walkers and "down he goes in flames"—all that sort of MGM rot. It was difficult during the first twenty years of aerodynamic theory to establish that all this was a genuine contribution to our understanding of physical phenomena. Even now, if I may harken toward a low-grade consideration, those great institutions in our country which are responsible for making grants in support of scholarly research projects, they also have difficulty in seeing that a history of aerodynamical theory could be anything but mere technology-plus-adventure-tales. They too are blinded by the high school myth that if one means to piddle about with aviation this means doing what bicycle engineers and hot-rod motorcyclists did in the 1920's; but how could all that be a real contribution in the tradition of Euler and Bernoulli?

This is rather like what I am talking about in general. If and when you make it possible for a kid, when he raises a question which seems peripheral, if then you make it possible for him to feel encouraged, if he could be shown that although his query is slightly to one side of the central subject matter, the very determination of what *is* the central subject matter is itself undertaken largely for purposes of convenience, and administration, and for budgetary problems in teaching; *then* I think such a student might be heartened more to explore at the foundations and in the interim regions of the sciences.

Tomorrow's scientists may learn fewer long numbers via what I am advocating here, but their whole attitude might be inestimably improved nonetheless.

DR. PHIL SMITH: Do you think that the cultivation of an attitude in teaching the physical sciences is equally as important or more important than the cultivation of certain knowledges?

DR. HANSON: Far more important. Go to I.B.M. up in Binghamton, New York; you'll find slide-rule soldiers in abundance there; chaps who can trot out the factorial of any magnitude you please, quickly and efficiently. (One almost wonders who plugs them in each morning.) But ask them about something really fundamental like, "Are you satisfied with the current algebraic techniques in quantum field theory?" You'll get a sort of wide-eyed stare, and a "but I use it every day" retort. "I know you use it every day. You do lots of things every day, but isn't there something about renormalization techniques that *upsets* you? You *are* interested in the history of ideas?" The answer is usually that he is not, and that I.B.M. is not, interested in the history of ideas at all.

But this reminds me of a remark that Reynolds (of "Reynolds number" fame) made in 1903: freely rendered, the claim was, "Physics is all finished as intellectual discovery. It is just a question of graduate students running out more decimal numbers for the old prof's theories now. We have got a kind of periodic table for all physics set up." This in 1903; in 1905 we get the two Einstein papers on the Brownian motion and on the photo electric effect. Things began to rumble then, and we're still quaking.

What Reynolds was saying was a clear reflection of the compartmentalization standard late in the nineteenth century. It's also interesting to note that, in the *vive voce* part of his M.A. examination, Einstein had a difficult time because some of his responses didn't fit into his examiner's conception of what a well designed scientific discussion should be like.

The attitude is all important; this is what distinguishes the great men in history—not just that they got the numbers right. Some of Michelson's determinations were wrong, but he certainly had the right idea about how to learn of light's velocity. The conception, the overall attitude, the sorts of questions one asks; these are what I am getting at. That's the kind of interest we ought to cultivate more in high schools and colleges. That's what we can easily do. But when, as now, we turn scientific training into a kind of rehearsal of quantitative magnitudes, we lose an opportunity to encourage *thought*. It's necessary, a little bit—I did make that remark about *rote* repetition. We've all got to go through a little bit of it. If we make all scientific education a kind of navel contemplation, an adoption of *postures* toward problems in physics, then it gets too much like philosophy; this isn't altogether a bad thing, but it is a different subject. We must straddle these things a bit. But if *I* had to put the pedagogical center of gravity somewhere, it would definitely be on the student's attitude.

Dr. Gage: If I may follow up what you are saying, it means if I were a teacher, I would have trouble in telling the difference between a student who asks a profound question like, "What is gravity?" and one who is faking. A psychologist of reading I know about had a theory that reading deficiencies are caused by an absence of some juice in the brain—acetylcholine.

Dr. Hanson: Carrot juice.

Dr. Gage: And what the psychologist hadn't done or what the bright eight-year-old or fourteen-year-old hadn't done who asks, "What is gravity?" or "What causes it?" was his homework. My reaction is they are not really entitled to be asking questions. The psychologist wasn't really a physiologist. He didn't know enough physiology. He hadn't done his homework, and he had no right to make up theories about reading deficiency as a result of this lack of acetylcholine in the brain. So I say to him, "Get out of this or go do your homework." And I'd say to the bright eight-year-old or the fourteen-year-old, "Don't ask these unsettling profound questions until you learn your twelfth-grade physics. Then you earn the right to ask proper questions. But you can't really get into the act—you haven't bought your ticket yet—until you have learned your ninth-grade algebra and other prerequisite subjects."

DR. HANSON: Well, Professor Gage, we are *really* in disagreement. It was the thrust of my exposition to counteract just what you have expressed. I'll never forget when I used to attend the quantum field theory seminars of Dirac at Cambridge—a very great physicist. Some highly paid help came to the seminar and a very valuable encounter it all was. But even there questions would come up like, "What *is* gravity really?" Or, "What indeed is one prepared to say a law in micro-physics consists in?" These were even then dismissed as merely philosophical questions.

DR. GAGE: Now those men had bought their tickets. They had done the homework.

DR. HANSON: No, there is no such thing. Nothing corresponds to "buying the ticket" here. There isn't some prerequisite course which terminates in *permitting* the student to ask a question like, "What is gravity?" The very rails are made out of such questions. Unless the point of these questions can be felt right from the very beginning all the other jazz about doing the calculations and working out the numbers will operate at quite a different level—the level of the calculational engineer rather than that of the problem-solving physicist. I am in a slightly compromised position here because I have to admit the point about rote repetition. To that extent we are agreed: if a kid systematically won't do his homework and doesn't give a tinker's damn about how $a = o$ when $F = ma$ and $\Sigma F = o$, then it is clearly difficult even to converse with him about *why* $F = ma$ and about the significance of the Fs in mechanics. But once he has done this bit, that he *has* done only a bit doesn't in itself serve as a measure of the perfunctoriness of his question. A man doesn't have to do much classical mechanics in order to be asking questions like, "What is the nature of this attraction in F $\propto \gamma\, Mm/r^2$?" Berkeley did not know much—he was not I.B.M. material—but his questions constituted some of Newton's greatest challenges. It is the *beginning* stages of a theory that must be understood in order to grind out the numbers. Yet it is also those beginnings which are most difficult to comprehend.

"Who said that a body free of impressed forces would move in a straight line ad indefinitum uniformly?" *Let* the lad ask it! Can *you* give him *any* answer? What *is* the empirical evidence for this claim? These are genuine questions which could be asked at any level. If the teacher cannot answer, why *should* the student accept everything that hinges on the Law of Inertia?

DR. GAGE: Well, let me put it another way. I recently glanced a little bit at a book that you probably know of better than I do, *The Structure of Scientific Revolutions.*

Dr. Hanson: Kuhn's.

Dr. Gage: I think he says that most scientists are really just devoting their careers to mopping-up operations. The paradigms get set by a Newton or an Einstein or a Mendel or whoever, and the rest of the people in that discipline just clean up after him for a long time. I think what you are saying is that every Tom, Dick, and Harry has a right to try to be a Mendel or a Newton or an Einstein and ask the fundamental questions. I think I am inclined to say that most of us are doomed to be mopper-uppers.

Dr. Hanson: I am certainly saying that everyone has the *right* to ask them. There isn't any legislation from Tom Kuhn or anyone else about this. Incidentally, about his book, what does Tom mean by "a paradigm"? He doesn't make it clear. After four hundred pages Tom says that sooner or later they are the kinds of things which, if upset, will result in a scientific revolution. Okay, so now we have another term here. Now, "What is a revolution in science?" Answer: That's the kind of thing that happens after you get a *paradigm upset.* It looks as if this is a big wheel going around in small circles. So you say: "Well, look here, I can remark the following three important events, each one of which is usually recorded in history books as a scientific revolution in some important sense. But there was no paradigm upset in any of these cases." Then Tom tells us, "They weren't really revolutions, despite what the historians say." Then you add: "Look, here is a cluster of paradigms; the organization, the entire discipline at this particular time, the group of chaps—*all* cleave to this paradigm set. And there has been a most serious challenging of such paradigms amongst practitioners of the sciences. But lo—nothing that one would call a 'scientific' revolution has resulted." Tom says, "Not really paradigms then." You see, this gets like saying, "Why does opium put one to sleep? Because of its soporific properties—and what's a soporific property? It's what opium has got such that it puts you to sleep when you take it." Well, really! This thesis goes around and around. Kuhn starts out with an *informative* historical thesis—a contingent, factual thesis—to the effect that when you find a revolution in science you should look for an upset in some paradigm and vice versa. Now this actually conveys something, and is informative in that it makes good sense to suppose his claim to be false, but *in fact* it happens to be true. Or it happens to be true 98 per cent of the time. But Tom is so impressed with the fully general thesis that when chaps begin to bring up possible counter-instances Kuhn kicks them into the general pattern by definition. So he ends up by transforming what was originally an informative historical claim into a specifically Kuhnian definition. It couldn't be false, and if it couldn't be false in these terms then it could not really be both true and informative.

Thus for Tom Kuhn the only level on which one can effect a scientific revolution is to challenge the super capital-lettered-purple-inked paradigms about which Tom has so much to say. He says it all in a highly illuminating and in a very informative way; but the kinds of questions that I have been posing here with respect to classical physics can be posed equally well in quite narrow and special disciplines like the history of science. If you get a man who uses templates for setting out transistor circuits—for *pouring* the things instead of having to solder wires—he might use the technique gratefully. Yet he might have many questions concerning why it is that when the stuff is put on in liquid form it has other effects later on when dried. Or he can ask "simple" questions about radio-set circuitry in general; but it's the *nature* of the question and the nature of the *attitude* he adopts toward them that strikes me as being so important.

I fly an airplane, a fifteen-year-old Navy fighter which needs lots and lots of attention. I can always remark the repair shops where they have the mechanic I would want to do my work *by the nature of his questions*. The chap who gives it a lick and a rub on the outside, but doesn't check the magneto falloff, the fuel pressure, or the tank filters —such a man I am not quite so interested in as in he who takes any little imperfection to be a possible sign of something that might in the long run cause mischief.

The average physicist who goes to graduate school today and develops a concern with problems that involve weak interaction at high energies—he gets into formal problems over "renormalization," "ghost states," etc.; the class of physicists divides at that juncture. Some will feel profound nagging perplexities about using techniques over which mathematicians would get sick. Others say, "Look, we are grinding out the right numbers in predictions, let's not look for any trouble. So long as we keep quiet and get the correct magnitudes we are doing what we are supposed to be doing." Now it's this division which requires our attention. The chaps who ask the nagging questions are not necessarily getting any more or any better numbers. They are (in a sense) holding back the seminars and discussion groups from grinding out finer determinations and setting up new experiments. But in the long run the nagging problems that the "worriers" raise might be the critical ones. There is no given moment in a man's scientific development when he is for the first time qualified to ask questions like this. I think he is entitled to ask these questions right at the beginning; indeed, if he does not, he does not really understand what is being ladled into his head.

Dr. Schwab: Indeed it would be nice if teaching were a narrative of inquiry in which the profound and the small questions are exhibited in their relations to one another.

Dr. Hanson: Well, this is actually done. Eric Rogers of Princeton has written a book, *Physics for the Inquiring Mind*. This is for senior high school students and for freshmen in college. There is no compromise here. This is not a cheap popularization. It is a serious work, but it is written with a specific focus on the kinds of questions that I have been calling your attention to here. Now you might very well point out that no student in Rogers' courses will, from that alone, become a hot candidate for I.B.M. employment. True! But such a fellow might be better off in the long run. He might even end up teaching at Princeton. Worse things have happened to Ph.D.'s.

Dr. Gage: In the chemistry lab the high school student is asked to, say, do an experiment in which he is supposed to get the atomic weight of carbon. He knows very well it's supposed to be 12 but he's sloppy and it comes out to be 12.01, so on Thursday he might say, "I am going to challenge the whole structure of the theory underlying atomic weight," and chases off in that direction. Then on Monday he comes back to the lab and he gets an inexact figure for the molecular weight of water. When is a student supposed to know that he should take certain things for granted and not rock the boat, and when is he supposed to start rocking the boat? If he rocks the boat every time he gets an inexact answer he'll—well, he won't get past the first lab assignment.

Dr. Hanson: What one must do is develop judgment and discrimination in this sort of thing, as with anything else; and the earlier one starts, the better. You know perfectly well that learning the difference between chemical atomic mass and physical atomic mass constituted a profound discovery which was made—when in the hell was it made?

Dr. Gage: Oxygen in 1820.

Dr. Hanson: No, much later. (After the discovery of oxygen's *isotopes*.)

Dr. Gage: I agree with you if the judgment that most students come to is that 99 per cent of the things that they are asked to do in laboratories or learn out of books they had better well take for granted and only after they have won their spurs and are in graduate school or working on a dissertation can they start rocking boats. But most students—and I think I was an average student—maybe that's why I was an average student—but most of us learn to receive or take for granted, to accept what is in the books. This judgment is something we do learn. That's why we are able to go ahead and take courses one after the other.

Dr. Schwab: At the dissertation level the professors are still asking them not to rock the boat, so naturally the guy who gets 12.1 instead of 12 never discovers isotopes.

DR. BEREITER: I think that this might be clarified a little by pointing out that there is a difference between taking for granted that somebody else's empirical results might be a little better than the ones you have gotten and knowing what other things you might take for granted and what ones not. I would also like to add a little empirical finding here. We did some experiments using some artificial sciences. Graduate students in physical science were taught their sciences and given some data to work on. They were carefully told at the outset that they should not assume that any physical laws that they believed in necessarily held in this imaginary universe. Invariably the next question they would ask would be, "Could we assume that mathematical laws hold here?" Now it was staggering to think that they would feel that you could suspend mathematics hypothetically the same way that you could suspend facts. Then after we assured them that mathematics still works here they would be constantly wrestling with the question, "What can we assume and what can't we?" Now there was vast ambiguity here. We used some terms that were familiar to them such as "charged," and I remember an electrical engineer who looked me straight in the eye and said, "Can we assume that unlike charges attract and like charges repel?" I said, "I can't tell you that." So they looked at each other and arrived at the conclusion that unless you assumed this everything collapsed. So they decided they would assume that this held. Although it's a matter of empirical fact, it was mathematical to them. We did the same experiment using bright high school students. None of them had the slightest bit of trouble with any of this and the outcome was that they were much more successful.

DR. HANSON: Well, if I may follow this up with Professor Gage's question (it wasn't really a question, it was a torpedo). Obviously a man doesn't show his originality by working out his own logarithm tables. There are some things that you just take up because you must learn to: one must learn how to operate with the slide rule, how to use a retort, how to use the several balances, etc. You have to know how to make appropriate inferences, how to use the most fitting language. This is the ground floor of any discipline, and any student who would rather be asking the "philosophical" questions I've been discussing here *instead* of learning his ABC's, he is not the kind of chap I am talking about. And I'm not concerned with the bright brat who is forever bent on badgering the busy teacher.

I am saying that if a student, in addition to doing his homework, is *also* asking these more fundamental questions, then everything should be done to encourage him. Now I mentioned to someone here that a close friend of mine started his university life as one of my students at

Cambridge University; and I don't know how he will finish—but he certainly used to worry me. I've never encountered such an aggressive, nasty, mean student. Actually he was quite serious, but he was quite mean, too! He made my life miserable—until I discovered that he behaved even worse in his physics courses. I noticed one thing leading to another and asked a senior Nobel physics prize recipient, "How do you get along with John now?" He said, "Oh, he is the bane of my existence. I have never met a man like that." Well, to make a long story short, Newton is supposed to have received 16 "alphas" in his Part Three Mathematical Tripos exam; my friend, John, got 18 "alphas"! He's really a pretty electric sort of guy. I don't know what one is to say about him. Certainly his complete mastery of algorithms was at least comparable to that of all the other chaps around him. The only way that I can distinguish him from the others is to note that, in addition, he was always probing beneath the algebra, asking, "Why this?" "Why that?"

Just one final twist of a quarter-turn. Here's the kind of thing one finds in some of Newton's recently published notes and papers: he makes two statements (in adjacent paragraphs) which are really pregnant. No person in Newton's time called attention to this. He granted Kepler's law of $1/r^2$ as giving the falloff in the intensity of radiation from a light source. Thus if I have a given point source of light at radius 1 from us, and if then we move that light out to radius 2, it will only appear $1/4$ as bright. If I move it out to radius 3 it will appear only $1/9$ as bright, etc.

In the next paragraph Newton then calls attention to what we now call "the cosmological principle"; the actual population of the stellar warehouse goes up as r^2 if one supposes that in each spherical spatial shell enclosing us the stars are distributed homogeneously and relatively equally. Then the number of stars 2 radii away will be 4 times as great as they had been at radius 1; and at 3 radii away there will be 9 times as many stars—so the fact that each one of them appears but $1/9$ as bright as they would have seemed at radius 1 is, in effect, compensated for and cancelled out altogether. In short, it follows that from each spherical shell, from each new distance, there is a positive increment of light radiation, *such that at midnight the sky should be blindingly bright.* Now these two correlations—r^2 for the stellar population increase, and $1/r^2$ for the radiation falloff—these are well accepted facts. Any student in high school could go through these with no trouble. But if a kid puts these two together and makes of them what Clairveaux and Olbers made of them—he has gone beyond the normal requirement of his homework. Any student might notice this particular correlation; by easy steps it leads to Olbers' Paradox, The Red Shift, and lots of other things in modern cosmology. Fully to explain how it is that despite these two correlations being true it is nonetheless not bright at midnight—that's the kind of question that has marked the great illuminations in the history of ideas. Such queries are quite compatible with learning one's homework; but the teacher who is *so* concerned with getting the homework across that he suppresses questions like this is stifling the attitude toward physical inquiry that constitutes the real excitement of physics. More, he is failing fully to make clear the very material he *does* want to teach— for even to manage the formulae properly requires some "natural philosophy."

---

6. What is Life?

G. Sommerhoff

THE NEED OF CRITICAL ANALYSIS

At the time of writing, scientific theory can show no unified body of thought which offers an explicit scientific formulation, critical analysis, and interpretation of the general nature of observed life, and which, strictly speaking, deserves to be called 'theoretical biology.' Modern biology has made immense strides in explaining the 'part events' of vital activities and the material matrix in which life functions, but it has failed to explain the *general* nature of observed life, and to enlighten the contemplative mind of Man about the place of life in the general scheme of things. Consequently, the influence of modern biology on Man's world-view has often been misleading rather than illuminating, and it has tended to foster immature forms of rationalism, some of whose repercussions have been world wide.

It is sometimes suggested that this failure of biology to deal with the general nature of life must be attributed to the far-going specialization of modern science and to the resulting inability of many scientists to see the wood for the trees. But the reason lies deeper. It must be seen mainly in the fact that biology has not so far been able to analyse and paraphrase in precise and exact scientific, i.e. physico-mathemat-

Reprinted by permission from *Analytical Biology* by G. Sommerhoff, pp. 1–36 (New York and London: Oxford University Press, 1950).

ical, terms, the really fundamental characteristics of observed life in the full and original meaning of that word: that *apparent purposiveness* and goal-directed character of vital activities which make the distinction between living and non-living systems in nature one of the most important distinctions Man draws among the objects of his environment: those characteristics of observed life which invite us to think of living things as somehow endowed with a soul, as somehow capable of personal relationship; those characteristics which invite us to think of living nature as permeated by intelligence and purpose, and whose loss we mourn when death occurs.

A question of the type 'What is so-and-so?' may mean at least two very different things. On the one hand, 'so-and-so' may be an expression wholly unknown to us, which we wish to see defined intelligibly. 'What are diophantine equations?' we may ask. On the other hand, 'so-and-so' may be a term which is already common currency and of whose connotation we may have an adequate, although as yet quite intuitive and vague, grasp. We now ask, 'What is "so-and-so"?' in order to see this more or less intuitive knowledge crystallize into an explicit and articulate formulation which will enable us to realize its place in the general scheme of things. When Man's urge for knowledge and his desire to feel more at home in the universe, prompts the question 'What is life?' it is undoubtedly in this latter sense that the question is put. And if it is conceded that of the many functions of science the most important in the long run is to satisfy these desires, then we must admit that any biology which cannot answer the question 'What is life?' in this sense, fails in a vital part of its mission.

In biochemistry and biophysics, modern science has given the world an advanced analysis of the physical and chemical 'part events' occurring in animate matter, and throughout this book the principles and results of these sciences will be accepted without question. We shall also accept the conclusion to which their results point, viz. that we have every reason to believe all the events occurring within animate matter to be fully accountable for in terms of the laws of physics and chemistry.

But the progress of science has failed to supplement this advance by an equally critical analysis and scientific formulation of the objective phenomena and relations which constitute the observed fact of *animation* as such. And as long as we fail in explicitly formulating and analysing these really fundamental characteristics of observed life in exact scientific terms, no scientific explanation of life can be forthcoming. It is obvious that nothing can be scientifically explained unless it can first be explicitly formulated in scientific terms. The most detailed physical description of the raindrops and their attendant electro-magnetic fields, fails to be a scientific explanation of the rain-

bow as long as it fails to refer explicitly to the fundamental characteristics of the phenomenon, i.e. to the type of linear colour sequence
which the word 'rainbow' connotes.

Similarly, the most detailed physical account and explanation of the
events occurring within the boundaries of a living organism fails to be
an account of life as such, so long as no explicit mention is made of the
true characteristics of the organism as a whole. We are not dealing here
with an unusual scientific case: it is widely known in the scientific
world that the most important step towards the solution of a problem
or explanation of a phenomenon is its exact formulation. The first step
towards a theoretical biology, therefore, must be a critical analysis
of the idea of life as such and an attempt on the strength of this
analysis to find an exact formulation of the most truly distinguishing
characteristics of life.

Broadly speaking we may distinguish three main groups of contemporary biologists.

The first and largest group is of those whose attitude towards the
general nature of life is simply to point out physico-chemical constituents and reactions which are typical of living organisms and to show
how they might be accounted for by the laws of physics and chemistry,
or how their origin can be explained in terms of modern evolutionary
theory. Although this attitude yields scientific answers to many questions, it does not answer the main question at issue. The fundamental
characteristics of life remain unformulated and unexplained. In a
certain sense, this school of thought explains life away. Even if all
concrete life processes could be traced down and explained, to the
movement of the last electrons involved and the last resonance effects
between them, we should have advanced no further towards a solution
of the general riddle of life. The mistake of this school of thought is
that it explores the denotation of life in terms of existing physical
and chemical concepts instead of its connotation with the aid of new
concepts. Some adherents have gone so far as to assert that since on
these lines no satisfactory distinction between living and non-living
systems can be found, the terms 'life' and 'living' must be regarded as
meaningless as far as the exact sciences are concerned. This, of course,
is a counsel of despair. The fact that scientists have so far proved
unable to paraphrase the meaning of life in exact scientific terms,
should not lead them to abandon the concept as meaningless, but
rather urge them to double their efforts. Any other course of action
reduces biology to an ultimate irrelevancy. The riddle of life is not
solved by abolishing life.

The second group of biologists abandons *faute de mieux*, whenever
it comes to the general problem of life, the canons of exact scientific
thought, and descends to the vague language of philosophical specula-

tion. Thus we get explanations of life in such vague and unscientific terms as the 'emergence of a new type of order,' 'psychic' or 'hormic' forces, 'wholes which are more than the sum of their parts' and other vague phrases. No matter how sincere and profound these attempts at wider generalization may be, and no matter how valuable as expressions of personal insight, they cannot fail to disappoint the serious seeker after scientific truth. These are not scientific answers and their inclusion in scientific books is misleading. They are valuable only in their place, which is among the broad generalizations of speculative philosophy. But science has stolen the thunder of metaphysical speculation, and, having once breathed the pure air of exact scientific thought, the modern mind insists on scientific answers to its questions.

The third prominent group of biologists comprises those who are vaguely aware of the bankruptcy of both the above schools of thought, yet do not know how to break away, and in consequence fight shy of the general problem of life altogether. We thus witness the paradoxical situation to-day that the best biologists are often the most difficult scientists to interest in the riddle of life, and to convince that over and above the special problems on which they are engaged there still exists the one fundamental and general problem.

In order to find the solution of the general problem of life, biology must therefore make a fresh start. It must begin with a critical analysis of the idea of life as such and a determined attempt to paraphrase the connotation of that word in exact scientific terms, i.e. in terms of clearly defined spatio-temporal relationships between quantitative variables. In other words, theoretical biology must begin by being *analytical*. It is with the object of establishing such a new and analytical approach, and with a view to illustrating at once its possibilities and its power to add to our understanding of the general nature of life, that this book has been written.

THE APPARENT PURPOSIVENESS OF LIFE PROCESSES

What are the fundamental characteristics of observed life in the sense of the preceding section? If we abandon scientific exactitude and provisionally attempt to express these fundamental characteristics of living systems in non-scientific and largely metaphorical language, we may say that they consist in the apparent purposiveness of vital activities and in the manner in which this apparent end-serving or goal-seeking quality integrates the part events of living systems into the self-regulating, self-maintaining, and self-reproducing organic wholes which we recognize as living individuals. That is to say, the distinguishing character of vital activities is their apparent subservience to biological needs which lie in the future, and to such fundamental biological ends as development, self-maintenance, or reproduction. Biological adaptation ('futurity adaptation' as some writers have called it), adaptive behaviour, physiological-, behavioural-, or morphological regulation, nervous and muscular ('anticipatory') coordination—are outstanding examples of vital activities which have this end-serving character. It is the all-pervasive presence of this apparent purposiveness in life processes, and the resulting possibility of thinking of living systems in terms of the 'goals' towards which their activities are directed, which is mainly responsible for the radical difference between the ways we think about living and non-living things.

How characteristic and pervasive a feature of vital activities this purpose-like character is, only those can fully appreciate who are able to survey the whole realm of biological phenomena. With the possible exception of that fringe of creatures which the conventional denotation of the word 'life' assigns to the borderline between the organic and inorganic world, it would be hard to find any level of organic activity which does not invite us to think of vital activities as being somehow purposive, as being subject to tendencies which are directed towards the fulfilment of specific and mutually interrelated ends. On the phenomenal level from which all science must proceed, life is nothing if not just this manifestation of apparent purposiveness and organic order in material systems. In the last analysis, the beast is not distinguishable from its dung save by the end-serving and integrating activities which unite it into an ordered, self-regulating, and single whole, and impart to the individual whole that unique independence from the vicissitudes of the environment and that unique power to hold its own by making internal adjustments, which all living organisms possess in some degree. It is this purpose-like subordination of the parts to the whole which, as Claude Bernard wrote, makes of the complex creature a connected system, a whole, an individual.

In other words, the failure of science to analyse and interpret the fundamental characteristics of life, is caused by its failure to analyse and interpret in exact scientific terms the nature of this purposelike character of life processes. The first task of analytical biology, therefore, must be to tackle this problem, and, without loss of scientific precision, to distil from the modern physico-chemical description of living nature that element of apparent purposiveness and organic order which nature parades so patently in all its organic manifestations, and which so far has appeared instantly to dissolve at the touch of scientific concepts. To put it naïvely, the fundamental problem of theoretical biology is to discover how the behaviour of myriads of blind, stupid, and by inclination chaotic, atoms can obey the laws of physics and chemistry, and at the same time become integrated into organic wholes and into activities of such purpose-like character.

It is not difficult to see why exact science has been unable to cope with this purposive or goal-directed aspect of organic nature: science still lacks really exact concepts in terms of which it can even as much as describe it, let alone interpret it. Biologists have been too keen to explain things before they were able to state in exact terms what they wanted to explain and what objective system-properties they were studying. Instead of scientific theories about the exact spatio-temporal relations and types of order involved in the organization of living systems, we find but hazy descriptions of the various purposive aspects of life in terms of such vague and often anthropocentric concepts as 'adaptation', 'subservience', 'coordination', 'regulation', 'integration', 'organization', 'final causation', &c., none of which, as they stand, attain to that standard of exactness which modern mathematical theory has shown to be indispensable to a strict and deductive scientific system. The result is a welter of discordant opinions about the general nature of life, and that typical inability to reach agreement, which so often accompanies the use of philosophical concepts whose inherent vagueness allows of almost as many readings as there may chance to be readers. None of these traditional biological concepts tell us much more than that there is in nature something analogous to the purposive behaviour of Man; but what this is biologists have so far been unable to say with precision. It is the main task of our analytical biology to remedy this failure.

Questions concerning the intrinsic meaning of the purpose-like quality of organic activities, and of the characteristic order found in living nature, have long been stock questions in the philosophy of life. In particular the relation of this apparent purposiveness to the determinism of classical physics has been the focus of many philosophical disputes. It is a commonplace that, ever since Descartes forged his rigid separation between mind and matter, the world has been struggling without success to bring the two together again. And the sterile controversy in biology between the scientists who postulated the existence of mysterious psychic agents or directive forces in the organism to account for its purposiveness, and the mechanists who treated the organism as little more than a complicated machine, is but a reflection of this struggle. In the main stream of Greek thought there was no room for such controversy. The essence of an organism was identified with its 'form', i.e. with the principle of its organization, and nature was a single, organic, and striving whole. In few branches of philosophy have discordances of opinion been of greater detriment to the sanity of Man's world-view than these. But for these discordances it would hardly have seemed possible for the adherents of the conflicting viewpoints which divide East and West to-day, to entrench themselves so uncompromisingly behind the alleged primacy of matter on the one hand and of the spirit on the other. The result of our work will, I hope, throw new light on these philosophical questions and will perhaps advance some distance towards reuniting mind and matter. Meanwhile the only safe conclusion to be drawn from the persistence and dogmatic temper of these controversies is that the philosophical concepts in terms of which they are conducted are too vague to allow the formulation of conclusive arguments. Quine once said that the less a science is advanced, the more does its terminology tend to rest on the uncritical assumption of mutual understanding. In the philosophy of life this uncritical assumption has obviously proved unjustified. New concepts, new rigour and precision are required.

This means that the critical analysis of life which was demanded above must go hand in hand with a determined effort to construct new and precise concepts, adequate to replace the traditional ones without loss of meaning, thus enabling the discussion to be raised to the required level of precision. The logical and linguistic structure of such traditional concepts as 'adaptation', 'integration', 'organization', &c., must be exposed and then paraphrased in exact scientific terms. We must, in effect, discover how to express the concerns of the vitalists in the exact scientific language of the mechanists. Carnap has adopted the term *explication* for the process of giving an old and vague concept a precise and more explicit meaning. In this technical sense the term has since gained widespread currency, and we shall use it throughout this work. He calls the old and the new concept the 'explicandum' and the 'explicatum' respectively. In this terminology, therefore, we may say that the primary task of our analytical biology is to present the biologist with suitable scientific explications of the vague concepts which we are accustomed to use for describing the general nature of life.

This process of explication is not unlike the early analysis and refinement which the concepts of mechanics had to undergo before this branch of natural philosophy could become the exact theoretical science which it is to-day. From a theoretical point of view, biology is still in a pre-Galilean stage, and the early history of mechanics illustrates well the procedure we have to adopt. In those early days scientists disputed about the 'power', 'resistance', 'magnitude', and 'efficacy' of motions in much the same vague way in which we to-day talk about the 'adaptiveness', 'purposiveness', and 'integration' of organic behaviour. And their discussions were as inconclusive. Only when a precise mathematical definition had been found for the 'magnitude of motion'; only when the single concept of 'resistance' was replaced by the mathematical concepts of 'inertia' and of 'resisting forces'; only when d'Alembert's mathematics had shown the dispute between the

Leibnizians and Cartesians on the efficacy of motion to be a mere dispute about words; only when 'mass' and 'power' had been replaced by adequate mathematical concepts—only then could theoretical mechanics come to full fruition, and could physicists reach a constructive measure of agreement on questions which had previously issued merely in a plethora of discordant philosophical speculations.

The main difficulty which besets the metaphorical concepts we are accustomed to use in a description of the purposiveness of vital activities and organic order, is that they imply a reference to some future goal towards which the respective organic activity is directed, and that this reference seems to be an essential and unalienable part of their meaning. They are, to say the least, quasi-teleological. When we say that the behaviour of an animal is 'adapted' to a given environment, we mean that it is so adapted from the point of view of some hypothetical goal towards the attainment of which we conceive this behaviour to be directed. It may be a proximate goal, as when an animal captures its prey, or an ultimate goal such as the survival of the individual or of the species. All the other concepts which we have mentioned in this connexion, such as 'coordination', 'co-operation', 'regulation', 'integration', 'organization', have the same finalistic reference.

It is impossible to deprive these concepts of their reference to the future without doing violence to their essential meaning. A good example of the emasculation which any of them may suffer from such treatment may be seen in the meaning which the concept of 'adaptation' has acquired in the hands of some mechanists. Deprived of its implicit reference to the future, the statement that an animal is adapted to its environment, becomes no more than a trivial affirmation that both the animal and the environment exist, and that the former is alive in the latter. It is this essential reference to the future which is responsible for all the confusion that has surrounded these concepts, and which, of course, is the main bone of contention between vitalists and mechanists.

The various ways in which the vitalists have dealt with this reference to the future are well known. The impossibility of incorporating their vague teleological concepts into a strictly scientific description of nature proved fatal. To-day it is fairly common ground among scientists that living nature is not teleological in the sense of employing anything akin to 'finalistic causation', and the attempts of vitalists to account for the apparent purposiveness of vital activities by invoking mysterious 'purposive agents', 'vital forces', 'entelechies', or other non-material components alleged to be present in living matter, have faded out of the main currents of biological thought. The interpretation of the process of organic 'becoming', in terms of the 'potential' or 'future' purposively forcing its way into the 'actual' or 'present' in the manner of such finalistic causation, has already come to be regarded as not merely scientifically sterile, but, in concrete scientific terms, an absurdity. These, however, are details of a dead controversy.

The mechanists were undoubtedly right in rejecting the teleology of the vitalists as scientifically sterile and as making nonsense of physical science. Yet they undid all they had gained by failing to realize that the unique manner in which vital phenomena appear to be tailored to the application of teleological concepts and positively invite their use, points to very real differences between animate and inanimate matter—differences whose objective foundation in some kind of spatio-temporal relationships it seems hardly possible to deny, even though we may not know what exactly these spatio-temporal relationships are. They also failed to realize that it should be the first task of biology to unmask these relationships.

Consider a concrete example. If we say that we 'try' to catch a fly, we regard this as a perfectly legitimate use of the verb 'to try.' But if we next say that the fly in the hollow of our hand will 'try' to escape, our modern scientific training intervenes and warns us that in the second case we are committing an illicit anthropomorphism. The fly, we are warned, is not a conscious rational agent, and therefore does not in any literal sense 'try' anything. This rigour of thought is very laudable. Yet in spite of these wise injunctions the incontrovertible fact surely remains that there is a unique something about the observed behaviour of the fly which quite emphatically invites this anthropomorphism and which renders this behaviour far better suited to such an analogy and teleological conception than, say, the behaviour of a falling stone.

What is this elusive something? What is its foundation in the objective realm of spatio-temporal relationships and functional interdependences between material events? How can it be scientifically defined and analysed? How can it be extracted from the physical description of the fly's behaviour? That, in a sense, is the crucial question. It is inconceivable that this goal-directed character of observed life should lack an underlying physical reality. At the same time it is a question which the vitalists have most persistently muddled and the organicists begged, while the mechanists have preferred the devil of scepticism to the deep sea of vagueness.

The doctrine that there is no place in exact science for a distinction between living and non-living systems, is often based on the argument that in the light of modern knowledge we can arrange known systems into a continuous sequence which passes without interruption, and unobtrusively, from obviously living systems to the obviously nonliving. Any scientific distinction between life and the lifeless, therefore, could do no more than draw an arbitrary line across such an intrinsically continuous ladder of being. This argument ignores the fact that the obviously living systems are characterized by a distinct and unique behaviour of a kind that renders it of the greatest practical and theoretical importance to distinguish them by our terminology. The observation that different material systems display these purpose-like and organizational characteristics in varying degrees and some in doubtful degrees, seems hardly relevant to the desirability of using a nomenclature and dichotomy which recognizes their occurrence and significance. One would hardly consider influenza an unworthy subject for scientific study, or a scientifically superfluous concept, on the grounds that some people may contract it in doubtful degrees.

VITAL ORGANIZATION AND ANALYTICAL BIOLOGY

The ground lost by the vitalists in recent generations was only in part gained by the mechanists. Vitalism was not without heirs, at least temperamentally: men who rightly remained puzzled by the apparent purposiveness shown by the behaviour of living matter and who continued to recognize this to be the real hard core of the riddle of life.

They advanced beyond vitalism in recognizing that the cause of the purpose-like behaviour of living systems lies in the presence of special organizational relationships. Thus the emphasis shifted to the concept of *organization*, and a number of schools of thought developed around this concept. Emergencism, holism, and organicism are probably the best-known philosophical currents in this stream of thought. In the view of these writers a living organism is distinguished from inorganic matter by a higher level of organization.

But none of these schools manage to tell us in precise scientific terms what exactly is meant by 'organization' and what exact spatio-temporal relationships distinguish a higher form of organization from a lower. Their philosophical speculations are as a vague and obscure as those of their predecessors.

A related but, on the whole, sounder line of thought was followed by those biologists who accepted the concepts of 'organization' and 'levels of organization' as capable of expressing the fundamental and distinguishing characteristics of observed life, but who also realized that the mere introduction of these concepts did not as such provide an answer to the problem of life. Their persistent cry that the central problem of biology was the problem of biological organization no doubt pointed in the right direction and did service to biology even if they had no other contribution to make. For while the concept of 'organization' keeps the purpose-like character of vital processes continuously before our eyes (since it is only through the apparent purposiveness of the activities to which they give rise that the existence of higher levels of organization can be detected), it yet implies that the purpose-like character of life processes has a foundation in objective spatio-temporal relationships. And, hence, it implies the possibility that some day it may prove possible to express—as indeed our analysis will attempt to do—the really fundamental character of life in exact scientific terms, and to incorporate it in a single and consistent scientific picture of the universe. In this sense the modern emphasis on organization has no doubt paved the way for the analytical approach which we are about to undertake.

To sum up. The main aim of our analytical approach to the study of life is to form a set of deductively employable concepts which will enable theoretical biology to deal with the really fundamental characteristics of observed life, viz. its apparent purposiveness. In order to achieve this aim we shall

(a) analyse the characteristic purposiveness of life-processes and clarify the spatio-temporal relations which underlie it;

(b) show how the results of this analysis may be formulated in terms of exact mathematical relations between quantitative variables, thus exposing the objective foundation which the apparent purposiveness of life has in the universe of physics;

(c) use these results to replace by accurate scientific concepts the vague concepts biologists and philosophers are accustomed to employ in the description of the purposiveness of natural events;

(d) show how this increased precision of thought may serve to throw new light on many features of life which were hitherto understood only imperfectly; and

(e) indicate some of the theoretical consequences which follow from our demonstration that the purposiveness of natural events has an objective basis in time and space, and may in fact be regarded as a *physical* property, as real and genuine as any property of matter studied by modern physics.

OUTLINES OF THE FACTUAL BACKGROUND

For the benefit of the non-biologist and for those who like to inspect the factual background before embarking on a theoretical discussion, I shall give a short sketch of the ways in which the purposiveness of vital activities and biological order manifests itself most markedly. Biological adaptation, regulation, coordination, co-operation, and integration are some of the outstanding phenomena we shall have to deal with, and the following pages may serve to illustrate these and others in turn.

Biologists most often speak of *adaptation* if a living organism undergoes changes which appear to serve its survival. Changes of this type may either accompany the evolution of a species or the development of a single organism and we speak of 'phylogenetic' and 'ontogenetic' adaptations accordingly. However, it is also customary to speak of end-serving behaviour as 'adaptive' behaviour. The 'end' of adaptive changes or adaptive behaviour need not necessarily be the ultimate survival of the organism or of the species, but may be a more proximate condition which in certain cases may bear no relation to the organism's survival, and may even be detrimental to it. When a monkey grabs a fruit, this is called an adaptive movement irrespective of whether the fruit is wholesome or poisonous. Again, the movement of panic-stricken animals which are about to rush to their certain death in a forest fire, may just as properly be described as adapted to the obstacles in their path as when the animals are running to safety.

An instance of other important facts to be borne in mind in any attempt to grasp in full what adaptation means, is this: If a chameleon changes its colour in the normal way to match the shade of its environment, we call that an instance of adaptive behaviour, but if it happens to fall into a pot with the right colour of paint we would not seriously call that adaptive behaviour. I say this merely to put the reader on his guard and to dispel at once any facile optimism that the concept of adaptation is a simple one, or empty of real problems.

The impact of modern learning and education on the development of the adolescent often leaves a young student with a strangely confused attitude towards the many adaptations in nature which strike his eye. His first conscious awareness of phylogenetic adaptations concerns the relation between form and function. In observing the innumerable morphological adaptations of our flora and fauna, the child makes his first acquaintance with the solutions nature has found for the engineering problems which different forms of existence raise: the streamlined fish, the winged bird, the long-necked giraffe, and many others. Later his imagination is stirred by the intricate and ingenious arrangements of our garden plants for securing fertilization, preventing self-fertilization, and for the dispersal of their seed: the honey and scents with which they attract insects, the colours which guide these from afar, and the markings which serve as their further signposts. In the Calceolarias he fancies a saddle provided for the insect to sit on and he will recognize little stirrups in other flowers. He admires the spring-like action developed by Crucianella to shoot pollen at the insect, and the opening mechanism of the pea flower. Then there are the parachutes, slings, catapults, pepper pots, bristles, winged planes, and other contrivances used by our flowers to disperse their seed. In his botany lessons he studies the tropisms of young shoots and

roots, the plant movements, the climbing devices, or even the manner
in which Linaria bends back the stalk bearing the seeds after fertilization, twists around so that the faded flowers face the wall instead of
the sun, and gradually pushes the seed into some cranny between the
bricks.

Then again, the young naturalist marvels at the protective colora-
tion found in the animal kingdom, the mimicry, or the advanced
technique of counter-shading, ruptive markings, illusions of false relief, marginal shadows, &c. And he finds their appeal further enhanced
when they are supported by matched patterns of behaviour. There are,
for instance, the geometrid caterpillars which resemble little twigs and
if disturbed take up correspondingly rigid positions, the innocuous
insects which mimic some ferocious relative, the butterflies whose
wings resemble withered leaves or copy the colour shades of flowers
and grasses on which they rest, the moth which orients itself so that its
markings coincide with the veins of the leaves on which it lives.

As his knowledge matures he comes to recognize the principle of
the lever in the human arm, the principle of the pulley in the *obliquus
superior* muscle of the eye, and much elementary physics in the cli-
matic adaptations of leaf structure in plants.

But then arrives the day when he learns how most of these phenomena can be causally accounted for in terms of physics and chemistry, and the hit-and-miss of natural selection. The romance comes to
a sudden end, his original wonder and sense of divine mystery suddenly find themselves opposed by authoritative scientific voices telling
him to regard all these phenomena as no more than the chance results of essentially blind physico-chemical forces, and as cosmologically
insignificant. From a social and religious point of view a valuable
attitude of mind is often lost thereby. Living nature ceases to be something with which Man can enter into personal relationships.

Which of these opposing tendencies finally sways his thought and
feeling will largely depend on his temperament and the influence of
his teachers. But few, indeed, are those who can steer the middle
course and emerge with a detached scientific attitude which realizes
the importance of avoiding facile romanticism about the harmony and
purposiveness of nature, and yet recognizes this purpose-like character
of life and organic order to be immensely significant. Few are those
who recognize these phenomena for what they are: a type of order
which, in spite of all biophysical, biochemical, and genetical discoveries, has remained a challenge to clear thinking.

Instinctive behaviour provides another large store of conspicuous
phylogenetic adaptations. Their popular appeal has made many of
these examples commonplace. The thoughts of every naturalist are
provoked by the manner in which birds hatched from incubators

instinctively know how to build their nests and assume their parental responsibilities. Even more striking examples from the insect would also jump to the mind. In the instinctive behaviour of the social and other insects, it is particularly easy to allow striking examples such as that of the spinning ants, *Oecophylla smaragdina*,[1] to blind us to innumerable other, less spectacular, but no less intricate and significant patterns of coordinated activities. It is also easy to be provoked to romanticize. William Morton Wheeler recalls the beetle *Rhynchites betulae* which makes two transverse incisions into a birch leaf and folds the apical portions into a compact cone. These lines of incision have been shown to be mathematical curves of such a nature as to represent the evolute of an evolvend and so to produce the leaf area precisely suited to the beetle's purpose. He cites the romantic significance attached to this behaviour by Wasmann and others who saw in this evidence of an intelligence which solved these complicated mathematical problems millions of years before the genius of Man discovered their solution. It is easy to overlook how rigid and unadaptable such behaviour patterns may be, and they lose some of their emotional appeal once this is realized. *Rhynchites betulae* may be able to draw the evolute of an evolvend but, presumably, could not produce a straight incision to save its life. On emerging from the ground after hatching, the caterpillar of the butterfly *Porthesia crysorrhoea* is strongly heliotropic and if it is placed in a jar which contains food on one side but a strong light on the other its stereotyped heliotropic behaviour prevents it from finding the food even to the point of death through starvation.

In passing from such phylogenetically adapted but comparatively rigid behaviour patterns to the adaptive and flexible responses which the organism currently makes to the flux of environmental events, we enter a further large realm of natural phenomena possessing a strongly purposive quality. This ranges all the way from the literally purposive behaviour of Man down to the simple activities of protozoa. For although adaptability of behaviour exists far more extensively in the higher forms of life than in the lower (and is in fact often used as a criterion for this distinction), even the simplest tropisms usually involve some small degree of adaptability.

Between phylogenetic modifications and the behaviour of living adults stand the modifications which the individual undergoes in the course of ontogenesis and in passing through his life cycle. Even if we postpone for the moment the question of embryonic development, it is easy to find numerous illustrations of ontogenetic adaptations which the living organism undergoes in response to special demands made by

---

[1] Teams of which draw the edges of leaves together while their companions bind these together with silk spun by the larvae.

the environment. Familiar examples are the enlargement of our striated muscles in response to persistent external demands; or the degree to which our epidermis can adapt itself to exceptional and protracted mechanical demands by thickening and becoming resistent. Connective tissue and growing bones have similar adaptive powers.

Habituation and learning also involve ontogenetic adaptations. Habituation or 'acclimatization', as it is often called, is the more widespread of these phenomena in the animal world. Behavioural habituation is known to be present in such low forms as sea anemones, and physiological habituation is known even in the very lowest forms of life. Thus, paramecia and other protozoa can acclimatize within individual clones to increased salinity of their environment, and the power of bacteria to increase their resistivity to drug action has also recently attracted attention.

So far we have mainly touched upon adaptations in morphological and behavioural phenomena, which are often the ones most easily observed in the study of living nature. But behind these easily observable activities there lies a world of hidden chemical and physical events which modern physiology is only gradually revealing. These physiological events show modes of adaptation as characteristic as any of the others. Here, too, we have innumerable phylogenetic adaptations, such as, for instance, the adaptations of the animal metabolism to the normal diet of the species.

With these examples we may for the present leave our illustrations of the extensive range and diversity of adaptation and adaptability in vital activities. It must be remembered, however, that adaptability is never unlimited. It may be very extensive, as in the higher organisms and especially in Man, but no living organism has the power to cope with all the conceivable challenges of its environment. On the contrary, the environmental changes which are possible in the normal routine of events are often so limited that, as someone has put it, few animals have a chance to show how foolishly they would act under irregular circumstances.

The concept of *regulation* in its most common biological uses refers to activities which 'aim' at ensuring the constancy of some environmental or internal condition. The latter case is the more common, for it seems to be the rule that the possibility of an organism maintaining itself as a going concern is contingent on its power to maintain a certain constancy of its 'milieu interne.' The regulative responses by means of which the living organism meets and offsets any disturbance of this constancy again furnish typical examples of the apparent purposiveness of organic behaviour. This is as true for the lower as for the higher forms of life, although once more the latter show progressively greater powers of regulation.

The body fluids play an essential part in the organism's internal environment. The proper functioning of the body requires of many substances that they should be present in this fluid matrix in certain critical concentrations. Many physiological mechanisms serve the regulation of these concentrations. The great sensitivity required of some of these physiological regulations is shown by such facts as that a frog's heart is killed if fluids are sent through it which have an excess acidity corresponding to about one part by weight of hydrogen ions to one billion parts of water. The delicacy of the actual regulative reactions is illustrated by the fact that purified pituitary hormone has been found to be appreciably active in concentrations of one part in 18,000 million. It is also interesting to note the different rapidities with which some of these regulations take place. In Man, nervous inexcitability following the passage of a nerve impulse is said to last normally for only about a millisecond; excess of carbon dioxide in the blood lasts for a few seconds; excess of bromide may last for weeks; and of lead for years.

Some of the mechanisms involved in physiological regulation may be comparatively simple, such as the disposal of excess water through the kidneys, or excess carbon dioxide from the blood through increased pulmonary activity. But the complete reorientation of feeling and behaviour and the psychological reorganization which a human being undergoes in extreme thirst, show how complex and comprehensive a mechanism the body may be able to mobilize in real need. The regulation of the blood's osmotic pressure and oxygen content, or of body temperature, are other familiar examples, and a particularly striking illustration of the self-regulating powers of the body and their purpose-like character is the fact that in starvation, when the body proteins have to be broken down, the body will break them down in the reversed order of their physiological importance, so that the most vital tissues will be preserved longest.

It would be wrong to give the impression that these regulative mechanisms are separate and isolated functional units, each with its separate task. Many organs serve a variety of functions. The liver is a good case in point. Conversely, there often exists more than one mechanism to deal with any one type of regulation. For instance, in regulating its temperature the body makes use of such diverse mechanisms as the relaxation or constriction of peripheral blood-vessels, sweating, panting, shivering, or adrenalin secretion.

In surveying these case of internal regulation it must not be forgotten that many animals also possess extensive powers of regulating their external environment. Nearly every animal at some stage of its life possesses motility and during this period it can regulate its environment by migration or otherwise. In some cases, as in Man, the animal has the power to regulate conditions in its environment not only by selection but also by direct modifications.

Embryological processes show very wide powers of regulation. Here, to quote Needham,[2] the concept of regulation denotes 'the extensive power embryonic forms of life have to continue a normal or approximately normal development or regeneration in spite of experimental interference by ablation, addition (implantation), exchange (transplantation), fusion, etc.'. And he adds: 'The processes thus revealed operate in all embryos to a greater or lesser extent and may be regarded as part of the sum total of processes whereby the organism is rendered more or less independent of its environment.' It has been shown that the cells of the blastulae of some animals, for instance sea urchins, may be completely separated even up to the thirty-two-cell stage and yet each of these fragments will eventually give rise to a complete individual. Far-going transplantations of tissue can be carried out in young embryos without affecting the outcome of the embryonic development. In the case of the amphibian embryo, Spemann showed that, before gastrulation has begun, nearly all parts of the embryo are interchangeable with other parts without preventing the development of a complete and viable animal.

Remarkable, too, is the extensive regulation which regenerative processes may display. The regeneration of amphibian limbs, for instance, has been studied extensively alongside amphibian embryology. The amputated leg stump in adult newts can reorganize any mass of competent tissue grafted on to it, and regenerate a complete limb from it. But we must not let these spectacular examples and others, such as the power of any of a dozen fragments into which a flat-worm may be cut to regenerate a complete individual, or of a single Begonia leaf to regenerate an entire plant, cast into the shade the extensive powers of regeneration possessed by most living organisms from the single cell upwards. For instance, although Man's power of regeneration is more limited than in some lower forms of life, very extensive regulation and reorganization is nevertheless involved in the processes of wound healing or the repair of fractured bones. In both cases a large number of the cells involved come to assume new functions and undergo a considerable internal reorganization. Other striking examples of purpose-like activity in repairing organic injuries are the adjustments which higher organisms can make to interferences with their nervous system—although they have no power actually to replace destroyed nerve cells. The increased subtlety and discrimination which the human auditory faculties develop after loss of sight is a case in

---

[2] *Biochemistry and Morphogenesis*, Cambridge, 1942.

point. If the semicircular canals of a bird are injured, recovery is possible through a gradual substitution of optical impulses for the missing labyrinthine ones in maintaining postural control. In the transplantation of a nerve of the dog it has been claimed that functionally correct innervation takes place without any preceeding incorrect movements. Similarly, in the transplantation of muscles it has been observed that the proper movement occurs immediately after removal of the bandage.

Closely akin, as far as its purpose-like character is concerned, is the fact of reconstitution as it is found in lower forms of life. The slime-mould, *Physarium polycephalum*, is not killed by being ground in a mortar with quartz sand and can pass without harm through soft and hard filter-paper. The Mycetozoa can 'creep' through cotton in fine strands which soon flow together again on the other side and form an organism having the same behaviour as before. In certain sponges, for instance, cells isolated by squeezing a part of the sponge through fine silk, will later reunite into little sponges.

Finally, mention must be made of another form of regulation which has a distinctly purpose-like quality. I mean the power of living organisms to create defensive substances in response to the entrance of foreign organic matter into vital parts of the system. The full extent of these immunological powers of living organisms are still imperfectly explored and little is known about the exact manner in which these foreign proteins or antigens are acted upon by the highly specific antibodies which the organism creates in its defence.

When a number of simultaneous organic activities which are not mutually dependent in any direct causal sense nevertheless seem to be directed to a single common goal—each proceeding, so to speak, as if it were aware of the others—or when they behave as if they were governed and dovetailed by a central, purposive, controlling agency, we are wont to speak of *coordinated* activities. The coordination of our voluntary muscles is an obvious example. A list of all the voluntary muscles or their antagonists which actively enter into a single human walking movement would be formidable indeed. The function of the central nervous system is, of course, primarily that of a coordinating organ. But coordinated animal and plant movements without the agency of any nervous system are also possible. For instance, the spiral movements of paramecia are due to a particular form of coordinated activity by its cilia.

The actual disengagement or dissociation of normally coordinated processes which can be brought about experimentally shows that coordination is a connective relationship which may allow considerable independence to the related parts. The experimenter can, for instance, secure the disengagement of growth from differentiation in embryonic tissues, nuclear division from cellular division, metabolism from either growth or differentiation.

A particularly wide field of coordinated activities is found in mutual co-operation and division of labour in higher animal associations. Insect societies have already been mentioned, and many additional examples could be chosen, ranging from the most primitive forms of family life to the complex coordinated activities of a modern nation at war.

Lastly, a word may be said about *integration*. Many of the purpose-like activities illustrated in this section are not, as such, necessarily exclusive properties of living organisms. In smaller measure they may be found in one form or another also in automata, servo-mechanisms, and other machines. An exclusive characteristic of life, however, is the way in which these purpose-like activities are dovetailed and unite the component parts or processes of living systems into actively self-main-taining, self-regulating, developing, and reproducing organic wholes —into living individuals. To denote this dovetailed mutual adjustment and collaboration of purpose-like activities the term 'biological inte-gration' has gained wide-spread currency and we shall take it up in the same sense.

To express the differences in the degrees of integration, biologists often speak of different 'levels' of integration. It is largely according to these levels of integration that the biologist has come to form the idea of individual organic wholes possessing varying degrees of au-tonomy, and has come to speak, for instance, of 'cellular', 'metameric', and 'social aggregates.' The higher the level of integration of an organic whole, the greater, obviously, the suppression of local inde-pendence. In the lower multicellular organisms we find a very con-siderable independence of the parts. The beheaded earthworm will exhibit most of the responses of the intact animal except, for instance, the burrowing reaction. Associations of multicellular organisms also show varying degrees of integration. From mere aggregations which are held together by tropistic or sensory responses, and loose-knit food associations or biocoenoses, we ascend the scale to reproductive associations and families, to the large assertive associations of flocks and herds, thence to insect societies, to the societies of monkeys and apes, and finally, to the complex fabric of human societies. All these show conspicuous organizational relationships, and, alive to more subtle forms of organization, some biologists have not hesitated to extend the idea of an organic whole to include the entire realm of living nature. Such conceptions are often based on the reciprocal nutritional dependence of the animal kingdom and the plant king-dom. Sometimes also they are based on the comparatively stable

balance which nature keeps between different animal or plant popula-
tions. References to such facts as that cholera bacilli may divide every
twenty minutes and that, therefore, each bacillus could in theory
generate 7,366 tons of bacilli per day, are obviously misconceived and
irrelevant. But it is true that an extensive increase in any one animal
population may bring about a series of checks which bear some
analogy to the self-regulating powers within individual organisms.

THE LANGUAGE OF THE PHYSICAL SCIENCES

The main subject-matter of this book is the purposiveness of life
processes and the manner in which this integrates living systems into
organic wholes, for we have recognized these to be the fundamental
characteristics of observed life. In the preceding sections these characteristics were discussed and illustrated in terms of such concepts as
'adaptation', 'regulation', 'coordination', 'integration', &c., and the
upshot of our general remarks was that a theoretical biology cannot
be born until these concepts can be translated into the physico-
mathematical language of exact science, i.e. into clearly definable
spatio-temporal relationships between quantitative variables. A fresh
and primarily analytical start must be made.

This statement of our aims may have stirred up a number of the
reader's prejudices. Words like 'adaptation', 'regulation', 'coordination', 'purpose', are good plain English words, and the reader may feel
that nothing can be gained by any attempt to paraphrase them in a
physico-mathematical language. Nothing can be clearer, they may say,
than good plain English. Other readers may be put out by the very
mention of mathematics in this context, for it may bring to their
minds those many mathematical efforts in biology which can be considered as little more than fanciful and sterile titivations unrelated to
the real problems biologists want solved.

These objections could be met simply by a plea to await the results
of our method in the later parts of the book. The new light which
these results shed on the general nature of life, will no doubt dispel
hastily formed prejudices. Yet, it will not lead us too far astray if we
briefly deal with one or two of these prejudices forthwith.

In the first place, it is important to recognize that while such plain
English words as 'adaptation', 'purposiveness', &c., are good enough
for ordinary discourse and for those simple deductive arguments to
whose conclusions we can at any time apply an intuitive and common-
sense check, they are far too vague for intricate deductive arguments,
and for an elaborate logical theory or axiomatic system (e.g. for discovering whether two axioms are consistent). The concept system of
the physical sciences and the language of physics is the most advanced

system of thought and symbols which the human mind has been able to develop for the interpretation of nature. The physical sciences owe their immense success primarily to the manner in which their mathematical language has overcome the intrinsic shortcomings of the natural languages for difficult informative and theoretical purposes.

Secondly, modern physical science has developed an immensely advanced and comprehensive picture of the universe in terms of mathematical relations between quantitative variables, and until we can translate the fundamental characteristics of observed life into that language we cannot bring the general phenomenon of life into a logical relation with the theoretical framework of modern physics, and incorporate it in a single comprehensive picture of the world. Nor can we rigorously examine such special issues as the compatibility of the purpose-like character of vital activities with the causal principles of macroscopic determinism upheld by modern physics.

Finally, such mathematics as we shall use will extend no further in relation to living organisms than (a) to treat the organism as a physical system, i.e. as a material system whose current state is in principle specifiable by means of quantitative parameters; (b) to employ the idea of one-one correspondences or functional relationships between certain sets of values of such parameters; (c) to use the customary mathematical symbols for such functional relationships, and (d) to use the idea of the derivative of a function, i.e. of the rate at which a change in one of a number of dependent parameters is accompanied by a change in one of the others. Moreover, these mathematical ideas will be used only qualitatively, i.e. for the purposes of introducing an indispensable degree of precision into our thoughts and symbols, and not for computative or prognostic purposes.

The main problem of any advanced informative language, particularly of any scientific use of language, is to find expressions and statements concerning whose meaning it is intrinsically possible to establish universal agreement and uniformity of interpretation among scientists. Men communicate with one another by means of conventional signs which can never mean quite the same to those who use them. The power of the scientific language lies in the degree to which it has succeeded in overcoming this inherent weakness, and in avoiding ambiguity or vagueness. This has made possible a measure of agreement among scientists about the facts they study and about possible interpretations for them which is unparalleled in any branch of human knowledge. Moreover, without this possibility of agreement and uniformity in interpreting the signs used the pooling of information and the scientific collaboration which is at the back of modern technical progress would have been unthinkable.

One reason for this need to avoid ambiguity and vagueness is that agreement about the meaning of a statement is an obvious prerequisite for agreement about its truth. Most scientific propositions are universal propositions and can, strictly speaking, never be more than tentatively accepted hypotheses. For no universal proposition can be strictly verified. Yet, agreement about the meaning of an hypothesis must obviously precede any agreement about its acceptability or about the question whether any particular experiment confirms or falsifies it.

But for the purpose of theory construction the most important reason why the informative use of language is vitiated by ambiguity or vagueness, is that ambiguous or vague meanings can invalidate any formal process of deduction and thereby make any deductive system of thought or theory impossible. It is well known that the classical syllogism may lead from correct premises to false conclusions if the verbal identity of the middle term fails to be accompanied by the real identity of the objects denoted in the two contexts, i.e. if the middle term is used ambiguously. To illustrate the mischief which the existence of a single ambiguity can do in a reasoned argument, a simple example may be cited which some readers may remember from their schooldays. Assume that in trying to define a certain expression, say the expression 'pure quantity', someone makes it clear that he means this expression to denote finite real numbers, but leaves it open whether or not this is to include the number zero. Under these assumptions the premise that any 'pure quantity' is divisible by any other 'pure quantity'—which would be true if zero is excluded—allows us to arrive by simple mathematical reasoning (which assumes, however, zero to be included) to arrive at the conclusion that $1 = 2$ and hence that any 'pure quantity' is equal to any other.[3]

This power of even so (*prima facie*) insignificant an ambiguity to lead to an infinite number of absurd or conflicting conclusions, is the bane of speculative philosophy. It is one of the main reasons why speculative philosophy has failed to interpret any aspect of reality in terms of a deductive system of thought on which a significant amount of agreement could be reached by philosophers. It is also the reason why instead of one comprehensive theory of life we have to-day but a collection of discordant and inconclusive philosophies of life, and why the best part of our efforts must go towards achieving real exactitude

---

[3] The 'proof' runs as follows:
Assume that a and b are two equal numbers; then
$$a = b$$
$$\therefore \quad ab = b^2$$
$$\therefore \quad ab - a^2 = b^2 - a^2$$
$$\therefore \quad a(b-a) = (b-a)(b+a)$$
$$\therefore \quad a = b+a$$
$$\therefore \quad a = a+a$$
$$\therefore \quad 1 = 2.$$

in the discussion of the fundamental characteristics of life. Only against this background of language and the intrinsic difficulties of its informative use can we come to see the physical sciences and the physico-mathematical language in their true perspectives.

To appreciate how the physical sciences have overcome these difficulties, it is necessary to distinguish between the two main sources of ambiguity or vagueness which exist in the informative use of language.

The first source of possible ambiguity or vagueness lies in the reference which the words or symbols used have to the world of perception, i.e. to the objects which they are meant to denote. Of any word or symbol which refers to the world of perception, the speaker must be able to make it absolutely clear what exactly the word refers to.

The second source of ambiguity or vagueness concerns the formal structure of the speaker's statements and their mode of statement composition. We may distinguish these two types of possible ambiguity and vagueness by calling them 'semantic' and 'formal', respectively. Which is the more important? Which the more fatal to the informative use of language? The answer is that either can be fatal, but that semantic vagueness is by far the more dangerous because in the past Man has been far less critical of it than of the formal correctness of his propositions and inferences. Logicians have for over two thousand years devoted themselves to the formal aspects of language, but only in our own age are men slowly beginning to grow alive to the importance of semantic precision.

An instructive example to show how very important this semantic precision is, may be taken from the general relativity theory. A cornerstone of the theory is Einstein's recognition that even so familiar, and to all appearances innocent, a concept as that of 'simultaneity' proves too ambiguous and vague when we try to establish by means of measurements whether or not it is fulfilled by distant events. Hence, the strict discipline of physical theory demands the rejection of the concept in this context. How much vaguer than the concept of 'simultaneity' are the concepts in terms of which we are accustomed to think of the fundamental characteristics of life!

How does the language and method of the physicist overcome the twin dangers of formal and semantic vagueness or ambiguity? It overcomes the first by resorting for all purposes of intricate deduction to the rigorous and precise formalism of mathematics; and it overcomes the second, as we have just seen, by operating with only such concepts and only such mathematical expressions that any reference which these expressions are intended to have to the world of perception can, either directly or indirectly, be made publicly clear and definite by the specification of a set of practical procedures (viz. operations of experiment and measurement) in terms of which it can in principle be ascertained whether the empirical conditions denoted by these expressions are, or are not, fulfilled in any given case. These two methods are linked together by the concept of *number* which allows the results of measurements to be expressed in the symbols of mathematics and hence enables us to apply mathematical reasoning to recorded empirical observations.

It is important to realize the fact that the only final way of making definite the meaning of any symbolic expressions which refer to the world of perception, and of securing uniformity of interpretation of such expressions, is by giving them so-called 'demonstrative definitions', i.e. by publicly demonstrating the objects or conditions which they are meant to denote. And the ultimate reason why operations of measurement can serve to give a definite meaning to a difficult physical concept is precisely that, since they consist of practical operations, they can be described entirely in terms of demonstratively definable expressions. If, for instance, the physicist is asked what exactly he means by the 'temperature' of a water-bath, he can make his exact meaning publicly clear by saying 'I mean the number indicated by a thermometer of such and such a construction and calibrated in such and such a way, when it is immersed in the water', and all the terms involved in this specification which have any reference at all to the world of perception, are in the last resort definable demonstratively. Alternatively, of course, he may give a merely formal thermodynamical definition of temperature, but in that case the concepts in terms of which he gives his definition admit—again either directly or indirectly by means of a further reduction—of being given a definite and public definition in terms of practical laboratory operations and measurements. It is true that in physical measurements it may not always be possible to reach agreement on the exact reading of a given instrument pointer, but it is as a rule possible to reach complete agreement on the limits between which its true reading lies, and since this margin of possible error can be formally taken account of in the mathematical evaluation of a given measurement, this difficulty is irrelevant in the present context.

In pure mathematics and symbolic logic a similar situation prevails. The rules according to which mathematical expressions may be formed and transformed (as in adding, subtracting, &c.) can be made clear in a public way by the simple act of demonstrating them on a piece of paper. Similarly, the rules for the combination and transformation of the signs used in modern logic can be made public and clear by—as Bridgman has put it—'demonstrable paper and pencil operations.'

In short, the secret of the success of the physical language in the description and interpretation of nature lies in the degree to which it eliminates the intrinsic vagueness of the natural languages by using demonstratively definable laboratory operations (viz. experiments and measurements) to correlate the facts of experience with a set of formal elements (viz. numbers), whose permissible combinations and transformations (adding, subtracting, &c.) are also publicly definable.

It is sometimes said that the secret of the physicist's success lies in the ultimate 'testability' of his propositions. In a certain sense this is merely another way of stating what we have already said, but I think it misleads by emphasizing a derivative rather than a primary aspect of the matter. Before a proposition can be tested it must first be accepted as a significant hypothesis, i.e. we must be clear about its meaning.

Avoiding vagueness or ambiguity in scientific concepts must not be confused with avoiding elasticity of such concepts. While vagueness must be condemned, elasticity may yet be highly desirable. The use of a concept is elastic if its users remain prepared in the light of experience to consider alternative definitions for it, and to revise its precise meaning. In the early stages of a scientific theory the existence of such elasticity may be of considerable importance. As long as the alternative definitions are sufficiently precise there is no contradiction between the elimination of vagueness and the maintenance of elasticity in the use of a concept. The ideas of 'number' in mathematics and of 'temperature' in physics are good examples in which precision was combined with elasticity in the course of their historical development. And in the development of suitable new concepts to deal with the phenomena of biological order we shall also endeavour to combine a minimum of vagueness with a maximum of elasticity. The concepts in terms of which Man chooses to think about the real world are the only things over which he has absolute power. He can make and unmake them. There is no such thing as the 'real' meaning of a concept to which its use has to conform. Although Man has, of course, 'real' habits and conventions of using certain words in certain ways, which it would be foolish to disregard in defining a word.

The superiority of physics in the realm of empirical thought is often loosely dismissed with a phrase to the ultimate effect that the world is made out of three types of elements: measurable quantities such as weight and temperature: unmeasurable quantities such as utility, desire, adaptation, organization, and qualities such as beauty; and it is said that physics has, as it were, an unfair advantage over the other sciences by confining itself to the study of the first type of element only. This mode of thought is very misleading. It is a serious confusion to project this threefold distinction into the objective world whereas it properly belongs only to the definiteness and precision of the concepts we use in thinking about that world. It is wrong to regard physics as a science whose subject-matter is objectively limited in this way. We must look upon physics as a science with an unlimited subject-matter but with a definitely limited conceptual apparatus, viz. one which is confined to concepts rigorously satisfying the strict formal and semantic requirements outlined above. It is important to realize this clearly, for unless we appreciate that the physico-mathematical system of to-day is not merely a set of propositions developed about an intrinsically limited aspect of nature, but a body of thought whose only limitation is the strict discipline imposed upon the choice of its concepts and upon the structure of its propositions, we may fail to see why it is both possible and desirable to extend this physico-mathematical discipline to other fields—such as in this case to the phenomena of biological order and organization. The distinguishing features of the physical sciences are not impressed upon them by their material, but by ideals of clear thinking.

Many important questions still lie well beyond the scope of physical thought, and speculative philosophy has this in common with all other bodies of theoretical thought which fail to satisfy the standards of precision achieved by modern physics, that it recognizes the power of language to convey, although not literal truth, at least some form of insight to suitable audiences. Thus it is prepared to discuss metaphorically and inconclusively rather than not at all the many important questions which physico-mathematical thought has so far been unable to reach. A. N. Whitehead's works are attempts to say significant things about the nature of organic order in such metaphorical terms. In some respects, indeed, he strains his metaphorical language almost to the limits of our associative faculties. No doubt such efforts are valuable, and their colourful phraseology contrasts strongly with the drabness of the physical language, but, however beautiful and masterly, such metaphorical systems of thought can never achieve the same conclusiveness and the same possibilities of agreement as scientific theories. There will always be as many conflicting philosophies as there are philosophers.

A clear distinction, therefore, can be drawn between physical theory and philosophy. The one sacrifices inclusiveness in the interest of conclusiveness, the other conclusiveness in the interest of inclusiveness. We need not on this account condemn either for its deficiencies. Our attitude towards them should be determined by the obvious recognition that the ideal must be the attainment of both inclusiveness and conclusiveness.

Finally, a word must be said about what is sometimes called the 'hypothetico-deductive' character of physical theory. This expression refers to the fact that the formal basis of physical theory, as of any theory in the empirical sciences, consists of interpreted axiom systems.

An axiom system is a set of mutually consistent and very general formulae which are put forward without regard to any reference they may have to matters of fact and without regard to the question whether we can know them to be true or false, but solely on the ground that a certain larger collection of given and less general formulae can be deduced from them. An interpreted axiom system is one in which the collection of given formulae refer to matters of fact and consist of significant propositions which may be true or false. We are prepared to accept an interpreted axiom system as true if we can find no evidence that any consequences derivable from the axioms are false and know of some that they are true. Scientific theory attempts to explain empirical facts by developing suitable axiom systems and suitable rules for their interpretation. An empirical fact is 'explained' by a scientific theory if the propositions expressing it can be shown to be a consequence of the axioms of the theory. The foremost aim pursued in the development of any scientific theory is to find the simplest set of axioms which will enable all the observable phenomena studied by the branch of science concerned to be explained in this manner. For instance, in classical mechanics it was found that all the phenomena studied could be shown to be consequences of Lagrange's Equations of Motion. These equations were therefore accepted as a suitable set of axioms. Similarly, Maxwell's equations proved to be a suitable set of axioms for explaining the phenomena of electrodynamics.

The part played by induction in the development of scientific theory often tends to obscure this purely hypothetical character of the universal propositions of science and of the 'laws of nature' which science proclaims. Induction is a psychological process. It is a process in which we jump from the observation that this man was mortal and that man was mortal to the hypothesis that all men are mortal. The framing of an hypothesis is essentially a process of free invention; but when we pass from the observation of a very large number of men to the hypothesis that all men are mortal, this process of invention is, of course, a comparatively simple psychological step. When an hypothesis is based on induction it may derive special weight from our knowledge that it is *ipso facto* confirmed by a large number of test cases, but it still remains merely an hypothesis. Induction and deduction are therefore in all respects quite different. Deduction is a formal process in which one proposition is derived from another as a necessary consequence. It has logical compulsion. Induction, on the other hand, is a psychological process. It has, at best, psychological compulsion and can lead to falsehood as well as truth.

In the present volume we are only concerned with critical analysis and not with the construction of axiom systems. Nevertheless, the process of substituting new concepts for old ones is based on a process of free invention not unlike the invention of hypotheses, and the reader will fail to see this work in its proper methodological perspective unless he realizes the essentially hypothetical character of scientific theory.

---

7. Teleological Explanation and Teleological Systems

Ernest Nagel

THE ANALYTICAL METHODS of the modern natural sciences are universally admitted to be competent for the study of all nonliving phenomena, even those which, like cosmic rays and the weather, are still not completely understood. Moreover, attempts at unifying special branches of physical science, by reducing their several systems of explanation to an inclusive theory, are generally encouraged and welcomed. During the past four centuries these methods have also been fruitfully employed in the study of living organisms; and many features of vital processes have been successfully explained in physico-chemical terms. Outstanding biologists as well as physical scientists have therefore concluded that the methods of the physical sciences are fully adequate to the materials of biology, and many of them have been entirely confident that eventually the whole of biology will be simply a chapter of physics and chemistry.

But despite the undeniable successes of physico-chemical explanations in the study of living things, biologists of unquestioned competence continue to regard them as not entirely adequate for the subject matter of biology. Most biologists are in general agreement that vital processes, like nonliving ones, occur only under determinate physico-chemical conditions and form no exceptions to physico-chemical laws. Some of them nevertheless maintain that the mode of analysis required for understanding living phenomena is fundamentally different from that which obtains in the physical sciences. Opposition to the systematic absorption of biology into physics and chemistry is sometimes based on the practical ground that it does not conform to the correct strategy of current biological research. However, such opposi-

Reprinted by permission from *Vision and Action: Essays in Honor of Horace Kallen on his Seventieth Birthday*, edited by S. Ratner, pp. 192–222. (New Brunswick, New Jersey: Rutgers University Press, 1953).

tion is often also supported by theoretical arguments, which aim to show that the reduction of biology to physico-chemistry is inherently impossible. Biology has long been an arena in which crucial issues in the logic of explanation have been the subject of vigorous debate. It is therefore instructive to examine some of the reasons biologists commonly advance for the claim that the logic of explanatory concepts in biology is distinctive of the science and that biology is an inherently autonomous discipline.

What are the chief supports for this claim? Let us first dispose of two less weighty ones. Although it is difficult to formulate in precise general terms the differences between the living and nonliving, no one seriously doubts the obvious fact that there are such differences. Accordingly, the sciences of the living are concerned with special questions that are patently different from those with which physics and chemistry deal. Biology studies the anatomy and physiology of living things, and investigates the modes and conditions of their reproduction, development and decay. It classifies vital organisms into types or species; and it inquires into their geographic distribution, their descent, and the modes and conditions of evolutionary changes in them. It also analyzes organisms as structures of interrelated parts, and seeks to discover what each part contributes to the maintenance of the organism as a whole. Physics and chemistry, on the other hand, are not specifically concerned with such problems, although the subject matter of biology also falls within the province of these sciences. Thus, a stone and a cat when dropped from a height exhibit behaviors which receive a common formulation in the laws of mechanics; and cats as well as stones therefore belong to the subject matter of physics. Nevertheless, cats possess structural features and engage in processes in which physics and chemistry, at any rate in their current form, are not interested. Stated more formally, biology employs expressions referring to identifiable characteristics of living phenomena (such as "sex," "cellular division," "heredity" or "adaptation") and asserts laws containing them (such as "Hemophelia among humans is a sex-linked hereditary trait") that do not occur in the physical sciences, and are not at present definable or derivable within the latter. Accordingly, while the subject matters of biology and the physical sciences are not disparate, and though the former science makes use of distinctions and laws borrowed from the latter, the science of biology does not at present coincide with the sciences of physics and chemistry.

It is no less evident that the techniques of observation and experimentation in biology are in general different from those current in the physical sciences. To be sure, there are tools and techniques of observation, measurement, and calculation (such as lenses, balances, and algebra) which are used in both groups of disciplines. But biology also requires special skills (such as those involved in the dissection of organic tissues) that serve no purpose in physics; and physics employs techniques (such as those needed for producing high vacua) that are irrelevant in present-day biology. A physical scientist untrained in the special techniques of biological research is no more likely to perform a biological experiment successfully than is a pianist untutored in playing wind-instruments likely to perform well on an oboe.

These differences between the special problems and techniques of the physical and biological sciences are sometimes cited as evidence for the inherent autonomy of biology, and for the claim that the analytical methods of physics are not fully adequate to the objectives of biological inquiry. However, though the differences are genuine, they certainly do not warrant such conclusions. Mechanics, electro-magnetism, and chemistry, for example, are prima facie distinct branches of physical science, in each of which different special problems are pursued and different techniques are employed. But these are quite obviously not sufficient reasons for maintaining that each of those divisions of physical science is an autonomous discipline. If there is a sound basis for the alleged absolute autonomy of biology, it must be sought elsewhere than in the differences between biology and the physical sciences that have been noted thus far.

What then are the weightier reasons which support that allegation? The main ones appear to be as follows. Vital processes have a prima facie purposive character; for organisms are capable of self-regulation, self-maintenance, and self-reproduction, and their activities seem to be directed toward the attainment of goals that lie in the future. It is usually admitted that one can study and formulate the morphological characteristics of plants and animals in a manner comparable with the way physical sciences investigate the structural traits of nonliving things. Thus, the categories of analysis and explanation of physics are generally held to be adequate for studying the gross and minute anatomy of the human kidney, or the serial order of its development. But morphological studies are only one part of the biologist's task, since the latter also includes inquiry into the *functions* of structures in sustaining the activities of the organism as a whole. Thus, biology studies the role played by the kidney and its microscopic structures in preserving the chemical composition of the blood, and thereby in maintaining the whole body and its other parts in their characteristic activities. It is such manifestly "goal-directed" behavior of living things that is often regarded as requiring a distinctive category of explanation in biology.

Moreover, living things are organic wholes, not additive systems of independent parts, and the behavior of these parts cannot be properly understood if they are regarded as so many isolatable mechanisms. The parts of an organism must be viewed as internally related members of an integrated whole. They mutually influence one another, and their behavior regulates and is regulated by the activities of the organism as a whole. Some biologists have argued that the coordinated, adaptive behavior of living organisms can be explained only by assuming a special vitalistic agent; others believe that an explanation is possible in terms of the hierarchical organization of internally related parts of the organism. But in either case, so it is frequently claimed, biology cannot dispense with the notion of organic unity; and in consequence it must use modes of analysis and formulation that are unmistakably *sui generis*.

Accordingly, there are two main features that are commonly alleged to differentiate biology from the physical sciences in an essential way. One is the dominant place occupied by *teleological* explanations in biological inquiry. The other is the use of conceptual tools uniquely appropriate in the study of systems whose total behavior is not the resultant of the activities of independent components. We must now examine these claims in some detail.

Almost any biological treatise or monograph yields conclusive evidence that biologists are concerned with the functions of vital processes and organs in maintaining characteristic activities of living things. In consequence, if "teleological analysis" is understood to be an inquiry into such functions, and into processes which are directed toward attaining certain end-products, then undoubtedly teleological explanations are pervasive in biology. In this respect, certainly, there appears to be a marked difference between the latter and the physical sciences. It would surely be an oddity on the part of a modern physicist were he to declare, for example, that atoms have outer shells of electrons in order to make chemical unions between themselves and other atoms possible. In ancient Aristotelian science categories of explanation suggested by the study of living things (and in particular by human art) were made canonical for all inquiry. Since nonliving as well as living phenomena were thus analyzed in teleological terms— an analysis which made the notion of final cause focal—Greek science did not assume a fundamental cleavage between biology and other natural sciences. Modern science, on the other hand, regards final causes to be vestal virgins which bear no fruit in the study of physical and chemical phenomena; and because of the association of teleological explanations with the doctrine that goals or ends of activity are dynamic agents in their own realization, it tends to view such explanations as a species of obscurantism. But does the procedure of teleological explanations in biology and the apparent absence of such explanations from the physical sciences entail the absolute autonomy of the former? We shall try to show that it does not.

Quite apart from their association with the doctrine of final causes, teleological explanations are sometimes suspect in modern natural science because they are assumed to invoke purposes or ends-in-view as causal factors in natural processes. Purposes and deliberate goals admittedly play important roles in human activities; but there is no basis whatever for assuming them in the study of physico-chemical and most biological phenomena. However, as has already been noted, there are a great many explanations that are counted as teleological which do not postulate any purposes or ends-in-view; for explanations are often said to be "teleological" only in the sense that they specify the *functions* which things or processes possess. Most contemporary biologists certainly do not impute purposes to the organic parts of living things whose functions are investigated; and most of them would probably also deny that the means-ends relationships discovered in the organization of living creatures are the products of some deliberate plan on the part of a purposeful agent. To be sure, there are biologists who postulate psychic states as concomitants and even as directive forces of all organic behavior. But they are in a minority; and they usually support their view by special considerations which can be distinguished from the facts of functional or teleological dependencies that most biologists do not hesitate to accept. Since the word "teleology" is ambiguous, it would doubtless prevent confusions and misunderstandings were it eliminated from the vocabulary of biologists. But as it is, biologists do use it, and say they are giving a teleological explanation when, for example, they explain that the function of the alimentary canal in vertebrates is to prepare ingested materials for absorption into the blood-stream. The crucial point is that when biologists do employ teleological language they are not necessarily committing the pathetic fallacy or lapsing into anthropomorphism.

We must now show, however, that teleological (or functional) explanations are equivalent to nonteleological ones, so that the former can be replaced by the latter without loss in asserted content. Consider some typical teleological statement, for example, "The function of chlorophyll in plants is to enable plants to perform photosynthesis." But this statement appears to assert nothing which is not asserted by "Plants perform photosynthesis only if they contain chlorophyll," or alternatively by "A necessary condition for the occurrence of photosynthesis in plants is the presence of chlorophyll." These latter statements, however, do not explicitly ascribe a function to chlorophyll, and in that sense are therefore not teleological formulations. If this example is taken as a paradigm, it seems that when a function is ascribed to a constituent of some organism, the content of the teleological statement is fully conveyed by another statement which simply asserts a necessary (or possibly a necessary and sufficient) condition for a certain trait or activity of that organism. On this assumption, therefore, a teleological explanation states the *consequences* for a given biological system of one of the latter's constituent parts or processes; the equivalent nonteleological explanation states some of the *conditions* (though not necessarily in physico-chemical terms) under which the system persists in its characteristic organization and activities. The difference between teleological and nonteleological explanations is thus comparable to the difference between saying that *B* is an effect of *A*, and saying that *A* is a cause or condition of *B*. In brief, the difference is one of selective attention, rather than of asserted content.

This point can be reinforced by another consideration. If a teleological explanation had an asserted content which is different from the content of every nonteleological statement, it would be possible to cite procedures and evidence for establishing the former which are different from the procedures and evidence required for confirming the latter. But in point of fact, there appear to be no such procedures and evidence. Thus, consider the teleological statement, "The function of the leucocytes in human blood is to defend the body against foreign micro-organisms." Now whatever may be the evidence which warrants this statement, it also warrants the statement that "Unless human blood contains a sufficient number of leucocytes, certain normal activities of the body are injured," and conversely. Accordingly, there is a strong presumption that the two statements do not differ in *factual* content. More generally, if as seems to be the case the conceivable empirical evidence for a teleological explanation is identical with the conceivable evidence for a certain nonteleological one, the conclusion appears inescapable that these statements cannot be distinguished with respect to what they *assert*, even though they may differ in other ways.

However, this proposed equation of teleological and nonteleological explanations must face a fundamental objection. Most biologists would perhaps be prepared to admit that a teleological explanation *implies* a nonteleological one; but some of them, at any rate, would maintain that the latter does not in general imply the former, so that the suggested equivalence does not in fact hold. This latter claim can be forcefully stated as follows. If there were such an equivalence, it may be said, not only could a teleological explanation be replaced by a nonteleological one, but a converse replacement would also be possible. In consequence, the customary statements of laws and theories in the physical sciences must be translatable into teleological formulations. In point of fact, however, modern physical science does not appear to sanction such formulations; and physical scientists would doubtless resist their introduction into their disciplines as an unfortunate attempt to reinstate the point of view of Greek and medieval science. Thus the statement, "The volume of a gas at constant temperature varies inversely with its pressure," is a typical physical law, which is entirely free of teleological connotations. If it were equivalent to a teleological statement its presumed equivalent would be, "The function of a varying pressure in a gas at constant temperature is to produce an inversely varying pressure," or perhaps, "Gases at constant temperature under variable pressure alter their volumes in order to keep the product of pressure and volume constant." But most physicists would regard these latter formulations as preposterous, and at best as misleading. There must therefore be some important differences between teleological and nonteleological statements which the discussion has thus far failed to make explicit.

The attitude of physical scientists toward teleological formulations in their own disciplines is doubtless as alleged in this objection. Nevertheless, the objection is not completely decisive on the point at issue. Two general comments are in order which will at least weaken its force.

In the first place, it is not entirely accurate to maintain that the physical sciences never employ formulations that have at least the appearance of teleological statements. As is well known, some physical laws and theories are often expressed in so-called "isoperimetric" or "variational" form, rather than in the more familiar form of numerical or differential equations. When laws and principles are so expressed, they undoubtedly seem to be akin to teleological formulations. For example, the elementary law of optics that the angle of incidence of a light ray with a surface is equal to the angle of reflection, can also be rendered by the statement that a light ray travels in such a manner that when it is reflected from a surface the length of its actual path is the minimum of all possible paths. More generally, a considerable part of classical as well as contemporary physical theory can be stated in the form of "extremal" principles. What these principles assert is that the actual development of a system is such as to minimize or maximize some magnitude which represents the possible configurations of the system.[1]

The discovery that the principles of mechanics can be given such extremal formulations was once considered as evidence (especially by Maupertuis in the eighteenth century) for the operation of a divine plan throughout nature. Such theological interpretations of extremal principles is now recognized almost universally to be entirely gratuitous; and no competent physicist today supposes that extremal prin-

[1] It can in fact be shown that when certain very general conditions are satisfied, all quantitative laws and principles can be given an "extremal" formulation.

ciples entail the assumption of purposes animating physical processes. The use of such principles in physical science nevertheless does show that it can formulate the dynamical structure of physical systems so as to bring into focus the incidence of constituent elements and processes upon certain properties of a system taken as a whole. If physical scientists dislike teleological language in their own disciplines, it is not because they regard teleological notions in this sense as foreign to their task. Their dislike stems in some measure from the fear that, except when such teleological language is made rigorously precise through the use of quantitative formulations, it is apt to be misunderstood as connoting the operation of purposes.

In the second place, the physical sciences unlike biology are in general not concerned with a relatively special class of organized bodies, and they do not investigate the conditions making for the persistence of some selected physical system rather than of others. When a biologist ascribes a function to the kidney, he tacitly assumes that it is the kidney's contribution to the maintenance of the living animal which is under discussion; and he ignores as irrelevant to his primary interest the kidney's contribution to the maintenance of any other system of which it may also be a constituent. On the other hand, a physicist generally attempts to discuss the effects of solar radiation upon a wide variety of things; and he is reluctant to ascribe a "function" to the sun's radiation, because there is no one physical system of which the sun is a part that is of greater interest to him than any other such system. And similarly for the law connecting the pressure and volume of a gas. If a physicist views with suspicion the formulation of this law in functional or teleological language, it is because (in addition to the reasons which have been or will be discussed) he does not regard it his business to assign special importance (even if only by vague suggestion) to one rather than another consequence of varying pressures in a gas.

However, the discussion thus far can be accused with some justice of naïveté if not of irrelevance, on the ground that it has ignored completely the fundamental point—namely, the "goal-directed" character of organic systems. It is because living things exhibit in varying degrees adaptive and regulative structures and activities, while the systems studied in the physical sciences do not—so it is frequently claimed—that teleological explanations are peculiarly appropriate for the former but not for the latter. Thus, it is because the solar system, or any other system of which the sun is a part, does not tend to persist in the face of environmental changes in some integrated pattern of activities, and because the constituents of the system do not undergo mutual adjustments so as to maintain this pattern in relative independence from the environment, that it is preposterous to ascribe any function to the sun or to the solar radiation. Nor does the fact that physics can formulate some of its theories in the form of extremal principles—so the objection continues—minimize the differences between biological and purely physical systems. It is true that a physical system develops in such a way as to minimize or maximize a certain magnitude which represents a property of the system as a whole. But physical systems are not organized to *maintain* extremal values of such magnitudes, or to develop under widely varying conditions in the direction of realizing some particular values of such magnitudes.

Biological systems, on the other hand, do possess such organization, as a single example (which could be matched by an indefinite number of others) makes clear. There are complicated but coordinated physiological processes in the human body, which maintain many of its characteristics in a relatively steady state (or homeostasis). Thus, the internal temperature of the body must remain fairly constant if it is not to be fatally injured. In point of fact, the temperature of the normal human being varies during a day only from about 97.3° F. to 99.1° F., and cannot fall much below 75° F. or rise much above 110° F. without permanent injury to the body. However, the temperature of the external environment can fluctuate much more widely than this; and it is clear from elementary physical considerations that the body's characteristic activities would be profoundly curtailed unless it were capable of compensating for such environmental changes. But the body is indeed capable of doing just this; and in consequence, its normal activities can continue, in relative independence of the temperature of the environment—provided, of course, that the environmental temperature does not fall outside a certain interval of magnitudes. The body achieves this homeostasis by means of a number of mechanisms, which serve as a series of defenses against shifts in the internal temperature. Thus, the thyroid gland is one of several that control the body's basal metabolic rate; the heat radiated or conducted through the skin depends on the quantity of blood flowing through peripheral vessels, a quantity which is regulated by dilation or contraction of these vessels; sweating and the respiration rate determine the quantity of moisture that is evaporated, and so affect the internal temperature; adrenalin in the blood also stimulates internal combustion, and its secretion is affected by changes in the external temperature; and automatic muscular contractions involved in shivering are an additional source of internal heat. There are thus physiological mechanisms in the body such that its internal temperature is automatically preserved, despite disturbing conditions in the body's internal and external environment.[2]

Three separate questions that are frequently confounded are raised

[2] Cf. Walter B. Cannon, *The Wisdom of the Body* (New York, 1932), Ch. 12.

by such facts of biological organization. Is it possible to formulate in general but fairly precise terms the distinguishing structure of "goal-directed" systems, but in such a way that the analysis is neutral with respect to assumptions concerning the existence of purposes or the dynamic operation of goals as instruments in their own realization? Is the fact, if it is a fact, that teleological explanations are customarily employed only in connection with "goal-directed" systems, decisive on the issue whether a teleological explanation is equivalent to some nonteleological one? Is it possible to explain in purely physico-chemical terms—that is, exclusively in terms of the laws and theories of current physics and chemistry—the operations of biological systems? This third question will not concern us in this paper; but the other two require our attention.

There have been many attempts since antiquity at constructing machines and physical systems which simulate the behavior of living organisms in one respect or another. None of these attempts has been entirely successful, for it has not been possible thus far to manufacture in the workshop and out of inorganic materials any device which acts fully like a living being. Nevertheless, it has been possible to construct physical systems which are self-maintaining and self-regulating up to a point, and which therefore resemble living organisms in one important respect. In an age in which servo-mechanisms no longer excite wonder, and in which the language of cybernetics and "negative feed-backs" has become widely fashionable, the imputation of "goal-directed" behavior to purely physical systems certainly cannot be rejected as an absurdity. Whether "purposes" can also be imputed to such physical systems, as some expounders of cybernetics claim,[3] is perhaps doubtful, though the question is in large measure a semantic one; in any event, the issue is not relevant in the present context of discussion. Moreover, the possibility of constructing self-regulating physical systems does not constitute proof that the activities of living organisms can be explained in exclusively physico-chemical terms. However, the occurrence of such systems does suggest that there is no sharp division between the teleological organization which is often assumed to be distinctive of living things, and the goal-directed organization of many physical systems; and it does offer strong support for the presumption that the structure of such organization can be

---

[3] Cf. Arturo Rosenblueth, Norbert Wiener, Julian Bigelow, "Behavior, Purpose and Teleology," *Philosophy of Science*, Vol. 10 (1943); Norbert Wiener, Cybernetics (New York, 1948); A. M. Turing, "Computing Machines and Intelligence," *Mind*, Vol. 59 (1950); Richard Taylor, "Comments on a Mechanistic Conception of Purposefulness," *Philosophy of Science*, Vol. 17 (1950), and the reply by Rosenblueth and Wiener with a rejoinder by Taylor in the same volume.

formulated without the postulation of purposes or of goals as dynamic agents.

With the homeostasis of the temperature of the human body before us as an exemplar, let us now state in general terms the structure of systems which have a goal-directed organization.[4] The characteristic feature of such systems is that they continue to manifest a certain state or property G, or to develop "in the direction" of attaining G, in the face of a relatively extensive class of changes in their external environments or in some of their internal parts—changes which, if not compensated by internal modifications in the system, would result in the vanishing of G or in an altered direction of development. This feature can be formulated more precisely though schematically as follows.

Let S be some system, E its external environment, and G some state or property which S possesses or is capable of possessing under suitable conditions. Assume for the moment—this assumption will be presently relaxed—that E remains constant in all relevant respects, so that its influence upon S can be ignored. Suppose also that S is analyzable into a structure of parts, such that the activities of a certain number of them are causally relevant for the occurrence of G. For the sake of simplicity, assume that there are just three such parts, the state of each of which at any time can be specified by a determinate form of the complex predicates "A," "B," and "C," respectively; numerical subscripts will serve as indicators of such determinate forms. Accordingly, the state of S at any time causally relevant to G will be expressed by specializations of the matrix "$(A_x B_y C_z)$." One further general assumption must now be made explicit. Each of these state-variables (they are not necessarily numerical variables) can be assigned any determinate values that are compatible with the known character of the part of S whose state it specifies. In effect, therefore, the states which can be values for "A_x" must fall into a certain class K_A; and there are corresponding classes K_B and K_C for the other two state-variables. The reason for this restriction will be clear from an example. If S is the human body, and "A_x" states the degree of dilation of peripheral blood vessels, it is obvious that this degree cannot exceed some maximum value; for it would be absurd to suppose that a blood vessel could acquire a mean diameter of, say, five feet. On the other hand, the possible values of one state-variable at a given time will be assumed to be independent of the possible values of the other state-variables at that same time. Accordingly, any combination of values of the

---

[4] The following discussion is heavily indebted to R. B. Braithwaite, "Teleological Explanation," *Proc. of the Aristotelian Society*, Vol. 47 (1947), and G. Sommerhoff, *Analytical Biology* (London, 1950). Cf. also Alfred J. Lotka, *Elements of Physical Biology* (New York, 1926), Ch. 25.

state-variables will be a permissible specialization of the matrix "$(A_xB_yC_z)$," provided that the values of each variable belong to the classes K_A, K_B, and K_C respectively. This is tantamount to saying that the state-variables which are stipulated to be causally relevant to G are also postulated to be capable of having values at a given time which are mutually independent of one another.

Suppose now that if S is in the state $(A_0B_0C_0)$ at some given time, then S either has the property G, or else a sequence of changes will take place in S in consequence of which S will possess G at some subsequent time. Call such an initial state of S a "causally effective state with respect to G," or a "G-state" for short. Not every possible state of S need be a G-state; for one of the causally relevant parts of S may be in such a state at a given time, that no combination of possible states of the other parts will yield a G-state for S. Thus, suppose that S is the human body, G the property of having an internal temperature lying in the range 97° F. to 99° F., A_x again the state of peripheral blood vessels, and B_y the state of the thyroid glands; it may happen that B_y assumes a value (e.g., corresponding to acute hyperactivity) such that for no possible value of A_x will G be realized. It is also conceivable that no possible state of S is a G-state, so that in fact G is never realized in S. For example, if S is the human body and G the property of having an internal temperature lying in the range 150° F. to 160° F., then there is no G-state for S. On the other hand, more than one possible state of S may be a G-state, though only one of them will be actual at a given time; but if there is more than one possible G-state, we shall assume that the one which is realized at a given time is uniquely determined by the actual state of S at some previous time. In short, we are assuming that S is a deterministic system with respect to the occurrence of G-states. The case in which there is more than one possible G-state for S is of particular relevance to the present discussion, and we must now consider it more closely.

Assume again that at some initial time, t_0, S is in the G-state $(A_0B_0C_0)$. But suppose now that a change occurs in S so that in consequence A_0 is caused to vary, and that at time, t_1 subsequent to t_0 the state variable "A_x" has some other value. Which value it will have at t_1 will depend on the particular changes that have occurred in S. We shall assume, however, that there is a range of possible changes, and that the values which "A_x" may have at time t_1 fall into some class K'_A (a sub-class of K_A) which contains more than one member. To fix our ideas, suppose that A_1 and A_2 are the members of K'_A; and assume further that neither $(A_1B_0C_0)$ nor $(A_2B_0C_0)$ is a G-state—that is, a variation in A_0 alone would take S out of a G-state. Accordingly, if the changes mentioned thus far were the only changes in the state of S, S would no longer be in a G-state at time t_1. Let us, however, make the contrary assumption. Assume S to be so constituted that if A_0 is caused to vary so that the value of "A_x" at time t_1 falls into K'_A, there will also be further compensatory changes in the values of some or all of the other state variables. More specifically, these further changes are stipulated to be of the following kind: if K'_{BC} is the class of sets of values which "B_y" and "C_z" have at time t_1, then for each value of "A_x" in K'_A there is a unique set in K'_{BC} such that S continues to be in a G-state at time t_1; but these further changes unaccompanied by the first-mentioned ones would take S out of a G-state—that is, if at time t_1 the state-variables of S have a set of values such that two of them belong to a set in K'_{BC} while the remaining one is not the corresponding member in K'_A, then S is not a G-state. For example, suppose that if A_0 is changed into A_1, the initial G-state $(A_0B_0C_0)$ is changed into the G-state $(A_1B_1C_1)$ with $(A_0B_1C_1)$ not a G-state; and if A_0 is changed into A_2, the initial G-state is changed into the G-state $(A_2B_1C_0)$, with $(A_0B_1C_0)$ not a G-state. In this example, K'_A is the class $\{A_1\ A_2\}$, and K'_{BC} the class of sets $\{[B_1, C_1], [B_1, C_0]\}$, with A_1 corresponding to $[B_1, C_1]$ and A_2 to $[B_1, C_0]$.

We now introduce some definitions, based upon the above discussion. Assume S to be a system satisfying the following conditions: (1) S can be analyzed into a structure of parts, a certain number of which (say three) are causally relevant to the occurrence in S of some property or feature G; and the causally relevant state of S at any time can be specified by means of a set of state-variables. These state-variables at any given time can be assigned values independently of each other, though the possible values of each variable are restricted to some class of values. (2) If S is in a G-state at some time t_0 during period T, and a variation occurs in one of the state-parameters (say "A") such that this variation alone would take S out of its G-state, then the possible values of this parameter at time t_1 subsequent to t_0 but still in T fall into a certain class K'_A. Call this variation a "primary variation" in S. (3) If the state parameter "A" varies in the indicated manner, then the remaining parameters also vary so that their variation alone would take S out of its G-state, and so that their possible values at time t_1 constitute sets belonging to a class K'_{BC}. (4) The elements of K'_A and K'_{BC} correspond to each other in a uniquely reciprocal fashion, such that when the state of S is specified by these corresponding values S is in a G-state at time t_1. Call the variations in S which are represented by the members of K'_{BC} the "adaptive" variations in relation to the variations represented by members of K'_A. When these assumptions hold for S, the parts of S that are causally relevant to G will be said to be "directively organized during the period T with respect to G"—or more shortly "directively organized," if the reference to T and G can be taken for granted. This definition can be easily generalized for a larger number of state-variables, and for the primary variation of more than one state-variable; but the present incompletely general definition will suffice for our purposes.

It will be clear from this account that if S is directively organized, the persistence of G is in a certain sense independent of the variations (up to a point) in any one of the causally relevant parts of S. For although it is the state of these parts which by hypothesis determine the occurrence of G, an altered state in one of them may be compensated by altered states in the other parts of S so as to preserve S in its G-state. The structure or character of so-called "teleological" systems is therefore expressed by the indicated conditions for a directively organized system; and these conditions can be stated, as we have seen, in a manner not requiring the adoption of teleology as a fundamental or unanalyzable category. What may be called the "degree of directive organization" of a system, or perhaps the "degree of persistence" of some trait of a system, can also be made explicit in terms of the above analysis. For the property G is maintained in S (or S persists in its development which eventuates in G) to the extent that the range of K'_A of the possible primary variations is associated with the range of induced compensatory changes K'_{BC} such that S is preserved in its G-state. The more inclusive the range K'_A that is associated with such compensatory changes, the more is the persistence of G independent of variations in the state of S. Accordingly, on the assumption that it is possible to specify a measure for the range K'_A, the "degree of directive organization" of S with respect to variations in the state-parameter A can be defined as the measure of this range.

We may now relax the assumption that the external environment E has no influence upon S. But in dropping this assumption, we merely complicate the analysis, without introducing anything novel into it. For suppose that there is some factor in E which is causally relevant to the occurrence of G in S, and whose state at any time can be specified by some determinate form of the state-variable "F_w." Then the state of the system S' (which includes both S and E) that is causally relevant to the occurrence of G in S is specified by some determinate form of the matrix "$(A_x B_y C_z F_w)$"; and the discussion proceeds as before. However, it is generally not the case that a variation in any of the internal parts of S produces any significant variation in the environmental factors. What usually is the case is that the latter vary quite independently of the former; that they do not undergo changes which compensate for changes in the state of S; and that while a limited range of changes in them may be compensated by changes in S so as to preserve S in some G-state, most of the states which environmental factors are capable of assuming cannot be so compensated by changes in S. It is customary, therefore, to talk of the "degree of plasticity" or the "degree of adaptability" of organic systems in relation to their environment, and not conversely. However, it is possible to define these notions without reference to organic systems in particular, in a manner analogous to the definition of "degree of directive organization" already suggested. Thus, suppose that the variations in the environmental state F, compensated by changes in S so as to preserve S in some G-state, all fall into the class K'_F; then if a measure for this class is available, the "degree of plasticity" of S with respect to G in relation to F can be defined as the measure of K'_F.

This must suffice as an account of the structure of "teleological" or "goal-directed" systems. The account is intended to formulate only the gross pervasive features of such systems, and undoubtedly suffers from neglect of many important complications. Moreover, it does not pretend to indicate what the detailed mechanisms may be which are involved in the occurrence of such systems. It is therefore deliberately neutral with respect to such issues as whether these mechanisms are explicable entirely in physico-chemical terms, or whether the notion of "feed-back" is required in analyzing them. But if the account is at least approximately adequate, it implies a positive answer to the question whether the distinguishing features of "goal-directed" systems can be formulated without invoking purposes and goals as dynamic agents.

However, there is one matter that must be briefly discussed. The definition of directively organized systems has been so stated that it may apply both to biological as well as to nonvital systems. It is in fact easy to find illustrations for it from either domain. The human body with respect to the homeostasis of its temperature is an example from biology; a building equipped with a furnace and thermostat is an example from physico-chemistry. But though the definition is not intended to distinguish between vital and nonvital systems—the difference between such systems must be stated in terms of the *specific* properties and activities they manifest—it *is* intended to set off systems which have a prima facie "goal-directed" character, from systems which are usually not so characterized. The question therefore remains whether the definition does achieve this aim, or whether on the contrary it is so inclusive that almost *any* system (whether it is ordinarily judged to be goal-directed or not) satisfies it.

Now there certainly are many physico-chemical systems which are ordinarily *not* regarded as being "goal-directed," but which appear to conform to the definition of directively organized systems proposed above. Thus, a pendulum at rest, an elastic solid, a steady electric current flowing through a conductor, a chemical system in thermodynamic equilibrium, are obvious examples of such systems. It seems therefore that the definition of directive organization—and in consequence the proposed analysis of "goal-directed" or "teleological" systems—fails to attain its intended objective. However, two comments are in order on the point at issue. In the first place, though we admittedly do distinguish between systems that are goal-directed and those which are not, the distinction is highly vague, and there are many systems which cannot be classified definitely as being of one kind rather than another. Thus, is the child's toy sometimes known as "the walking beetle"—which turns aside when it reaches the edge of a table and fails to fall off, because an idle wheel is then brought into play through the action of an "antenna"—a goal-directed system or not? Is a virus such a system? Is the system consisting of members of some species which has undergone certain lines of evolutionary development, a goal-directed one? Moreover, some systems have been classified as "teleological" at one time and in relation to one body of knowledge, only to be re-classified as "nonteleological" at a later time when knowledge concerning the physics of mechanisms had improved. "Nature does nothing in vain" was a maxim commonly accepted in pre-Newtonian physics, and on the basis of the doctrine of "natural places" even the descent of bodies and the ascent of smoke were regarded as goal-directed. Accordingly, it is at least an open question whether the current distinction between systems that are goal-directed and those which are not has an identifiable objective basis (*i.e.*, in terms of differences between the actual organization of such systems), and whether the *same* system may not be classified in alternative ways depending on the perspective from which it is viewed and on the antecedent assumptions that are adopted for analyzing its structure.

In the second place, it is by no means clear that physical systems such as the pendulum at rest, which is not usually regarded as goal-directed, really do conform to the definition of "directively organized" systems proposed above. Consider a simple pendulum which is initially at rest, and is then given a small impulse (say by a sudden gust of wind); and assume that apart from the constraints of the system and the force of gravitation the only force that acts on the bob is the friction of the air. Then on the usual physical assumptions, the pendulum will perform harmonic oscillations with decreasing amplitudes, and will finally assume its initial position of rest. The system here consists of the pendulum and the various forces acting on it, while the property G is the state of the pendulum when it is at rest at the lowest point of its path of oscillation. By hypothesis, its length and the mass of the bob are fixed, and so is the force of gravitation acting on it, as well as the coefficient of damping. What is variable, is the impulsive force of the gust of wind, and the restoring force which operates on the bob as a consequence of the constraints of the system and of the presence of the gravitational field. However, and this is the crucial point, these two forces are *not* independent of one another. Thus, if the effective component of the former has a certain magnitude, the restoring force will have an equal magnitude with an opposite direction. Accordingly, if the state of the system at a given time were specified in terms of state-variables which take these forces as values, these state-variables would not satisfy one of the stipulated conditions for state-variables of directively organized systems: for the value of one of them at a given time is uniquely determined by the value of the other at that same time. In short, the values at any specified time of these proposed state-variables are not independent. It therefore follows that the simple pendulum is *not* a directively organized system in the sense of the definition given. And it is possible to show in a similar manner that a number of other physical systems, currently classified as nonteleological, fail to satisfy this definition. Whether one could show this for all such systems is admittedly an open question. But there is at least some ground for holding that the definition does achieve what it is intended to achieve, and that it states the distinctive features of systems commonly characterized as "teleological."

We can now settle quite briefly the second question we undertook to discuss, namely, whether the supposed fact that teleological explanations are usually reserved for "goal-directed" systems casts doubt on the claim that teleological and nonteleological explanations are equivalent in asserted content. But if such systems are always analyzable as directively organized ones, in the sense of the above definition, the answer to this question is clearly in the negative. For the defining characteristics of such systems can be formulated entirely in nonteleological language; and in consequence, every teleological explanation (that is, every explanation which contains a teleological expression) must be translatable into an equivalent statement (or set of statements) which is nonteleological.

Why, then, does it seem odd to render physical statements such as Boyle's law in teleological form? The obvious answer is that we do not usually employ teleological statements except in the context of discussing systems which are assumed to be directively organized. A teleological version of Boyle's law appears strange and unacceptable, because such a formulation is usually taken to imply that any gas enclosed in a volume is a directively organized system, in contradiction to the tacit assumption that it is not such a system. In a sense, therefore, a teleological explanation does assert more than its prima facie equivalent nonteleological translation does. For the former tacitly assumes, while the latter often does not, that the system under consideration is directively organized. But if the above discussion is sound in principle, this "excess" meaning of teleological statements can always be expressed in nonteleological language.

On the assumption that a teleological explanation can always be equated to a nonteleological one with respect to what each asserts, let us now make more explicit in what respects they do differ. The difference appears to be as follows: Teleological explanations focus attention on the culminations and products of specific processes, and upon the contributions of parts of a system to its maintenance. They view the operations of things from the perspective of certain selected wholes to which the things belong; and they are therefore concerned with properties of parts of such wholes only in so far as these properties are relevant to some complex features or activities assumed as characteristic for those wholes. Nonteleological explanations, on the other hand, place chief emphasis on certain conditions under which specified processes are initiated and persist, and on the factors upon which the continued operation of given systems are contingent. They represent the inclusive behavior of a thing as the operation of certain selected constituents into which the thing is analyzable; and they are therefore concerned with features of complex wholes only to the extent that these features are related to the assumed characteristics of those constituents. The difference between teleological and nonteleological explanations, as has already been suggested, is one of emphasis and of perspective in formulation.

It is sometimes objected, however, that teleological explanations are fallaciously parochial; for they tacitly assume a privileged status for a special set of complex systems, and so make focal the role of things and processes in maintaining just those systems and no others. Processes have no inherent termini, so it is argued, and cannot rightly be assumed to contribute exclusively to the maintenance of some unique set of wholes. It is therefore misleading to say that *the* function of the white cells in the human blood is to defend the human body against foreign micro-organisms. This is admittedly *a* function of the leucocytes; and it may even be said to be *the* function of these cells from the perspective of the human body. But leucocytes are elements in other systems as well—for example, in the system of the blood stream considered in isolation from the rest of the body, in the system composed of some virus colony as well as these white cells, or in the more inclusive and complex solar system. These other systems are also capable of persisting in their "normal" organization and activities only under definite conditions; and from the perspective of *their* maintenance the leucocytes possess other functions.

One obvious reply to this objection is a *tu quoque*. It is as legitimate to focus attention on consequences, culminations and uses, as it is on antecedents and conditions. Processes do not have inherent termini, but neither do they have absolute beginnings; things and processes are not in general exclusively involved in maintaining some unique whole, but neither are wholes analyzable into a unique set of constituents. It is nevertheless intellectually profitable in causal inquiries to focus attention on certain earlier stages in the development of a process rather than on later ones, and on one set of constituents of a system rather than another set. And similarly, it is illuminating to select as the point of departure for the investigation of some problems certain complex wholes rather than others. Moreover, as we have seen, some things are parts of directively organized systems, but do not appear to be parts of more than one such system. The study of the unique function of such parts in such unique teleological systems is therefore not a preoccupation that assigns without warrant a special importance to certain systems. On the contrary, it is an inquiry which is sensitive to fundamental and objectively identifiable differences in nature.

There is nevertheless a point to the objection. For the operation of human interest in the construction of teleological explanations is perhaps more often overlooked than in the case of nonteleological analyses. In consequence, certain end-products of processes and certain directions of changes are frequently assumed to be inherently "natural," "essential" or "proper," while all others are then labelled as "unnatural," "accidental" or even "monstrous." Thus, the development of corn seeds into corn plants is sometimes said to be natural, while their transformation into the flesh of birds or men is asserted to be accidental. In a given context of inquiry, and in the light of the problems which initiate it, there may be ample justification for ignoring all but one direction of possible changes, and all but one system of activities to whose maintenance things and processes contribute. But such disregard of other wholes and of other functions which their constituents may have, does not warrant the conclusion that what is ignored is less genuine or natural than what receives selective attention.

One final point in connection with teleological explanations in biology must be briefly noted. As has already been mentioned, some biologists maintain that the distinctive character of biological explanations appears in physiological inquiries, in which the functions of organs and vital processes are under investigation, even though most biologists are quite prepared to admit that no special categories of explanation are required in morphology or the study of structural traits. Accordingly, great stress has been placed by some writers on the contrast between structure and function, and on the difficulties in assessing the relative importance of each as a determinant of living phenomena. It is generally conceded that "the development of functions goes hand in hand with the development of structures," and that neither does vital action exist apart from a material structure, nor does vital structure exist save as a product of protoplasmic activity. In this sense, structure and function are commonly regarded as "inseparable aspects" of biological organization. Nevertheless, eminent biologists believe it is still an unresolved and perhaps insoluble problem "to what extent structures may modify functions or functions structures," and regard the contrast between structure and function to present a "dilemma." [5]

But what is this contrast, why do its terms raise an apparently irresolvable issue, and what does one of its terms cover that allegedly requires a mode of analysis and explanation that is specific to biology? Let us first remind ourselves in what way a morphological study of a biological organ, say the human eye, differs from the corresponding physiological investigation. A structural account of the eye usually consists in a description of its gross and minute anatomy; and such an account therefore specifies the various parts of the organ, their shapes and relative spatial arrangements with respect to each other and other parts of the body, and their cellular and physico-chemical compositions. The phrase, "structure of the eye," therefore ordinarily signifies the spatial organization of its parts, together with the physico-chemical properties of each part. On the other hand, a physiological account of the organ specifies the activities in which its various parts can or do participate, and the role these parts play in vision. For example, the ciliary muscles are shown to be capable of contracting and slackening, so that because of their connection with the suspensory ligament the curvature of the lens can be accommodated to near and far vision; or the lachrymal glands are identified as the sources of fluids which lubricate and cleanse the conjunctival membranes. In general, therefore, physiology is concerned with the character, the order, and the consequences of the activities in which the parts of the eye may be engaged.

If this example is typical of the way biologists employ the terms, the contrast between structure and function is evidently a contrast between, on the one hand, the *spatial* organization of anatomically distinguishable parts of an organ and, on the other hand, the *temporal* (or spatio-temporal) organization of changes in those parts. What is investigated under each term of the contrasting pair is a mode of organization or a type of order. In the first case, the organization is primarily if not exclusively a spatial one, and the object of the investigation is to ascertain the spatial distribution of organic parts and the modes of their linkage; in the latter case, the organization has a tem-

---

[5] Cf. Edwin G. Conklin, *Heredity and Environment* (Princeton, 1922), p. 32, and Edmund B. Wilson, *The Cell* (New York, 1925), p. 670. In a more recent volume, Conklin declares that "the relation of mechanism to finalism is not unlike that of structure to function—they are two aspects of organization. The mechanistic conception of life is in the main a structural aspect, the teleological view looks chiefly to ultimate function. These two aspects of life are not antagonistic, but complementary." *Man: Real and Ideal* (New York, 1943), p. 117.

poral dimension, and the aim of the inquiry is to discover sequential and simultaneous orders of change in the spatially ordered and linked parts of organic bodies. It is evident, therefore, that structure and function (in the sense in which biologists appear to use these words) are indeed "inseparable." For it is difficult to make sense of any supposition to the effect that a system of activities which has a temporal organization is not a system of spatially structured parts manifesting these activities. In any event, there is obviously no antithesis between an inquiry directed to the discovery of the spatial organization of organic parts, and an inquiry addressed to ascertaining the spatio-temporal orders that characterize the activities of those parts. A comparable distinction between inquiries can also be introduced in the physical sciences. Descriptive physical geography, for example, is concerned primarily with the spatial distribution and spatial relations of mountains, plains, rivers, and oceans; historical geology and geophysics, on the other hand, investigate the temporal and dynamic orders of change in which such geographic features are involved. Accordingly, if inquiries into structure and function were antithetical in biology, a comparable antithesis would also occur within the non-biological sciences. Any inquiry involves discriminating selection from the great variety of patterns of relations that are exhibited by the subject matter; and it is undoubtedly convenient to direct some inquiries to certain kinds of such patterns and other inquiries to different kinds. There seems to be no reason for generating a fundamental puzzle from the fact that living organisms exhibit both a spatial and a spatio-temporal order of their parts.

What then is the unsolved or irresolvable issue raised by the biological distinction between structure and function? Two questions can be distinguished in this connection. It may be asked, in the first place, what spatial structures are required for the exercise of specified functions, and whether a change in the pattern of activities of an organism or of its parts is associated with any change in the distribution and spatial organization of the constituents of that system. This is patently a matter to be settled by detailed empirical inquiry, and though there are innumerable unsettled problems in this connection, they do not raise issues of fundamental principle. There is a school of philosophers and biological theorists, for example, which maintains that the development of certain comparable organs in markedly different species can be explained only on the assumption of a "vital impulse" which directs evolution toward the attainment of some future function. Thus, the fact that the eyes of the octopus and of man are anatomically similar, though the evolution of each species from eyeless ancestors has followed different lines of development, has been used as evidence for the claim that no explanation of this convergence is possible in terms of the mechanisms of chance variation and adaptation; and that fact has been used to support the view that there is an "undivided original vital impulse" which so acts on inert matter as to create appropriate organs for the function of vision.[6] But even this hypothesis, however vague and otherwise unsatisfactory it may be, involves in part factual issues; and if most biologists reject it, it is largely because the available factual evidence supports more adequately a different theory of evolutionary development.

In the second place, one may ask just why it is that a given structure is associated with a certain set of functions, or conversely. Now this question may be understood as a demand for an explanation, perhaps in physico-chemical terms, for the fact that when a living body has a given spatial organization of its parts it exhibits a certain pattern of activities. When the question is so understood, it is far from being a preposterous one; for although we may not possess answers to it in most cases, we do have reasonably adequate answers in at least a few others, so that we have some ground for the presumption that our ignorance is not necessarily permanent.

However, such explanations must contain as premises not only statements about the physico-chemical constitution of the parts of a living thing and about the spatial organization of these parts, but also statements of physico-chemical laws or theories; and at least some of these latter must assert connections between the spatial organization of physico-chemical systems and their pattern of activities. But if the question continues to be pressed, and an explanation is demanded for these latter connections as well, an impasse is finally reached. For the demand then in effect assumes that the temporal or causal structure of physical processes is deducible simply from the spatial organization of physical systems, or conversely; and neither assumption is in fact tenable. It is possible, for example, to give quite an accurate account of the spatial relations in which the various parts of a clock stand to one another. We can specify the sizes of its cog-wheels and the linkages between them, the shapes and positions of its pointers, the location of the mainspring and the escapement-wheel, and so on. But although such knowledge of the clock's spatial structure is indispensable, it is not sufficient for understanding how the clock will operate. We must also know the laws of mechanics, which formulate the temporal structure of the clock's behavior by indicating how the spatial distribution of its parts at one time is related to the distribution at a later time. However, this temporal structure cannot be deduced simply from the clock's spatial structure (or its "anatomy"), any more than its spatial structure at any given time can be derived from the general laws of mechanics. Accordingly, the question why a given biological

[6] Cf. H. Bergson, *Creative Evolution* (New York, 1911), Ch. 1; and the brief but incisive critique of views similar to those of Bergson in George G. Simpson, *The Meaning of Evolution* (New Haven, 1949), Ch. 12.

structure is associated with specified functions may be irresolvable, not because it is beyond our capacities to answer it, but simply because the question in the sense intended asks for what is *logically* impossible. In short, structure does not *logically* determine function, though as a matter of *contingent* fact the specific structure possessed by an organism does set bounds to the kinds of activities in which the organism can engage. And conversely, the pattern of behavior exhibited by an organism does not *logically* imply a unique anatomical structure, though in point of *contingent* fact an organism manifests specific modes of activity only when its parts possess a determinate structure of a definite kind.

It follows from these various considerations that the distinction between structure and function covers nothing which distinguishes biology from the physical sciences, or which necessitates the use in the former of a distinctive logic of explanation. It has not been the aim of this paper to deny the patent differences between biology and other natural sciences with respect to the role played in them of functional analyses. Nor has it been its aim to cast doubt on the legitimacy of such explanations in any domain in which they are found to be appropriate because of the special character of the systems investigated. The objective of this essay has simply been to show that the prevalence of teleological explanations in biology does not constitute a sufficient basis for the claim that the pattern of explanation in biology is fundamentally different from what it is in the physical sciences, nor for the further claim that for this reason biology must be regarded as an inherently autonomous discipline.

---

8. The Structure of the Natural Sciences

Joseph J. Schwab

I SHALL TREAT THREE TOPICS: first, the short-term syntax of the sciences, or, to give it another name, the syntax of stable enquiry; second, the long-term syntax of the sciences, or, alternatively, the syntax of fluid enquiry. I shall then turn to a sketch of the substantive structures of science.

THE SYNTAX OF STABLE ENQUIRY

Let us begin by examining the description of science which has its origin in John Dewey's *How We Think*. This starting point is almost mandatory, for the Deweyan formulation, which describes science as taking place in a sequence of steps, has appeared and reappeared in so many textbook prefaces that it has taken on an official character.

Let us begin our analysis of the useful but misleading details of this formulation with an instance of the sort of enquiry the step-wise description attempts to embody.

Imagine a scientist in the early days of modern biology who noted that most living cells contained small, dark-staining bodies called nuclei near the middle. The scientist wondered what role these dark-staining nuclei played in the economy of the cell. Because of their near universality among cells, he suspected that they played an indispensable role and decided to test this possibility. He did so by means of an experiment intended to provide him with some cells (or, rather, cell fragments) that contained no nucleus as well as with cell fragments that did possess a nucleus. The experiment consisted simply of shaking a number of cells in an appropriate solution. By this means, the experimenter obtained the materials he desired. Let us suppose that he obtained 100 non-nucleated fragments and 100 nucleated fragments of cells. He then proceeded to note the fate of each of these fragments. He found, let us say, that 85 of the non-nucleated fragments died within 24 hours; 10 more of these non-nucleated fragments died in 36 hours, and the remainder in about 48 hours. Meanwhile, he found that 21 of the fragments with nuclei died within 24 hours; a few more died in the ensuing two days, but 65 survived for 13 days. At the end of 30 days a few of these nucleated fragments still lived. On the basis of these results, the scientist asserted that the nucleus was necessary to the life of any cell that has one.

The traditional textbook formulation of scientific method sees in this procedure five distinct steps. The first step is the noting of relevant data. In our example, this corresponds, presumably, to the scientist noting that most cells have nuclei. The second step is the forming of a hypothesis. This would correspond to our biologist supposing that the nucleus is indispensable to the life of the cell. The third step is a plan for test of the hypothesis—the intention to obtain and compare fragments with nuclei and fragments without. Step Four is said to be the execution of the plan (the shaking), and Step Five the drawing of the conclusion from the data so obtained.

One of the most misleading aspects of this description of scientific syntax is contained in the description of the last step as the drawing of a *conclusion*. "Conclusion," as you know, conveys two meanings. It suggests, first, that something has been brought to a close. Second, because it is a logical term, referring to a statement derived correctly from presumably true premises, it suggests that the statement it refers to is true. Therefore, to call the last step of a bit of scientific enquiry the drawing of a conclusion is to suggest that the scientist (a) terminates an enterprise and (b) that he has the truth.

Neither of these characteristics holds good for the case in point nor for most scientific enquiries. This becomes clear if we contrast the formulation of the conclusion (that "the nucleus is necessary to the life of any cell that has one") with the data on which the statement is based. Note, first, that the statement derives, not from a study of all cells or all kinds of cells that possess nuclei, but only a few cells of one kind. Notice, too, that even these limited data did not present a clear picture of non-nucleated cell fragments that died instantly or of nucleated fragments that persisted indefinitely. Quite the contrary, the data were "messy." Some nucleated fragments died as soon as non-nucleated ones, and some non-nucleated fragments survived for many hours.

In no sense, then, ought we to consider the scientist's "conclusion" as conclusive. If there is soundness to his assertion, it derives from something more than the data obtained from this one experiment. It rests not only on the data from this experiment but on numerous other items selected from the body of biological knowledge and taken as true (assumed). It is based on knowledge of the similarity of different kinds of cells, a knowledge that permits generalizing to most cells from an experiment performed on one kind only. It is based on the knowledge that any cell, even under the best of conditions, may die from a number of causes. It rests on experience which suggests that the rough handling involved in the experiment may have contributed to the mortality of the nucleated fragments. It rests even on the decision to ignore the difference between cell *fragments* and whole cells.

Some of these bits of assumed biological knowledge are based on data as "messy" as those underlying the present experiment. Further, these bits of knowledge are *selected* bits. We can expect, then, that later enquiries may reverse or modify some of these basic bits. Another enquirer may make a different selection from the body of scientific knowledge and thus come to a different "conclusion" from that reached by our enquirer, even though he used our enquirer's data. In brief, the typical, isolated scientific enquiry yields neither a terminus to research on the problem nor an unequivocal, logically proved conclusion. Rather, it is a temporary plateau, a momentary equilibrium, which permits the experimenter to go on to other matters, other problems, and other enquiries which will bring him back to his original problem with a new insight or a new method or new data and therefore a revision of his understanding.

Let us, therefore, describe the last step of a short-term enquiry, not as the drawing of a conclusion, but as an *interpretation of data*. This is no mere polite shift of language, for to say "interpretation of data" is to convey a notion of the tremendous flexibility permitted to the scientist in his treatment of data and to rule out the misleading suggestion that each such short-term enquiry leads to a definitive end.

We are led to an even more far-reaching change of view if we take note of the fundamental illogic involved in the notion that an experiment of the kind we have described could be asserted to be a "proof" of a hypothesis. The basic logical pattern involved is that of a hypothetical syllogism. In its purely logical form, this pattern is as follows:

If A (our hypothesis) be true

Then, B (a certain outcome, a definite state of affairs accessible to observation) should follow;

If not A, not B.

In practice, it is often easy to fulfill the first half of this logical form. We are often able to say that if our hypothesis (A) be the case, then certain phenomena, consequences of the actual existence of A, should follow. In almost no case, however, can we fulfill the second half of this logical form. We are almost never in a position to say that *only* our hypothesized condition can give rise to the expected outcome, B. We may be sure that the alternatives to hypothesis A which we have conceived will lead to some outcome other than B, but we cannot be sure that there are not still other alternatives, unimagined by us or our colleagues, which would lead to precisely the same outcome as does the one we think we are testing. Hence, the discovery of consequence B does not prove that A is "true."

We can, indeed, have only reasonably good assurance that we have *dis*proved an hypothesis. Suppose that a certain hypothesis, A, must lead to outcome B. Suppose that we have searched diligently under what we conceive to be the appropriate conditions for outcome B and have failed to find it. We may then equate our failure to find the outcome with its non-existence and conclude that our hypothesis, A, is false. However, there is always the possibility that what we fail to find does indeed exist but was sought in the wrong place or by the wrong means.

The improbability of obtaining definitive proof or disproof suggests that it might be wise, for purposes of teaching, to treat science not as a process of proof or verification at all but rather as a process of discovery, a process of disclosing events in nature and of discovering ways of relating these events to one another in such a fashion that our understanding is enhanced. In any case, we cannot avoid the realization that science is a process of *constructing* bodies of *tentative* knowledge, of discovering *different* ways of making data coherent, and "telling" about a given subject matter. Ultimately, the test of such tentative bodies of knowledge concerns their usefulness—their usefulness in practice, their usefulness in satisfying our demand for a coherent account, their usefulness in leading to further enquiry.

We turn now to Step Two of the schoolbook version of science, the formation of a hypothesis. In one very large class of short-term enquiries the discrimination of such a step is entirely justified. Consider the physicist who supposes the existence of a minute particle that by definition is inaccessible to observation. Consider the later physicist who assigns to some of these particles a "spin" of a certain speed and direction. Consider the biochemist who constructs a model of the possible structure of the gene. Such hypotheses are "black box" hypotheses in the sense that they are, either by definition or by the limitations of existing techniques, inaccessible to immediate observation. If they are to be "verified" in any sense at all, it must be by the discernment of outcomes and consequences of the matter hypothesized.

Further, each such hypothesis represents a major act of constructive imagination. The scientist takes account of a vast variety of data which must be accounted for. He treats each datum as a limitation on what may be conceived as accounting for the whole range of data, and within the boundaries of these complex limitations he conceives a solution to the problem. Many important researches, especially in the physical sciences, are pursued through the use of such "black box" hypotheses. For such enquiries, we have every reason to discriminate the formation of a hypothesis as a distinct step or act, a step intrinsic to the method used in these researches.

Consider, however, another large class of enquiries. An investigator notes that the pancreas secretes digestive enzymes in large quantities into the small intestine only when food is present in the small intestine. He wishes to determine how the pancreas is stimulated to secrete at the appropriate time. Past knowledge teaches him that the two most likely means are nerve connections from intestine to pancreas or the secretion by the wall of the small intestine of a hormone that is carried by the blood to the pancreas. He looks for such nerve connections and finds them. He tries to extract such a hormone from the intestinal wall and succeeds. The nerve he locates is anatomically discernible and when stimulated at the intestinal end can be shown to convey an impulse to the pancreas. The hormone he extracts is capable of being analyzed chemically, even of being synthesized. Shall we say that the search for such a nervous connection or for such a hormone is instigated by "the formation of a hypothesis"? We may if we wish. If we do, however, we should distinguish between "black box" hypotheses and these "glass box" affairs that refer to things or events that are immediately (or almost immediately) accessible to observation. Further, we should note that because they are accessible to observation, these "glass box" hypotheticals and the processes of enquiry which lead up to them and follow from them differ markedly from those of the "black box" variety. Our biologist *saw* nerve fibres leading to the pancreas; he *saw* that the small intestine and the pancreas were well supplied with blood vessels. His "verification" involved no painful search for consequences that would permit application of some version of the hypothetical syllogism. Rather, he needed only to suppress one of the two possible pathways to determine whether the pancreas still secreted. Better still, he could locate nerve fibres whose stimulation led to pancreatic secretion or isolate a substance from the small intestine which led to pancreatic secretion when injected into the blood.

The importance of noting that such "glass box" hypotheses exist lies in the fact that their transparency, both as to possibility and to verification, makes the isolation of hypothesis-making as a discrete, named step pretentious and over-emphatic. In such cases it is enough to say that the investigator poses the *problem*, "to determine whether the intestinal walls secrete a hormone which stimulates the pancreas." This permits recognition of a pattern of enquiry in which hypotheses, though present in some formal sense, are dim. Thus, we make way for the protests by scientists in certain fields that they make no hypotheses but only observe. Investigators in these fields are much better described as trying to "find out what organ is present," "what animals occupy a given region," "what happens when food is present in the intestines," etc. Such investigators are *looking for* rather than *testing*. In brief, we see again a sense in which science is a process of discovery rather than of proof.

Perhaps the most revealing weakness of the schoolbook version of enquiry is its omission of a step preceding Step One. Step One refers to the discrimination of relevant data but fails to tell us in what way relevance and irrelevance are determined. It further fails to take account of the fact that data are relevant to something, that "relevance" must have a reference. What then are these "relevant" data relevant to and how can we tell when they are?

The answers to these questions require us to recognize the existence of substantive structures and one of the roles they play as principles of enquiry. The role in question is that of giving us our problems for enquiry. We saw one example of this in Chapter 1 [*The Structures of Knowledge and the Curriculum*], where the conception of "tropism" guided early enquiries into animal behavior. Let us take a further case in point. An anatomist, let us suppose, has just completed a reexamination of the adrenal gland. It had formerly been supposed that this part of the body was homogeneous. The anatomist has just discovered that it is made of two distinct kinds of tissue to which he has given topographical names—cortical tissues and medullary tissues. A physiologist reads the anatomist's report of his study and remembers the "function" that has been assigned to this gland. Immediately he says to himself, "In all probabiilty this function is not one function but two. I shall determine where the dividing line is and which function belongs to which tissue of the adrenal gland." He goes to the laboratory, removes the adrenal cortex from a number of animals, leaving the medulla intact; from others he removes the medulla, leaving the cortex intact. Eventually, he and his colleagues succeed in discriminating the function into two and of assigning each to different tissues of the adrenal gland.

What is important here is, first, that this enquiry was initiated, not merely by the gathering of "relevant data" but by the recognition of a *problem*. It was the question "What are the functions of the adrenal cortex and of the adrenal medulla?" which made it possible to decide what data were relevant, what further data were wanted, and what experiment to perform. Second, these questions could not have arisen had there not been in the mind of the investigator and in the habits of the science he represented the pattern of enquiry which revolved around the conception of structure and function. In this particular conception of the subject matter (the substantive structure), the living body is a city, a political state; the organs, the servants of this state, are each discriminable anatomical parts; hence, any newly discriminated anatomical part immediately becomes an object of enquiry, an object to which the question addressed is, "What is its function?" In brief, what data are relevant, what further data are wanted, what experiments ought to be performed, are matters determined by a prior act—the formulation of a problem. The problem, in turn, derives from the prevailing substantive structure guiding enquiry in the field, together with such "index phenomena" as point to the proper place to address the problem.

Let us summarize these criticisms and what they imply in a revised version of the schoolbook study of the short-term syntax of the sciences.

    1. The formulation of a problem (from juxtaposing a principle of enquiry—a substantive structure—and index phenomena).

2. The search for data that will suggest possible solutions to this problem.

3. Reformulation of the problem to include these possible solutions.

4. A determination of the data necessary to solve the problem.

5. A plan of experiment that will elicit the data desired.

6. Execution of the experiment and accumulation of the desired data.

7. Interpretation of the data by means of the guiding substantive structures together with previous knowledge possessed by the investigator.

THE LONG-TERM SYNTAX OF THE SCIENCES

It would be well to point out why I have called the pattern described above the short-term syntax of the sciences, or the syntax of stable enquiry. The enquiries that fit this pattern—and they constitute the vast bulk of scientific enquiries—are stable in the sense that their authors think they know exactly what to do. There is no wavering about what questions to ask or what substantive structures to employ. If the current principles of physiology are organ and function, the stable researcher in physiology busies himself discovering the function of first one organ and then another. If the conception of unit gene is the going conception in genetics, the stable enquirer in that field tries to find how many genes and which ones control each of a number of identifiable traits.

Such enquiries are short-term in the sense that separate problems can be pursued separately; each such problem, such as the function of organ X, can be settled in a relatively short time. The substantive structures are accepted as if they were eternal principles; organs obviously exist; equally obviously, each organ has a function. There is no upsetting of the apple cart by asking whether the organism is well understood in terms of organ and function or better understood in some other way. The principle guides the enquiries but is never, itself, the subject of an enquiry.

The syntax of fluid enquiry or the long-term syntax of sciences arises when what the short-term enquirer takes for granted is treated as a problem. The moving force behind fluid enquiry is the demand for increasing validity of substantive structures. Let us recall how we defined validity in Chapter 1. We said there that the criterion of validity demands that the substantive structure, which points to the problems and the data of enquiry, reflect, as much as possible, the richness and complexity of the subject matter to which it is applied. We said also that as investigations proceed under the guidance of one or another substantive structure, we begin to detect inconsistencies and disparities of various sorts. Suppose, for example, that we have developed our physiology under the guidance of a very simple substantive structure. This structure, a simple version of the notion of structure and function, dictates a simple experimental pattern in which we remove an organ and try to determine what aspects of the behavior of the entire organism are missing in consequence. Suppose that by this experimental pattern we have determined that organ X has function A, while organ Y has function B. Then, by accident or design, an experimenter removes both organ X and organ Y from the same animal, only to discover that the result is something far different from the expected mere sum of the losses of function A and function B. Here, then, is a startling disparity between what is expected on the basis of the substantive principle and what is actually disclosed. In other cases, the inconsistency may be between two different bodies of data. Suppose, for example, that removal of organ X under one set of circumstances leads to the conclusion that it performs function A. The removal of the same organ from animals under different living conditions discloses, apparently, the presence of another function, B.

In either case, there appears to be something wrong with the substantive structure, something inadequate relative to the subject matter itself, a failure of complete validity. Our organism turns out to be more complicated than the structure supposes it to be. In the case of the first disparity (between two organs removed separately and the two removed together), we discern a degree of *interaction* between organs which our principle does not include. In the second instance (where removal of the same organ under different circumstances yields evidence pointing to different functions), we see the possibility that even if, as we supposed, organs perform certain functions, the organs may be more flexible as to function than our principle has led us to believe.

When such disparities occur—and they occur periodically in all the sciences—they instigate a new kind of enquiry. We call it fluid enquiry for the obvious reason that matters are no longer fixed and stable in the science. Its underpinnings, its basic principles, are called into question, and a new set of principles, and their test are required. We call it long-term syntax because, in a sense, it is a form of enquiry that proceeds through each and every stable enquiry that takes place in the science. For, if scrutinized in the right way, every attempt to put the question dictated by a given principle of enquiry is a test of that principle. Each such stable enquiry is likely to have its incoherencies and inconsistencies, which are ignored or explained away in the interest of the conduct of the stable enquiry. Thus, for example, the primitive experiment on the role of the nucleus in the cell yielded inconsistencies of data, with respect to what cells died and how quickly, and which cells lived longer, which were "washed out" in the interest of pinning down some role of the nucleus. In other hands or under other circumstances these same disparities might have become the most relevant of the data involved, pointing to the possible inadequacy of the very notion of single, unchanging roles for cellular parts.

The fluid enquirer has three aims: first, to be alert to the moments of enquiry which reveal inadequacies of principle; second, to obtain such clues as he can from current stable enquiries which will point to the specific weakness or inadequacy that characterizes the principle in question; finally, to devise a modification of the existing structure, or a new structure to replace it, that will embrace more of the richness of the subject matter and take account of the specific weaknesses discovered in the older principles.

Since stable enquiries constitute the bulk of enquiries, they also absorb the attention of most scientists most of the time in any given field. In consequence, fluid enquiry is not equally well recognized among all sciences as the important affair it is. Indeed, there are some scientists (if not some sciences) who would deny the very existence of fluid enquiry because they deny the existence of conceptual frames (substantive structures) as underpinnings of their work. Many men feel much more emotional stability and readiness for work if they permit themselves to believe that the notions that guide their work represent "the facts" and are stable and eternal. It was once possible to maintain the fantasy of such stability for a lifetime. Relatively few men were engaged in research, and research itself was not an organized enterprise. Substantive structures, in consequence, had a long life; and the interval between revisions was often longer than the lifetime of a generation of scientists. This is no longer the case. Scientific enquiry is a vast and organized enterprise, and revisions of principle occur frequently. As a result, we find fluid enquiry accorded great honor in some sciences and in others, recognition, at least. The theoretical physicist is a man of honor in his field. The chemical physicist is recognized and rewarded for his contributions to fluid enquiry in the field of chemistry. Even in biology a grudging recognition of the necessity for fluid enquiry has appeared within the last ten years.

It is virtually impossible to provide a step-by-step description of the method of fluid enquiry, for, while stable enquirers permit themselves some flexibility in the interpretation of data, there is practically no limit to the flexibility with which the fluid enquirer may work. The detection of inadequacies in current structures is an act of creative "insight" which has no known method. The revision of a structure or the invention of a new one is an act of creative imagination for which, again, there are no known methods. Even the timing, the occasion, for fluid enquiry is indefinitely variable. In one case, a courageous man, Edward Murray East, undertook a piece of fluid enquiry well before there was general recognition of any need for it. In the years between 1900 and 1914, the newly opened study of heredity was doing very well with a simple conception of the hereditary trait and the hereditary unit. The ruling conception dictated the recognition of hereditary traits as "either/or" phenomenon. One had blue eyes or brown eyes. One had curly hair or straight hair, and so on. The conception of the unit of heredity, the gene, was similarly either/or. One had gene A or one had its substitute gene *a* (and in unusual cases a third or a fourth substitute), but whether the alternatives were one or several, one had or did not have a given gene. There were no bits of genes. The effect of this simple conception of trait and genetic unit was such that the study of hereditary patterns was apparently limited to the study of traits that could be distinguished as either/or. The possibility of accounting for such "continuously variable" traits as height, weight, number of rows of kernels on an ear of corn, and so on, was remote. Yet, at this time, there were still plenty of either/or traits to be investigated and only a few men were particularly worried about the limitations of the existing conceptual structure. Yet, in 1916, East published papers on the inheritance of size and on the inheritance of rows of kernels of corn, papers that were designed to exhibit the way in which the conception of the gene and its action could be so modified as to make possible the study of such continuously variable traits. By contrast, many other revisions of conceptual structure took place only when the need was desperate.

We said above that there are three objectives of fluid enquiry: detection of the inadequacy of a conceptual structure, identification of its particular weaknesses, devising of replacements. In fact, there is a fourth objective of fluid enquiry which shares with these three their "fluidity," their flexibility of method, but which is much more open to study than acts of creative insight or imagination. This fourth objective consists of the political-rhetorical-scientific hard work of obtaining acceptance of a new conceptual scheme by one's fellow scientists. This task, political-rhetorical though it be, is as much a part of the scientific enterprise as obtaining data, or persuading one's colleagues that one's interpretation of data is appropriate.

When new conceptual structures are proposed in the intellectual marketplace of science, four major criteria are usually brought to bear by the community of scientists in determining whether or not to accept the proposed new structures. I have given commonplace names to these criteria as follows: adequacy, interconnectivity, feasibility, and continuity. As we shall see, these criteria are often in conflict or tension with one another in the sense that maximizing one of them may be achievable only by minimizing another. Since the criteria often are in competition, the fact that they also tend to reflect widely differing preferences on the part of different scientists leads to an even more complex and unpredictable patterning of fluid enquiry than we have already suggested. Let us look briefly at each of these criteria.

The "adequacy" of a proposed new principle refers to its most obviously needed characteristic—its ability to establish such connections *within* the subject matter that the incoherencies and inconsistencies exhibited by the use of earlier principles will be repaired. For example, to be an adequate successor to the principle of the simple conception of structure and function described earlier, a principle would have to enable us to conceive of interactions among organs and among their functions, together with an even higher level of interaction which would lead to detection of and response to changes in the environing state of the organism. More specifically, we would need to make our conception of the anatomy and physiology of an organism so flexible that we could investigate the possibility that one organ, responding to a change in the environment, so affected a second organ that the second one underwent a change in its fine structure leading to a change in its activity which made it a more helpful contributor to the over-all economy of the body under the new conditions. Few scientists would underestimate the importance of the criterion of adequacy in judging a proposed new conception. Yet, in its application, many may prefer a less adequate conception as a price worth paying for obtaining greater "continuity."

The criterion of continuity brings into sharp relief the operation of conservatism in science. Clearly, the advantages of a radically new conception lie in the future—enquiries not yet undertaken and bodies of knowledge not yet envisaged. Anxiety is roused in many scientists by considering such a radical change. Furthermore, there is ground for anxiety since a radical departure is bound to be a costly affair. The old body of knowledge will require extensive reformulation. There must be sweeping rewriting of textbooks and reorganization of courses and training programs for graduate students. Much of this work may fall on the shoulders of those who were responsible for the development of the bodies of knowledge now scheduled for oblivion. Little wonder then that such radical proposals may often be resisted on the ground that sufficient advance could be made in enquiry with principles far less radical, that is, with principles exhibiting much more unity of content and connection with the principles being discarded. It is this view that I summarize under the heading of "continuity."

Where the criterion of adequacy refers to the richness of connection which a new structure establishes among elements or parts *within* a subject matter, interconnectivity refers to the extent and richness of connection which new conceptions promise to establish *between* subject matters formerly held separate. This criterion is emphasized by scientists who are concerned with the unification of science, for, obviously, conceptions that establish connections among subject matters lay a ground for enquiries that cover them both at once and therefore promise unification of what was formerly two bodies of knowledge. Newtonian mechanics is a case in point in that it established connection between terrestrial and celestial motions. John Dalton's "A New System of Chemical Philosophy" contains a similar emphasis on the criterion of interconnectivity. His argument for an atomic concept as the guiding principle for chemical enquiry emphasizes again and again the point that such a principle would relate the subject matter of chemical analysis and synthesis to problems of falling bodies, the planets, and the motions of bodies generally, through its connection with the dynamical conception of force.

The criterion of feasibility shares the conservative tendency of the criterion of continuity. When new conceptual structures are proposed, they are proposed as *working* principles: they must lead to enquiries that can be carried out within the limitations of existing techniques, skills, and facilities. Yet they normally call for new experimental patterns, for unfamiliar forms of data, for new ways of collating and arranging data, even for new technical devices. Hence, proposed new principles are scrutinized closely to determine the relative ease, cost, precision, and reliability with which the data they require can be collected and analyzed. A principle will be resisted if the cost of putting it into operation is extremely high or if there is no clear promise of the desired degree of precision and reliability. Consequently, many defenses of new structures do not appear to be primarily proposals of new conceptions at all. Rather, they are reports of experiments actually performed and data actually collected, the data and the experiments being those evoked by a new conception. The point, of course, is to make clear by example rather than by argument the feasibility of the principle in question.

As we have said, these several criteria are applied differently by different men at different times. There is sometimes quick success of radically new, highly adequate, or interconnecting principle. At other times, the shift of principle is mild indeed, hewing closely to the criteria of continuity and feasibility. In all cases, however, the shift of principle re-energizes enquiry in the field and gives it new directions.

SUBSTANTIVE STRUCTURES

If it is difficult to sketch the course of fluid enquiry, it is impossible to describe the substantive structures of the sciences in general. These structures are not only extremely numerous but extremely varied.

They are so because of the very character of substantive structures and the role they play. They are designed to fit given subject matters as known at a given moment of their investigation. And whether these subject matters differ from one another *sub specie eternitatis,* or only appear to differ because previous principles for enquiry into them have differed, is beside the point; they do differ. As a result, the substantive structures used in psychology belong to psychology and differ radically from those appropriate to biology, physics, or chemistry. We can, however, sketch briefly a few of the forms or shapes that principles in the sciences can take on.

Many of the effective principles in the sciences have been of a kind we may call *reductive.* Reductive principles instruct the enquirer to treat his subject matter as something that takes on all its important properties from its own elements or parts and from the connections relating these parts to one another. Thus the properties of the larger whole are accounted for by the summations, combinations, and interactions of the constitutive parts. The principles of nineteenth-century chemistry provide a case in point. First, these principles instructed the chemist to treat the subject of his enquiry as compounds of material, chemical elements. Second, these principles then provided means for identifying and distinguishing one element from another and for distinguishing an element from a compound. Third, the same principles included a conception of binding factors (affinities or valences) which established investigable relations among elements in compounds. Thus chemical substances are *reduced* to simple chemical substances and connections between them. In the same way, early atomic physicists reduced the 92 kinds of chemical atoms to two or three kinds of smaller physical "atoms." Early psychologists developed the same sort of reductive principle. The complex of behavior was reduced to simple combinations of learned and unlearned units of behavior (conditioned and unconditioned reflexes).

Of course, the sort of unit or element and the kind of connection between them which are used in reductive principles vary with the subject matter. It is a far cry from the psychical elements (id, ego, and super-ego) of the Freudian theory of personality to the 92 elements of nineteenth-century chemistry. There are even very important differences between the 92 chemical elements and the elemental particles of early twentieth-century physics. Nevertheless, all such structures have this in common: some chosen whole is understood, "explained" in terms of (a) its particular constituents, and (b) the relations that bind these constituents together in a certain way. Meanwhile, the constituents themselves go unexplained. They are the irreducible elements, invariant and independent of one another, which simply "are" for the sake of explaining that which they compose.

The second kind of scientific principle we may call "organic" or "holistic." Such principles are superficially the opposite of reductive ones. Where reductive principles instruct us to find our explanation of larger wholes in their constituent parts, organic principles instruct us to treat the larger whole as simply "being" (i.e., not explained). Then, provided with this stability of the whole, we are told to explain its parts by reference to the describable but unexplained whole. This is well illustrated by the kind of common-sense statement which runs, "Cities being what they are, we must expect slums to develop." Or, "Since the State exists to regulate the behavior of its members so as to maximize their well-being, we can now identify the essential function of each of its parts. The legislative part exists to identify the conditions of well-being and to state the rules of behavior which will lead to realization of these conditions, etc."

When such principles are used in sciences, we see, first, that certain wholes are identified, bounded, and described. (They are only described, however, not explained.) Then, various parts of the described whole are discriminated and "explained" in terms of the contribution they make to the bounded whole. Such principles as these are probably even more numerous than reductive principles and give rise to the commonest form of knowledge—classificatory schemes. The operation of such principles is most easily seen in the traditional physiology that first assigns certain fixed activities as descriptive of an organism (e.g., ingestion, digestion, excretion, reproduction) and then describes each part of the organism by reference to what it contributes to one or another of these defining activities. Finally, such principles enable us to classify all sorts of organisms according to the activities they have or do not have and according to the sorts of organs or parts that contribute to each such activity.

Finally, let us take note of still a third form of principle, which we may call "rational" without implying that reductive or organic principles are in any sense irrational. Where, roughly speaking, reductive principles describe wholes in terms of their parts, and organic principles describe parts in terms of their contribution to a whole, rational principles instruct the scientist to treat his subject matter as determined or explained by some system, often some purely mathematical or rational structure of relationships within which the subject matter exists and acts. Take, for example, an early field or gradient theory in embryology. The parts of the developing animal are taken as the subject matter. The laws of their development is the knowledge sought, the "explanation" desired. This knowledge is then sought, not in terms of particular constituent parts, or of the action of particular causes but in terms of the entire environing system created by the interactions of each of these developing parts with every other developing part.

When we explain the whole system of the heavens as well as the behavior of any one planet by referring to the properties of ellipses and the consequences of centripetal forces which vary as the square of distance, we have another example of the use of rational principles.

Rational principles usually require a special language. Ordinary language is well suited to analyzing things, taking them apart. On the whole, too, ordinary language is well designed to describe things or the visible behavior of things. Rational principles, by contrast, forbid us to seek explanations by isolating bits and pieces of things, events, or characteristics. They ask us, instead, to talk in terms of an entire system. Furthermore, the system is usually a system of relationships treated apart from the things in the relationship. Thus, the system we are required to deal with is not only a system but an abstract system. We require, then, a language capable of coping with abstract systems. Mathematics is the principal source of such languages. Hence, the knowledge that arises from the application of rational principles is usually formulated in the form of equations, many of whose terms do not refer to simple, measurable, physical quantities.

We should close, I think, by pointing out that some principles arise from the attempt to avoid principles. Two such anti-principles are conspicuous. In the physical sciences we are periodically confronted by the plea to avoid all such conceptual structures as particles and waves, even such accepted notions as force and mass. Instead, say the proponents of anti-principles, we should limit science to the description of measurable, related changes. For example, according to this view we should not assert that $F = MA$ but, rather, only report the different accelerations imparted to a given object by impact from balls of different weights.

In biology we sometimes have recourse to the simple search for the sequence of common events. If we are interested in event A, such as the secretion by a gland, we ask what event Z immediately precedes it, what further event precedes that one, and so on.

PART THREE
History and the Social Sciences

9. Grounds for a Reconsideration of Historiography

Charles A. Beard

I F A DESIRE TO advance learning or increase precision of knowledge requires any justification, practical, as well as theoretical grounds may be put forward to warrant a plea for a reconsideration of historiography—the business of studying, thinking about, and writing about history. Practical persons—academic and lay—concerned primarily with public or private affairs and absorbed in "the instant need of things," are, to be sure, likely to question at once the truth or relevance of this contention. By such "practitioners" history is often, if not commonly, regarded as a kind of old almanac or as an ancient, if sometimes amusing, chronicle, without utility or pertinence in framing and executing policies for the conduct of affairs, public or private.

When leaders in politics, business, labor, agriculture, or other activities deemed "practical," set about forming programs for action they seldom, if ever, think of devoting long weeks and months to the study of history as possibly germane to their procedure. On the contrary, when in the presence of a problem to be handled, they are inclined to employ their impressions derived from current experiences in such affairs; and, if supplements are regarded as desirable, to make use of treatises on law, economics, government, and foreign affairs, or other special works presumably directed to practical ends. To practitioners in general the idea of having recourse to history in a search for firm guidance to effective action would therefore seem to be a waste of time if not absurd.

Yet in the speeches and declarations made by articulate persons among practitioners—economists, reformers, politicians, business men, labor leaders, for instance—and in the newspapers and journals published for their information and satisfaction appeals to "history" occur with striking frequency. The word flows with ease from the pens of publicists, editors, columnists, and other writers for the general public; it crops up in the periods of orators, radio commentators, and special pleaders engaged in advancing practical interests, or for that matter

Reprinted by permission from *Theory and Practice in Historical Study: A Report of the Committee on Historiography,* Bulletin 54, pp. 3–14 (New York: The Social Science Research Council, 1946).

advocating impractical, even dangerous, delusions. History is indeed often treated as the court of last resort by such instructors of the public when they are impressed by the need of "proving" the validity of their propositions, dogmas, and assertions. Men and women who could not demonstrate the simplest proposition in mathematics, chemistry, or physics, or pass a high school examination in history feel perfectly competent to demonstrate the soundness of any public or private policy they espouse by making reference to history, or at least feel competent enough to use history in efforts to support that soundness.

Among the phrases which appear in the speeches and writings of or for practitioners, the following are so common as to be clichés:

> All history proves.
> The lesson of history is plain.
> History demonstrates.
> History shows.
> History teaches.
> History affirms.
> History confirms.
> History repeats itself.
> History makes it clear.
> An understanding of history settles the question.
> All that belongs to ancient history.
> If history is taken as our guide.
> The verdict of history has been pronounced in our favor.
> His place in history is secure.
> The verdict of history is against any such folly.
> The truth of history corroborates.
> History admits no such contention.
> Let us turn to history and see.
> The history of that matter is definitely closed.
> All history up to the present has been the history of class struggles.
> American history must be taught in the schools.

The appeals of publicists to history in short form are frequently supplemented by efforts on their part to "historicize" long arguments for one cause or another; that is, to make what purports to be more or less elaborate statements of historical facts, real or alleged, in a resolve to sustain in this fashion the invincibility of their assertions and contentions.

Although there is no way of measuring the influence of historicizations on public opinion, the immense circulation they attain seems to indicate that laborious students of history probably have less influence in national life than men of science had, let us say, in the New Eng-

land of Cotton Mather. Great applause is given to works which purport to be authenticated by references to history but in fact bear
about the same relation to historical knowledge that astrology bears to
astronomy.

Thus recent and current experiences present to workers in historiography a dilemma pertaining to the nature and uses of their work.
History is treated as having little or no relation to the conduct of
practical affairs and yet is constantly employed in efforts to validate
the gravest policies, proposals, contentions, and dogmas advanced for
adoption in respect of domestic and foreign affairs. Either historians
have failed in giving precision, limitations, and social significance to
their work or, by their writings, have lent countenance to the idea that
almost any pressing public question can be indefeasibly answered by
citations or illustrations selected from historical writings. History
can scarcely be at the same time a useless old almanac and the ultimate source of knowledge and "laws" for demonstrating the invincible
validity of policies proposed or already in practice.

Here then is a contradiction in contemporary thought which involves nothing less than the fundamentals of historiography in relation
to practical affairs of the gravest import. On this ground alone a call
for the reconsideration of historiography appears to have ample justification wholly apart from the love of knowledge in itself or the advancement of learning for its own sake.

Reasons involving a still wider reach of philosophic understanding,
and yet with a bearing on practical affairs, also justify such a reconsideration. The Western world has long been at a crisis in thought and
learning, as well as in practice—the most widespread and tumultuous
crisis of the kind since the beginning of recorded history. This is a
contention which scarcely needs a supporting argument. The state of
things human around the globe demonstrates the soundness of the
proposition. If it be urged that the calamities from which mankind suffers are really due to "economic maladjustments," it can hardly be denied that these maladjustments have occurred *in* history-as-actuality [1]
and have, in some measure at least, grown out of defects in practical

---

[1] Owing to the loose uses of the term "history" it is necessary in the interest of precision to make preliminary definitions of terms. Otherwise confusion may be confounded.
In these pages, history-as-actuality means all that has been felt, thought, imagined, said,
and done by human beings as such and in relation to one another and to their environment since the beginning of mankind's operations on this planet. *Written-history* is a
systematic or fragmentary narration or account purporting to deal with all or part of this
history-as-actuality. *History-as-record* consists of the documents and memorials pertaining
to history-as-actuality on which written-history is or should be based. Of course for recent
history, a writer may use in part his own experiences and observations and oral statements
by his contemporaries which he has heard and remembered or written down. Unless
these distinctions are made clear by the context they should be explicitly set forth whenever the word "history" is used.

knowledge of history and out of incapacity for thinking about ways and means of preventing them or overcoming them. And if we are to mitigate or overcome them, effective intellectual operations of some kind must precede or accompany effective action in respect to them, unless forsooth action is to be taken thoughtlessly, on impulsive opinions alone.

Since this crisis in thought has occurred *in* and is an aspect of history-as-actuality, then in the nature of things efforts to deal with it in terms of the realities out of which it came involve knowledge of and interpretations of this history. In every attempt to "explain" how we have come into the present state of things, recourse is had, even by persons wholly uneducated, to events, ideas, interests, and personalities of history-as-actuality recent in time. All public policies and personal designs framed with a view to bringing about an ideal or better state of things either present interpretations of history-as-actuality or are based on assumptions, explicit or tacit, respecting the nature of that actuality, past, present, and in the process of becoming. Broad and sweeping as this generalization appears, it is, I believe, incontrovertible and presents one of the supreme intellectual challenges of our time.

Even in times called "normal" similar reliances on interpretations of history-as-actuality occur. Such times are in fact only "epochs" or "stages" of history, general or local or regional. They are epochs characterized by peace or relative peace, in which economy is fairly prosperous or stable, and governments, besides being stable, are less active than in wartime and intervene less in what is called "the natural course" of private affairs—the economic and other undertakings of individuals and concerns.

The idea of "the natural (or normal) course" in human affairs is itself an interpretation of history. By its very terms it implies that such a course is as predominant or general in history as processes are in physical nature and that if broken or interrupted it will or can be recovered or restored, as physical nature tends to overcome aberrations or eccentricities. It assumes furthermore that such a course in human affairs is natural, without inquiring whether *all* nature is taken into account, and that other courses are unnatural, without wondering how and why a part or period of history can be "natural," that is, nature-like, and another part or period can be "unnatural." Here is a dualism in history which arbitrarily breaks the interrelations of events, ideas, interests, and personalities known to exist in history-as-actuality. In addition, it raises one of the most fundamental of historical questions: Does history repeat itself, so that the state of affairs prevailing in some past epoch—as distinguished from merely analogous or similar conditions—will be or may be restored or recovered?

Under the sway of the idea of the normal or the natural—an idea essentially historical—public and private policies are frequently based on the assumption that there will be a return to former conditions or that given actions can bring it about. Statesmen assume that if they act in a particular manner or refrain from action, the return they desire will occur in history to come. Directors of private economic affairs likewise make their calculations on the assumption that the course of history in the past has in fact disclosed, or has permitted, such exact returns, and that the future course—a continuation of the past and present flow—will be or may be made in conformity to expectations. It has been said, even with justification, that military men generally base the beginning of every new war on the experiences of the last war rather than on an exploration of the new potentials or on Napoleon's maxim of "act and then see" (*on s'engage et alors on voit*).

It appears, therefore, that the idea of history which bulks large in discourses and writings of practitioners and their spokesmen enters also into the daily calculations for action in "normal" as well as "critical" times. Hence, all branches of learning that deal with practice come into any comprehensive consideration of history-as-actuality, and of the nature and uses of written-history.

Indeed all the humanistic sciences—that is, organized bodies of knowledge and thought pertaining to human affairs—including historiography and the social sciences, whether concerned with theory or practice, are a part of history-as-actuality and rest upon assumptions respecting the nature of that history.[2] It is true that workers and writers in these sciences—economics, politics, sociology, anthropology, psychology, ethics, esthetics, etc.—may show little interest in history as such, may indeed claim to discard written-history as irrelevant or useless. Yet all the data of all these humanistic sciences are selected from the data of human experience in time and space, the actuality called history; and the humanistic sciences certainly consist of abstractions drawn from knowledge of phases of human life as lived in history—particular phases such as economic, political, esthetic, or ethical interests and activities—and in turn these sciences become aspects of history-as-actuality.

Great thinkers in the humanistic sciences employ abstractions drawn from knowledge of history-as-actuality and thus covering less than the totality of human life in its time-span. In analyzing, selecting, and organizing their data, they make these abstractions serve their

[2] Such assumptions, for example, presuppose that things will continue very much as they are, that some former state of affairs will be more or less restored, or that one or more of certain current tendencies will become dominant through change. In any case here appears a theory of a continuum of some kind, a rejection of the idea that history-as-actuality is a senseless chaos of unrelated events, and a penchant for the old or the new which enters into the selection and ordering of "facts" and "dicta" for presentation as economics, sociology, political science, etc.

purposes as constructs or fictions [3] based on emphasized particularities, or phases, of history-as-actuality. By making use of such constructs or fictions they advance their respective sciences.

For example, Adam Smith was deeply impressed by the existence of moral sentiments in history. He wrote a book on the subject. Yet when he came to formulating his influential work on *The Wealth of Nations*, he put moral sentiments aside and created the abstraction known as "the economic man" to guide him in his study and writing. In adopting this fiction, Smith evidently assumed that moral sentiments and other manifestations of human history could be taken for granted, would remain more or less constant or at all events would not vitiate the correctness of his economic reasoning and conclusions. He drew upon knowledge of history-as-actuality and his observations of history in the making around him for the data he employed, for information respecting the policies he deplored or approved, and for illustrations of the policies he condemned or advocated. His work was an expression of history-as-actuality and of thought about it in his own age, and his powerful polemic entered into the shaping of history.

The fiction of the economic man was highly useful for many purposes in examining and predicting the behavior of human beings in relation to the production and distribution of wealth. It is still highly useful. Without it we should know a great deal less than we do about the nature of human affairs and we should not be as well equipped to deal with many situations of life, large and small.

But as Adam Smith proceeded he almost became a victim of his own fiction. When he confronted the issue of justifying his emphasis on the economic man and explaining how it came about that general good resulted from the avid pursuit of material interests by acquisitive individuals, Smith lamely referred to the "invisible hand," to some mysterious providence which turns individual greed into collective beneficence. Here he introduced something besides the economic man and sought to escape the moral question that he himself had raised. Here, in effect, he made a fundamental interpretation respecting the nature of all history-as-actuality in which economic men operate.

"The political man"—likewise an abstraction from history—is an over-arching fiction employed by political scientists and is useful to them in forming categories, framing maxims and axioms, and attempt-

---

[3] "*Fictio* means, in the first place, an activity of *fingere*, that is to say, of constructing, forming, giving shape, elaborating, presenting, artistically fashioning; conceiving, thinking, imagining, assuming, planning, devising, inventing. Secondly it refers to the product of these activities, the fictional assumption, fabrication, creation, the imagined case." Students and practitioners in law and natural science openly make use of fictions. In law "an act of God" is a convenient fiction. For natural science, the infinitive extension of space and the infinite divisibility of matter are fictions. Indeed matter itself is a fiction. Hans Vaihinger, *The Philosophy of "As if"* (New York, 1924), 81.

ing predictions respecting political behavior. It also rests upon assumptions concerning the nature of history-as-actuality, the changing contexture or relationships in which political behavior arises, takes forms, and changes. Like economics, political science draws upon knowledge of history recent or distant for its data for classification, deduction, and illustration.

The ancillary abstractions or fictions of political science, such as democracy, aristocracy, monarchy, dictatorship, and oligarchy, if stripped of the concreteness of historical content, are in truth meaningless and useless to common sense and for practice. As Croce has said of philosophy, so it may be said of political science that, "pursued for its own sake and outside historical knowledge, [it] is only to be found as a profession among others by which man earns his living, and as such is worth little because it has been removed from its live source whence it arose and in which it can renew itself." [4]

It is generally agreed that the axioms and arguments of the one powerful work on political science produced in the United States, *The Federalist*, are anchored in studies of history and directed to concrete ends. Its authors are often disingenuous, if not worse, in pleading their case. They emphasize and they conceal; such indeed is the habit of human beings seeking to inform, persuade, and inspire to action. But they never depart so far from concreteness as to disappear in the fogginess of abstractions devoid of historical content. Besides, *The Federalist* has one quality generally lacking in academic political writings. It has style, that is, the ringing verve of realistic thought directed toward the end of action in fulfilment of a great purpose openly avowed. It is a polemic, of course, but that does not necessarily detract from its science. Nearly all the influential writings in political philosophy or political theory, so called, are polemics directed to ends.

Useful as a fiction or abstraction, like the economic man or the political man, is or may be for limited and practical purposes, it becomes harmful, as Havelock Ellis has said, "when we regard it as hypothesis and therefore possibly true." Certainly great harm was done when writers of small caliber treated the fiction of the economic man as possibly true or as wholly and positively true and shut their eyes and minds to other aspects of history. In another way, Adam Smith himself did harm when, instead of facing boldly the question of the general good, he resorted to a mystical effusion—"the invisible hand."

The crowning weakness of Smith's work lay in his assumptions concerning the nature of all history-as-actuality and historical thought; in his failure to reckon with other aspects of history, with the creative and unique as well as routine activities of mankind, with the impacts of other than economic propensities upon the operations of the

---

[4] Benedetto Croce, *History of the Story of Liberty* (London, 1941), 138–139.

economic man. It was in fact the introduction of historical economics and the resort to the study of the history of specific economic activities, toward the end of the nineteenth century, that disclosed to those who had eyes to see and minds to grasp the limitations and unrealities of the Smithian creed which had then been driven into absurd extremities.

Since all the humanistic sciences, such as economics and politics, are based on abstractions from knowledge of history-as-actuality, that is, are selective emphases on particular aspects of history, they can be in no respect independent, free-moving sciences. The degree of truth in them, the degree of their correspondence to reality, depends not merely on their logic or cogency of statement but also on the extent to which they cover the relevant and necessary facts in the case. In other words, to ascertain the degree of truth in them, it is imperative to check them against comprehensive knowledge of the actuality of history. Furthermore in seeking to discover the long-term validity of any among these sciences, we must take into the reckoning changes in human societies before that science was formulated, the circumstances in which it was formulated and by whom, changes since its formulation, and the probabilities discernible in recent historical tendencies. Certainly this process of checking abstractions against comprehensive knowledge of history is as necessary in the interest of truth-seeking as checking the conflicting schools to be found within any humanistic science against one another or resorting to a logical analysis of their discrepancies. Indeed such checking against historical knowledge seems to be the chief intellectual operation likely to increase the degree of truth in any of the sciences.

This checking of abstractions in the humanistic sciences against knowledge of history is analogous to the procedure followed in physical sciences—verification by observation of physical performances. The analogy is, of course, far from exact; it is indeed purely figurative in nature, for the observer of human affairs can only "see" the past through the media of documents and memorials. He cannot observe it directly. He may recall memories of events and personalities belonging to his own past but they are at best extremely limited and fragmentary. It is mainly by the use of constructive and informed imagination in the interpretation and exposition of documents and memorials that he is able to describe with any degree of exactness the outstanding features of any situation or age beyond his own past, and even then he is limited by the number and nature of the documents and survivals available to him. If this is discouraging to those who expect the exactness of physics and chemistry in the humanistic sciences, nevertheless the fact remains that for validity any humanistic science must be checked against comprehensive knowledge of history-as-actuality when truth-seeking is pressed toward the limits of the possible.

In some ways history itself, as actuality, passes judgment on the validity of propositions in the humanistic sciences. If, for example, Adam Smith's economics is to be taken as describing what is or will be, as distinguished from a plea for what "ought to be," history has already passed judgments on it. The public policies which he recommended as calculated to increase the wealth of nations were extensively adopted by Great Britain near the middle of the nineteenth century; and this adoption, to his enthusiastic disciples, seemed to herald universal triumph. But in fact, whatever the shortcomings of our present historical knowledge, there is a consensus of competence on the following proposition: Smith's system was not so extensively applied in other countries as in Great Britain and marked tendencies in public policies during the past fifty years, even in Great Britain, have been against, rather than in favor, of the Smithian system. History-as-actuality may be described as cruel and senseless, but, whatever it is, it has passed and is passing judgments on Smith's economics as predicted practice up to the present; and if the spirit of natural science is to prevail in the humanistic sciences this judgment, however deplorable, must be accepted as a historical verdict.

The desirability of resorting to knowledge of history as a check on humanistic sciences is reinforced by the fact that, while they all depend on history for data and ideas, they are, in a large sense, antihistorical. Most, if not all of them, purport to describe "what is" and perhaps "what will be," despite human aspirations and distempers. Except for what may be called historical sociology, they usually make abstractions from a brief or limited span of years, even when they draw, as did the authors of The Federalist, upon the writings of antiquity for illustrations. They are concerned primarily with repetitions, routines, constants in history-as-actuality. When they use the vague phrase "other things being equal" in attempting to support the validity of their abstractions, they are in effect seeking to escape history, to evade the historical changes which may and probably will invalidate their propositions.

On the other hand, historians are especially concerned, doubtless too much, with the uniqueness of events and personalities, with what is growing and becoming, with changes and creations. Owing to the very nature of history-as-actuality, historians, if true to their subject matter, are bound to exercise this concern. The political scientists, if cautious, may with due propriety and for convenience speak of the regimes of Caesar, Cromwell, and Napoleon as dictatorships, but the historian, adhering to the records, points out dissimilarities among them, the uniqueness of each in the circumstances of its origin and functioning and in its intrinsic character.

Accordingly, to treat any humanistic science as living and scientific and to look upon history as a kind of old almanac compiled by and for curious creatures called historians is to disregard relevant facts in the total case and to give a false security and assurance to that alleged science. To divorce any humanistic science from history is to introduce confusion into the intellectual processes by which we acquire knowledge of human affairs; by which we are enabled to evolve workable statements or formulas that represent the utmost truth attainable to us and that promise to be serviceable in the wiser and better ordering of human affairs.

Nor is the cause of utmost and serviceable truth well served by resorting to the use of analogies drawn from the natural sciences, such as a biological analogy, "the cross-fertilization of related sciences." As analogy of this kind is merely a bit of rhetoric utterly inconceivable in real terms. "Cross-fertilization," like many other words, such as "social forces," falls into the category of figurative expressions, which, as Dubois-Reymond has pointed out, "one uses when the idea is not clear enough to be directly formulated."

Workers in the several humanistic sciences may undoubtedly learn from one another and should endeavor to do so. But history is not just "one" of the related humanistic sciences. History-as-actuality, with which historians are bound by their very office to be concerned, includes all the humanistic sciences and all the data upon which they draw for formulas, axioms, proofs, demonstration, and illustrations; and it is against knowledge of this comprehensive history that the abstractions of the humanistic sciences are to be checked for validity.

The economist, the political scientist, or sociologist may say in reply: "I have read a lot of history and I find in it many features of an old almanac and very little help in enlarging my knowledge of economics or politics or sociology or in checking my abstractions." Anyone well acquainted with historical writings must admit that there is some justice in the complaint as well as some injustice. It is here that the primary distinction must be re-emphasized. History-as-actuality is one thing; written-history purporting to describe all or part of history-as-actuality is still another thing.

For the purpose of truth-seeking in the humanistic sciences this distinction must be clearly and severely maintained in our thinking; for, when the word history is used, especially by laymen, *written* history is usually meant, that is, a kind of book or books written by some person or persons, in a time and place, about history-as-actuality in general or some phases or "periods" of that actuality. And, to speak frankly, a large part, if not all, of the written history, even the best of it, falls far below the highest conceivable level of intellectual performance. It is at this point that the supreme problem of the business before us arises and the obligation of historians to examine their assumptions, procedures, and results appears in full force.

This is not to say that historians have been less intelligent and effective in producing true and workable statements than their colleagues in the other humanistic sciences. To prove such a proposition one way or the other would be a task in historical operations that is probably beyond human powers. But it seems correct to assert that Brooks and Henry Adams, for example, who worked primarily in history, demonstrated a comprehension of events taking place around them between 1870 and 1914 and made predictions as to the probable course of American and world affairs which justify a judgment that they displayed a higher degree of understanding than did most of their colleagues working in economics, sociology, law, or politics. With startling emphasis history-as-actuality since 1900 has verified many of their predictions.[5]

It would be idle, however, to dwell long upon the intellectual merits or demerits of past performances in historiography or any of the humanistic sciences, although we may undoubtedly learn from the analysis and study of such performances. The task before historians, if they are thoughtful rather than fretful, may be put in homely terms: "What do we do now and how?"

Or to break the general question down into subsidiary questions:

Just what intellectual operations does the historian perform in studying and writing history?

What does he think he is doing in performing these operations?

According to what axioms, maxims, assumptions, and methods does he proceed?

For what reason, if any discernible reason, are particular aspects of history chosen for emphasis and other aspects excluded?

Why, for instance, are many ideas, interests, institutions and activities usually excluded from general history and why in particular are one half of the human race—women—except a few queens and courtesans, so completely ignored, even in histories purporting to be "general" or "cultural" in nature?

How can a larger degree of comprehensiveness and exactness be achieved in historical writing?

How can a consensus of competence be secured on the formulas of procedure in historical study and writing best calculated to attain the ends of greater comprehensiveness, exactitude, and utility for theory and practice in the world of thought and action?

In what ways may the abstractions, formulas, and categories of the other humanistic sciences be used to broaden and give precision to historical studies in themselves and as auxiliaries to those other sciences?

[5] Charles A. Beard, Introduction to Brooks Adams, *The Law of Civilization and Decay* (New York, 1943).

By what actions may the most effective cooperation be attained among the parties to this common cause?

The "problem" indicated by these questions is no doubt highly complicated, and the Committee on Historiography, after long discussion, decided that neither the time nor the resources at its disposal would permit it to attempt a comprehensive treatment of the theme. Upon due consideration the committee came to the conclusion that in the circumstances it should simply direct its attention to the formulation of a program relevant to the problem and offer suggestions for further procedure.

In this program the following elements appear: (1) a series of fundamental propositions on the nature and limits of historiography; (2) a discussion of various frames of reference or schemes of thought which have been employed as operating fictions or controlling conceptions in the writing of history in the United States; (3) an illustration of the ways in which frames of reference have been employed by historians in dealing with a selected theme of American history, namely, the Civil War and Reconstruction; (4) a glossary dealing with a few, but primary, terms used in historiography, with a view to concentrating attention on the nature and limitations of such terms; and (5) a bibliography of selected works on historiography, which should be helpful to students who wish to have some idea of what they are doing when they are examining the documents of history, determining the authenticity of records, selecting facts, ordering facts, drawing inferences, exercising the art of constructive imagination, and writing history.

---

10.   Controlling Assumptions in the Practice of American Historians

John Herman Randall, Jr. and George Haines, IV

ISTORICAL INVESTIGATION," says Santayana, "has for its aim to fix the order and character of events throughout past time in all places. The task is frankly superhuman, because no block of real

Reprinted by permission from *Theory and Practice in Historical Study: A Report of the Committee on Historiography*, Bulletin 54, pp. 17–52 (New York: The Social Science Research Council, 1946).

existence, with its infinitesimal detail, can be recorded, nor if somehow recorded could it be dominated by the mind; and to carry on a survey of this social continuum *ad infinitum* would multiply the difficulty. The task might also be called infrahuman, because the sort of omniscience which such complete historical science would achieve would merely furnish materials for intelligence: it would be inferior to intelligence itself. . . . An attempt to rehearse the inner life of everybody that has ever lived would be no rational endeavour. Instead of lifting the historian above the world and making him the most consummate of creatures, it would flatten his mind out into a passive after-image of diffuse existence, with all its horrible blindness, strain, and monotony. Reason is not come to repeat the universe but to fulfil it. Besides, a complete survey of events would perforce register all changes that have taken place in matter since time began, the fields of geology, astronomy, palaeontology, and archaeology being all, in a sense, included in history. Such learning would dissolve thought in a vertigo, if it had not already perished of boredom. . . . The profit of studying history lies in something else than in a dead knowledge of what happens to have happened." [1]

In view of the situation Santayana thus graphically depicts, it is clear that, as Proposition VI states, "Every written history, particularly that covering any considerable area of time and space, is a selection of facts made by some person or persons and is ordered or organized under the influence of some scheme of reference, interest, or emphasis —avowed or unavowed—in the thought of the author or authors." [2] This means that the historian must employ some principle of selection: he must choose what he will include as significant for his history. In writing the history of the United States, he must decide what is "basic" for that history. Even though he permit himself four lengthy volumes to set forth *The Rise of American Civilization*, and can hence afford a broader base, he cannot escape the need for a principle of selection.

Moreover, if seventeen years elapse between the two written histories, the principle of selection employed in the later one will probably differ appreciably from the principle that served for the earlier. This will be not only because in the interval the historian has found out more "facts," and has a greater store from which to choose those that are really "basic" for a much shorter work. It will be due fully as much to the circumstance that he has grown in the stature of his wisdom. He has come to understand the world and its ways and the pattern of human experience with more maturity and insight, per-

---

[1] George Santayana, "History," *Reason in Science* (New York, 1906), 51–53.

[2] A reference is here made to oral as well as written history; it is stipulated that any historical interpretation "conform to the rules of critical scholarship." [Editor's Note:]

haps; at least he now understands it differently. And he understands
it differently in large part because there is now something different to
understand. The history-that-has-happened during those seventeen
years—the history as "actuality"—has not stood still. That history,
like all the histories-that-happen, has been progressive and cumulative. In 1944 the United States is not what it was in 1927. Hence the
historian, facing the problem of selecting those facts in the American
past that seem "basic" for 1944, will not be able to make just the same
selection that he made in 1927.

Thus the history the historian will write, and the principle of selection he will employ, will be undergoing continual change. For the
meaning and the significance of the past is continually changing with
the occurrence of fresh events. Of course, what *did* happen, as brute
events, does not change with further events. But, as we have seen, the
historian is not and cannot be concerned with all that did happen.
He is and must be concerned with those particular events that did
happen which turn out to be "basic" for his history. He is not concerned only with the "basic" or significant past. And it is precisely
this "basic" past, this meaning and significance of the past, that is
continually changing, that is cumulative and progressive. Writing the
history of the United States, the historian uses what is basic and
significant in that history-that-happened for 1927, or for 1944, as the
principle that will control his selection of material. What is significant
in American history he will understand in one way in 1927, and in a
somewhat different way in 1944. For the historian's understanding of
the significant past, like that past itself, is progressive and cumulative.

There is really nothing mysterious about this obvious fact that men's
understanding of what is significant in their history changes with the
lapse of time. For all understanding is in terms of causes and consequences. Now, our understanding of causes naturally changes and
deepens as we find out more about the operation of causes; and
equally naturally, our understanding of consequences changes with
the working out of further consequences in the history-that-happens
itself.

In the first place, the understanding of causes changes as we manage
to extend and build up our sciences of man's social behavior. When
we are content to explain what groups of men do by attributing their
actions to the guiding hand of Providence, we will, like the early
New England historians, write histories of the operation of God's
will, and we will select facts that illustrate it. Or, like Bancroft, we
will record "the movement of the divine power which gives unity to
the universe, and order and connection to events." When we have
come to understand the mysterious ways in which God performs His

wonders as the working out of the God-given genius for politics of
the Teutonic race, we will, like H. B. Adams, trace the "origin" of
the New England town-meeting to the primitive German mark.
When we have read John Stuart Mill's *Logic*, and absorbed his
Baconian conception of the nature of science, we will eschew all
guiding hypotheses and indefatigably collect "facts," hopefully trust-
ing that somehow good, in the form of some "synthesis" that will
make it all clear, will be the final goal of all this ill. We will be strictly
"scientific" and "critical" historians, like those great pioneers who
won respect for "history" as an academic discipline in the seminars
set up during the eighteen-eighties at Johns Hopkins, Columbia, and
elsewhere. When we have seen a great light, and been converted to
the gospel of St. Marx, we will write histories like those of Simons,
Gustavus Myers, or Lewis Corey. When we have learned from James
Harvey Robinson that the historian must master all the social sciences,
and have read—or at least abstracted—all the books in that wide field,
we will understand the past in terms of all the different hypotheses of
all the social sciences, and will, like Harry Elmer Barnes, adopt a
"multiple causation" theory as our principle of selection. Our understanding of the causes of what has happened will change in these ways
with our changing—and, we trust, increasingly adequate—schemes of
scientific explanation.

Secondly, the understanding of consequences, and hence of the
"significance" of past events, changes with further history-that-happens
—with what comes to pass in the world of events as a result of the
possibilities inherent in what has happened. Thus World War I was
understood in one way as leading to the adoption of the Covenant of
the League of Nations. It was understood in another way as the Russian Revolution worked itself out, and began to appear as a much
more significant consequence of the war than the abortive effort at an
international organization. The war took on a still further significance
with the rise of the Fascist and Nazi regimes, and with the resumption
of German expansion. It is now beginning to look like the first stage
in the Russian domination of Europe. Or take the matter of American
participation in that struggle. Ten years ago, the entry of America into
World War I was understood as the result of British propaganda and
the machinations of munition-makers. It was hard to believe that
Americans had been so stupid as to think they were really "making
the world safe for democracy"; reputable historians preferred less
simple-minded and more diabolical explanations. The years since
1939 have changed profoundly our understanding of American participation in World War I. After Pearl Harbor, it was seen as the first
and unsuccessful attempt to curb German aggression and establish a

military alliance to guarantee the status quo. With the resumption of
Russian and British power politics, our participation in that earlier
war may well come to be seen in still another light.

New consequences flowing from past events change the significance
of the past, of what has happened. Events which before had been
overlooked, because they did not seem "basic" for anything that followed, now come to be selected as highly significant; other events that
used to seem "basic" recede into the limbo of mere details. In this
sense, a history-that-happens is not and in the nature of the case
cannot be fully understood by the actors in it. They can not realize
the "significance" or consequences of what they are doing, since they
cannot foresee the future. We understand that history only when it
has become a part of our own past; and if it continues to have consequences, our children will understand it still differently. In this sense,
the historian, as Hegel proclaimed, is like the owl of Minerva, who
takes his flight only when the shades of night are gathering, and the
returns are all in. The significance of any history-that-happens is not
completely grasped until all its consequences have been discerned.
The "meaning" of any historical fact is what it does, how it continues
to behave and operate, what consequences follow from it.

For example, at a historic moment Winston Churchill said: "With
the fall of Singapore we are beginning to realize the meaning of Pearl
Harbor." Note the word "beginning." For the "meaning," that is, the
cumulative consequences of that specific event, were not completed
when Churchill was speaking. They have not been completed yet.
They depend on how things will turn out in the future.

In this sense, we understand my history-that-has-happened in terms
of the future: our principle for selecting what is basic in that history
involves a reference to its predicted outcome. Our "emphasis" will be
determined by what we find going on in the present. But what we
find there is not yet fully worked out. Rather, the present suggests
what will eventuate in times to come. Thus we understand what is
basic in a history in terms of what we call some "dynamic element" in
the present, some "present tendency" directed toward the future. The
present is full of such tendencies: it suggests many different possible
futures, according as different tendencies now at work prove controlling. The historian selects one of these possible futures as "just
around the corner," and uses it as a principle by which to select what
is basic among the multitude of facts at his disposal.

For example, our papers are today full of attempts to understand
what has been happening, the recent history of the different phases of
the war. Most of this discussion inevitably turns out to be a prediction
of what is going to happen: we cannot understand what has happened
without reference to a projected future. Thus we cannot understand

the Administration's foreign policy—toward the French, toward the Italians, toward Spain, toward Poland—we cannot understand what is "basic" in its history, without trying to predict how it is going to turn out. As we say, we are now beginning to see its significance, as we find out what it has already led to.

The historian must thus choose among the various possibilities of the present that tendency, that predicted future, which he judges to be dynamic or controlling. He chooses as his principle of selection the "real pattern of events," what is "being realized," what is "working itself out." Now, since the future is not foreseeable in detail—though many elements in it can be predicted, and all human action is based on such predictions of what will happen if other things occur —the historian's choice of a principle of selection necessarily involves a certain choice of allegiance, an act of faith in one kind of future rather than another. Thus, to take the growth of science as the basic factor in the intellectual history of modern times, means that we judge it to be of most significance today. "The future lies with it," we say, meaning we are for it. No devout Catholic, for instance, would choose that factor as basic. For him, the future will be different, and consequently he will have a different understanding of the past. In the same way, to take the growth of group control of technology as the principle for selecting what is basic in our economic past, is to express an allegiance. It is to make the problem of establishing such control central in the present. In terms of that principle of selection, the dominance of laissez faire during the nineteenth century will be understood as a "stage" in the reconstruction of the earlier medieval group controls. No "rugged individualist" would choose that focus: in his history he would select a different past.

But to say that a principle of selection is "chosen" does not mean that such choices are arbitrary. Men do not arbitrarily "choose" their allegiances and faiths, even when they are converts. Their faiths are rather forced upon them. Grace, we are told, is prevenient, and it is God who sends faith. The history-that-happens itself generates the faiths and allegiances that furnish the principles for selecting what is important in understanding it. Men do not "choose" arbitrarily to be Catholics—or rugged individualists—any more than they "choose" not to be. Some men indeed have their faiths and allegiances forced upon them by "facts," by knowledge; though presumably for none is this wholly the case. For such men, facts do force the selection of the controlling tendencies, the implicit ends, in the present, in terms of which they can understand the past. For such men, knowledge does declare what has to be done: the furtherance of science, the socialized control of industry, the achievement of international organization.

This is especially true when they are in responsible positions, and have to act to get something done. Thus Mr. Hoover, though a rugged individualist, was compelled by facts to go further than any of his predecessors in setting up group controls. This practical knowledge of what has to be done, like the technical knowledge of how to do it, is relatively free from the "arbitrariness" and irresponsible "relativism" —the "subjective relativism"—of so-called "theoretical knowledge," which is not knowledge at all, but a mere "having of ideas," mere "ideology." In terms of these ends that have to be achieved, these goals forced on us by facts, men understand the present and the past, using these ends as principles for selecting what is basic in the histories they write.

Indeed, there are so many facts and so many patterns of relation discernible in the history of anything, and it is so impossible to include them all, that any selection will remain "arbitrary" and "subjective" unless it is dictated by some necessary choice or problem generated in that history itself. Only by realizing that these are the fundamental problems and choices today, or that they were fundamental in some past period, can we hope to understand or write the history of anything "objectively." Only thus we can understand objectively, for example, the history of the Romantic era. It is notoriously difficult to find any common traits or common pattern in that movement. But we can find the common *problems* in terms of which we can understand its history. As Jacques Barzun writes, "Clearly, the one thing that unifies men in a given age is not their individual philosophies, but the dominant problem that these philosophies are designed to solve. In the romantic period this problem was to create a new world on the ruins of the old" [3]—to criticize the inadequate synthesis of the eighteenth century, and to reconstruct a more adequate one.

The historian must make a selection. From the infinite variety of relatednesses that past events disclose, he must select what is basic for his particular history. If that selection is not to be merely what is important *for him*, if it is not to be "subjective" and "arbitrary," it must have an "objective" emphasis or focus in something to be done, something he sees forced on men. The history of what is basic *for that problem*—of the conditions that generated it, the resources men had to draw upon, how they dealt with it—will then be perfectly "objective," in a sense in which no mere recording of arbitrarily selected "facts" could ever be. This is the "objective relativism" that is characteristic of all types of knowledge. Knowledge can be "objective" only *for* some determinate context; it is always a knowledge of the relations essential for that context. In historical knowledge, the context is always that of a problem faced by men, of the causes of that problem,

---

[3] Jacques Barzun, *Romanticism and the Modern Ego* (Boston, 1943), 21, 22.

the means for its solution, and the course actually adopted. In that context, the relation of cause and consequence, of means and end, will thus be quite "objective."

This objective relativism of the principles of selection and interpretation necessary to the historian's enterprise is set forth briefly in certain of the propositions laid down in this handbook.[4] It has been here elaborated with a little more detail. It is the aim of this essay to illustrate it in terms of the principles of selection and interpretation actually employed by certain of the major American historians of the last two generations. We shall pay special attention to the assumptions controlling the work of those "scientific" and "objective" founders of the profession in this country who claimed to make no assumptions and to have no principles of selection. We shall endeavor to set forth what assumptions they actually adopted, what problems they faced that led them to their principles, and why they made the choices they did.

II

Critical and scientific historical investigation, associated with instruction on a graduate level, began in the United States with the inauguration in 1876 in the newly-founded Johns Hopkins University of study in "History and Politics," and the setting up of an historical seminar under Herbert Baxter Adams. Four years later John W. Burgess founded the School of Political Science at Columbia, which came to rival Adams' seminar in providing training for professional historians. Michigan, Cornell, and Wisconsin, as well as Harvard and Pennsylvania, soon developed able graduate instruction in historical research.

These university scholars were of course not the first American historians to employ critical methods. Many a local historian, as far back as the eighteenth century, had displayed an ability to use sources critically, a zeal for "objectivity," and a range of concerns far wider than the rather narrowly political concentration of the new academic scholars.[5] Bancroft, who took his degree at Göttingen under Heeren in 1820, brought back to America an enthusiasm for the painstaking methods of the new German school of historical scholarship, of whose giants Heeren was so accomplished a forerunner. By the 'sixties the trickle of pilgrims in the sources of German learning had already swelled to a respectable stream. The year 1857 saw three German-

---

[4] The handbook referred to here stipulates that historiography is to be characterized by rules of scientific method. [Editor's Note.]

[5] See Richard H. Shryock, "American Historiography: A Critical Analysis and a Program," *American Philosophical Society Proceedings*, 87 (1943), 35–46; also Michael Kraus, *A History of American History* (New York, 1937).

trained scholars, Henry Torrey, Francis Lieber, and Andrew D. White, installed in chairs of history at Harvard, Columbia, and Michigan respectively—though according to J. Franklin Jameson as late as 1880 there were only eleven professors of history in the United States.[6]

The significance of Adams and Burgess does not lie primarily in the methods they had learnt across the seas and how ably taught their American students. It lies rather in the fact that they were establishing a new learned profession. They were introducing a new university discipline on an educational scene just groping, rather self-consciously, to provide itself with postgraduate professional training. The new graduate schools were painfully aware that they had yet to prove their worth in terms of the rigorous standards of their German models. The social studies in particular were on their mettle to justify their pretensions to rank as critical disciplines employing an exacting "scientific" method. And none was under greater compulsion than history to vindicate its new claim to a serious place among the circle of research sciences the emerging American universities were beginning to cultivate.

It is the great achievement of those scholars who began teaching history in American universities after 1880 that in the course of a single generation they completely succeeded in this basic aim. By 1910 the historical profession was firmly entrenched in institutions of higher learning. It was universally recognized as a research discipline as rigorous and exacting—if not quite so exact in its conclusions—as any university study not mathematical in its methods. Its ablest practitioners had won reputations equal to those of their European counterparts; its organized seminars offered a training that did not suffer in comparison with that of Europe. Perhaps most remarkable of all, the practice of historical writing had been transformed from the literary avocation it had been in nineteenth-century America into a highly professionalized discipline. If the academic scholars did not actually monopolize the field of historiography, they had come to dictate its aims and standards. Even the general educated public, though it still preferred the more readable works of the popularizers and journalists, felt guiltily it was getting its history second-hand, and was delighted to discover a work it could enjoy by a real scholar and "authority."

This professionalization and institutionalization of the practice of history in America we are apt to take as a matter of course. Actually, however, it has been the major factor controlling the way the Ameri-

[6] W. Stull Holt, Ed. *Historical Scholarship in the United States, 1876–1901* (Baltimore, 1938), 8.

can historian has regarded his work for the last two generations; it has dictated his methods and his aims and concerns. It is hardly too much to say that for twenty-five years after 1880 the central problems faced by the historian in America were institutional, involved in vindicating the standing of his profession in the learned world. Thus, in an age enormously impressed by the achievements of natural science, and convinced that even literature and the arts must be studied with "scientific methods," the historian too had to be "scientific" at all costs. Because men still construed the aim of science as the sheer discovery and direct reading of the structure of things, this meant that the historian had to be "objective." Since there was as yet little explicit appreciation of the role of hypothesis and theory in scientific procedure, it meant he must try to establish above all as many "facts" as possible. The only hypotheses he could afford to permit himself were those his German and English models accepted, like the Teutonic origin of English and American political institutions, or the colonial character of the colonies. Since his models were concerned with the problems of legal and constitutional origins, he too must prove his weapons on that aspect of the American past. After all, was he not trying to establish himself in a school of political science?

These pioneer critical historians had explicit principles of selection and definite schemes of understanding the past, as well as plenty of class and individual biases reflecting their background. But those principles and schemes were very largely determined by the problems of establishing a profession, which dictated the approved political subject-matter and the respectable European ways of understanding it. Historians were hardly free to make central the new economic problems already insistently emerging in American life. Their own institutional problem left them little liberty to employ the new ways of understanding that generation was working out—new conceptions of the very nature and method of science, a wealth of new knowledge about man and human society, new philosophies and new ways of looking at human affairs.

After 1900 the historians' position was pretty secure. In this new-found confidence it was possible to go on to question the limitations to which the pioneer historians had perforce submitted. The decade of the nineteen-hundreds began to hear the demand to focus on other problems, to include other aspects of the past, economic, intellectual, religious and cultural. Men of ranging mind, inspired by the new sciences of man to which a great series of pioneer thinkers were just giving a characteristic American stamp, began to use their hypotheses as heuristic principles in historical investigation.

But the profession had now itself become stabilized and institutionalized; it had developed traditions of selection and method to which its practitioners had grown intensely loyal. When shortly after 1910 men like Becker, Thorndike, Turner, Robinson, and Beard proposed to cultivate these new interests and to employ these new tools, their programs might have been welcomed—as indeed they were by the nonprofessionals—as a promising extension of horizons. But most of the professionals took this natural expansion of history as an attack on all they stood for. What might have been a shift of interest springing from the steady growth of knowledge and the emergence of new problems became instead a controversy. Historians argued heatedly about the "proper" field and concern of "history." They debated the extent to which the historian should be permitted to use ideas and hypotheses as principles of interpretation. Was it compatible with the scientific standing of the profession to explore what light might be thrown on the familiar outlines of political history by such newcomers as "sectionalism" or the "economic factor"?

Traditionalists were forced to formulate their own assumptions with some care; for the first time "scientific" history became really conscious of its presuppositions. Their critics were naturally led in turn to make exaggerated claims for the ideas and methods they found illuminating: "the new history" or "economic determinism" would give the final answer to all the historian's problems. Before they could go on to show what their programs could accomplish, they had to argue interminably for their right as "historians" to do so. There was now an established profession that had to be converted to any new departure. Thus in another but still controlling sense, the central problems of even the more heretical historians remained institutional and professional. Whatever new ideas or approaches gave promise of illuminating the past had to be first adjusted to the requirements of the profession. Thus socialists might employ the Marxian theory fruitfully to bring to light fully documented "facts." But what they wrote could hardly be reckoned as "history": they frankly had an axe to grind.

The geographical determinism and the sectional hypothesis of Turner, which seemed radical enough when first advanced in 1893, were sufficiently in line with the tradition, and were developed with enough skill and judgment, to enable them to pass muster. It is significant of the state of American historical thought that his "frontier theory" could stand for several decades as the major principle for interpreting the American past, and could exert such influence on the younger Beard and on Parrington.[7] That a theory of such limited

[7] Cf. Charles A. Beard, An Economic Interpretation of the Constitution of the United States (New York, 1913), 5f.

scope [8] could have enjoyed the controlling vogue it did makes clear how eager American historians were becoming to seize upon and generalize any fruitful idea presented with the proper professional credentials.

By the nineteen-twenties the critics of the traditionalists had won their fight: they were free to write the kind of history they wanted, economic interpretations, social and cultural history, intellectual history. The monumental works of Parrington and Beard appeared; Schlesinger and Fox started their series. Under pressure of the economic problems of the 'thirties, even writings with a strong Marxian tinge were admitted as "history." Most important of all, the profession now felt so secure that its leaders could begin to challenge the very conception of "science" on which "scientific" history had based its triumphs. Instead of self-consciously asserting the claim that their knowledge is as "scientific" as the next man's, they could now take it for granted that their knowledge is genuine knowledge, and go on to inquire precisely what kind of knowledge historical knowledge actually is.

With its head start of several generations, Continental history had achieved that degree of professional self-confidence by the eighteen-eighties, and had already produced a great literature of self-examination and criticism. Venturesome Americans now began to explore this literature—not always, to be sure, with full awareness of its theoretical presuppositions, or of its foundation in general philosophical theories and epistemologies which they would probably not be prepared to accept. A few pioneers, like Becker and Lynn Thorndike, had indeed dared to raise such issues at the time of the earlier controversies around 1910, and had done so in terms of more American philosophies. The profession had then been hardly ripe for such questions. But now more general searching of heart and debate ensued. Once more theoretical issues were filtered through the screen of professional and institutional interests.

III

These salient facts of the institutional development of the historical profession in the United States have been emphasized, because they

[8] Cf. Charles A. Beard, "The Frontier in American History," New Republic 97–98 (1938–39), 359–362. "Turner overemphasized, in my opinion, the influence of frontier economy on the growth of the democratic idea, on the formation of national policies and on constitutional interpretation. . . .

"The freehold frontier did have a lot of influence on American development, but how much and what kind is still an open question for me. That it does not 'explain' American development I am firmly convinced" (361).

provide the framework indispensable for understanding the assumptions and principles of selection American historians have actually employed. They were controlling for the pioneer "scientific" historians who claimed to make no assumptions. With few exceptions, our historians have not only not been very critically aware of their own presuppositions. They have had little independent interest in the philosophical currents or the winds of doctrine that have swept the American scene. When they have absorbed and expressed current attitudes, it has been largely without deliberate intent. The pioneers, carefully trained by their German teachers to eschew any "philosophy of history"—an ever-present temptation and snare in the German situation —found every interest of professional respectability reinforcing this scientific caution. It is rather remarkable that the long line of historical students exposed to the intellectual ferments of the German universities should have carried over so little of the philosophies they there heard expounded; a political thinker like Burgess stands out as a striking exception. It is still more remarkable, in view of the stirring developments in the social sciences in our country during the last two or three generations, that historians, again with outstanding exceptions like Robinson, should have been so slow to reflect these more homely intellectual issues so vigorously debated by the other students of man.

The great idea of evolution did indeed find many repercussions among the historians.[9] Yet even here it is hard to point to any historian before Robinson who made it really central in his work. John Fiske was as widely known for his popularization of the Spencerian version of evolution as for his later historical writing. His humanistic and religious reformulation of Spencer, so influential on the liberal theology of the last generation, is a landmark in American thought.[10] Yet it is difficult to discover much influence of his distinctive Spencerian views on his dramatic historical narratives. Of all American historians Henry Adams had the greatest interest in general ideas. His long search for "the law of history" began with the idea of evolution; in the 'seventies he prefaced his course on medieval history at Harvard with a study of primitive society. Then, unable to reconcile Grant's administration with a belief in cosmic progress, he became the leading philosophical heretic against the reigning religion of evolution. Yet his admirable political history antedated his most distinctive theoretical views, which have themselves remained without effect on historical writing. The great debate between "religion" and "science" did indeed

[9] Cf. Merle Curti, The Growth of American Thought (New York, 1943), 568f.
[10] Cf. Herbert W. Schneider, "The Influence of Darwin and Spencer on American Philosophical Theology," Journal of the History of Ideas, 6 (1945), 5, 10; Richard Hofstadter, Social Darwinism in American Thought, 1860–1915 (New York, 1944).

stimulate some notable historical works, like those of Draper, White, Lea, and Robinson. But the abundant American materials bearing on this issue have only begun to be exploited in the less heated atmosphere of our own generation.

Of course, those who have written American history without concern for the standards of the professional guild have never attempted to conceal their own assumptions and principles of selection. The earliest New England historians, like the Mathers, were convinced that events in the Holy Commonwealth revealed the guiding hand of Providence. They wrote in praise of God and Massachusetts, and their histories were designed to magnify both for their strong interest in each other. This Providential view persisted in the years of national self-glorification that followed the establishment of the Republic, though it was no longer the epic of Massachusetts, but the epic of America, that men now celebrated in their nationalistic histories. "God winnowed the nations of Europe and reserved this continent for his chosen people."

But when George Bancroft began his thrilling story in 1834, God had become a humanized and moralized Unitarian Deity whose main concern was to work out in America the culmination of secular political liberty. Bancroft can hardly be said to have brought back from Germany any one of those precisely elaborated philosophies of the *Zeitgeist* in which that generation of German thinkers were reformulating the doctrine of Providence. Göttingen, the university of the Prince Regent's province of Hanover, would hardly predispose a man toward the Hegelian glorification of the Prussian State. But Bancroft certainly did absorb the reigning theological idea of the immanence of God in the world and in human affairs, which made the whole of history the working out of a divine plan.

More significant, however, than the continuation of this Providential view in secularized and political form was Bancroft's conviction that God spoke with the voice of Jacksonian Democracy. The Divine Plan might have employed as its chosen instruments those brave refugees from tyranny and oppression who colonized the land; it might have culminated in the unique achievement of the Founding Fathers who brought forth the Constitution. But it now worked through a party program of organized democracy on which hung the world's hope of happiness. Richard Hildreth, Bancroft's chief rival as a nationalistic glorifier, viewed the American past rather with the eyes of an anti-Jeffersonian Federalist. Acceptance of the Providential view in no wise precluded a strong partisan bias: God was obviously on the side of sound politics.

In the next generation the terminology had changed. Providence was now dressed up as Evolution. But that inspiring idea, now happily enshrined in the very heart of the new science, still spoke in much the same accents of manifest destiny. Between the vaguely idealistic religious optimism of Bancroft and the vaguely religious evolutionary optimism of John Fiske, the difference is slight; each equally could glorify the heroes of the American past. But the horizons are now broader. Where Bancroft traced the epic of liberty in America from its Puritan sources, Fiske expanded it into an epic of the English-speaking peoples, an epic that began in the German forests, came down in unbroken continuity through the constitutional achievements of the British nation, and culminated in the complete working out of the spirit of 1688 in the American Revolution and the Constitution. Fiske does indeed strike a new note. His Spencerian evolution now definitely chooses the middle class as its instrument, and it is by their valiant efforts that the torch of liberty is handed on.

IV

It was against such a background of popular national feeling and self-esteem, reinforced by whatever rationalization of the guiding hand of God was in vogue, that the new professional historians had to vindicate their claim to scientific impartiality and academic standing. They faced two alternatives. They could radically transmute history into a sociological and evolutionary science, drawing their inspiration from Comte, Quételet and Marx, and from the sociology of Spencer and Taylor. The hope of formulating "the laws of history," in the ultimate interest of predicting the future, has fascinated a certain strain of American historians, from Buckle's disciple Draper down. The classic instance is found in Brooks and Henry Adams, who drew on thermodynamics to combat the prevailing gospel of biological "progress." In our own day a science of history has been sketched with much more sophistication by Teggart.

The other alternative was not to transform history into something else, but to investigate and write "history" itself by means of "scientific" methods. It was at this point that their German training and model proved decisive for American professional historians. Ranke and his expert disciples taught them how to be "scientific" without ceasing to be historical.[11] This meant not only the critical use of contemporary documents, henceforth established as the cornerstone of the historian's technique. To be "scientific" meant also to divest oneself of the "prejudices of the present," indeed, to eschew all attempts at generalization or interpretation, and to set forth "facts," to record

[11] Cf. Carl Becker, "Some Aspects of the Influence of Social Problems and Ideas upon the Study and Writing of History," *American Sociological Society Publications*, reprinted in *American Journal of Sociology*, 18 (1912–13), 641–675; esp. 657ff.

"exactly what happened" *wie es eigentlich gewesen ist*. It meant to take toward the historical "facts" the same objective and detached attitude of mind with which the scientist was supposed to regard natural phenomena.

Now, those scholars who during the 'thirties and 'forties were setting the course of German historical methods had made their own appeal to "facts" for somewhat different reasons, and in a rather different atmosphere, from the Americans of the 'eighties. They too were inspired by the professional aim of establishing history as a *Geisteswissenschaft* in the learned world. But they were also living in a generation facing grave political and constitutional questions. They were above all concerned with combating the French Revolutionary ideas of natural rights and natural law by an appeal to traditional German institutions. In seeking the "facts" of the German past they were in search of those political forms that might be gradually developed in the present, in contrast to all abstract speculations and universal principles. They were turning to German experience and German tradition and historic German rights—to "facts" as against "vain speculations." Hence even Ranke found his aim of objectivity in no conflict with the prevailing notion of a dominant *Zeitgeist*, and he could entertain enthusiasm for the development of the Prussian *Geist* from Luther to the Hohenzollerns.

In the German historians, objectivity and the appeal to facts were thus an instrument of German nationalism as well as of professional prestige, and throughout the century they could consequently both extend their critical and "scientific" methods and become increasingly nationalistic at one and the same time. For the Americans, "scientific" history was rather an escape from the prevalent exploitation of nationalistic prejudices into the exalted company of the pure scientists. For them, "facts" were not the revelation of a normative tradition of historic rights; they were not, as for Ranke, the exemplification of those great ideas whose conflict constitutes the meaning of history. Facts had become detached from any hypothesis or interpretation. Their chief claim to "scientific" importance was that they were beyond peradventure of doubt "so." In an extreme case, McMaster, "facts" were whatever happened to appear in the public press.[12] In general, "facts" were the single element in the historian's subject-matter that were indubitably "scientific." His techniques in laboriously establishing them were the one part of his procedure that could claim to be a "scientific method." Generalizations and "syntheses" could be admitted only if they forced themselves as the direct deliverance of "facts."

[12] *Cf.* Shryock, "American Historiography," 43.

This view, of course, involved the unquestioned acceptance of a definite philosophy of science and scientific method. It was the philosophy stamped on that generation by John Stuart Mill, whose *Logic* (1843) still served as the Bible of scientific method. Deriving his own ideas from Francis Bacon rather than from actual scientific procedure, Mill consciously rejected any "anticipation" of nature in the scientist's work. In his view, the scientist does not elaborate an hypothesis which he proceeds to test by comparing its consequences with relevant facts, selected for their bearing on that hypothesis. Rather, he arranges a large number of "facts" in tables in the hope that the Canons of Induction will enable him to see in those facts the connections that are there. The facts must be gathered first; the generalization will then emerge from their comparison. This "inductive" method was applied to history in the *Introduction to the Study of History* by Langlois and Seignobos, which H. B. Adams recommends as the best handbook for the historian. The analytic determination of the facts must precede any raising of the question of "synthesis."

This way of escaping all speculation, prejudice, and one-sidedness appealed strongly to the scientific historians. First you gathered all the available "facts"—presumably entered on index cards. Only then could you go on to undertake a "synthesis." Burgess well states this procedure:

> The University professor . . . must *construct* history out of the chaos of original historic atoms. . . .
>
> We seek to teach the student, first, how to get hold of a historic fact, how to distinguish fact from fiction, how to divest it as far as possible of coloring or exaggeration. We send him, therefore, to the most original sources attainable for his primary information. If there be more than one original source upon the same fact, we teach him to set these in comparison or contrast. . . . We undertake . . . to teach the student to set the facts which he has thus attained in their chronological order, to the further end of setting them in their order as cause and effect. And we seek to make him clearly comprehend and continually feel that the latter procedure is the one most delicate and critical which the historical student is called upon to undertake, in that he is continually tempted to account that which is mere antecedent and consequent as being cause and effect. . . .
>
> After the facts have been determined and the causal *nexus* established we endeavor to teach the student to look for the *institutions and ideas* which have been developed through the sequence of events in the civilization of an age or people.[13]

[13] John W. Burgess, "The Methods of Historical Study and Research in Columbia College," *Methods of Teaching and Studying History*, ed. G. Stanley Hall (2nd ed., Boston, 1885), 218–220.

In the light of any present day analysis of scientific methods, it can only be said that if this is indeed the proper procedure in historical investigation, history is the only field of knowledge in which such a pure inductive method without hypotheses or guiding principles obtains. Yet in the eighteen-eighties this seemed the very essence of scientific procedure.

Into the set of assumptions that governed the work of the new professional historians there thus went the conviction, reinforced by the reigning "inductive" theory of scientific method, that any principle of interpretation would lead away from "facts" to speculation, and eventually to a "philosophy of history." This devotion to "the fact," combined with the strong professional sense of having painfully staked out a "field" of their own, now under attack, is perhaps most revealingly expressed in a paper by George Burton Adams, written in 1909 when critical voices were already making themselves heard.[14] Adams distinguishes between the "scientific" study of history, and the science or philosophy of history which seeks "laws."

> It is one thing to raise the question, Is human action dominated by law, and can we by discovering those laws construct a science of history, in the sense in which there exists a science of chemistry? It is quite a different thing to ask, Can methods of investigation which are strictly scientific be applied to the study of the past action of the race in such a way as to give our knowledge of what happened greater certainty? The school of Ranke has never endeavored to go beyond this last question, but their answer to it has been a clear and, I believe, an indisputable affirmative. The actual result has been a science of investigation, and a method of training the future historian, which it is not too much to say, have taken complete possession of the world of historical scholarship. At any rate it is true that all technically trained historians for more than fifty years have been trained according to these ideas and they have all found it exceedingly difficult to free themselves from the fundamental principle of their school that the first duty of the historian is to ascertain as nearly as possible and to record exactly what happened.[15]

Adams goes on to complain of the "attacks" made upon such scientific history by parvenus encroaching upon its "field," who dare to use principles of interpretation, and actually want conclusions from its "facts."

> During the last four decades of that century, and especially during its last quarter, there arose a variety of new interests, new

[14] George Burton Adams, "History and the Philosophy of History," *American Historical Review*, 14 (1909), 221–236.
[15] *Ibid.*, 223.

groups of scholars formed themselves, new points of view were occupied, new methods were loudly proclaimed, new sciences were born and named, all concerned with the same facts of the past which it is our business to study. So closely are these new interests related to us, and to one another, in the common body of materials which we must all use, that we are tempted to call them off-shoots of history. . . . but the statement . . . would be neither historically nor logically correct. Certainly their attitude towards traditional history has not been that of dutiful children towards a parent. So uniformly and severely critical have they been of the methods and purposes of the political historian, if we may use that term as a means of differentiation for the historian by name and profession, that we may almost regard their rise as an attack upon our position, systematic and concerted, and from various points at once. This is hardly the literal truth and yet it behooves us to understand clearly that after three-quarters of a century of practically undisputed possession of our great field of study, during which the achievements of the political historian have won the admiration and applause of the world, our right to the field is now called in question, our methods, our results and our ideals are assailed, and we are being thrown upon the defensive at many points.[16]

Adams lists five principal lines of "attack." There is political science: "in many of its members the tendency is strong to assume that the chief end to be served by the historian is to furnish material for their science." There is the geographers' "movement," "somewhat more aggressive in spirit." There is the drive to give economic explanations: "We do not count the economic historian proper among those who would drive us from the field." But "there is a great difference between economic history and that which calls itself the economic interpretation of history." Finally, there are sociology and social psychology. All five have for their main endeavor "to construct a science or a philosophy of history." [17]

"Are we passing from an age of investigation to an age of speculation?" Adams asks. "There are I think on all sides, in many ways, signs that this may very possibly be the case."

For more than fifty years the historian has had possession of the field and has deemed it his sufficient mission to determine what the fact was, including the immediate conditions which gave it shape. Now he finds himself confronted with numerous groups of aggressive and confident workers in the same field who ask not what was the fact—many of them seem to be comparatively little interested in that—but their constant question is what is the ulti-

[16] *Ibid.*, 224.
[17] *Ibid.*, 226.

mate explanation of history, or, more modestly, what are the forces which determine human events and according to what laws do they act? [18]

Adams can only exhort the scientific historian to preserve the faith:

> What should the historian do in view of the threatened invasion of his domain by ideals and methods not quite his own? . . . To those whose methods of work are fixed. . . . I must have one word of comfort. It is this. All science which is true science must rest upon the proved and correlated fact. . . . At the very beginning of all conquest of the unknown lies the fact, established and classified, to the fullest extent possible at the moment.[19]

V

This devotion to "the fact," to objectivity and to Mill's theory of induction, did not actually prevent the early "scientific" professional historians from making certain important assumptions which exerted a controlling influence on their work. First, they had a definite principle of selection: "history" was for them not only political history, it was, in its technical and scientific phases, legal and constitutional history, with a strong emphasis on the development of local institutions. Secondly, they were greatly impressed by the persisting continuity of political institutions, and traced the "germ" of the later developments of American liberty and order back through English forms to the primitive German forests. Both H. B. Adams and Burgess were as deeply committed to this Teutonic origin hypothesis as more popular writers like Fiske. Thirdly, and bound up with this principle of continuity, they were addicted to the "comparative method," with all its dubious assumptions about a unilinear evolutionary development. In view of these three controlling presuppositions alone, it is difficult to take seriously protests like those of G. B. Adams against the use of other and more adequate hypotheses.

All three of these major assumptions the Americans took over in professional emulation of their German teachers and of the English models that so impressed them. But the first, their concentration on political development, was for them, too, closely bound up with the characteristic problems faced in the mid-nineteenth century. Over the library of the historical seminar at Johns Hopkins was inscribed the motto from Freeman: "History is past politics; politics is present history." But Adams himself, like Burgess, interpreted this to mean the kind of constitutional and legal history practiced by Bluntschli and his other teachers at Heidelberg, and by Stubbs and Maine in Eng-

---

[18] *Ibid.*, 229.
[19] *Ibid.*, 235–236.

land. "I have no ambition to be known as a Professor of American History," he wrote President Gilman. "I do not object to the phrase 'Institutional History,' for that describes very happily the nature of my university work in class and seminary." Burgess, whose controlling interest was to develop American political science on the German model, likewise made institutional development the center of his attention in history. "This I might term the ultimate object of our entire method of historical instruction. With us history is the chief preparation for the student of the legal and political sciences." [20]

Ultimately, both the Germans and the Englishmen whom these Americans were following were selecting from the past what would throw light on the pressing problems of nineteenth-century constitutional development with which they were themselves vitally concerned. Adams' teacher Bluntschli, under whom he completed a course and took his degree in historical and political science in 1876, and who, we are told, exercised the strongest influence on his growing mind,[21] was a leader among the German liberals. For him history was always the handmaid of politics. His interest in the development of local institutions of self-government was focused on expanding them into a liberal federal constitution for a united Germany. Stubbs, Maitland and Maine were likewise facing very practical problems of legal and constitutional adjustment. In America, too, for the generation of Adams and Burgess, living in the aftermath of the Civil War, the political unification and consolidation of more local communities still seemed the central American problem. The historical profession, in fact, came into existence, in this country as earlier in Germany, as an integral part of the first serious training in political science. Its founders cultivated "past politics" in this institutional sense precisely because such "political" problems were those of which they were most acutely aware.

Even as late as 1910 Becker could write: "Since the importance of intellectual and religious development has been comparatively slight, apparently at least, historians, in abandoning the purely political point of view, have limited themselves for the most part to exhibiting the influence of economic and social conditions upon political history. For this purpose, American history presented exceptional opportunities, especially in respect of the Colonial period and the period from 1815 to 1860." [22] When economic factors were introduced, they were brought in, as in Beard's early work, not as themselves central, but for

---

[20] Burgess, "The Methods of Historical Study and Research in Columbia College," *op. cit.*, 220.

[21] John M. Vincent, *Herbert B. Adams, Tributes of Friends* (Baltimore, 1902), 39.

[22] Carl Becker, "Some Aspects . . ." *American Journal of Sociology*, 18 (1912–13), 653.

the light they could throw on institutional changes. Thus Burgess' student Osgood, who developed such institutional history most completely, and who was for his time unusually sensitive to the importance of its economic conditions, in 1898 defended the older political emphasis: "The political and constitutional side of the subject, it seems to me, should be given the first place, because it is only through law and political institutions that social forces become in a large sense operative. The directions which these forces take are also largely determined by the political framework within which they act." [23]

During the depression of the 'thirties many Americans came to feel that it was economic rather than political problems that were of primary importance. With the situation Becker described in 1910, just before the full swing to the economic interpretation of politics set in, we have only to compare a book like Louis M. Hacker's *Triumph of American Capitalism*, in which political events appear as the symptoms of fundamental economic changes, to realize the complete shift of incidence. And though interest in American intellectual history, awakened by Tyler, had been growing steadily since Parrington's impressive work—Becker's remark sounds curiously remote today—it took the great ideological conflicts so sharply raised during the last decade to give us histories of American thought like those by Ralph H. Gabriel, Merle Curti, and R. B. Perry.

How the crucial problems later shifted to economics and to ideas is clear enough. What is harder to realize is that the pioneer "scientific" historians were equally concerned with what they saw as the crucial problems of their own day, and that it was these problems that determined their selection of "political" material in the past. Just what that selection was, and the professional influences that played upon him, H. B. Adams has himself set down in a revealing passage.

> The idea of studying American Institutional and American Economic History, upon co-operative principles, beginning with local institutions, and extending ultimately to national institutions, developed gradually from an interest in municipal history, first awakened in the Seminary of Prof. Erdmannsdoerffer at the University of Heidelberg, where, in 1875, while reading the *Gesta Friderici Imperatoris*, by Otto of Freising, seminary discussion turned upon the Communes of Lombardy and the question of Roman or Germanic origin of city government in medieval Italy. This awakened interest, quickened by the reading of Carl Hegel, Arnold, Von Maurer, Fustel de Coulanges, was ultimately directed toward England and New England by a suggestion upon the last page of Sir Henry Maine's *Village Communities*, where, quoting Palfrey's *History of New England* (II, 13, 14) and certain

[23] Cited in D. R. Fox, *Herbert Levi Osgood* (New York, 1924), 86.

remarks in the *Nation* (No. 273) upon the passage by Professor
William F. Allen of the University of Wisconsin, Sir Henry calls
attention to the survival of Village Communities in America.
This suggestive idea, verified in all essential details with reference
to Nantucket, Plymouth Plantations, Cape Ann, Salem, and the
oldest towns in New England, has been extended gradually to a
co-operative study of American local institutions in all the older
States and throughout the Northwest, where, in Wisconsin, Professor Allen, the original pioneer, had joined in the work, supported by his Seminary of advanced students.[24]

Here we see clearly how the selective interests developed by Germans and Englishmen to bring their medieval past to bear on their
contemporary problems were turned by Adams to American political
concerns. After his return to the United States Adams is said never to
have opened his German notebooks.[25] He trusted his students to apply
critical methods to American materials; from the beginning he encouraged Turner's interests. Unlike Burgess, he did not insist that they
complete their real education in Germany. It is interesting that the
original impetus to colonial history, in which the "scientific" historians
did their most impressive work, came from that sturdy enthusiast for
the Northwest, William Allen of Wisconsin, where Turner also
carried on the war against the dominance of the historians of the
seaboard.

In the 'seventies and 'eighties the two other major assumptions of
the "scientific" historians, the Teutonic "germ" theory of political
institutions and the comparative method, went hand in hand in this
country. Both were vigorously advocated and taught by H. B. Adams
and Burgess alike. During the 'nineties, however, their students
pushed both into the background; and even the comparative method,
which lasted the longer, is little heard of after 1900. Adams' able pupil,
C. M. Andrews, as early as 1893, while still defending a qualified comparative method, summarizes the evidence against the Teutonic
theory, in what is probably the most competent early discussion. He
had criticized Adams' Teutonism severely as far back as 1883, as had
Osgood also.

The Teutonic theory originated amongst the leaders of the German
national revival, Grimm, Eichhorn, and Savigny. Carried to England
by Palgrave and Kemble, it was there used to fan the self-esteem of

---

[24] H. B. Adams, "Co-operation in University Work," *Johns Hopkins University
Studies in History and Political Science*, 1 (Baltimore, 1883), 80, 81. In a briefer account in *Contributions to American Educational History*, No. 1 (Washington, Bureau
of Education, 1887), 173, Adams mentions also "the Harvard School of Anglo-Saxon
law," referring to a volume of studies by Henry Adams' students, *Essays in Anglo-
Saxon Law* (Boston, 1876).

[25] Albion W. Small, *Origins of Sociology* (Chicago, 1924), 328 note.

the "Anglo-Saxon race," not only by popular writers like Charles Kingsley, but by historians like Freeman, and was even adopted by the more cautious Stubbs and Green. But with Americans of the eighteen-eighties it hardly bore the same "racial" stamp, though it lent itself to a scholarly version of American political superiority.[26] By them it was accepted, together with the comparative method, primarily as part of the body of evolutionary ideas they found their teachers applying to social development. It was the continuity of political institutions, and the cultural heritage the colonies received from England, rather than any "racial" theory, that impressed them as being in line with evolutionary thought. The biological continuity was incidental, and the term "race" was very loosely used, even in a man like Moses Coit Tyler. Adams is revealing:

> The science of Biology no longer favors the theory of spontaneous generation. Wherever organic life occurs, there must have been some seed for that life. History should not be content with describing effects when it can explain causes. It is just as improbable that free local institutions should spring up without a germ along American shores as that English wheat should have grown here without planting. Town institutions were propagated in New England by old English and Germanic ideas brought over by Pilgrims and Puritans.[27]

The biological analogy is significant; but even more significant is Adams' real point, the cultural continuity with England. This does not prevent him from going on: "Thus, English historians, Green, Freeman, and Stubbs, recognize their fatherland. The origin of the English Constitution, as Montesquieu long ago declared, is found in the forests of Germany." [28]

More important and lasting was the comparative method, which came not only with the authority of the philologists and the legal historians, but also bearing all the promise of the new evolutionary anthropology of Tylor and Spencer. As Andrews explained in 1893, "The philologists were its sponsors, Grimm and Maurer used it in Germany, Kemble brought it to England, and Sir Henry Maine applied it and extended it from a local to a universal method." [29]

> As the study of anthropology continues, it becomes apparent that the people of this earth are not to each other as though they

---

[26] See Edward Norman Saveth, "Race and Nationalism in American Historiography: the late Nineteenth Century," *Political Scinece Quarterly*, 54 (1939), 421–441.

[27] H. B. Adams, "Germanic Origins of New England Towns," *Johns Hopkins University Studies in History and Political Science*, 1 (Baltimore, 1883), 8.

[28] *Ibid.*, 10.

[29] Charles M. Andrews, "Some Recent Aspects of Institutional Study," *Yale Review*, (1892–93), 384.

were inhabitants of different planets; that following the general lines of historical advancement, these people have developed from tribal life to political life in much the same manner; that the stages in their growth have had, from the necessities of the case, certain points of similarity, in consequence of which certain principles of development can be established; which, it is inherently probable, will apply to all peoples when they have reached a similar stage in social and political growth. We must, therefore, compare not anything and everything, but only that evidence which, so far as it can be determined, belongs to corresponding periods in the life of a people, and which alone we have an historical right to compare.[30]

The assumptions involved in the comparative method are here clearly stated. Everywhere society was supposed to have followed the same fixed line of development, and to have passed through the same "stages," from a primitive communism and promiscuity to the "higher" forms of present-day Western civilization. Illustrations of this unilinear pattern could hence be drawn from anywhere, and, torn out of context, fitted into the neat scheme. Little attention was paid to the means whereby these changes were effected; they came "by evolution." Burgess states the essence of the method as applied to institutional development:

> What we most insist upon, however, is a critical comparison of the sequence of facts in the history of different states or peoples at a like period in the development of their civilizations. If this be done with patience, care, and judgment, the student who possesses a moderate degree of true logic will soon learn to distinguish, to some extent at least, antecedent and consequent from cause and effect.[31]

By 1893 Andrews is already qualifying the comparative method, in the light of the criticisms of Fustel de Coulanges, Seebohm, and Vinogradoff—who were at the same time the major instruments in effecting the overthrow of the Teutonic theory.

> Every people [says the comparative method] of whom we have sufficient knowledge to determine the fact, has passed or is passing through certain stages of institutional and social development. . . . But all people will not develop wholly alike; everywhere will there be seen local and racial divergencies from any common type. Inherent ethnological traits, climate, geographical location, adjacency to certain forms of animal life, completeness of commercial relations, attrition of nations and many other influences, will

---

[30] *Ibid.*, 385.
[31] Burgess, "The Methods of Historical Study and Research in Columbia College," *op. cit.*, 220.

bring about marked social and political peculiarities, out of which
has sprung that peculiar people's contributions to the civilization
of the world.[32]

And he goes on to ask that historians correct "the natural tendency
of the older method to conceive of all phases of social, economic, and
political life as merely evolutions of something which has gone before. For there is at present a too general willingness to eliminate
the influence of extraneous factors, and an unwillingness to allow for
direct personal or legislative interference in originating or altering a
phase of institutional life." [33]

The Teutonic germ theory was a developmental hypothesis, the
comparative method was a procedural postulate. Both have been long
since abandoned. More significantly, from the point of view of the
claims of the "scientific" historians, neither could remotely be said to
have been implicit in "the facts" they were actually used to "antici-
pate." Each had been developed in Europe as a tool to deal with
certain problems; both were applied in America to a quite different set
of problems. More broadly, they were both part of that body of ideas
by which nineteenth-century thinkers supposed they were applying
"the principles of the evolutionary philosophy" to social development.
As the latest fashion in scientific theory, they were eminently suited
to establish the historical profession on a basis of intellectual respectability. And in the long list of scholarly monographs that began to
appear at Johns Hopkins and Columbia, among the best of which was
the *Introduction to the Local Constitutional History of the United
States* (1889) by Adams' student, George Elliott Howard, they proved
their value as leading principles of historical investigation. That they
were superseded by more adequate and fruitful hypotheses in the next
generation goes only to show that like any heuristic principle they led
to the discovery of facts which forced their own modification. They
were instruments by which that evolutionary generation sought to
understand the past of the problems that concerned it. In the light of
their many virtues, there is irony in the fact that the one function they
clearly did not and could not serve was that of depicting the past *wie
es eigentlich gewesen.*

An excellent summary of almost all the ideas that dominated the
first decades of critical, "objective" and "scientific" history—that is, of
its assumptions and presuppositions here analyzed—is to be found in
the list of "Fundamental Principles of American History" which Albert Bushnell Hart wished "to leave sharply defined in the minds of
the students."

---

[32] *Op cit.*, 388, 389.
[33] *Ibid.*, 400.

1. No nation has a *history disconnected* from that of the rest
of the world: the United States is closely related, in point of time,
with previous ages; in point of space, with other civilized countries.

2. *Institutions* are a *growth*, and not a creation: the Constitution of the United States itself is constantly changing with the
changes in public opinion.

3. Our institutions are *Teutonic in origin*; they have come to
us through English institutions.

4. The growth of our institutions has been *from local to central*: the general government can, therefore, be understood only
in the light of the early history of the country.

5. The *principle of union* is of slow growth in America: the
Constitution was framed from necessity, and not from preference.[34]

VI

The greatest achievements of the methods of the pioneer "scientific" historians, and the clearest illustrations of whither their aims and
assumptions could lead, are the monumental studies of colonial institutions produced by Herbert L. Osgood, student and colleague of
Burgess, and by Charles M. Andrews, trained under H. B. Adams.
Here if anywhere is unadulterated devotion to "the fact," especially in
Osgood's crammed pages. And here is the cardinal instance of what
can be done even if, in accordance with their principle of selection,
the "historical fact" be limited to the development of local legal and
political institutions. Here is the true American fruit of Bluntschli and
Stubbs and Maitland and Maine. Here is the "comparative method"
transformed from a speculative evolutionary hypothesis into a factual
comparison of the different British colonies. Neither Osgood nor
Andrews ever accepted the Teutonic theory. But its core, the basic
continuity between English and Colonial institutions, is the controlling assumption of both. Osgood sees English law, administration and
imperial policy as the foundation of the colonies, which were a natural
outgrowth of the history of England during the middle ages, and preserved their institutional and organic connection; their history is
concerned largely with certain medieval survivals. This is the one
"correct general idea" Osgood makes central. The whole struggle
culminating in the Revolution was but an episode in the development
of the English colonial system.[35]

Andrews likewise made central the colonial and British character of
the colonies. "The colonial period of our history is not American only

---

[34] A. B. Hart, "Methods of Teaching American History," *Methods of Teaching and
Studying History*, ed. G. Stanley Hall, 3.

[35] *Bulletin* of the Columbia Department of History (1896), quoted in D. R. Fox,
Herbert Levi Osgood (New York, 1924), 71–73.

but Anglo-American"—"The years from 1607 to 1783 were colonial before they were American or national, and our Revolution is a colonial and not an American problem." This controlling assumption runs through all his volumes; he always insists that colonial history must be approached from the "English end." His magnum opus, not published until the nineteen-thirties, seems particularly conservative because of this thoroughgoing emphasis on the earlier evolutionary idea of continuity, in contrast to the idea of the "mutations wrought by environment" in America which the influence of Turner had made central.

Osgood originally had broad interests in economic history: he had studied under Schmoller and Adolf Wagner. But his position was cautious: "Social and economic forces should be treated as contributing to and conditioning historical development, but the historian must never lose sight of the fact that they operate within a framework of law." [36] In reviewing Osgood's posthumous work, Andrews took him to task for his neglect of economic forces:

> To pay almost exclusive attention to politics, government, and administration and to pass by with only an occasional reference all consideration of economic and social forces, the significance of rising prices, debt, and the cost of living, the growth of regional and radical feeling, and the bearing of commerce and the increase of wealth on legislation is to run at times pretty near the surface and to miss some of the deeper currents of colonial life. . . .
>
> Professor Osgood's position of viewing all details of his subject from the standpoint of the colonies tends to create in him a disrelish—I would not call it a prejudice—for the British system and all who upheld it, and to make it difficult for him to understand just what was the British outlook before 1763.[37]

On Andrews' charge of anti-British prejudice, it is interesting to read what Osgood himself said of Fiske:

> Two political societies of quite different type were thus brought into conflict, and to the reviewer it seems clear that the historian is bound to do justice to the character and aims of both. . . . The truth is until American historians cease the attempt to defend a dogma, and begin in earnest the effort to understand the aristocratic society which existed in England and the democracy which was maturing here, and the causes of the conflict between the two, we shall not have a satisfactory history either of the colonial period or of the revolution.[38]

[36] *Ibid.*, 70.
[37] C. M. Andrews, review of Osgood in *American Historical Review*, 31 (1925–26), 536, 537.
[38] Review of Fiske's *American Revolution* (1891), cited in Fox, *op. cit.*, 50f.

Thus does the impartial objectivity of one generation become the biased prejudice of the next.

To complete the story, let us compare this judgment of Andrews on Osgood with the judgment passed in the next decade by a frank employer of methods of economic interpretation on Andrews himself:

> It must be concluded that his history is animated by a conservative spirit. His legalistic approach, his preoccupation with the legal foundation of property rights, and his emphasis upon the role of leaders in colonial history (particularly those of the English upper and upper middle classes) suggests such a conclusion. He assumes that legal and political institutions are the most important elements in the internal history of the colonies, assigning to economic factors a minor role. . . .
>
> In treating colonial economy he is content merely to describe a few products and activities without probing into the workings of economic forces, without considering wages, prices, profits, creditor-debtor relationships, and the distribution of income and wealth, and without showing the impact of such factors on law, government, and policy. Without mentioning the productive labor of the servants in New England he describes them as an undesirable, immoral element. . . .
>
> In brief, Professor Andrews has written the history of the legal foundations of colonial government and property rights.[39]

As Professor Nettels points out, "Professor Andrews certainly does not belong to that group of historians who regard themselves as judicial because they refrain from judging." Andrews did not in fact claim to be "objective": "Complete objectivity would be as undesirable as it would be impossible." Yet he also maintained: "Objective history is merely nonpartisan history. To write objectively is merely to write with the detachment of the onlooker rather than with the prejudice of the advocate and to draw conclusions from the evidence itself and not from prepossessions already existing in the writer's mind. History viewed through Whig or Tory spectacles . . . and used to defend a doctrine, a theory, or a philosophy—all such history is a bad guide for the public because it does not tell the truth." [40] Professor Nettels is probably right in suggesting that if ever an historian looked at the past through Tory spectacles, it was Andrews. His whole work is colored by his defense of the British mercantilist policy and by his contempt for the American "radicals" and for the lower classes in general.

In Andrews the "scientific" institutional school had completed the

[39] Curtis Nettels, review in *New England Quarterly*, 10 (1937), 793–795.
[40] C. M. Andrews, "These Forty Years," *American Historical Review*, 30 (1924–25), 243, 244.

circle. The profession was now so firmly rooted that an historian could afford to give rein to his "strong convictions," and in the process bring out more significant facts than the pure devotees of "the fact." For the moral of the judgments passed by Osgood on Fiske, by Andrews on Osgood, and by Nettels on Andrews, is not only that ways of understanding the past change, and that therefore the historian does not "tell the truth." It is also that in seeking "the truth" in his own way, and in terms of his own assumptions and presuppositions, the historian does manage to add significantly to that store of knowledge we possess about the past.

VII

The first major break with these ideas of the early "scientific" historians came with Frederick Jackson Turner. His paper, "The Significance of the Frontier in American History," read at Chicago in 1893, was, in the words of Beard, "destined to have a more profound influence on thought about American history than any other essay or volume ever written on the subject." [41] Turner is conventionally identified, much too narrowly, of course, with this frontier hypothesis. Actually, he had an extremely broad conception of history, and of the various approaches and hypotheses by which the past might be illuminated. Although he did not himself follow them all up, there is hardly a way of exploring and interpreting the American past employed by later historians that is not suggested in his writings. And from the first he was clear upon the role of interpretative hypotheses in historical investigation.

Superficially, Turner's great influence came from the fact that he had delivered for American history a Declaration of Independence from the domination of the seaboard historians and their problems of colonial "origins." He broadened its central theme into the building of a continental nation. He encouraged a host of writings on the various phases of American internal expansion, and on the conflicts of the democratic agrarian freehold economy with its rivals in the East and South. Many of his disciples had much narrower perspectives than Turner himself, and went further in identifying a distinctive American "democracy" with the crudities of frontier life—although he cannot be wholly absolved from responsibility for the loose and superficial dilution of the "democratic idea" to cover anything and everything.

More significant in the long run in changing concepts of historical method was the very fact that Turner had dared to advance explicitly

[41] Beard, "The Frontier in American History," *loc. cit.*, 359.

not only a new principle of selection, but also a full-fledged hypothesis to guide the investigation and interpretation of historical facts. And he went on to a second, the importance of sectionalism in American life, conceived in intellectual and cultural as well as in economic terms. This hypothesis of the divergent and conflicting interests and ideas of different economic and cultural "sections" or regions has entered deeply into all later investigation of our history. It has colored and cut across even the class-conflict theory of the Marxian 'thirties, and has given a distinctive American stamp to all serious economic interpretations of our national life. Perhaps most important of all, Turner's economic sectionalism for the first time made such economic interpretation respectable.[42]

Finally, in identifying what was distinctively American with the "democracy" of the freeholding frontier, Turner was fully aware that he was making central, for understanding the past as well as for acting in the present, the new problems that had succeeded the earlier ones that still dominated the schools of Adams and Burgess. The issue of national unification had in fact given way to the struggle between the agrarian interests of the Populists and early Progressives against Eastern capitalism. The epic of the slow building of a federal structure out of local institutions now in Turner likewise gave way to the epic conflict between Jeffersonian and Hamiltonian principles. For those who understood the significance of Turner, "detachment" and sheer worship of "the fact" were over. One might not be committed, like Turner, to the agrarian cause. One might not even distinguish the protagonists in the struggle quite as simply as he did. But one could not fail to perceive the illumination that came from reading it in the light of present problems. It would still take several decades to overcome the institutionalized inertia of the profession. But for those who grasped Turner, the battle was over. Principles of interpretation were fruitful, and they were most fruitful when related to continuing problems.

In actual fact, of course, Turner was not for the first time introducing assumptions into "scientific" history. He was making explicit the assumptions already there. And he was doing it, not by opposing those presuppositions radically, but rather by modifying them in detail. Thus, he did not challenge the accepted principle that the central concern of the historian should be the development of American political institutions. Rather, he viewed those institutions in a new light, as the democracy of the frontier; he turned to the interplay of forces that constituted the history of that development.

Turner had had many discussions at Johns Hopkins with Woodrow

[42] Cf. Beard's, An Economic Interpretation of the Constitution of the United States, 5.

Wilson as to what constitutes the distinctive basis of American nationalism.

> Thus the advance of the frontier has meant a steady movement away from the influence of Europe, a steady growth of independence on American lines. And to study this advance, the men who grew up under these conditions, and the political, economic, and social results of it, is to study the really American part of our history.[43]

Here too, in transforming the national epic into the history of the shifting West, Turner was actually doing just about what the Easterners had long been doing for their own sections. He was as much if not more of a nationalist than they. He often went as far in identifying Middle-Western with American institutions and attitudes as his teacher William F. Allen, who had a fine enthusiasm for the North-West as the key to the "imperial destiny of the United States," and to its national policy.[44]

This side of Turner has recently come in for a good deal of criticism by Easterners, who speak of the "intra-United States tendency" of Turnerian study, and even of his "isolationism." [45] But two years before his Chicago address, in 1891, Turner himself had written:

> Not only is it true that no country can be understood without taking account of all the past; it is also true that we cannot select a stretch of land and say we will limit our study to this land; for local history can only be understood in the light of the history of the world. There is unity as well as continuity.[46]

Thus from the beginning Turner viewed the development of distinctively American institutions as an extension and modification of the history of Western civilization, though the concern with the American phase gradually came to overshadow for him the larger whole within which it orginally had its setting.

Moreover, Turner was as much of a social evolutionist as the other historians of the 'eighties, and even more anxious to make use of biological concepts. But, uninfluenced by the idealistic evolutionary thought of the Germans, he was closer to Darwinian ideas of variation under different conditions. Where those who had studied in Germany, following the European lead, had emphasized the side of continuity

---

[43] *Early Writings of Frederick Jackson Turner* (Madison, 1938), 189.

[44] William Francis Allen, "Place of the North-West in General History" (1888), William Francis Allen, *Monographs and Essays* (Boston, 1890), 110–111.

[45] *Cf.* G. W. Pierson, *Pennsylvania Magazine of History and Biography*, 64 (1940), 449ff., and *New England Quarterly*, 15 (1942), 224ff. Pierson gives credit to Richard H. Shryock and Dixon Ryan Fox.

[46] "The Significance of History," *Early Writings*, 57.

with remote "origins," he brought to the fore the modifying influence of the new American environment, its function in selecting and adapting new forms, new institutions, new patterns of thought.

> The outcome is not the old Europe, not simply the development of Germanic germs, any more than the first phenomenon was a case of reversion to the Germanic mark. The fact is, that here is a new product that is American. . . . The existence of an area of free land, its continuous recession, and the advance of American settlement westward, explain American development. . . . American democracy is fundamentally the outcome of the experience of the American people in dealing with the West.[47]

Turner seems to have derived his evolutionary ideas more from Darwin than from Spencer: his references to biological theory are direct. But he expanded his evolutionary environmentalism in the direction of the sociologists who were emphasizing geographical influences. He owed something to Buckle, and more to Ratzel and Albion Small; [48] he was early struck by Josiah Royce's study of California as a distinctive "province." There is much in his conception of a "section" that resembles the "region" of the sociologist and the "culture area" of the anthropologist. The firm hold the sectional theory came to obtain was undoubtedly strengthened by its congeniality with that type of thought. Turner himself apparently worked out the idea in relative independence. But his historical hypothesis was part of a broad movement toward environmentalism in all the evolutionary social sciences, which developed in criticism of the overemphasis on continuity and origins in the generation of Spencer and Tylor.

Turner was no narrow geographical determinist. He specifically denied that any single factor is determinative, or absolutely dictates to man, and he advocated a "multiple hypothesis" scheme of historical interpretation, providing room for "stock," inherited ideals, and spiritual factors.[49] Indeed, his contention was that the conditions of the frontier, on the "hither edge of free land," did not force any particular institutions on men. They rather freed men from the compulsions of habit and law, and made it possible for them to work out new experiments in institutional forms. The frontier was not coercive but emancipating, not a limit to be accepted but a challenge to be faced actively. Turner's social evolutionism saw no automatic process,

[47] Frederick Jackson Turner, The Frontier in American History (New York, 1920), 4, 1, 266. Cf. Merle Curti, "The Section and the Frontier in American History: the Methodological Concepts of F. J. Turner," Methods in Social Science, ed. S. A. Rice (Chicago, 1931).

[48] Fulmer Mood, "Turner's Formative Period," Early Writings, 3ff.

[49] But cf. Shryock, "American Historiography," 37, 38.

coming either from a growing "germ" in continuous development or from the pressure of an external environment. He had freed himself both from the evolving *Geist* of the Germans, and from the mechanical progress of the Spencerian sociologists. He was working his way toward that humanistic, experimental, and pragmatic conception of social evolution as the human use of natural conditions and materials, which came to the fore in American social thought around 1910, to find its philosophic formulation in John Dewey, and its exemplification among historians in Carl Becker and Charles Beard.

From the beginning Turner was conscious of the relation between his hypotheses for interpreting the past and the new problems he faced as a Wisconsin Progressive. He made his functional conception of history clear in his early essay of 1891 on "The Significance of History."

> The historical study of the first half of the nineteenth century reflected the thought of that age. It was an age of political agitation and inquiry, as our own age still so largely is. It was an age of science. That inductive study of phenomena which has worked a revolution in our knowledge of the external world was applied to history. In a world, the study of history became scientific and political.
>
> Today the questions that are uppermost, and that will become increasingly important, are not so much political as economic questions. The age of machinery, of the factory system, is also the age of socialistic inquiry. . . .
>
> Each age tries to form its own conception of the past. *Each age writes the history of the past anew with reference to the conditions uppermost in its own time.* . . . 'The whole mode and manner of looking at things alters with every age,' but this does not mean that the real events of a given age change; it means that our comprehension of these facts changes.[50]

In his presidential address to the American Historical Association in 1910, in the midst of the struggle between the Progressives and the Old Guard, he emphasized the close relation between his way of understanding the past and the political struggles among conflicting economic interests central in his own day: "There is disclosed by present events a new significance to these contests of radical democracy and conservative interests." [51] The whole long history of American development was thus brought to a focus in the issues of 1910, and illuminated by them.

This functional conception of the historian's principles of interpre-

[50] *Early Writings*, 51, 52.
[51] "Social Forces in American History," *Frontier in American History*, 328.

tation, so clearly entertained by Turner and applied in his own distinctive hypotheses, led far beyond the particular struggles of the Progressive era in terms of which he himself read the American past. As the crucial issues themselves deepened with growing industrialization, it demanded the further elaboration of those hypotheses. In effecting such an extension, subsequent historians were remaining true to Turner's spirit, however far they might depart from his letter. In 1910 it was natural, and still possible to identify the spearhead of "radical democracy" with the Middle-Western heirs of the old frontier. Another decade, of Wilson and of war, broadened the contest to include as a central protagonist the working class of the great industrial cities. Turner's agrarian perspective began to seem too narrow. Historians like Beard, who had started with an economic regionalism close to Turner's, were led to emphasize the past role of other factors and other economic interests which Turner had neglected but whose historical importance now stood revealed. As the basis and the very texture of American democratic programs shifted more and more to the demands of the urban industrial classes, there stood out in sharper relief the significance, in past conflicts also, of the democratic impulses of Eastern idealism, and of the long story of labor organization.

Thus Turner's own principles pointed to that very extension and supplementation of his particular limited hypotheses which has formed the main task of more recent historical interpretation. With the shifting and broadened incidence of the major economic conflict, Turner's championship of the Middle West and of frontier agrarian democracy came to be balanced by a juster recognition of the importance, in the complex interplay of forces in American history, of other sections and of other economic groups.

During the 'twenties this more adequate and less simplified version of economic sectionalism was still carried on within the framework set by Turner's assumption of the distinctively American character of American history. American problems continued to dominate the historian, and he plunged into an eager investigation of the background of the struggle of competing ideas and economic interests on the contemporary scene. For the great majority this concentration on rather narrowly national issues was even intensified by the depression of the 'thirties. Most historians then reflected the widespread desire to find somewhere in the American past a distinctively American answer to all our economic difficulties. Those who did look beyond the seas turned back in alarm, convinced that our country must be different, and must be kept unique. Turnerian nationalism, conceived primarily in economic terms, but now with a new ideological emphasis on "the American way," seemed everywhere in the ascendant.

To be sure, the 'thirties also saw the rise of new schools of interpretation to challenge this basic nationalism. But it would not be too much to say that even this further break with Turner's underlying assumption was still exemplifying his own functional principle. Face to face with new issues that seemed to them to transcend the too narrow limits of a purely American economic conflict, these minority schools were compelled to understand even the American past in more universal ways and in a broader setting. Thus the Marxians saw America not as unique, but as a cardinal instance of the common pattern of capitalistic development. Their histories consequently abandoned Turner's nationalistic perspective, and tried instead to bring out in the American past all those traits it shared with the general history of Western industrialism. For they were setting out from the problems of a world-wide depression and a world-wide conflict of interests and ideas; they were trying to understand why America too had been swept into the world current. They read American problems in the light of world issues.

In the post-Marxian present, there are many signs that America's radically changed status among the nations, bringing with it a host of new international problems, is provoking a fundamental reaction against the whole nationalistic emphasis that has dominated American historians for a generation. These new and unfamiliar issues will doubtless express themselves in a further reorientation of the way in which historians will understand our past. Indeed, there is already emerging a major conflict between two perspectives for interpreting American history. On the one hand stand those, still in the great majority, who hold to Turner's assumption of a distinctive American development, in economic organization and problems as well as in democratic ideals and ways of life. On the other hand stand those who see the growth of America as an integral part of the history of the western world in which she now holds so commanding and responsible a position. If the second group are likely to increase in number and influence, this is to say, with Turner, that "the conditions uppermost in our own time" have profoundly altered, and that, confronting significantly new problems, we must of necessity find other aspects of our past more basic than those we have recently emphasized. Those who would supplement Turner's own nationalism with such a broader perspective are really vindicating his fundamental conception of historical understanding.

VIII

In Turner are to be found, at least implicitly, nearly all the ideas more recent American historians have pushed further. Above all, he revealed the assumptions of the "scientific" and "objective" school for what they were. In proposing alternatives, he raised the whole question of the basis for choosing principles of selection to be employed. He strikingly illustrated the utility of hypotheses of interpretation. He suggested the expansion of the "field" of history to include social, cultural, and intellectual developments. And he was among the first to conceive the whole enterprise of history in the functional terms of the new humanistic and pragmatic philosophy that was emerging from the American social sciences.

During the decade of the nineteen-hundreds all these suggestions were rapidly exploited in their several directions. Most obvious was the sheer broadening of the possible subject-matter of the historian to embrace any or all aspects of civilization and culture. Lamprecht's visit in connection with the St. Louis Exposition proved a great stimulus to what was loosely called "the new history." These unsettling ferments created alarm in the more institutionalized members of the profession, whose precious traditions went back as far as the eighteen-eighties. Then around 1910 the heretics began to take the offensive, proclaiming their own programs and vigorously attacking in unmeasured tones the presuppositions of the founding fathers of the profession.

At the same meeting of the American Historical Association in 1910 at which Turner read his presidential address on "Social Forces in American History," James Harvey Robinson presented a paper on "The Relation of History to the Newer Sciences of Man." He started a controversial discussion, in which George L. Burr defended the conservatives and George H. Mead supported Robinson. The same year Carl Becker, in his article on "Detachment and the Writing of History," in the *Atlantic Monthly*, had launched the first of his major attacks on "the fact" to which "objectivists" were proclaiming their undying devotion. In the *Popular Science Monthly*, writing on "The Scientific Presentation of History," Lynn Thorndike made similar sharp criticisms of the methodology of the scientific school. In 1910 and 1911 appeared two economic interpretations: A. M. Simons' *Social Forces in American History*, definitely socialist, and Gustavus Myers' *History of Great American Fortunes*. In 1912 Robinson issued a collected volume of his essays on *The New History*. The same year Becker delivered his address on "Some Aspects of the Influence of Social Problems and Ideas upon the Study and Writing of History," perhaps the clearest early statement of the functional and pragmatic view. In 1913 was issued Beard's *An Economic Interpretation of the Constitution*.

A bare list like this suggests how thick and fast the rebels were hurling their shafts against the older "scientific" history. And they won the day. After a few years of vigorous controversy, serious opposition subsided. Enterprising historians were henceforth free, if not exactly encouraged, to select what aspect of the past they might choose, and to employ what principles of interpretation they might find illuminating. Gradually their results ceased to be impugned on the ground that as "historians" they had no right to start with such assumptions. Assumptions came slowly to be judged by the competence and brilliance with which they were used to explore the past, and to be criticized in their own terms in the light of their interpretative value. The older political historians were not indeed driven from the "field." They continued to form the majority, and, like Andrews, to produce very substantial work. But their ideas were now on the defensive. It was generally recognized that they too had principles of selection and methods of interpretation, and those principles and methods now had to justify themselves, like any others, by their fruits.

With this practical recognition of the functional nature of historical knowledge, American historiography had come of age. To be sure, there was to be continuing controversy over the efforts of reflective historians like Carl Becker and Charles Beard to formulate in theoretical terms their conceptions of the historian's enterprise. The profession, even in its outstanding leaders, can hardly be said even as yet to have achieved complete clarity as to its methodological principles. And large numbers, who greatly admire in others the fruits of the practice of a functional history, and perhaps ably carry it on themselves, nevertheless in their own theory of history retain many elements from the assumptions of earlier days. But in this lag the historical profession is scarcely unique. It is notorious that most natural scientists are apt to be none too clear when they try to analyze all that is implied in the very methods they themselves may be so brilliantly exemplifying. In stating their methods, they are very likely to fall back on what they early learned their methods should be, oblivious of how they themselves have improved on what they were taught. In this, historians by and large can well claim that they are thoroughly scientific. Theoretical clarity as to method seems to be possible only after that method has been painfully elaborated in practice.

The major achievements in American history after 1920 are frankly functional; the fact needs no belaboring. They employ principles of selection and of interpretation of which their authors are clearly conscious. That selection and that interpretation have been brought to a focus upon the critical problems that have successively confronted the American people. There are still those who, recognizing this present practice of our historians, regard it with regret as a lapse from the high standards of those who raised American historiography to a position of prestige. This essay, as indeed this whole volume, maintains rather that it is rooted in the nature of the historical enterprise itself. We have endeavored to show that this was in fact the practice of those "scientific" and "objective" founders of the profession in America who in theory denied it. In becoming aware of their controlling assumptions, and in consciously striving to work out hypotheses and principles of interpretation that would contribute most fruitfully to the understanding of basic American problems as they have seen them, our more recent historians have actually been following the lead and carrying on the work of the great pioneers of the last generation. They have been able to do it more critically and more intelligently, because they have realized more clearly just what it is they are doing.

---

11. Explanation and Human Action: Applications to Social Science

A. R. Louch

ANTHROPOLOGY

R ECALL FIRST that the anthropologist was at the beginning a traveller. By virtue of his acquaintance with parts of the world out of reach of most of us, he could tell stay-at-homes interesting stories about the diet and economy, the religious and sexual practices of alien and often exotic peoples. His talk looks to be of a piece with that of one's neighbour who has just come back (with slides) from Bermuda or a tour of the Western Parks.

Why is not every traveller an anthropologist? For one thing, it is a matter of acuity of observation. This is not something that can be formulated into anything as impressive (or oppressive) as a methodology. It is a matter of patient watching, and watching from a point of view that makes the alien behaviour intelligible by drawing likenesses and marking differences between practices abroad and at home. For another thing, the anthropologist faces barriers in communication and understanding beyond anything faced by the English traveller in France, or the American in Scandinavia. Differences are greater when

Reprinted by permission from *Explanation and Human Action* by A. R. Louch, pp. 159–182 (Berkeley and Los Angeles: University of California Press, 1966).

it is a matter of the Englishman or the American among the Dobu or Andaman Islanders. A human practice among such groups is much more likely to be misinterpreted by the anthropologist than are the actions of one's cultural neighbours by the less venturesome tourist. Eating one's enemy's brains or dodging out of the way of an approaching sister are not easily identifiable acts, in the way that a bargaining Italian or the ceremonial embrace among Frenchmen can be understood. There is a discontinuity of meaning here which requires a way of understanding and explaining behaviour different from anything that can be noticed in accounting for one's own or one's neighbours' behaviour.

This is the primary sense, it seems to me, in which the anthropologist might be said to explain what he observes. He shows that a highly puzzling act is the done thing, he exhibits the beliefs which provide the rationale for such conventions or ceremonies. The same might be said for sociological explanations except that they are offered with respect to practices already understood and engaged in, and so these accounts seem unnecessary and pretentious. Once we are able to say 'his sister is taboo', or 'he wants to assimilate his enemy's mana', we have explained the sudden decision to walk another and quite inappropriate way or the peculiar fervour, not to be confused with enjoyment, with which the brains are gulped down.

How does the anthropologist come to see behaviour in this way? For one thing, he asks people. Of greater importance, he comes to live the life of the people he investigates. He develops the capacity for identifying objects and situations and ceremonies after their lights. And this might be called research, and so be thought of as a scientific enterprise. Nothing would be wrong with this, except that philosophers and social scientists have interpreted terms like research and science in rather special ways. This is our old acquaintance: scientific explanation consists either in (a) inductive generalization or (b) the construction of hypotheses embracing a great number of cases, and from which further instances can be shown to follow. It is difficult to assimilate the anthropological traveller to either (a) or (b). Consequently anthropology is only a collection of traveller's tales with no particular scientific significance, or else it is really theoretical after all, and anthropologists of the past, in their methodological naïvety, have failed to formulate hypotheses with sufficient rigour to allow for observations or experiments which would support them in a decisive way.

I shall argue for the first of these options, but without prejudice, that is, without the pejorative 'mere' or 'only' qualifying the terms. Travellers' tales can be, as much as scientific theories, contributions to human knowledge; they can be better or worse, more or less accurate. Moreover, they are not the first and random comments that some day will be organized into a scientific theory. They are sufficient unto themselves. The pattern of explanation in anthropology is not a poor approximation of the generalizing and experimental and predictive capacities of the methods of science, but moral explanation, within which instances may be judged more or less adequate.

Let me illustrate this, first by reference to amateur accounts, to travellers' tales, rather than to the possibly more self-conscious work and writing of the professionals. Laurens van der Post, having spent much time among the Bushmen, and being willing to enter into a strange way of life, is able to say quite different things about the practice of exposing the aged than is another man, like Robert Ruark, whose conception of the African was governed by the rituals of his own culture. The latter describes the practice of leaving the old on the savanna to die as if it were a case of complete moral indifference, animal rather than human behaviour. The Africans to him simply have no finer feelings. In van der Post, on the other hand, we see the abandonment performed in a vivid ceremony, emphasizing the continuity of the race, and ensuring its perpetuity. He does not fail to notice, as Ruark does, the solemn grief at parting, as the young leave their aged to the mercy of the lions and hyenas, if not to a worse death. He sees also the acceptance of this practice by those so condemned, and the necessity of it forced on the Africans by the rigours and want that characterize their life. Is the difference here merely a choice of prejudices or values? It is surely a matter of values. Ruark sees the practice as an isolated piece of grist for his own moral mill; he makes no attempt to place the practice in its context. And this makes the difference. Ruark makes a moral judgment, but van der Post arrives at a moral assessment. The first requires nothing beyond one's arsenal of moral convictions and a case to which to apply them. The second requires a much more detailed description of what might be called the moral ecology within which the practice is observed. The first reflects the interference of values with accurate description which social scientists rightly deplore. The second is a case of moral explanation, based upon the most detailed factual picture possible.[1]

Still, someone committed to a rather different way of talking about human affairs might argue that what is seen here is a typical pattern of apology or attack. The example betrays an inclination to count as understanding, anything that justifies conduct. This is perhaps one sort of answer that is commonly anticipated to the question 'why?'

---

[1] For the views of van der Post cf. his *Lost World of the Kalahari* (Penguin, 1962), and *The Heart of the Hunter* (Penguin, 1965). As for Ruark, this, it seems to me, was the substance of his remarks in a television interview several years ago. I am unable to recall the exact occasion. It is, in any event, a common enough attitude among colonials, and anyone looking at foreign customs simply as departures from his own.

So the mother's despairing 'why?', as once more her child forgets to leave his dirty overshoes in the hallway, or the lover's bewildered 'why?' to his partner's infidelities. But it can, or should, be replaced by a question having a different sense.

I do not know whether a different kind of answer *can* be given. Indeed, though it is common enough for philosophers of science or of mind to decide what questions can and can't be asked of a given subject matter, I am not quite sure what is to be accomplished by such a piece of logical legislation, or how it is to be accomplished. It often appears to be a matter of second-guessing the future course of science by constructing logical necessities out of current theories. So positivists and logical empiricists have given the green light to the construction of hypotheses in sociology, and some disciples of Wittgenstein have, on the other hand, suggested that what the sociologist must do is to provide accounts which appeal rather to conventions or rules of the game. But it can be very embarrassing to a philosopher to demarcate with papal authority the domains and procedures of the several branches of knowledge only to discover that somewhere or other someone is doing quite successfully just what the philosopher told him he couldn't possibly do.

Beyond matters of caution and self-protection, however, it does appear that such philosophical theories are usually sustained by the analysis of sample theories, explanations, or other sorts of knowledge claims taken to be standard or paradigm. Thus the question as to what *can* be merges very readily into the question what should be.

I do not believe that current practice of social scientists is vitiated because they have fixed on the wrong paradigm. They have not had success with that paradigm, but that is a different thing. Hypothetico-deductive accounts in sociology are grotesque parodies of sciences like mechanics, and the anthropologist, seeking accuracy by recording native dances on tape and film, and then analysing them into their component steps, is no doubt caricaturing rather than using 'scientific' procedures of measurement, in order to assure himself a place in science's promised land. These are misuses of the physicist's ways of devising hypotheses and gathering evidence, not because these methods cannot or should not be applied to human beings, but because this aspect of the sociologist's work is out of step with the rest of his inquiry. The concepts that shape sociological thinking include status and role, convention and function, and these concepts force us to view society in ways that defeat the application of scientific rigour and method. For these are concepts which belong to the moral realm of discourse. To identify instances of status or role, convention or function, is already to understand them. Thus, theories and statistics as means of explaining are otiose in these fields. In the remainder of this section and in the next, I shall argue this thesis, first with respect to the concepts that cluster around 'convention', and second, those that cluster around 'function.'

'Convention' embraces a number of other concepts, among them status and role. They have in common the sense of carrying out instructions, doing assigned tasks, and playing one's part. If behaviour is seen as a performance, it is automatically explained in a certain way. A priest celebrating mass, a merchant bargaining in the market-place, a Park Avenue heiress walking her poodle, are, among hosts of others, events or actions which do not need explaining. This is not because they are difficult, opaque, or too unique to afford the accommodation of general theory, but because they are transparent. A way of life provides the capacity to observe and identify such acts. Since a way of life is essentially a repository of action-guiding reasons acquired in a moral education, this observation and explanation is, properly speaking, moral observation and explanation. To know that a priest is celebrating mass is, in general, to know why he is doing it. The note of novelty and research is sustained in the anthropologist's account, because he investigates the actions of those whose moral instruction differs from his own. The discordant note of redundancy in the sociologist's account is produced by the clash of a proposed method of research with actions already explained by the moral education common to the investigator and investigated.

The picture often given of sociology is of a vast assemblage of facts or 'data' which require mathematical trimming so that the underlying structure accounting for them is revealed. This aim is most clearly seen in the work of Parsons in sociology and Nadel in anthropology. But when the structure is described, as it is by Parsons and Nadel, through the use of terms like status and role, it is no longer clear why hypotheses or more rigorous mathematical treatment are necessary or appropriate. A book like Nadel's *Theory of Social Structure* is an extraordinary remove from the anthropological data with which, allegedly, it is to cope.[2] Nadel feels that anthropology is ready for the techniques of mathematical logic, but the relationships he formalizes are conventional in nature. They are roles based on age, sex, kinship, leadership, skill, service, partnership, and a group of rather shaky (for symbolization) creative or 'belief' communicative functions, like those of the artist and the orator (compare his chart, p. 53). When the nature and prerequisites of the role are clear, formalization is neither necessary nor helpful. When they are not, symbolization only succeeds in giving a false sense of security.

If the relationship between two or more individuals or groups is

---

[2] S. F. Nadel, *Theory of Social Structure* (Free Press, 1957).

understood as the practice of a role, the action is thereby explained conventionally. The convention that governs a role, together with the suitability of the agent to perform the role, entitles the individual or the group to act as he or it does. The relation of entitlement is a logical relation; if we understand the convention we must understand the actions which follow from it. If we are able to identify an individual as the possessor of a certain role, we also know why he acts as he does.

In a recent monograph Peter Winch argues along similar lines, suggesting that sociology ought therefore to be thought of as a business of conceptual analysis, akin to philosophy instead of empirical science.[3] His argument, it seems to me, needs a good deal of restating. It applies with some force to the logic of explanation of conventional actions. But (1) it leaves out of account the manner in which conventions are deciphered and (2) it gives the impression that the sociologist or anthropologist is concerned only with intra-cultural or intra-conventional actions.

As to (1), if we have the convention in hand, so to speak, it is perhaps only a piece of conceptual analysis that leads us to the entailed or entitled actions. But for every convention in the hand, there are two in the bush. There are obscurities in much of human action which can be clarified by deciphering the conventions governing these actions, if we can first get at the convention in question. How we discover or disclose the conventions governing action is a complicated story. But surely it is not a story of conceptual analysis, but of the arduous and detailed observation of behaviour. A book like William H. Whyte's *The Organization Man* may serve as an example. In it one sees much of the behaviour of the managerial class in the United States stemming from rules of a rather unusual game or code. But the code itself is not written up in rule books or on bronze plaques for Whyte to read and apply to the behaviour of the organization people. The code is itself extrapolated from the behaviour and the talk, which then become understandable as conventional. This is empirical research in a straightforward sense. Evidence is collected, compared and tabulated. But the explanation is not some further device, brought to bear upon the generalizations that emerge from the behaviour; it comes when the investigator sees the actions of this class as rule-abiding. It would be odd to insist that the explanation should now extend to further instances, after the manner of the application of an explanatory hypothesis in science, and in a way that implies that further evidence is required to support the explanation. Further evidence would show only that the rules are more widely practised; it would not support or shore up the application to the original cases.

[3] Peter Winch, *The Idea of a Social Science* (Routledge & Kegan Paul, 1958).

(2) raises a different order of problems. The actions of individuals or groups may appear conventional. But what of the drift and variability in the conventions themselves? A man may act in certain ways because he is a father. But why do some cultures prescribe some kinds of conduct to fathers, and other cultures assign quite different roles? Why, even further, do kinship regulations have the kind of universal application and adoption that anthropologists can show in their surveys of cultures? These and other questions about human habits and institutions are surely legitimate, even though the answers customarily given to them are equivocal and metaphorical. Indeed, they might be regarded as among the more pressing and important questions for anthropologists to answer. One kind of answer or method of providing an answer to such questions is the thesis usually labelled functionalism. I shall now turn to an examination of this thesis, and the disputes that arise between functionalists and their methodological competitors.

FUNCTION

The functional thesis is most closely associated with the name of Malinowski, and I shall be basing my remarks largely on his sponsorship of the thesis in A Scientific Theory of Culture.[4] His thesis is much like that of Wittgenstein's with respect to the meaning of language. Where Wittgenstein says, ask not for the meaning, but the use, Malinowski says, ask not what the culture trait is, but what is its use (p. 118). The nature of a trait cannot be discovered by its form, which may be universal, but by the way in which it combines with other traits to carry on social activities (pp. 148–9).

Let us apply this thesis first to tools, which provide obvious cases for functional analysis. Very little has been said about a tool in classifying it according to its form or material, stone or wood, core or flake, hafted or thonged. These items of archaeological description do indeed help delineate the patterns of distribution in space and time, facts which are sometimes ignored or depreciated by Malinowski. But that we choose to call them tools in the first place implies that we look at them in addition as designed to do a certain job, as performing a certain function. When Leakey a few years ago showed that one could skin an animal with a prepared core (or was it a flake?) he was offering evidence that the chipped stones liberally deposited in Palaeolithic deposits were tools. They could do the job.

To say that a thing is a watch is to say that it tells time, or at least that, cleaned, repaired and set, it would tell time. To say that a thing is a knife is to say that it cuts, if properly sharpened. But it is to say also

[4] Bronislaw Malinowski, A Scientific Theory of Culture and Other Essays (Oxford University Press: Galaxy Books, 1960).

that it is *used* to tell time, or to cut. Watches and other complicated machines are obviously the central or paradigm cases here. We feel no uneasiness in speaking of the use of an artifact dug up out of the soil and out of its context, or inferring all sorts of things about its users. But there are shadings and borderlines. Cases arise in which we become less comfortable, less secure, in calling the item in question a tool. It is much the same, of course, in philosophy. Following Wittgenstein's procedure, one is tempted to find uses in the automatic way that philosophers formerly assigned meanings to any assemblage of letters. Yet clearly language contains a great deal of dead wood. There are many words in the language similar in form or context to other words to which use can confidently be assigned, but which themselves are idling expressions. This is one of the difficulties in taking paradigms of descriptive or game-playing discourse so seriously that it is assumed that any linguistic act has at least the credentials for entrance into one of the classes of language act typified by the paradigm cases. Similarly, taking tools as a paradigm of anthropological investigation can lead to possibly grotesque results when applied to typical social habits and institutions. Is it the function of marriage to insure the care of the young, or of sexual taboos to underwrite marriage arrangements by placing a brake upon the socially disruptive effect of sexual urges? (Malinowski, p. 208). At least is this the function of marriage or taboos in the sense that it is the function of Leakey's chipped core to skin an animal or of a watch to tell time?

In one sense we *describe* something as functional, like a tool; in another sense we *appraise* something as functional. It is in this latter sense that the term applies to institutions and culture traits. Most members of a community marry and beget children, and recoil from sexual contact with relatives, but they do not individually do so to preserve the species, or provide a stable environment for raising children. To individuals the institutions are conditions of the environment which shape, inhibit or promote their desires, plans and actions. Anthropologists do not regard the bounty or parsimony of nature, or the soil, rainfall, rivers, mountains and harbours, as functional. But all of these conditions of the environment may be appraised as functional, and may be made use of accordingly. A man is born into society, as he is born into a physical environment, and he may make use of both to further his or others' ends. The institution of marriage and the features of the landscape may be *assessed* as functional. Tools, on the other hand, are *designed* to perform a function; it is not that they happen to or that they are found lying around and turn out to do the job. We might call design the strong and narrow, and assessment the weak and broad sense of function.

Human institutions are easy enough to appraise as functional. Consider, for example, Lévi-Strauss's description of kinship and marriage systems in *Man, Culture, and Society*.[5] There are for him certain conditions which social arrangements are designed to fulfil. A society needs to be able to assign a status to a new-born or newly-arrived member. Marriage arrangements are required, together with sexual taboos, to insure the possibility of determining a man's lineage, which is the simplest way of assigning an individual a place in society. The family supplies the key to social order, providing continuity and rank, together with an easily ascertainable way of deciding how to act toward another person in the group.

This account derives its power from the tradition of inherited status. If we look at social organization through the imperatives of rank and place (status and role), we can assess institutions of marriage and kinship as more or less effective instruments to this end. It becomes more difficult if one wonders why there should be such imperatives in the first place. For, like tools, institutions are facts, but unlike tools, the needs against which the function of an institution is to be measured are not biological or ecological constants, but are induced in part by the very institutions that are supposedly designed to satisfy them. In the case of a tool, there are certain conditions to be met and certain clear limitations on the manner of doing the job. One may choose not to do the job; instead of skinning the animal and preparing a core to do so, one may live on nuts and berries. Still the tool is the clue to the purposes of its users, and thus exhibits its functional character. The only condition that appears to be remotely analogous to this in the case of institutions is the necessity of providing some permanent organization to provide for the young. That every society has such institutions is thus ascribable to such needs. But the great variety in form of institutions cannot be explained as accommodations to this necessity. Kinship regulations, the assigning of status, and all the usual concerns of anthropologists acquire functional importance only given a conception of rules and regulations as a background to the functioning of institutions. The social forms are assumed to begin with.

The picture of functionalism that emerges is this. We approach the investigation of habits and institutions by way of the question we can also ask of tools, namely, what are they for? But the answer to this question varies, depending on whether we are entitled to talk about a designed or an appraised artefact or activity. An institution is not a piece of machinery designed to resolve antedating needs; it is rather the form which allows anthropologists to talk about needs. The need for family life is inconceivable outside the institution of the family.

[5] Harry L. Shapiro (ed.), *Man, Culture, and Society* (Oxford University Press: Galaxy Books, 1960), pp. 282–4.

Consequently it would be circular to speak of the institution as answering to that need. It is all too easy here to fall into the language of determinism. When we say marriage answers to certain needs (generated by the institution as part of the environment) it is as if we could also say circumstances caused or compelled the development of family life. But if the connexion were deterministic we would expect to find concomitant variation between the environment (physical and biological) and the institution. In a sense we don't even know quite what the scope of such variables are. How are we to pick out the relevant features in the environment, for example? And thus the putative causal relationship is apt to reduce to the trivial claim that there is family life in every physical environment. When we do succeed in disclosing relevant features of the environment, they turn out to be themselves cultural factors, that is, institutions, and thus appeal to the environment fails as an explanation of the institution.

Situations are seen as constituting needs because we have cast our observations in the language of purpose and goal. To understand that a situation embodies a need is not achieved by generalizing the connexions among observed particulars. It is to see the situation as valued. So to explain cultural phenomena functionally is to see patterns in actions and institutions in the light of goals and principles which these practices help or hinder. It follows that the institutions themselves must be in existence, as part of the situation to be appraised, for us to introduce notions like the satisfaction of need and function. Need, like function, is a term of appraisal. It notes a logical, not a factual relationship between ecology and action.

Anthropologists, like their sociologist colleagues, hanker after generality and causal laws, and the sort of fact-collecting that seems to add up to generalizations upon which theories may be built. Needs are made use of to tie together the facts by means of an explanatory theory, and so it looks as if they could be employed to state general truths about human and social development. But the generality achieved or hoped for, as Malinowski recognizes, is often so all-inclusive as to be vacuous. Social institutions are frequently explained as socially integrative. In a sense, of course, institutions are socially integrative, for that is what we mean by a society. If we break down such overblown formulae to informative size, the result is a set of piecemeal ascriptions of functions to various social practices in various groups. We don't want to talk about the function of the dance, but, for example, about the function of dancing among the Winnebagos or American teenagers. For the account of function cannot be given save in the particular circumstances which provide grounds for assessing needs, that is, within the framework of institutions and codes.

The explanatory role of function is only one of its uses in anthropology. Closer to Malinowski's heart is its use as a way of defining the unit of anthropological investigation, the elements that one describes in writing up reports of this or that culture. He argues (pp. 148–9, 176) that doctrines like diffusionism or evolutionism, or techniques like trait-comparison, rest upon the supposition that the object of anthropological interest is a physical unit, the form of an object or activity, and not the meaning of what is done, or the point of its manufacture.

I wish to endorse these arguments as they appear in the pages of A *Scientific Theory of Culture,* after having excised what I should regard as a certain intemperance in Malinowski's elimination of these alternate theories and procedures. Surely there can be nothing wrong with a description of the geographical or temporal distribution of culture traits, however defined, and it is in such descriptions that the essence of diffusionist or evolutionary hypotheses are to be found. It is or it is not the case that a core or a flake industry is found over a certain territory or that specified traits succeed each other in time. The difficulties with diffusionist and evolutionary hypotheses arise at the explanatory level, the diffusionist thesis because it rests upon the highly dubious principle of the parsimony of human invention, the evolutionist because the sorts of general evolutionary hypotheses that have been developed have confused logical and temporal orders, on the supposition, for example, that evolution is in the direction of complexity, or toward some favoured technique or manner of living. The question, *why* this or that particular pattern of diffusion or evolution, suggests a causal hypothesis, which pictures the changes in society as the result of something analogous to physical forces, like tides washing over the various human communities in the world. The evidence produced, however, suggests a very different picture. The anthropologist usually exhibits grounds for the adoption of a trait, in terms, for example, of the utility or the attractiveness of the trait adopted or modified. Frequently, of course, the story he offers is one in which traits are taken over by a community from a conquering, or more subtly dominating group, and this looks much more like a causal account. But it is not that sort of cause which would benefit from casting an account in the hypothetical or inductive forms that require predictions to nourish them. The act of conquest or manifest superiority in efficiency are the features of the context that justify or provide grounds for its adoption.

The same remarks may be offered with respect to Malinowski's criticism of the trait-comparison method. He accuses Frazer, among others, of this anthropological sin, which is, of course, the failure to see a trait embedded in its context. Thus Frazer can see, without further difficulty, the kinship of the Christian mistletoe, the castrated god of the Near East and the celebration of the mass. If the object of investigation is to assess the function of the trait, the business at hand could not be conducted out of context, and so it looks as if trait-comparison is excluded on methodological grounds. But nothing excludes the comparison of forms, for example, any ceremony where ritual eating or washing is involved, for this comparison may provide the basis for discovering the historical diffusion of traits.

The typical methodological quarrels among anthropologists thus appear to be unfounded. These arguments and anxieties have been sustained by the notion that one must first define the unit of one's investigation before engaging in substantive inquiries. Having done so, the typical anthropologist inveighs against his methodological neighbours, as if hypotheses of a different order than his own are logically misconceived. But one cannot criticize a description of the diffusion of the form of pottery on the grounds that the trait has not been defined functionally. It is simply a different, though related, enterprise. The mistake arises from the conception of anthropology as a unified science, in which a total description of culture is to follow from one set of laws harnessed together by means of a common and logically unified body of concepts. But anthropology, as Wittgenstein might say, is a medley of techniques, where the medley is a harmony of different interests and points of view, and not a dissonance of vying theories.

Having purged the Malinowskian theory of such theory-ridden excesses, it is now possible to see his arguments in a rather different light. Functional accounts do not occupy a low rung on a ladder with some envisaged or not too well envisaged theory at the top. The ladder of scientific progress is not climbed by rejecting functionalist in favour of physicalist rungs. Functional accounts are not crude approximations of physical theories, but accounts of a logically different kind. If the theoretical view is imposed on anthropologists, it is on the assumption that all successful descriptions and explanations of matters of fact begin with 'hard data'. There is a good deal of mystique surrounding the use made of this sort of concept by philosophers, aided and abetted by the way in which mathematics is made use of in the natural sciences to define and employ descriptive concepts with exceptional accuracy and precision. So it has seemed to some social anthropologists that techniques of quantification would tie down theories firmly to genuine and reliable data. Unfortunately, the steps in the dance, or the elapsed time required for a specific shuffle, no matter how often or painstakingly recorded, do not add up to the dance. If it is the dance and its role in the life of a community that interests the anthropologist, the quantitative analysis of steps and movements is out of place. Identifying dances, ceremonies and actions are also instances of genuine descriptions and observations. Such identifications begin from a different point of view, not involving the accuracy or precision characteristic of concepts in physical theory. However, they are the sort of thing we want to talk about. They have the virtue of relevance to human conduct, if they lack, in some measure, the virtue of certainty in the formulation of hypotheses concerning it.

Anthropology, then, is a normative discipline, in the sense that its inquiries are shaped by concepts like convention and procedures like the tracing of grounds for action. The intermingling of moral and empirical matters is puzzling only if moral categories are thought of as contaminating the descriptive possibilities of discourse. And this view turns on conceptions of purely empirical data like logical atoms or sense-data, which are meant to afford a starting point for any empirical inquiry. There are many things we want to find out, and to different aims and different subjects logically different items of observation are relevant. Norms and conventions, rules and grounds are the tools of moral judgment, but they are also the tools for describing social practice. The use of such concepts and procedures cannot, then, be stigmatized as mere airings of personal preferences, or isolated from the body of empirical knowledge as a priori or conceptual inquiries. Talk about human institutions and practices is already a moral cutting of the empirical cake.

SOCIOLOGY

Much the same arguments can be applied to sociology and history. Once again, moral reasoning has been misconstrued as causal hypothesis or general theory.

When Max Weber advanced his thesis implicating protestant theology in the rise of capitalism, he defended it on what he called 'rational' grounds, with the suggestion that the thesis might be fortified by evidence of a statistical nature. Most of his critics have countered by pointing out that this further evidence is, or must be, lacking. Weber, so this critique goes, needs to show that whenever Calvinist-like religious beliefs turn up, so do capitalist attitudes. Or, lacking such broad instances for comparison, he needs to break down his study into a multitude of connexions drawn between individual clerics and entrepreneurs. The criticism assumes that Weber's thesis is of the type described with monotonous frequency by philosophers of sciences and sociologists of a methodological bent. First, one notes regularities and then devises hypotheses to explain them. The explanation, or successful explanation, at any rate, is to be found in the deduction of new and verifiable consequences (normally predictions) from the hypotheses. Given this pattern of explanation, Weber's thesis is treated as a special case of a general law. Since the law is empty, the case remains unproven, or worse, a bit of speculation masquerading as theory.

Now Weber opens himself to the charge by formulating his hypotheses in causal form and subscribing to a methodology which puts forward ideal types as analogous, at least, to general laws, as the sort of thing that would require evidence of regularities. Winch rightly points to the logical gulf that divides the two procedures.[6] It is as if (a not uncommon problem among sociologists) Weber's way of talking about his work got in the way of the work itself. On this interpretation the historian and sociologist appeal to reasons and motives to explain actions just in the way that scientists and ordinary men appeal to the movements of some bodies to explain the movements of others. Reasons are taken to be *events*, followed by their effects, which, generally, are actions. But since reasons are hidden by the logically impenetrable wall of the mind, it is necessary to resort to the device of the hypothetical experiment, or some means of reliving others' lives, in order to suppose that we ever do succeed in offering such accounts. Once all this is assumed, it is very natural to argue, as Nagel does in *The Structure of Science* (pp. 482 ff.), that historians and sociologists who rely on the imaginative technique of identifying themselves with the subjects of their inquiries are confusing the manner of arriving at their hypotheses with the grounds for holding them. It is always possible, Nagel argues, that our conjectured plumbing of motives is quite mistaken, a possibility amply attested to in the history of history. But it is also possible that Weber's kind of sociology is open to a rather different interpretation to which Nagel's criticisms will not apply.

Weber's ideal types in *The Protestant Ethic*, for example, might be treated as characterizations or impressions of ways of thought and styles of living which enable him to compare them. The doctrine of the calling, with its emphasis upon worldly activity, and predestination, with its alienation of daily life from spiritual concerns, are exhibited as ways by which the emphasis upon money-making for its own sake could be justified. What Weber did *not* do was to show that, as a result of worming his way into the heads of clerics and commercial men, he could disclose in himself these religiously toned motives, and assess their influence upon economic practice and attitudes. It is not a business of discovery in that sense at all, but of the assessment of arguments. It is, as Weber himself called it, a rational inquiry, for its object is to discern logical connections among propositions expressing

[6] Winch, op. cit., pp. 111–20, especially p. 115.

beliefs about the world, or one's obligations, or the supernatural. In the theological context he is calling attention to the moral consequences inherent in Calvinist religious views. In the field of business ethics, as schools of business like to call it nowadays, he is showing what sorts of economic activities are permitted and encouraged by theological precepts, how, as Sombart, writing in the same field might say, economic practice can be clothed in religious sanctity.

History and sociology, so conceived, are branches of ethics. They focus attention on prevailing or important ingredients in a way of life, and show how these relate to and follow from other presuppositions, attitudes, and practices, whether these are religious, moral, scientific, political or economic. Such connexions serve to explain practice because principles can be seen at work which would justify the practice. This is Weber's theme and method. It is also, for example, the gist of Gibbon's theme, that a classical way of life is inconsistent with Christian beliefs and the *mores* of the barbarians. It is also the nature of the connexion frequently drawn between the philosophical views of the seventeenth and eighteenth centuries and the revolutions that accompanied or followed them. And lest this be thought of as an identification of history with the history of ideas, after the manner of Collingwood, it should be noted that this is also the nature of the connexion drawn between excessive taxation and those same revolutions. It has often been thought that attention to hard economic facts helps to replace the old moralistic procedures of historians with proper scientific methods. If this means that the historian who talks about taxation instead of philosophy is seeking correlations between variables which will serve as the basis for a causal theory, his evidence is shaky indeed. We should not ordinarily advance to the general theory that tax problems always cause revolutions on the basis of the handful of instances at our disposal. Moreover, if we read the historian's record closely, it is clear that he is not interested in such a general theory at all, and has no need for such a broadening of his view in order to talk, as he does talk, about the relation of taxation to the Dutch or English revolution. For he describes the taxation as excessive, that is, as constituting grounds for revolt.

If this is the way the historian and sociologist go about their business, their explanations do not require further evidence in the way that an account of physical movement is regarded as acceptable only if it extends to or embraces further cases. The way in which the background relates to the actions within which they are performed is not causal or statistical. Nor does it have the kind of capacity which requires the invention of theoretical 'models' to render the relation between them intelligible. The explanation is instead, moral; it presents features of the background as justifying or providing grounds for the action. This relationship is logical, not empirical. This appears to support Winch's view in *The Idea of a Social Science* that social analysis is conceptual or a priori. The social analyst is really the social philosopher and social inquiry an examination of the tools of communication by which we initiate and describe action. It is the meaning of institutions and practices, not their outward form, that concern us.

Winch draws much of the sustenance for this view from Wittgenstein, and particularly that dark saying, 'Language is a form of life.' This is taken by Winch as meaning that human action is governed by the concepts which describe it. Consequently, to understand the actions is to understand the concepts. Understanding concepts is surely conceptual inquiry, and conceptual inquiry is just as surely philosophy. So understanding social action is a philosophical, and therefore not an empirical, enterprise.

In the preceding paragraphs I have allied my arguments to those of Winch. I hope now to show that those arguments do not have the consequences envisaged by Winch for the nature of social inquiry.

In the first place, Wittgenstein's statement is open to a rather different interpretation. To say that language is a form of life may well have been a reminder that language is embedded in life and is a response to the needs and circumstances of its users. In this sense the text could be construed as an objection to a-priorism in philosophy, not a defence of it in sociology. It appears, indeed, that Winch is the victim of the kind of philosophizing to which Wittgenstein took exception. In saying, ask not for the meaning, but the use, Wittgenstein seems to have been reminding us that philosophers' categories are not eternal verities or absolute or exhaustive categories, but reflections on uses of language that can be seen to apply only in context. The moral for the social scientist, so far as he is concerned with the deliberate communication and the expressive behaviour of those whose actions he examines, appears to be: see how these communications and actions function in social contexts. It may be that the collection of statistics or the formulation of hypotheses do not enter here as explanatory moves, and this provides Winch with arguments for his view that sociology is as much a priori as empirical. But it is a matter of empirical discovery that people talk certain ways, for it is only in the context of the talk that we can claim to understand what they are doing and why they are doing it. So with my own variant of Winch's thesis. In morally explaining human practices the sociologist is not merely cloaking actions in the respectability of one's own moral convictions, but enriching the factual detail so as to see what it is in the situation that could provide the agent with grounds for acting.

I suspect that Winch has fallen victim to one of the philosopher's traditional dichotomies. It is a dichotomy especially associated with

the name of Hume, though Hume notes many cases which overlap or
lie outside of this dichotomy. First, the distinction of relations of ideas
and matters of fact appears to divide propositions into those known
and those probable. But among the relations of ideas are found relations of resemblance, which do not neatly line up with Hume's further
distinction between conceptual and empirical. But before long it
becomes easier for Hume to think of the knowledge/probability distinction in terms of its clearest cases, mathematics and causal judgments. And these illustrate the conceptual/empirical distinction as
well. In this way the two dichotomies merge, conceptual and known,
as against empirical and probable.

This is a merger made by many philosophers. Winch is in good company. But it is, I think, a confusion of major importance. He argues,
rightly I believe, that the explanation of an action is an inquiry which
cannot benefit from the strategies which one would enlist in order to
establish the probability of a causal hypothesis. It is thus easy for him
to make this stand as a denial also of the relevance of empirical
strategies to social inquiries altogether. It may indeed be absurd to
treat propositions and theories as experimental facts (as Winch notes
on p. 109), but it does not follow that our way of establishing a relation between putative theories or beliefs and the actions in which men
engage is a matter only of logical implication. Weber, once again, sees
capitalist attitudes as following from Calvinist theology or Lutheran
social doctrine. But this inquiry cannot be conducted simply by reading the *Institutes* and Ben Franklin's autobiography and showing that
the first entails the second. No logician would sanction such a deduction. It is rather that the two resemble one another in ways pertinent
to the assigning of grounds for acting. The connexion is not disclosed
by research into regularities, but by observation, and the collection
of vast amounts of evidence designed to fill out the theological and
economic pictures, so that they can be compared with authority. This
was in fact a matter which Weber fudged, for his comparisons are
often drawn from irrelevant stretches of time, or can be drawn between just the sort of theology and economy which he wished to claim
were not so connected. Thus his critics point to the arbitrariness with
which he joined sixteenth-century religious beliefs and eighteenth- or
even nineteenth-century economic attitudes and to the prevalence
or at least occurrence of Protestant-like moral injunctions from Italian
Catholics like Alberti. If these characterizations and the objections to
them are ejected from the empirical canon, it should lead us to question the appropriateness of the causal-probability conception of the
empirical, and not the empirical or factual character of these claims
and procedures.

That the explanation in such cases is a matter of finding grounds for the questioned action, suggests that explaining is a matter of presenting arguments or offering moral judgment. The argumentative feature seems to support Winch's a priori view, the moral feature the view of those who, like Collingwood, lay such stress on the historian's sympathy with his subject. But the grounds available to responsible historical or sociological scholarship consist in the events and circumstances which surround the investigated action. And this, surely, is a matter of observation, which can be done with more or less attention, thoroughness and accuracy.

Two of Winch's examples may illustrate the poverty imposed upon sociology by his interpretation. In the first, Winch points out (p. 127) that understanding the concept 'war' is both necessary and sufficient to understanding how belligerents will act. It is clear, for example, why a soldier operates a machine-gun while sitting in a foxhole. His nation is at war, and this means, among other things, that soldiers will act in this way. All well and good, but one wonders: if this is sociology, why does it need to be written at all? Assuredly, the concept war includes the notion of people trying, often under most unhappy circumstances, to kill one another. But does the concept also allow us to determine why two nations have gone to war? Winch admits (p. 130) under pressure from a colleague that certain kinds of social relation, 'particularly important for sociology and history', might not be of an intellectual, symbolic or conventional nature. He cites wars 'in which the issue between combatants [is] purely a struggle for physical survival (as in a war between hungry migrants and the possessors of the land on which they are encroaching)'. But he immediately reverts to the sense in which these wars can be stylized by the conventions issuing from the concept, that is, he reverts to an explanation of individual warlike acts. In doing so, he seems to dodge the criticism of Professor Rees, referred to in his footnote. For, if I read Winch's waiver aright, Rees's question has to do with the occasion of a war, not a description of its conduct. To appeal to the fact that, though as hungry as tigers, men do not quarrel over land as tigers do over meat, is irrelevant, for it is not the style of fighting but the occasion for it that is of major interest to the historian or sociologist.

Winch draws further comfort here from the supposition that some wars can be explained in conventional, symbolic, or intellectual terms. His case is unfortunately chosen, however. For it would lead us to think of the Crusades (his example) in terms of the propaganda which led people to go on them, that is, as Holy Wars. This would surely impoverish our historical accounts, which need to take into account sundry matters like trade routes, the position of the Papacy and its manœuvrings with increasingly powerful temporal princes, and the problems arising in a state divided between feudal and royal power. By the same token one could regard Soviet moves in Korea, Vietnam, Hungary and Czechoslovakia as wars of liberation, deducible from the premises of Communist theory, just as the Crusades are deducible from Christian theology or papal policy. Surely our understanding of these conflicts is immeasurably increased when we take into account the numerous factors in the situation suppressed or not noticed by the pamphleteers or official propagandists. The history and sociology that Winch can buy with his a priori currency is naïve indeed. No reputable observer would be inclined to accept it.

In the second example Winch wishes to reject a comparison of Christian baptism with other instances of ritual purification. The grounds for his rejection of these interesting comparisons are clear enough. If he is to explain baptism a priori, the rite must be deducible from a set of conventions or espoused theory to be found in Christian theology and ritual. If the historian were to find the roots of Christian baptism in earlier rites of purification, his thesis would entail assertions of temporal, perhaps causal sequence, requiring empirical research.

The comparison of baptism and lustral rites does not have the methodological consequence Winch fears it has, for it is not appropriate to support resemblances by the accumulation of statistics. But in the anxiety to avoid this possibility Winch is forced to exclude such comparisons altogether, and thus to insist wholly on the kind of understanding of baptism that follows from the rules that explicitly govern its practice. And so he is led by his fears to retreat from a middle ground which might well be held against his enemy. Recall that this enemy is not observation and its pertinence to social inquiry, but the kind of explanation in science that consists of generalization and prediction. Impressions formed of a subject or resemblances drawn among subjects are factual in the quite ordinary sense that they are based, if they are held responsibly, on arduous observation and close attention to the surrounding circumstances. What is irrelevant is the supposition that noting resemblances or forming impressions stands in further need of statistical evidence or hypotheses from which predictions will follow. In explaining conduct by appeal to conventions, or to aspects of the ecology of actions which provide grounds for them, no further factual information is required. But the descriptions and comparisons that support such explanations are surely matters of observation. This is the gist of Winch's objection to the remarkable passage which he quotes from Pareto (p. 105), who seems to suggest that we can only understand baptism by including it within a more general theory of which lustral rites and washings would be other instances. But his objections to Pareto should not scare him quite so quickly into his a priori lair.

Social customs and practices are rather less clearly governed by code-books than Winch can allow. Most human actions may be governed or guided by conventions, but to discover the rules in most cases involves close description of actions and their contexts. Winch quotes with approval a remark of G. E. M. Anscombe that to understand certain kinds of performance, like working a sum, is to be able to do them. This, presumably, is to serve as a model for social inquiry generally, but taken in that spirit it implies that the sociology of mathematics is the study of mathematics, the sociology of religion the study of theology and prescribed rites, and sociology generally the study of rational prescriptions of action. Sociologists and anthropologists, surely, would insist that habits and practices differ from the uttered or written doctrine, which has, after all, been codified by those pleading special interests. To appeal to such documents in the case of religion is to share Samuel Johnson's view that the proper study of Christianity is contained in the work of theologians.[7] This is no longer a sociological or anthropological, but a theological or philosophical study. Its method involves the logical assessment of arguments and assertions designed to support or refute their validity or application. To suppose that such appraisal could answer the question, 'why this religious practice?' in the way that the mathematician could answer the question, 'why did you take that step?' or that anyone could answer the question, 'what makes you think so-and-so is in town?' (The answer: 'I saw him') is to assume that our grounds for engaging in religious or more generally social acts are as perfectly and as rationally established as are the grounds for mathematical or scientific judgment or procedure. And this surely begs a very large question.

There is a gulf between moves designed to win a game or support a theory or carry out a prescribed ceremony and those which terminate in acquiring a wife, walking the dog, choosing an occupation, or running for office. It is not that these actions are unrelated to conventions. But the manner in which they are related is a good deal more complicated than Winch's view could allow, or than his rule-book cases indicate. Numbers of conventions, for example, are unacknowledged by those who engage in them. Some tribes in Africa, reported in Lévi-Strauss's essay on the family in *Man, Culture, and Society* (pp. 273-4), encourage marriages between two women, one of whom, through the unproclaimed affair of the other, plays the role of father to the children of the 'wife'. Much in this arrangement is a matter of strict convention. A marriage ceremony is performed, rules for inheritance invoked and applied, and roles assigned. Any reasonably in-

[7] The example occurs in Lienhardt's essay on 'Religion' in *Man, Culture, and Society*, pp. 310-11.

telligent member of the group could cite chapter and verse to explain these actions. But the peripheral and unacknowledged affair, by which children bless this union, is less easy to account for conventionally, except in that the rules and conventions of marriage contribute something to the background of the practice. The anthropologist explains the affair by showing how it is necessary in order to provide the 'husband', always a woman of noble lineage, with children so that the noble strain will not die with her. The conventional here rubs off on the clandestine, but one needs to assay a great number of details of the social situation of such tribes in order to draw the connexion of ground and action.

Such examples have an esoteric charm which might distract us from the point, which can be made just as easily by appeal to perfectly pedestrian cases. A businessman in Paris, after a certain amount of success, is apt to acquire a 'five o'clock' mistress, a denizen of more privileged housing in New York City will acquire a poodle. In America the distance between conversing males is greater than it is in France. We should not be able to deduce these actions from concepts or look them up in rule books, but we do infer that they are conventional once we see evidence of their persistent practice by a special group or class or nation. To say that an action is conventional is to say, among other things, that it is not idiosyncratic, and this is a truth that can be discovered only by observation. It is surely not discoverable by lexicography or grammar alone.

The conventions appealed to as explaining actions are not, in such cases, invoked through a priori acquaintance with concepts, or reading rule books or listening to the rationalizations of the actors. The last of these, taken religiously, would reflect a naïveté which would render us inadequate for the business of living, let alone anthropological observation. The second would restrict the scope of sociology to the degree that one would wonder what the point of it is. The first suggests the kind of automatic imposition of one's own ways on other patterns of life, a habit which supposedly went out with the missionary.

If Winch's a-priorism is tempting, it is perhaps because it so neatly pricks the sociologist's pretensions to provide, as newly discovered scientific truths, matters that we already know, and must know in order to live successfully in a society. The sociologist tells us in a formidable barrage of terminology and theory a good many things about our various roles which we must know about in order for the sociologist to have observed us playing them. We are able to do so as a result of instruction and example, and it is thus that we come to act as merchants or teachers or fathers or friends. For a sociologist to tell us about this with the air of novel discovery strikes us as redundant, not to say insulting.

If it is this redundancy that worries Winch, his remedy, according to which sociology is to be adopted as philosophy's foster-child, is misleading. The argument seems sound enough. Concepts make actions possible, and philosophers investigate concepts. Therefore, sociology belongs to philosophy's methodological family. But we learn concepts and we learn how to act by performing tasks, following directions, taking actions. If we understand in some transparent way why we act as we do, it is because we have learned the sort of actions which are appropriate to different contexts. It is not that sociology, in pursuing research methods, is perpetrating a logical howler like the man who would discover whether two and two make four by counting apples. It is rather that this barrage of techniques is quite unnecessary to the kinds of discoveries he proposes to make by its means. Social practice is much like playing games. The rules must be known to play, and playing is to understand what you are doing. If the game puzzles us, we need to appeal to players and umpires, and the social analogues of these in lawyers and business men, doctors and priests, patients and congregations, politicians and voters. Replies to such questions are suspect in proportion to the looseness of the conventions within which the agents act. They can only be removed by seeing very clearly *what* is done and *how* things turn out, discoveries which often serve to correct and amend the rationale of the participants. The anthropologist has the advantage over the sociologist here just because he is engaged in finding out about games which we don't all play. He learns these games by questioning the participants and learning to play himself.

But those who study man or society are engaged as well in a different kind of inquiry which involves comparison of games and practices. It has usually been thought that the point of such comparison is to give the comfort of added evidence to the accounts of specific institutions or practices, and so to treat these special commentaries as rudimentary forms of general laws. I have done what I can to endorse Winch's indictment of this conception of the method of social inquiry. But empirical knowledge must be narrowly conceived indeed to admit only statistical, theoretical or predictive statements to its company. Such a conception is surprising in Winch, for it is a view much more characteristic of those who wish to apply the methods of theoretical science to sociology. Theoretical procedures are adopted generally on the grounds that anything worth saying must observe the form of scientific theory. Winch, I would have thought, ought to be more ready to admit that there are many significant statements that depend upon observations other than those of a statistical or theoretical nature, and that these constitute the bulk of our non-scientific knowledge of the world and of human affairs. This would have been the point, one would have supposed, to his objections to theorizing in sociology. But he is trapped in Hume's dichotomy and thus forced, in rejecting the theoretical, to abandon the empirical. He is thus forced as well to reject the comparison of traits between different cultures, different games, for this too seems to him to have one possible point, the construction of general theories supported by statistical and experimental findings.

Sometimes, it is true, social inquiry is a business of learning a practice. Sometimes, however, it is a business of comparing practices in order to investigate the manner of their origin and diffusion. Thus it helps to place an institution like baptism alongside lustral rites, or attitudes toward the gods alongside father-child or king-subject relationships, or the idea of sacrifice alongside bribery. The social practices placed alongside one another do not thereby become the special consequences of a general theory; rather, the familiar cases are used as ways of exploring the conventions and functions that govern the puzzling case. Similarities suggest lines of geographical contact and temporal dissemination of traits. Exception can be taken to such procedures only if it is assumed that conventions and actions are in every case crystal-clear, which is surely false. Both conventions and actions, except in rule-book cases, are characterized by the sort of ambiguity that would require patient observation and study to diagnose. If diagnoses are tentative, it must be remembered that behaviour is often tentative; to suppose that such ambiguity cries out for scientific procedures is thus to misconstrue the kind of account that is given. Winch, I think, is frightened by the charge of ambiguity into limiting himself to clear cases like games and ceremonies.

Comparison of traits and practices can also serve to suggest lines of historical and geographical diffusion. This move is blocked by Winch, for it seems to suggest a way of accounting which is at odds with his picture of social science. But there appears to be no reason why such a diverse grouping of aims and subject matters as constitute the social sciences should admit of anything so monolithic as a 'methodology.' There can be no social science, if this means that all the ways we talk about human doings can be deduced from a set of laws or that all our inquiries into human action can be characterized by a common procedure. Neither the theoretical models that obsess sociologists nor the game or convention models proposed by Winch can be used to legislate the scope or direction of such inquiries.

12.   The Place of History in the Curriculum

John R. Palmer

DETERMINING WHAT TO TEACH and establishing the most appropriate sequence of learnings are fundamental problems in curriculum construction. Many theories have been tried and proven more
or less successful. It has seemed reasonable on occasion to proceed
from the simple to the complex, or from the familiar to the unfamiliar,
the concrete to the abstract, and so forth. Once well established, the
sequence of content exposure in any area of the curriculum has
tended to remain relatively fixed with an aura of sacredness about
it. Indeed, the shifting of a particular course in a given school from
Grade 9 to Grade 10, for example, has frequently been viewed with
great consternation and come about only after months of faculty
meetings and costly consultation with specialists.

It appears that we are now in "a time of troubles" when upheaval
and change in the curriculum, while not readily acceptable to all,
are occurring at an unusually rapid rate. One need only refer to the
recognition given the work of the Physical Science Study Committee,
the Chemical Bonds Approach Committee, and the University of
Illinois Committee on School Mathematics or to the immediate
popularity of Jerome Bruner's *The Process of Education* to provide
evidence of the trend. Although no such far-reaching proposals have
swept through the social studies, there have been signs of change
but without any clear indication of where they might eventually lead.

Committees of scholars, working in some cases with elementary-
and secondary-school teachers, from the fields of economics, geography, and anthropology are attempting to clarify and organize the
content to be taught from each of these fields in the public schools.
World history, to cite another example, is increasingly becoming
truly world in scope with the addition of major units or even separate courses in non-Western cultures.[1] These are representative

Reprinted by permission from *The School Review*, LXXI:2 (Summer, 1963), 208–221.
Copyright 1963 by the University of Chicago.

[1] Both of these trends are evident in the recent publication by Erling M. Hunt *et. al.*,
High School Social Studies Perspectives (Boston: Houghton Mifflin Company, 1962).
The National Task Force on Economic Education published its basic findings in *Economic Education in the Schools* (New York: Committee for Economic Development,
1961).

of the "bits and pieces" approach that seems to prevail in the social studies. A clearly delineated set of principles or criteria for selecting and ordering content and learning experiences is lacking. In the writer's opinion this is a highly undesirable state of affairs in a period of rapid and dramatic curriculum change. It can only be remedied by clarifying the issues that are basic to the establishment of a defensible program of social education. What follows is an attempt to examine one of these fundamental issues—the place and role of history as contrasted with the several social sciences in the total social-studies curriculum. The matter is approached through an analysis of written history and the tasks performed by the historical researcher as he writes about the past.

The study of history, the broadest of all studies of society, should begin with the recognition that there is something to be explained. Few historians are mere chroniclers of the past. It is necessary that they determine as accurately as possible what has taken place, but they must also attempt to understand and explain these happenings in terms of causes and consequences and find relationships between some of the sequentially ordered events. The historian and the history teacher are quite aware that while a chronicle gives information, it does little to promote understanding.

Consider, for example, the sequence of events surrounding the assassination of President Lincoln, an event of some significance in the history of our country. Much effort has gone into determining precisely what took place immediately before and after the attack in Ford's Theater. We know that the President visited Richmond on April 5, then returned to Washington and worked on plans for the conclusion of hostilities. Both in his last public address on April 11 and at his final cabinet meeting on April 14 Lincoln urged a conciliatory attitude. At 10:15 P.M. on the evening of the 14th, as he was sitting in his box at Ford's Theater watching *Our American Cousin,* he was shot by John Wilkes Booth. He was carried unconscious to a rooming house across the street and died there just before 7:30 A.M. on April 15. Vice-President Johnson took the oath of office as President three hours later.

This series of statements asserts the occurrence of particular events that took place one after the other. To be sure, a great many occurrences that might have been included are missing. As a matter of fact, an entire book has been written about only those things that took place in one twenty-four-hour period during these ten days. But the task of the historian is essentially the same regardless of the minuteness of the details. The assertion of the occurrence of the series of events is only the initial step that helps make possible the difficult and more important task of establishing the interrelations of specific actions and particular occurrences.

In recording the past, the historian almost inevitably explains to some degree each sequence of happenings and relates it to the broader context of events. The reader, as he is carried along by the rapid succession of events leading to Lincoln's assassination, is almost compelled to ask "Why?" to seek an explanation that will make what took place appear plausible. The historian is moved by a similar desire. Quite obviously, an historian's claim that any two events are causally related can be mistaken, but such claims are not made without the belief that the grounds are valid. Few historians claim any occult powers or infallible intuition concerning the connection that exists between individual events. Rather, they make such assertions of causal relationship only on the basis of generalizations derived from previous acquaintance with and knowledge of social and physical phenomena.

To get a better picture of this explanation process, we can look again at the example of the historian's treatment of Lincoln's assassination. If the accounts do not limit themselves to chronology, how is this affair dealt with? Two brief illustrations will suffice.

> But just five days after Appomattox, as he watched a performance of *Our American Cousin* in a Washington theater, Lincoln had been killed by the bullet insanely fired by John Wilkes Booth. All the world mourned. . . . With his passing the nation was to suffer grievously from a tragic failure of leadership.[2]

> At home, in the White House, there was little rest for Lincoln during those tumultuous days and nights of celebration following the surrender at Appomattox. Now, as always, the theater offered him an escape in a physical as well as a psychological sense. It was a place to go to get away from people and be alone while in their midst. . . . On the evening of April 14, 1865, he planned to seek that accustomed relaxation, this time at Ford's Theatre. . . . Mrs. Lincoln, troubled with a headache, suggested that they stay home, but he insisted on going out; otherwise, he said, he would have to see visitors all evening as usual. And so they went.[3]

At first reading these passages seem quite different, but if one considers what each author has done, they are very similar in certain respects. Notice the generalizations about human nature and human behavior that are implicit in them. In the first instance, the mental sta-

[2] Foster Rhea Dulles, *The United States Since 1865*, University of Michigan History of the Modern World, edited by Allan Nevins and Howard M. Ehrmann (Ann Arbor: University of Michigan Press, 1959), p. 7.

[3] J. G. Randall and R. N. Current, *Lincoln the President* (New York: Dodd, Mead and Company, 1953), p. 379.

bility of the assassin is brought into question. Although it is not explicitly stated, the author has apparently assumed that, given the circumstances—the period of crisis through which the country was passing, the great need for leadership which Lincoln was peculiarly suited to fulfil, and so forth—the act of assassination is only explicable on grounds of insanity. In a sense, then, this is not an historical explanation at all but a psychological one. Without listing them, the author has made use of psychological principles to account for an historical event. The average reader "understands," which is to say that he is well acquainted with how our culture views murder, particularly the murder of the President, and the psychological explanation usually given for it. The writer expects this of his readers and feels it is unnecessary to include the complete explanation in the narrative.

It can readily be seen that the second passage also relies heavily on psychological generalizations, but in this instance they are used to account for Lincoln's presence at the fateful performance. This time the author is more explicit in filling in the principles of human behavior he has brought into the explanation process. Some of them might be stated very roughly as follows: (1) Persons working under pressure are subject to fatigue and seek periods of escape; (2) It is possible in a theater to be isolated while in a crowd; (3) A person, once he has planned for and anticipated a pleasurable experience, usually resists interference in carrying out those plans. These generalizations and others like them make it possible for the historian to explain Lincoln's presence at Ford's Theater. Without them he can merely assert that Lincoln was, in fact, there.

In historical research the process of inquiry usually begins with a problem of interpretation triggered by a set of circumstances. It may involve, as in the instance discussed above, the activities of one or a few individuals, or it may involve large groups or an entire nation. But in any case the understanding of human behavior in a complex context of social and physical phenomena is at the heart of the matter. The social sciences, and occasionally the natural sciences, supply the ideas and generalizations with which the historian works. These disciplines provide him with an understanding of the many interdependent variables of a physical, social, economic, political, and intellectual nature that shape the structure and processes of human society.

The fields of economics, political science, sociology, geography, psychology, and anthropology have taken only some part of the total spectrum of human social behavior as their special domain. The historian, however, must always work toward a general synthesis and deal as far as it is possible with the totality of the situation. "His conclusion, if his analysis is successful, is a generalized statement of the nature and meaning of the sequence of events in this particular culture, and an *explanation* of the sequence in terms of the causal influences affecting it."[4] In doing this, he relies heavily on other disciplines.

Although the historian's task can be accomplished only by assuming and using general laws, historians do not see themselves as being involved in the formulation of historical generalizations.[5] Although such men as Arnold Toynbee and Oswald Spengler have tried to show that every society demonstrates a uniform pattern of change, none of these efforts has found wide acceptance among historians. They regard them as contributions to theology or sociology, perhaps, but not to history.[6] The generalizations historians do use tend to be probabilistic in character, which means that they possess a low order of generality. The concepts of which they are constructed are usually imprecise and of indefinite extension when compared to the terminology of the physical sciences or mathematics. Thus one could not have predicted with certainty that President Lincoln would go to the theater but, given the circumstances and his own desires in the matter, *one would expect most people* to have acted as he did. The social sciences generally must be content with such explanations and generalizations at present, but whether this is necessarily the case cannot be answered with certainty.

The reliance of the historian on other disciplines is further borne out by an examination of the terminology he uses. History is written in the vocabulary of the common man with liberal borrowings from other disciplines, particularly the social sciences. Imagine, if you will, writing the history of the 1930's without using such terms as "national debt," "social change," "social class," "conservation," "balance of trade," "socialism," "sound currency," "balanced budget," and so on. Returning to the accounts of Lincoln's assassination, one finds such words as "insanely," "mourned," "escape" (in the psychological sense), "relaxation," and "headache." It is difficult to call these historical concepts unless one is prepared to assert that all

[4] Social Science Research Council, *The Social Sciences in Historical Study*, pp. 104–5; Bulletin No. 64. (New York: Social Science Research Council, 1954.)
[5] Ernest Nagel, "Some Issues in the Logic of Historical Analysis," *Scientific Monthly*, LXXIV (March, 1952), 163; Patrick Gardiner. *The Nature of Historical Explanation*, p. 64. (London: Oxford University Press, 1952.)
[6] M. F. Ashley Montagu (editor), *Toynbee and History: Critical Essays and Reviews* (Boston: Porter Sargent, 1956), pp. 193, 312ff., 361, 371 ff. Edward T. Gargan (editor), *The Intent of Toynbee's History* (Chicago: Loyola University Press, 1961), pp. 11–24. H. Stuart Hughes, *Oswald Spengler* (New York: Charles Scribners Sons, 1952), Chapter 6.

words are peculiar to the study of history.[7] And yet a great variety of concepts is necessary in order to relate and explain historical data. It is essential that history presuppose a vast amount of knowledge, for it has little vocabulary and few generalizations of its own.

The tendency of historians has been increasingly to stress the fact that history is a study of social or cultural phenomena rather than merely an account of political and military events. This was the "New History" of an earlier generation of historians, and the continuing trend is an admission that history presupposes all the social sciences.

The schools have been operating under an illusion for a long time —the illusion that the history that is taught makes clear the "pattern of historical change and process." Curriculums have been formulated and social-studies teachers prepared as if what history explains is "history" itself. Our analysis indicates that it is clearly not the school subject called history that enables us to understand the past but science—economics, anthropology, psychology, and the other social sciences.[8]

This suggests that there are two fallacies in the current conception of the function of history in the curriculum—the "background" fallacy and the "ordinal" fallacy. It is commonly asserted that every student needs to study history for a number of years in order to build a background that will enable him to understand history. But this is fallacious. The study of history (as presently practiced) does not provide the student what he needs to know in order to understand history. If his memory is good he will acquire a backlog of associated names, dates, and events that has a very limited value in further historical inquiry.

There is the related circumstance that Abraham Kaplan has labeled the "ordinal" fallacy [9]—first this, then that; first I will achieve power, then use it for the public good; first I will learn about the past, then use it to comprehend society in general and the present and future in particular. In principle, of course, this seems to be quite right, but in practice often the preparatory phase is never completed so that one may move to the second phase. Doctoral students of history are

---

[7] Morton G. White, "Historical Explanation," *Mind*, LII (July, 1943), 212–29.

[8] It appears that all knowledge is historical knowledge in the sense that it is based on previous experience and learning. But the academic subject "history" as it has developed treats the past in very particular and limited ways. As a result, the term "historical knowledge" has taken on a very special meaning. The correspondence between the past in the fullest sense and the school subject "history" as well as the correspondence between all knowledge and that which is taught in history courses is meager indeed.

[9] Abraham Kaplan, *The New World of Philosophy* (New York: Random House, 1961), p. 60.

building background just as they were in grammar school. There is a sense in which everything we do or learn is preparation for what will follow, but in formal education it frequently happens that nothing follows except further preparation. Opportunities are not provided for the application of the history that has been learned to the analysis of historical change or present circumstances. It is possible, of course, that teachers of history seldom move to the application phase because little that is being taught in history courses can be utilized in this manner. If this be true, it tends to confirm our thesis.

It is illuminating to turn the pages of any history text used in the schools and consider what would remain if the concepts and the subject matter specific to the social sciences as distinct from history were removed. The answer is, of course, the residue would consist of a calendar of names, events, and dates of the barest sort. These are not unimportant, but neither are they all that we claim to teach when we teach history. From the point of view of the relatively naïve student, a history textbook or a history course is actually a multi-disciplinary approach to the human past. The student's understanding of history does not depend primarily on his knowing the calendar of events but on his comprehension of the explanations with which the events are clothed. These explanations consist largely of concepts and generalizations taken from the social sciences which, when properly related, serve to account for the occurrence of particular events or clusters of events.

As in the case of Lincoln's assassination, the historian (and too frequently the history teacher) assumes the student will understand the leaps from cause to effect, that he will be able to supply the economic, anthropological, psychological, or other generalizations that the historian had in mind but failed to write down. It should be emphasized that we are not attempting to pass judgment on the manner in which history is written but only to determine what generally is the case and what its significance may be for the teaching-learning process. The teaching of some part of written history to the future citizen for purposes of general education should be considered as quite distinct from the purposes and procedures of the historical scholar. The assumption has been made here that both tasks are significant and necessary, but that it is an error to attempt to superimpose the methods and purposes of one upon the other.

If this is a reasonably accurate description of the situation, from the standpoint of curriculum construction there appear to be two alternatives that might be seriously considered if we mean to teach history in a productive fashion. The first would involve following through with a chronological survey of the past but teaching con-

HISTORY AND THE SOCIAL SCIENCES

cepts and generalizations from the social sciences whenever they
are needed to provide understanding. If faithfully done, this is a
most difficult task. The complexity of many historical situations, and
therefore the knowledge required to make sense of them, is staggering
for the immature student. It is bold, indeed, to assume that all relevant
concepts, generalizations, and analytical techniques required to comprehend the French Revolution of 1789 or the Protestant Reforma-
tion can be presented by the teacher and grasped by the student at
the appropriate moment. It is also questionable whether or not a
particular generalization pulled from economics, for example, can
be understood and used correctly by a student who has little or no
acquaintance with the logically organized body of concepts and
relationships which make up the economic discipline. Can students
(do students now) achieve an adequate understanding of the structure, concepts, and generalizations of the several social sciences
through the study of history? At the very least, it is questionable.

History textbooks and the preparation of history teachers are pitted
against such learning. Although there are undoubtedly a few persons
with an adequate understanding of history as well as several of the
social sciences, it is probably fair to claim that most history teachers
in elementary and secondary schools are proficient in only one social
science (if any) in addition to history. This situation also seems to
prevail among those who write history textbooks. While many of
these books have a sociological, a political, or some other emphasis,
they are woefully weak in the precision and clarity with which they
present social-science materials. The teacher, being little better informed on many matters than the students, is prone to "teach the
book" when he is outside his areas of competence and thus reinforce
the inaccuracies and vague generalities contained in the texts.

The findings of a committee of the American Economic Association tend to substantiate this contention about history texts. Several
United States history textbooks used in secondary schools were examined "from the point of view of economists seeking information
on the presentation of economic topics." [10] The economists found
that economic topics are generally presented in a descriptive rather
than an analytic fashion, economic forces are not related to social
action, and topics fundamental to the understanding of an economy
are omitted. None of the books examined "adequately presents the
economic aspects of United States history as they are developing
today." [11] It is clear that these economists did not feel that the presentation of economic topics was handled in such a way as to promote

[10] Paul R. Olson, "This Is Economics in the Schools," *American Economic Review*,
LI (May, 1961), 564.
[11] *Ibid.*, p. 568.

understanding of economics. The history teacher not only needs to clarify and supplement the economic material contained in the texts, but he also must be able to detect errors, half-truths, and misinformation. His ability to do this is subject to serious doubt in the light of surveys which indicate that most history teachers have not completed even an elementary college survey of economics.[12]

The second alternative is suggested by the criticisms of the first. The study of written history does not directly provide the basic generalizations and concepts which are needed in order to comprehend human behavior and society, but, paradoxically, these are necessary if one is to read and study history with maximum understanding and profit. The solution for the schools seems to lie in teaching the fundamental concepts and generalizations of the several social sciences prior to the study of history.

It is not possible at present to do more than speculate about such matters as appropriate grade placement and the proper sequential arrangement of the knowledge encompassed by the social sciences. These questions can only be answered through experimental classroom trials and the co-operative efforts of scholars and teachers. But it is an essential first step to clarify the respective positions and roles of history and the social sciences as a basic guide for curriculum construction and experimentation. Our analysis has led to the conclusion that the emphasis should be on the content of the social sciences, at least through the elementary school, with the study of history coming near the culmination of the common school experience. This is not to suggest that nothing from the past enters into the study of the social sciences, for the past provides us with examples and illustrations that are useful in teaching these subjects. But this is very different than requiring the systematic study of particular periods of history.

There are, of course, the further important questions of what history to teach following the social sciences and how to teach it. Quite obviously it is foolish to speak of "the" history. Either we mean by this everything that has ever happened, which constitutes a subject matter so gargantuan as to be incomprehensible and unteachable, or we mean that selection from the past which happens to appeal to us but no one else. While neither of these is acceptable, some criterion for selection is necessary.

Recently it has been popular to consider "that which illuminates the present" as the primary criterion. This is not completely satisfactory, however, on at least two counts. Although every writer and teacher of history is influenced by present realities, each has weak-

[12] For example, the findings of Vernon C. Pohlmann and Frederick L. Wellman, "Are High School Social Studies Teachers Adequately Prepared?" *Social Education*, XXIV (November, 1960), 310–12.

nesses for certain parts of the past that hold a fascination quite apart from any ability to clarify our present predicament. We are all familiar with the American history teacher who spends six weeks on the military campaigns of the Civil War. Even more fundamental is the difficulty of finding any plausible theory as to why what has been selected by the historian or teacher does enable us to understand the present.

The attempt cannot be made here to deal conclusively with these difficulties, but some general observations can be made. Even though complete agreement may be impossible, there are many past occurrences and periods that generally assumed to be significant for the present. If these are able to provide perspective in which to view the present and the future they have served a useful purpose. At the same time, whatever history is studied should offer students the opportunity of dealing with social reality in its full complexity, as a system of interrelated variables representing the several aspects of human life.

By giving students prior preparation in the social sciences, history might serve as the course in the curriculum on which knowledge of all aspects of human society is brought to bear. The history class can provide an arena in which evidence from any area of knowledge may be presented and considered. Any ideas, any occurrences, the activities of any individual are admissible if their significance for the circumstances under consideration can be established.

Conceiving of the study of history in this way counteracts the tendency toward fragmentation of knowledge that is a continuing problem in formal education. It should also curtail the present tendencies in history classes to make superficial social generalizations and oversimplify historical and current problems. The student will be able to draw upon the findings of specialists in many facets of society to further his own understanding. In life situations the student-citizen is required to understand a total social context as it is in a given point in time, how it developed, and to what it may lead. This is the problem of the historian as well, and history courses can, if properly placed and taught, provide the student experience with this type of analysis.

We cannot and dare not rub out the past, but neither can we make it replace our present and our future. "What must be done is to face resolutely both the old world and the new, and to attempt once more the age-old task of adjustment and reconstruction. . . . We must understand what is new in terms of the ideas we already have; we have no others." [13] This necessarily involves reference to the past. But the study designated as "history" in the schools has certain peculiarities, as we have pointed out, that stand in the way of its fulfilling, in

[13] John Herman Randall, Jr., *Nature and Historical Experience* (New York: Columbia University Press, 1958), p. 8.

and of itself, the benefits to be derived from studying the past. In a very real sense all knowledge is needed, but more particularly the social sciences.

It is certainly true that history now dominates the social-studies curriculum throughout the elementary and secondary schools. Perhaps partly because this has traditionally been the case, the place and the treatment of history in the curriculum has been quite resistant to change. This is unfortunate because, while the social sciences have been developing and changing rapidly during the past half-century, the conception of history has also been undergoing significant changes. We are now able to speak of cultural historians, economic historians, political historians, and so forth. The discipline has greatly extended its scope and incorporated many things from the social sciences. During this same period the several social sciences have developed their research techniques and bodies of knowledge with greater precision and clarity. It now appears that history for purposes of common education can be more profitably studied and can better fulfil its functions, both in preparing the young as citizens and in enhancing their general intellectual development, if a fundamental revision is made in its place in the curriculum.

---

13. Generalization and History

D. Bob Gowin

A GENERALIZATION IN HISTORY, a wise old historian is reported to have remarked,[1] is anything two historians can agree on. This generous sense of senatorial courtesy in the academic community is

Reprinted by permission of the author and publisher from *Proceedings of the Twenty-Fourth Annual Meeting of the Philosophy of Education Society*, 1968 (Edwardsville, Illinois: Studies in Philosophy and Education, Southern Illinois University, 1968). This essay in part of a longer work on *The Structure of Knowledge in History* by D. B. Gowin and Mark M. Krug to be published by Random House, Inc.

[1] Alexander V. Riasanovsky and Barnes Riznik, *Generalizations in Historical Writing* (Philadelphia: University of Pennsylvania Press, 1963) 11. This book contains essays by H. Stuart Hughes, Isaiah Berlin, David M. Potter, Albert Guerard and Crane Brinton. Another book with a similar title which will also be referred to is edited by Gottschalk. Louis Gottschalk, *Generalization in the Writing of History* (Chicago: The University of Chicago Press, 1963). Part III of this book contains the best bibliography of writings on historiography and the philosophy of history that I have found. It was compiled by Martin Klein.

probably more a result of battles fought to an uneasy draw than a result of the identification and analysis of a most critical intellectual problem within the field of history. Testimony by scholars in history reveals that they think they have not paid enough attention to the problem of generalization.[2] If the academic disciplines cannot put their own intellectual house in order, then the recent recommendation that scholars in education should look to academic scholarship as their model seems wasted motion. But looked at in another light perhaps education is the place where important issues and problems come to a focus such that distinctions not made as well as those thought useful within academic fields can be tested and appraised for their validity. John Dewey was well aware of the usefulness of education as a laboratory for the expression and testing of philosophical distinctions. Perhaps the distinctions within the field of history when framed by the window of educational needs and practices can be given a test somewhat more rigorous than the chance agreement of professors of history.

The dangers of the amateur outsider are well recognized by me; I am such a person to the field of history. And it is apparent to me that I cannot do education without trenching on concerns that historians have or ought to have taken seriously. The questions simply put are these: What is subject matter content? How can we identify, select, define and justify *what* is taught in schools? What is the structure of knowledge in general and in history in particular? Where does history fit in the curriculum of our schools, what is its value for pupils and the general society? These questions of subject matter and curriculum are inescapable problems in education. I agree with Professor Schwab when he writes, "Of the four topics of education—the learner, the teacher, the milieu, and the subject matter (that which is intended to be taught or learned)—none has been so thoroughly neglected in the past half century as the last." [3]

The neglect is apparent in the social studies curriculum. Whether

---

[2] David M. Potter, *People of Plenty* (Chicago: The University of Chicago Press, 1954) xviii–xix. ". . . history for nearly twenty-five centuries after the time of Herodotus simply did not deal in generalization. It dealt with unique events, such as the conduct of a particular battle or the negotiation of a particular treaty, and all of the much-vaunted "historical method" was a method for determining specific events by means of rigorous textual criticism and severe rules for the evaluation of evidence. The arts or techniques of broad interpretation or of generalization from a mass of specific data were not part of the 'historical method . . .' In recent decades the historian's lack of systematic procedure in the practice of generalization has become a serious liability." Writers in the books cited in 1 support Potter's contention while at the same time doing something about reducing its severity by their own analyses.

[3] Stanley Elam (editor), *Education and the Structure of Knowledge* (Chicago: Rand McNally, 1964) 4. Professor Schwab is now at work on a two year financed study of the structure of knowledge.

we are talking about history or social science, elementary, secondary or higher education, there is and has been great confusion and lack of precision concerning *what* the subject matter content of the social studies is or should be. Curriculum reform efforts in other areas, notably the sciences and mathematics, have at least given us, whatever else their ultimate deficiencies may be, the idea that people in those fields could agree on some of the essential concepts and generalizations in their subject matter. A method much used recently for establishing agreement on content has been to ask academic scholars to identify and define the basic organizing ideas, to hold conferences among experts where these agreements were reinforced to some extent, to select individuals to write syllabi and then to try out and evaluate these materials with selected teachers in selected school systems. If the curricula survive this process, then the rest of us are obliged to adopt these materials and methods.

This pattern of work is being tried in history and the social studies but it does not appear to be nearly as successful as the other efforts. For some the reason seems obvious: History deals with the unique, the concrete, the particular; it does not deal with principles and generalizations and explanatory laws. Therefore there can be no organizing principles to historical knowledge such that the content in this area of human concern can be ordered neatly. So goes the argument.

It is held by some that there are doubt-free grounds for recognizing basically different orders of phenomena in nature and experience, each order of phenomena requiring a different discipline for its investigation because of the differences in the character of the phenomena. If we try to distinguish history and science we find the view that stresses the vast difference between the generality of natural phenomena (i.e., their predictability, the tendency of natural things to behave or be the same in instance after instance) and the particularity of human events, (i.e., the essentially unique and non-repeating character of acts notable in the behavior of man). Science seeks general laws that characterize the repeating behavior of natural things. History would seek to determine the precise, unique events that characterize each life, each era, each civilization or culture that it studied. Aristotle is supposed to have remarked that "Poetry is more philosophical than history," presumably because it gets at the universal by studying the essence of a particular individual. This remark may be the source of the distinction between two allegedly different kinds of sciences: the nomothetic, the sciences of abstract general laws for indefinitely repeatable events, and the ideographic—the sciences for understanding the unique and nonrecurrent. If we examine, if only cursorily, the statements found in science books and history books we will soon note that the statements of science are general in form and make few references to specific dates, places, objects. Statements in history, on the other hand, are liberally sprinkled with dates, places, names, and references to the particular.

A recent article by Professor Mark M. Krug sets the curriculum educational problem explicitly.[4] Krug undertakes an analysis of Professor Jerome Bruner's new social studies curriculum proposals. Since Bruner's committee report of the deliberations of a large group of scholars at Woods Hole in 1959, which was published as *The Process of Education*,[5] a lot of talk has arisen in education concerning the structure of knowledge. The claim is made that if pupils can grasp the structure of a discipline they then will have a kind of basic understanding far superior to the add-summative iteration of particular facts. Bruner writes: "The structure of knowledge—its connectedness and its derivations that make one idea follow another—is the proper emphasis in education. For it is structure, the great conceptual inventions that bring order to the congeries of disconnected observations, that gives meaning to what we may learn and makes possible the opening up of new realms of experience." [6] Elsewhere Bruner argues, if it can be called an argument, that for young people to adapt to changing conditions, they must study "the possible rather than the achieved." [7] Further, "It is the behavioral sciences and their generality with respect to variations in the human condition that must be central to our presentation of man, not the particularities of his history." [8] And Krug writes: "Thus, Bruner has made his choice. Without equivocation and without any attempt to becloud the real issue, he wants the social studies curriculum in elementary and secondary schools to be centered on the concepts and generalizations and skills from the behavioral sciences. He is willing and ready to abandon the teaching of history with its stress on the unique, the separate, the particular." [9]

Bruner, as a social scientist, picks out the generalizing feature of social sciences in order to establish the structure of knowledge about man, and Krug, as a historian, makes the claim that history deals with the particular. Both Bruner and Krug would seem to be correct. If we want the curriculum to reflect Bruner's structure-of-knowledge ap-

---

[4] Mark M. Krug, "Bruner's New Social Studies: A Critique," *Social Education*, October, 1966) 400–406.

[5] Jerome S. Bruner, *The Process of Education* (Cambridge: Harvard University Press, 1962).

[6] Jerome S. Bruner, *On Knowing* (Cambridge: Harvard University Press, 1962) 120.

[7] Jerome S. Bruner, "Education As Social Invention," *Saturday Review*, (February 19, 1966) 103.

[8] Idem.

[9] Krug, op. cit., p. 406.

proach, then, since such structures depend on identifying key concepts and generalizations, history is out. By the same token, if we want to be true to the nature of historical knowledge, then we cannot expect to teach it through the structure of knowledge, for history has no set of central, organizing generalizations.[10]

If both are correct, as they seem to be to this point, then our curriculum decision is simple: teach both the social sciences for their generalizing power, and history for its individualizing power. And, as seems reasonable, only those things should be in the curriculum which augment and add a different flavor to the total curriculum mix. But this solution is too facile and does an injustice to the nature of historical knowledge.

There are several terms we can use to talk about subject matter knowledge—facts, concepts, principles, generalizations among others. Since there is a special problem about generalizations in history, I will deal primarily with that term. If we read more than a little written history, and think about the kinds of statements found there, we may be surprised. Despite the disclaimer against generalization, there are to be found in history statements of a remarkably general sort. The main issue of this paper concerns the epistemological status of these general statements. In considering this issue, I will try to identify and describe some ways of thinking about generalizations in history. First, I will exhibit an example of a summarizing generalization and suggest a technique by which such summarizing generalizations could be converted to explicit generalizations which go beyond the particular study in which they arise.

Here is an example of a historical generalization found in a recent piece of historical analysis by a historian-philosopher. His topic is Chinese history, long a fertile area of historical research.

> "The power of the state apparatus and of the emperor steadily increased in later centuries. The history of Chinese thought by itself cannot, of course, explain completely this rise of despotism. Certainly related to it was the economic condition of the literati, the existence or nonexistence of enormously powerful families, the increase in the number of potential bureaucrats upon whom the state could draw, and the personality of powerful emperors, as well as some of the harsher accidents of military history." [11]

[10] Ernest Nagel, *The Structure of Science* (New York: Harcourt, Brace & World, Inc., 1961) 548. And of course, as the philosophers of science acknowledge, no conclusions concerning the actual character of specific things and processes in nature can be derived from general statements alone, because theories and laws must be supplemented by initial conditions, that is, by statements singular or instantial in form, if the generalizations are to serve for explaining or predicting any *particular* occurrence. The natural sciences are not exclusively nomothetic and the historical sciences are not simply ideographic.

[11] David S. Nivison and Arthur F. Wright (eds.), *Confucianism in Action* (Stanford: Stanford University Press, 1959) 14.

A paraphrase of this generalization could take the form: Power increases in time—(in China)—as a function of shifts in Chinese thought, the poor economic position of the literati, presence or absence of powerful families, increasing number of (pliant) bureaucrats, powerful emperors, and accidents of military power.

This generalization is a *summarizing* generalization. It brings together a number of observed factors. It seems to take the form of "If A happens, and we have records that it did, then A is correlated with other happenings. Some of these happenings, which we also have records for, are the following." And then the list is compiled. To document accurately just what these happenings are with which A is correlated is to make a generalization.

But it is difficult to work with a generalization in this form. It seems merely to record a correlation (to be sure of complex phenomena). Suppose we compose another generalization from Nivision's summarizing generalization. Thus:

> Despotic political power increases as a function of strong leaders, powerful families, less powerful literati, pliant bureaucrats, accidents of military history.

Even in this form it remains no more than a summarizing generalization. Two parts of the generalization are highly contingent: the presence or absence of powerful families and the harsher accidents of military history. These two parts seem to be specific qualifications which contribute to the shift in power, but their contribution is not one which we can generalize about. When Nivison comes to his explanation, we are able to compose a broader generalization. In his explanation he is trying to relate the loss of power of the intellectuals and the rise of despotic political power.

> ". . . in Ch'ing, by the 18th century, Chinese despotism had become as perfect as human things become; not only was the emperor's command of political power unqualified, but his moral authority, even his intellectual authority, was paramount, and the literati now accepted this situation as natural and right.
>
> "In retrospect, it seems that nothing else could have happened. There were many reasons why the literati lost the independent power and prestige they had enjoyed: stern and impersonal institutional forces and fickle whims of political fortune played their part. But the fate of Confucian utopia was the fate history so often metes out to bright illusions—to the hopes of the Roman Republic, of Rousseau, of Marx. The Neo-Confucian visionaries wanted a utopian totalitarianism, minus the trappings and sinews, the harsh reality, of power. What they got was not what they wanted. But it was what we might have expected." [12]

[12] Ibid., p. 23–24.

This is the moral of his story, so to speak. He seems to be asking this telling question: why do intellectuals with good ideas lose power and prestige such that other men, less good, even despotic, gain power and control? He says that the explanation—the reason why—cannot be found in the context of the intellectuals alone. Other powers entered in. But there is one factor common to effective intellectual life per se: it must not be cut off from other sources of power —economic, political, administrative. The explanation seems to be: force of ideas without force in the social order is illusory.

It is important to note that generalizations are different from explanations. Explanations give us reasons by which to interpret the phenomena described and summarized in generalizations. If we accept the reasons, we may claim to understand. Thus, there is a linkage of terms and statement forms: understanding comes from accepting the reasons given in the explanation; the explanation is of the summarizing generalization which is in turn based upon concepts which are signs pointing to a set of facts which serve as evidence for the generalization. In a sense, the farther we move away from facts along this linkage, the more interesting the narrative becomes but also the less confidence we may have in the final form.

I would now like to compose a generalization which goes beyond Nivison's summarizing generalization. I will call it #2.

> #2. "In social life, when ideas and intellectuals are separated from effective political power, the hope for the achievement of the ideas will be found to be just another bright illusion."

A statement in this form, #2, can be taken out of the context in which it was made and related to other contexts. For example, examine statement #3.

> #3. In the intellectual community of the university, when intelligent criticism of educational practices is separated from effective administrative power, the hope for the achievement of desirable educational change will be found to be just another bright illusion.

This generalization could have reference to a number of university educational practices. For example, the recent rise in students' criticisms about course offerings—the free university idea—turns out on some campuses to be merely an illusion when students are unable to exercise power over the selection of instructors, readings and meeting places. In Nivision's meaning, student intellectuals are not going to get what they want without facing up to the harsh reality of power.

This example may seem forced. Let us take a less complex example.

> #1a. "Those who have learned helpless submission are better
> prepared to exercise tyranny than to cooperate in social integra-
> tion."

This statement can be made into a broader generalization by exchanging some particular phrases for more general phrases.

> #2a. "Those who have learned to adapt to a social system are
> better prepared to act out all the old roles of that system than to
> create new social roles."

A generalization of this form does not, of course, have to be true. It
is a valid generalization from #1a, however. The generalization from
#1a to #2a begins by replacing "helpless submission' with "adapt to a
system." Adapting to a system is clearly a more general case of which
helpless submission is a particular case. Likewise, "to exercise tyranny"
is a particular form of "acting out the roles of a social system." And
"to cooperate in social integration" is one particular way of acting
whereas "to create new social roles" is more general.

What is the point to this generalizing? The point is that generalization #2a can serve as a kind of logical bridge from the context in
which generalization #1a was generated across to other instances not
seemingly related to that original context. For example, I can compose generalization #3a from #2a, but I might not have been able to
compose #3a from #1a. Thus:

> #3a. "Those who have become educated in formal schools are
> better prepared to follow the patterns of their teachers than to
> create new ways of acting for themselves and their pupils.

For most people experienced in teacher education, this is a common
observation that student teachers tend to teach as they were taught
and not as they were taught to teach. Is this stretching? Yes, but that's
what we want.

When the concept of generalization is thought about in this way,
we find that a form of reasoning can occur. We can use one set of
ideas as a logical bridge to another set of ideas. The technique for
generalization-making is a simple one and could easily be taught in
historical method. Standard logical cautions, including the following,
should be noted.

1. The new, broader generalization should be applicable to the
   older, less broad one.
2. It should not be presumed to be necessarily true.
3. The possibility of finding evidence for or against it must not be
   ruled out by the way it is stated.

This process of generalization, as described, is different from that described by Professor Phenix as characterizing mathematical generali-

zation.[13] Briefly, mathematical generalizations develop by dropping out particulars, according to certain rules of calculation and axiomatic and systemic consistency. This process of generalization as recommended for historical knowledge construction involves replacing some particulars in a generalization with other particulars each having a more general meaning.

This last example, and analysis, is merely a brief attempt to show that one can reconstruct historical knowledge into forms which will permit the same kind of generalizing power, or at least similar to that claimed for the social sciences. Lurking behind the notion of generalizing power of social science is the notion of the establishment of causal laws of nature. There have been statements by such historians as Buckle and Marx asserting that it is possible to discover the single causal law in history. Before we can disentangle this claim we must make three distinctions common to the definitions of history.[14]

We must distinguish between history-as-actuality, history-as-record and written-history. History-as-actuality means all that has been felt, thought, imagined, said, and done by human beings as such and in relation to one another and to their environment since the beginning of mankind's operations on this planet. History-as-actuality leaves a residue, a record. History-as-record consists of documents and other unwritten records, such as coins, monuments, photographs, recorded sound. These documents are the basis for written-history. Written-history is defined as a systematic or fragmentary narration or account purporting to deal with all or part of history-as-actuality.

Now those who seek causal laws seek regularities in the very process of history-as-actuality. Marx's view of the class struggle as underlying all other aspects of human history is the classic case in point. There are many reasons for rejecting the Marxian or single cause position; I will just mention the one that appeals to me. Suppose history-as-actuality leaves no record? We have examples within our own experience which give us evidence for believing that there are events which pass and vanish, leaving no perceptible record. For example, if I mark the position of a boat in the water by making an X on the water, in time no record is left. My own memory of the event lasts a while, but then it too will vanish. Suppose history-as-actuality is like that in important ways? If the records of the phenomena vanish, then the likelihood of man discovering the laws of history-as-actuality is greatly

[13] Philip H. Phenix, "An Analytic View of the Process of Generalization," *Studies in Philosophy and Education*, V (Spring, 1967), 245–66.
[14] *Theory and Practice in Historical Study: A Report of the Committee on Historiography* (Social Science Research Council Bulletin 54 (New York: 1946) 5.

reduced.[15] It is at this point that the claim of the nonrepeatability of
human events is characteristically applied to historical knowledge.

I think it is important to understand that historical knowledge is
knowledge of man and his doings. But I think that the question of the
reliability of historical knowledge is best resolved by looking at the
relation between history-as-record and written-history. The records are
before the historian as he works. They supply the evidence for his
inferences. And these records can be repeatedly examined. The jump
from evidence to inference can be made by many different historians
poring over the same documents. Whether reading an aerial photo-
graph of the fields of France (as Bloch did in his study of feudal
society) or reading the film record from a Wilson cloud chamber, the
process of reasoning from evidence to inference is alike for historian
or physicist. The historian uses a generalization as a summarizing
logical form; it is something to make sense of and to tie together a
lot of specific facts. Social scientists use generalizations as something
to be established in the logical form of "If A, then B, with qualifications." Or "Every case of A is also a case of B." And the social scientists are not too concerned that one particular set of facts is used, just
as long as some facts can be found.

We do not want to accept the historian's defense of his subject
matter on the ground of its being ideographic. He can and does use
generalizations, and perhaps should be encouraged to use them more
effectively and more often. But we do want to keep the historian at
work on the study of a set of specific facts. Why facts? Several reasons.
First we want evidence for our inferences. Second, we value truth,
especially in areas of human concern where it is easy to be deceived;
statements of facts help us to remember what happened. Third, a fact
(as referent to a statement of fact) is a factum, something done. If we
have factual evidence that something *did* happen, then we know that
an event like that *could* happen. Anything that did happen is possible.
Facts entail possibility. We do not have to suggest, although it is a
common suggestion to make, that if something did happen once then
it might happen again, and hence that historical knowledge serves as
a beacon into the future. The important thing is to realize that facts
entail possibility.

Facts, of course, are not simple things. Facts, too, are general. Carl
Becker saw this well in his paper entitled "What are Historical
Facts?" That "Caesar crossed the Rubicon in 49 B.C." turns out not
to be a simple fact, for there was Caesar's army to cross with him,

[15] I am reminded here of a remark attributed to Bertrand Russell which I have been
unable to locate. Roughly paraphrased, Russell said that while we have discovered some
simple causal laws in nature, it may not be that nature is simple and regular but only
that what we have discovered takes this form.

many acts and many words and many lesser facts go into one simple fact. It is the statement of the fact that is simple, not the fact, not the thing done. A fact is . . . "a simple statement which is a generalization of a thousand and one simpler facts which we do not for the moment care to use, and this generalization itself we cannot use apart from the wider facts and generalizations which it symbolizes." [16]

The historian differs from the experimental scientist in that the scientist generates his own facts whereas the historian must try to account for the particular set of facts he has before himself in the record. The ingenuity of the experimental scientist comes in setting up test conditions that are somehow unusual and artificial; in a sense he must find a novel way to interrogate nature. The experimental scientist manipulates events so they leave a mark, a record. The historian must find a new way to ask telling questions of the recorded facts he already has at hand. This difference seems to me to be the important difference between science and history, not the ideographic-nomothetic distinction. In thinking about the constructions of written history, it is helpful to distinguish three meanings of fact. $fact_1$ is the event that happened or the thing that was done, the factum; $fact_2$ is the record left behind of what was done; $fact_3$ is the statement of the thing done, based on the record, and placed in a context of other statements (a narrative). Of these three meanings, only $fact_1$ is a particular, unique happening; recorded facts and statements of fact may take the form of generalizations as Becker argues.

Thus far I have considered these aspects of the nature of historical generalization: (1) the existence of summarizing generalizations in written history, (2) a suggested technique for converting summarizing generalizations into explicit transferable generalizations which go beyond the data from which they were derived, and (3) the similarity and difference between facts and generalizations.

A generalization may also serve as the telling question of the historian. David Potter reports that he began his *People of Plenty* study with the simple question of the relation between economic abundance and American national character. What is the effect of abundance on Americans? Before he completes his study Potter relates abundance to: natural resources, equality, democracy, mobility, social classes, status, political methods, lack of intellectualism, political commitment, the mission of America, "frontier" influence, advertising, individual character formation, child rearing practices, housing, siblings, clothing, parents, physical maturation, and romantic love. Quite a list!

His study is not a simple set of statistical correlations. And it would be a mistake to extract the generalization "If abundance, then these

[16] Carl Becker, "What Are Historical Facts?" *The Western Political Quarterly*, VIII: 3 (September, 1955), pp. 327–40.

traits." Economic abundance and the life style of a people can be seen, however, as representing one form of social organization and individual choices. As representative, a historical study such as this both generalizes and particularizes. Historical studies of Greek life for example, as of any epoch, present a peculiar and individual combination of selected human qualities. Greek life may be thought of as a peak expression of the combination of the intellectual and esthetic. As long as free choice is real, any life *could* have that combination given the necessary conditions. It has been proven that it is possible. American life, as Potter shows, has a different and specific combination of human qualities which are representative of a life style of an age.

The volume of facts, concepts, generalizations when brought together by the historian create meaning. Meaning is a function of the context, the network of relations. I like the term "voluminosity" to characterize this aspect of historical knowledge. Each written history should have its central subject, and its richness of detail describing that subject. These organized centers and diversities create a kind of understanding of human beings just as surely as, but in a different way from, statistical measures of central tendency and estimates of standard deviations found in behavioral sciences. Take one other kind of historical work, the biography. How is it possible to get a generalization from the study of one individual person? If we think of an individual as the focus of energies which connect things in experience, then we can see that the study of an individual, like the study of a society, generalizes because it is representative of a center, a focus. Some things have been brought together and many other things have dropped out. Centrality of personal character is a generalization in human form.[17]

The root meaning of a generalization seems to me to be a statement of connections found in experience. Many linguistic forms—facts, concepts, laws, explanations, metaphors—also function as connectors, to stand for relations between variables. Note how each of the following perform this function: *poetic image* ("The force that through the green fuse drives the flower drives my green age"), *statistical generalization* ("75% of these sampled coffee beans are brown"), *empirical generalization* ("Laborers spend more per adult for food than do white collar employees with the same size income"), *law* ("The sui-

---

[17] The hero in history is a generalization even though he appears as a unique being. The hero is actually a combination of qualities of particular individuals, and extended into size and proportion that is greater than that of any one person. The hero serves to generalize across instances, not only in the way in which he was put together in the past but also as a guide to the future: we can imagine how the hero would have acted under circumstances like those we now face.

cide rate varies inversely with degree of social integration characteristic of any group"), *historical generalization* ("People will be influenced by the circumstances and conditions in which they live and collective responses to distinctive conditions will in time take the form of collective traits that are themselves distinctive").

We cannot expect historians to search out and find the dozen or so generalizations central to all historical knowledge. One attempt to do so, cited by Krug, is a three year Wisconsin study: A *Conceptual Framework for the Social Studies in Wisconsin Schools*, Social Studies Bulletin, issued by Angus B. Rothwell, State Department of Public Instruction, Madison, Wisconsin, December, 1964. From these three years of work the following five generalizations were reached:

1. Every effort at reform began as the private opinion of an individual.
2. It is difficult to separate fact from fiction. Every writer has his biases.
3. Facts may often be interpreted in more than one way.
4. Nations with great power may not always use it wisely.
5. Those who cannot remember the past may be condemned to repeat it.

The historians arrived at five glimpses of obvious, or the dubious, as the case may be. They represent nothing characteristically historical; they are not related to a certain kind of inquiry; and they summarize no specific set of historical facts. One might have picked up these statements from reading novels, or political science, perhaps even philosophy. Meyerhoff's generalization, "The only safe generalization about history is that it will always be rewritten," has at least the virtue of logic. Any piece of written history is also a piece of history-as-actuality, of history-as-record and may serve as data for the next historian to use. In a sense writing history makes history. It is a candidate for later criticism and interpretation. It is safe to generalize that history will be rewritten for the evidence for *that* generalization is found in the nature of historical process itself.

The answer to Bruner (and for Krug) is to devise a method by which we can uniformily analyze the structure of knowledge in *any* historical work. We need a method so we won't have to depend upon the chancy choice of scholars only infrequently interested in the difficult problems of education.

A generalization is only one term in a group of terms used in talking about the structure of knowledge. Other terms—and each one needs analysis—are concept, fact, principle, assumption, presupposition, explanation, interpretation, conclusion, value. If we could develop a method which would precisely and systematically cause us to discover these aspects about *each* historical work, then we would be on strong ground for getting at the structure of knowledge in history. The attempt to stretch history over the specialized definition of the behavioral sciences just won't work: historical knowledge is shaped by the kind of inquiry that produced it, and there are important variations in the types of inquiry useful to the study of mankind.[18]

Experience with its modes, its connections, its intersections is the primary ground out of which such things as generalizations are formed. Historical generalizations have a different logical form to the extent that they are products of a different form of inquiry. As Dewey writes of historical knowledge: "Nowhere is it easier to find a more striking instance of the principle that new (logical) forms accrue to existential material when and because it is subjected to inquiry." [19] Statements in a discipline are like words in a sentence —they take their meaning from the context, claims Schwab. To place the products of inquiries in the context of the pathway of inquiry is to get an insight into their logical form. To understand how constructed knowledge came to be is to understand one relation between human experience and knowledge. Bruner seems correct when he relates "structures" to the role they serve in bringing order to disconnected observations, to opening up new realms of experience. I seriously doubt, however, that he is correct in claiming that the structure of knowledge defined as the connectedness and derivations that make one *idea* follow another is the proper emphasis in education. Merely relating one idea to another can be the worst form of empty verbalism.

My last comment—more a comment than a conclusion—is this: The most general question we can ask about subject matter knowledge in an educational context is the relation between such examples of propositional knowledge and the nature of human experience. In my view historical knowledge can be considered distinctive and should be thought of in its own right but not in its own terms, for the historians' defense of their subject is often inadequate. This analysis may not do justice to the topic, but the topic is a just topic for full and complete analysis.

[18] It is only by convention that we fail to recognize that the celebrated repeatability of experimental science is also a historical phenomenon. Only by convention can we agree that experiments repeated are the "same." All knowledge is part of history-as-actuality and is historical in that sense.

[19] John Dewey, *Logic* (New York: Henry Holt & Co., Inc., 1938) pp. 230–39.

PART FOUR
Literature and the Arts

14. Art, Language, and Truth

Morris Weitz

IN CONTEMPORARY AESTHETIC INQUIRY there is a good deal of discussion about the linguistic character of art. Morris, Langer, Cassirer, Richards, Burke, Blackmur, Panofsky, Ducasse, Freud, and others have dealt extensively with this aspect of art. Parker has pointed out that, historically speaking, this is a rather new approach. Two other basic interpretations of art preceded this linguistic one, the dominant view of our era. First was the doctrine that art is essentially imitation, either of the universal features of reality, including human experience, or of the beautiful in nature. This doctrine, whose hegemony lasted some two thousand years and which was known as classicism, was unable to explain much of art, especially fantastic art; consequently, it was succeeded by the romantic theory, according to which art is essentially imagination. Further probings into the nature of art, especially in the last one hundred years or so, disclosed the social and communicative character of art, and led eventually to the contemporary view that art is essentially a language.[1]

The organic theory concurs with this prevalent conception of art. Because it stresses the expressive dimension of art, that is, the fact that all of its constituents may function as icons, indices, or symbols to spectators, it accepts the thesis that art is a language.

But to affirm that art is a language immediately provokes the query, what *kind* of language? The most imposing, perhaps even the most accepted, view today is that art is an *emotive* language. Ducasse and I. A. Richards are among the champions of this view. Ducasse writes: *"Art is essentially a form of language—namely, the language of feeling, mood, sentiment, and emotional attitude. It is thus to be distinguished from the language of assertion."* [2]

---

[1] DeWitt H. Parker, "Aesthetics," *Twentieth Century Philosophy*, ed. Dagobert D. Runes (New York: Philosophical Library, 1947), pp. 42–45.

[2] C. J. Ducasse, *Art, the Critics, and You* (New York: Oskar Piest, 1944), pp. 52–53 (italics in original).

However, it is Richards who has offered the details of the emotive theory. According to him (and C. K. Ogden), at least in *The Meaning of Meaning*, which constitutes the prolegomenon to Richards' later work, language has many functions. It symbolizes thought, expresses attitudes of the speaker, evokes attitudes in the listener, and promotes certain effects. But these can be sharply divided into two main functions, the symbolic and the emotive. Symbolic language, or the symbolic use of words, is the statement, recording, support, and communication of thought, whereas emotive language, or the emotive use of words, is the evocation, expression, or excitation of feelings and attitudes.

To illustrate: Suppose I say, "This painting is the work of Picasso." My statement is informative, referential, and true or false, depending upon whether or not the painting *is* Picasso's. But if I say, "This painting is excellent," then, according to Richards, I am not really saying anything *about* the painting; instead I am articulating or expressing my feelings of approval toward it, perhaps even in the hope of evoking similar feelings in my listeners.

This distinction between the emotive and the symbolic (referential) uses of language Richards regards as basic to the distinction between art, especially literature, which is his main problem, and science. To understand the emotive use of language and to use it exclusively is the function of art. Art ought to abandon its quest for knowledge and truth, for it is not necessary to know *what* things are in order to express our feelings toward them.[3]

In its semantical dimension, the emotive theory of Ducasse and Richards is the view that art, as a system of signs, does not embody propositions or referential assertions, that is, *truth claims*, but serves only as the expression or excitation of feelings, emotions and attitudes. Carnap has supplemented this view, which is essentially positivistic, by affirming the kinship of artistic (also metaphysical and ethical) language and certain body gestures. I laugh, I cry, I yell, or I stamp my feet. My laughing, crying, yelling, or stamping my feet expresses my feelings and attitudes. Linguistically, when I perform in these ways, I communicate something to my audience; and I may even inspire them to similar body activity. But I do not say anything; I state no fact; I make no claim. What I do is not true or false, but an expression of feeling. So too with art; it is also a form of emotional gesture, a kind of stamping of one's feet or clapping of one's hands, but ever so nicely! Thus, the language of art, from literature to music,

---

[3] C. K. Ogden and I. A. Richards, *The Meaning of Meaning* (New York: Harcourt, Brace and Company, 1923), esp. pp. 123–126, 147–151, 227–229, and 230–236.

is closer to body gestures than it is to the language of science or empirical statements.[4]

This theory raises an extremely important question, one which is central to the contemporary doctrine that art is a language. Is art merely an emotive language or is it referential and assertive as well? *Can art embody truth claims?*

Among contemporary aestheticians who have been engaging in debate on this issue, T. M. Greene has offered the most extensive defense of the doctrine that art does embody truth claims, and he maintains that all of the arts, not only literature, embody "propositional truth." His theory has been discussed in two recent books, by B. C. Heyl and by John Hospers. Both of these critics, I think, have succeeded in exposing the inadequacies of Greene's position, so that there would be no point here in entering into *their* particular dispute, especially if one, like myself, does not accept the premises of either side of the dispute.[5] Instead, we shall present a different solution.

Hospers, in his critique of Greene, comments: "Professor Greene might have sought a way out which in fact he does not, namely, to say that works of art are *implied* assertions (or else that they imply assertions)." [6]

This "way out" has already been indicated by DeWitt Parker, in his formulation of the concept of "depth meaning."

> Many poems and some works of plastic art possess what I like to call "depth meanings"—meanings of universal scope underneath relatively concrete meanings or ideas. Thus in the following line of one of Frost's little poems
> "Nothing gold can stay"
> the word "gold" has its usual surface meaning, but underneath that is its depth meaning, precious; so in addition to saying that nothing golden can endure, the poet is saying that nothing valuable can abide—a more universal statement.[7]

In my opinion, the introduction of Parker's concept of depth meaning offers us a new way of analyzing the problem of truth in art. I do not think that it solves the whole problem for us but it does seem to solve at least part of it, and in the following way. Let us, for the moment, grant the positivistic thesis that literature (with the trivial

---

[4] Rudolf Carnap, *Philosophy and Logical Syntax* (London: Kegan Paul, Trench, Trubner and Company, 1935), Chap. 1.

[5] T. M. Greene, *The Arts and the Art of Criticism* (Princeton: Princeton University Press, 1940), Chap. xxiii; B. C. Heyl, *New Bearings in Esthetics and Art Criticism* (New Haven: Yale University Press, 1943), Chap. iii; and John Hospers, *Meaning and Truth in the Arts* (Chapel Hill: University of North Carolina Press, 1946), Chaps. v–vi.

[6] John Hospers, *op. cit.*, p. 160 (italics in original).

[7] DeWitt H. Parker, *The Principles of Aesthetics*, second edition (New York: F. S. Crofts and Company, 1946), p. 32.

exception of those statements in it that are about historical figures and places, etc.) is primarily emotive. Still, it does not follow that none of it is also referential. For if we employ Parker's concept of depth meaning, we may assert that literature is emotive on one linguistic dimension, the surface meanings, and referential on the other, the depth meanings. We can then point out that the emotive theory possesses an initial credibility only because it neglects the entire realm of depth meanings in literature by confining itself to the meanings presented immediately through the *printed* page.

As an example of a work in literature that embodys certain truth claims through the presence of depth meanings, I will choose the recent American novel, *Native Son*, by Richard Wright.[8] The novel deals with a young Negro, Bigger Thomas, who is without faith in his poverty-stricken, frustrated life. His feelings and attitudes toward life are inchoate except that he deeply resents his status as a Negro. His tragedy begins when he accepts a charity job as a chauffeur given him by one of the millionaire landlords of Chicago's South Side slums, where Bigger lives. The millionaire has a daughter, Mary Dalton, who is having her fling with Communism. Naturally, she becomes interested in Bigger and desires to get a glimpse into his way of life. She and her boy friend trick him into acting as their guide to the Negro dives of the South Side.

During the course of the evening, Mary gets drunk and, after persuading her boy friend to leave her alone with Bigger on her way home, she makes advances to him. Bigger is not interested, knowing well the penalty that would be meted out to him if he accepted her invitation. Instead he takes her home and carries her into her bedroom, trying to keep her quiet and put her to sleep. Mary's mother, who is blind, hears the noises of her daughter and enters the room. Bigger, terrified at her presence, is forced to put a pillow over Mary's head, to stop her mumbling. Mrs. Dalton finally leaves and Bigger removes the pillow, only to discover that Mary has suffocated. Desperate, Bigger decides to burn his victim rather than to try to explain what happened. The rest of the story concerns the discovery of Bigger's guilt, his escape and second murder, then his arrest, trial, and finally his execution.

So much for the story. As a story it is all that an emotionalist could wish for: it is exciting and beautifully written, at a kind of white heat that keeps up with the plot. The question now arises, are there any truth claims in the novel? The answer, according to our hypothesis, depends upon the presence and nature of the depth meanings.

[8] This example and its analysis constitute a revision of the author's articles, "Does Art Tell the Truth?" and "The Logic of Art," *Philosophy and Phenomenological Research*, III (March, 1943), no. 3; and V (March, 1945), no. 3.

The first thing we notice as we read the novel is that it is not about an isolated Negro but about all Negroes and group minorities in America. Bigger Thomas, the subject of the novel, in the course of his experiences, epitomizes and embodies the truth claim that individual freedom is still an abortive ideal in America, since our social injustices cancel out individual development.

As contemporary novels go, however, this is a rather trivial thematic truth claim, and one might be led to infer from it that even if some novels do contain truth claims through their depth meanings, they are trivial and consequently aesthetically insignificant.

But a careful reading of Wright's novel will, I believe, reveal another depth meaning and truth claim that is far from trivial; in fact, it is so poignant that it saves the work from being merely another proletarian novel. It is to be found in the final pages of the novel where Bigger, having been sentenced to die, is talking with his lawyer, Mr. Max. Mr. Max is trying to soothe Bigger. He tells him that he will not die in vain, that he will be remembered as another martyr of exploitation. But all of this means nothing to Bigger, who is preoccupied with his own fate and his own life's meaning. The last paragraphs are especially significant:

> "Mr. Max, you go home. I'm all right . . . Sounds funny, Mr. Max, but when I think about what you say I kind of feel what I wanted. It makes me feel I was kind of right . . ." Max opened his mouth to say something and Bigger drowned out his voice. "I ain't trying to forgive nobody and I ain't asking for nobody to forgive me. I ain't going to cry. They wouldn't let me live and I killed. Maybe it ain't fair to kill and I reckon I really didn't want to kill. But when I think of why all the killing was, I begin to feel what I wanted, what I am . . ."
>
> Bigger saw Max back away from him with compressed lips. But he felt he had to make Max understand how he saw things now.
>
> "I didn't want to kill!" Bigger shouted. "But what I killed for, I *am!* It must've been pretty deep in me to make me kill! I must have felt it awful hard to murder . . ."
>
> Max lifted his hand to touch Bigger, but did not.
>
> "No; no; no . . . Bigger, not that . . ." Max pleaded despairingly.
>
> "What I killed for must've been good!" Bigger's voice was full of frenzied anguish. "It must have been good! When a man kills, it's for something . . . I didn't know I was really alive in this world until I felt things hard enough to kill for 'em . . . It's the truth, Mr. Max. I can say it now, 'cause I'm going to die. I know what I'm saying real good and I know how it sounds. But I am all right when I look at it that way . . ."
>
> Max's eyes were full of terror. Several times his body moved nervously, as if he were about to go to Bigger, but he stood still.

"I'm all right, Mr. Max. Just go and tell Ma I was all right and
not to worry none, see? Tell her I was all right and wasn't crying
none . . ."

Max's eyes were wet. Slowly, he extended his hand. Bigger took
it.

"Good-bye, Bigger," he said quietly.

"Good-bye, Mr. Max." [9]

This scene, especially as it is read in its relations to the rest of the
novel, contains a depth meaning that is a profound truth claim concerning the present state of man. Through Bigger, and in this speech,
especially, Wright is *claiming* that the only freedom left to man is the
freedom to destroy, first others and finally oneself. No other novelist
or poet has articulated this idea, so far as I know. Nor even has any
contemporary sociologist or philosopher. Here, then, is an example
where the artist not only asserts something important (which is true
or false) but is the only intellectual to have done so.

It is only when one comes to discern this depth meaning that the
novel takes on its basic significance. Until it becomes clear that
Bigger is more than a symbol of exploitation and represents *all* men
who struggle to realize themselves in a world full of evil, the novel
remains a mere adequate proletarian one. But it is this meaning that
gives the novel its universality. The symbol of Bigger, the killer of
white women, who is modern man in his own tortured self-destructive-
ness, vivifies the whole work and makes of each scene, especially the
courtroom scene, something much deeper than it could possibly be
when the novel is analyzed in terms of the other depth meanings
alone. The novel rises above the truth claim concerning the exploitation of minorities in America to signify what Wright regards as the
tragedy of modern man, that he can attain autonomy only by destruction and eventual self-destruction.

It is important to point out that the truth claims of literature are
not always true. Like the truth claims of science, they may be false,
too. Consequently, when we say that *Native Son* contains truth
claims, we do not mean to be asserting that it contains a number of
truths. It may very well be that the depth meanings of *Native Son* are
all false. But so far as our problem is concerned, that would make no
difference at all. The important thing is that much of literature contains truth claims, hence is as linguistically referential as science.

In fact, I find it incredible that aestheticians who read contemporary fiction should support the emotive theory of the language of
art. A survey of our own American realistic fiction, especially the

[9] Richard Wright, *Native Son* (New York: Harper and Brothers, 1940), p. 358; reprinted by courtesy of the publishers. (Eds.)

novels of Dos Passos, Hemingway, Faulkner, Steinbeck, and Farrell, cannot but reveal the presence of truth claims in the depth meanings of their work. The Farrell trilogy, *Studs Lonigan*, for example, contains as its basic depth meaning and truth claim the judgment that American life, dominated by bourgeois values, is vacuous and spiritually sick to the core.

What does it mean to say that a work of literature contains a depth meaning? That is to say, what is the logical status of a depth meaning and artistic truth claim? This is a large question, but at least part of the answer, I believe, is the following.

In *some* works of literature, where there are these depth meanings which do function as truth claims, there appear black marks on paper. These marks serve as signs of concepts or ideas of one sort or another to readers; and these ideas, in syntactical juxtaposition to each other, comprise the sentences and meanings of the work. But these are its surface or printed meanings, and they are, logically speaking, what we may call, according to the terminology of Russell's theory of logical types, "first-order" meanings. And if we grant the positivist his thesis that art is initially an emotive language, we may refer to these as emotive first-order meanings.

Now, besides these meanings, these works contain certain depth meanings which, logically speaking, are "second-order" in character. These meanings may be propositional in nature and function as truth claims. They are contained in the work of art even though they do not appear in print. To assert that they are contained in the work is to say that they are *implied* by the first-order meanings, where by implication we do not mean Russell's material or Lewis's strict implication, since neither of these conceives correctly our nonmathematical, ordinary sense of implication. Part of what is meant by implication in the sense in which we are using it has been formulated best by G. E. Moore when he writes, for example, "There seems to me to be nothing mysterious about this sense of 'imply,' in which if you assert that you went to the pictures last Tuesday, you *imply*, though you don't *assert*, that you believe or know that you did." [10] Thus, when we say that a literary work, such as *Native Son*, contains a second-order truth claim, what is meant is that some of the printed meanings imply the truth claim even though it is not expressed in the sense of appearing in print. Truth claims are second-order, then, because they depend upon and cannot exist without the printed first-order meanings. They are logical functions of the first-order meanings in the way that "Napoleon had all the characteristics of a great general" would be a second-order logical function of the first-order sentences, "Napoleon

---

[10] *The Philosophy of G. E. Moore*, ed. P. A. Schilpp (Evanston: Northwestern University Press, 1942), p. 542 (italics in original).

had courage," Napoleon had cunning," Napoleon had loyalty," etc., were these latter sentences to appear in a book on the printed page and the former not to appear in print at all but still be part of the total book.

Alfred Ayer, who supports the positivist position in its general orientation, has challenged its interpretation of the language of art. He denies that the language of art is emotive. In literature, even in poetry, the sentences are to be construed as linguistically referential in character. But, with the trivial exception of references to historical events, persons, etc., they are all false.[11]

This is an improvement upon the positivist theory of art, I think; but it, too, is incorrect, since not *all* the truth claims or referential statements of literature *are* false. There is more reason to believe that some of them (for example, that race prejudice in America thwarts individual growth) are true than there is for believing that all of them are false.

The emotive theory aside, the situation regarding the language of literature in relation to truth claims seems to me to include at least three different categories. First—and let us use examples from poetry throughout for the sake of simplicity, although let it be understood that the same analysis is applicable to drama, the novel, and the short story—there are many poems that contain truth claims as surface sentences, and not necessarily as depth meanings. Longfellow's "A Psalm of Life" contains the following lines:

> Life is real! Life is earnest!
>   And the grave is not its goal;
> Dust thou art, to dust returnest,
>   Was not spoken of the soul.
>
> Not enjoyment, and not sorrow,
>   Is our destined end or way;
> But to act, that each tomorrow
>   Find us farther than today.

Whatever we may think of this specimen, and it *is* pretty bad, we cannot deny that it makes a number of truth claims about the nature of life directly through the printed sentences of the poem.

So does this example from Shakespeare:

> Blow, blow, thou winter wind!
> Thou art not so unkind
> As man's ingratitude.

[11] A. J. Ayer, *Language, Truth and Logic* (New York: Oxford University Press, 1936), pp. 37–39.

Or this one:

> Let me not to the marriage of true minds
> Admit impediments. Love is not love
> Which alters when its alteration finds,
> Or bends with the remover to remove:
> O, no! it is an ever-fixed mark
> That looks on tempests and is never shaken.

In both of these the poet is actually stating something that purports to be as much a revelation of certain aspects of reality (namely, the world of human experience) as any statement in science. In neither of these examples is it even necessary to paraphrase the claim since it is made so clearly; and in each case, if we wish to do so, or if we regard it as aesthetically relevant to do so, we may raise the question of the actual truth or falsity of the claim.

Poetry affords us many, many examples of printed truth claims. It is futile to deny it and I think the reason distinguished readers of poetry like Richards have denied it is that they did not want the truth claims of poetry to enter into our evaluation of the poetry. But we must keep our problems separate. Our immediate problem is whether or not poetry is able to embody truth claims. The examples given show that some poems, good and bad, do embody these claims, and within the surface-printed sentences. In no way does it follow from the presence of these truth claims that they constitute the most important element in poetry; or that they are the whole of any poetic communication; or even that they are important or aesthetically relevant at all. All of these are quite different considerations. In fact, there are at least four different questions to keep straight, and we are at present dealing only with the first. These questions are: (1) does some or all art embody truth claims? (2) ought any art to embody truth claims? (3) does the presence of truth claims make a difference to our appreciation of those works that have them? (4) ought the presence of truth claims to make a difference in our appreciation of those works that contain them? If critics and aestheticians had kept these questions distinct, we might have avoided a great deal of unnecessary debate during the last twenty-five years.

We shall discuss the last three questions in our next chapter.[12] Let us now continue with the first and the enumeration of the categories of the language of poetry. Poetry can embody truth claims within the printed sentences; this is the first category. It can also embody truth claims as depth meanings. The truth claim of "Prufrock," namely, that there are two kinds of life and two kinds of death, is never stated

---

[12] This chapter is not included in this selection. (Eds.)

as a printed sentence anywhere in the entire poem; yet it is part of
the total poem as surely as the connotative overtones of coffee spoons
are within the poem, even though they are never printed either.

Another example of a poem that contains a truth claim presented
as a depth meaning is Yeats's "A Deep-Sworn Vow." [13]

This is an extremely poignant communication, full of passion and
paradox. Among its constituents is the depth meaning, not printed
but present nevertheless, that one cannot erace the memory of true
love; this constituent functions as a truth claim about the content of
human experience.

One could with no difficulty at all list hundreds of examples of
poetic communications in which depth meanings embody truth
claims that serve as artistic commentaries on human experience by
the poet. I conclude, therefore, that the emotive theory is simply
false in its assertion that no art contains referential meanings.

The only element of truth in the emotive theory, at least so far as
literature is concerned, lies in the third of our classifications. There
are many poems in which there are no printed or implied truth claims,
but instead articulations of wishes or commands or expressions of
attitudes.

In Longfellow's "A Psalm of Life," we have the following combination of a wish and a command:

> In the world's broad field of battle,
> In the bivouac of Life,
> Be not like dumb, driven cattle!
> Be a hero in the strife!
>
> Trust no Future, howe'er pleasant!
> Let the dead Past bury its dead!
> Act,—act in the living Present!
> Heart within, and God o'erhead!

In Elizabeth Barrett Browning's "How Do I Love Thee," we have
a pure expression of an attitude—of love—toward some object—the
beloved:

> How do I love thee? Let me count the ways.
> I love thee to the depth and breadth and height
> My soul can reach, when feeling out of sight
> For the ends of Being and ideal Grace.
> I love thee to the level of everyday's
> Most quiet need, by sun and candle-light.
> I love thee freely, as men strive for Right;
> I love thee purely, as they turn from Praise.

[13] From W. B. Yeats, *The Wild Swans at Coole* (New York: The Macmillan Company, 1919). The text of the poem, included in Mr. Weitz's essay, is here omitted (Eds.).

> I love thee with the passion put to use
> In my old griefs, and with my childhood's faith.
> I love thee with a love I seemed to lose
> With my lost saints,—I love thee with the breath,
> Smiles, tears, of all my life!—and, if God choose,
> I shall but love thee better after death.

Finally, consider E. E. Cummings's "Portrait," in which the poet expresses his cavalier, flippant attitude toward death, and in which there is no truth claim stated or implied:

> Buffalo Bill's
> defunct
>   who used to
>   ride a watersmooth-silver
>   stallion
> and break onetwothreefourfive pigeonsjustlikethat
>   Jesus
>   he was a handsome man
>   and what i want to know is
> how do you like your blueeyed boy
> Mister Death [14]

PAINTING AND TRUTH CLAIMS

So much for the emotive theory and the problem of artistic truth as it applies to literature. What can we say of painting and truth? Can paintings make truth claims?

Erwin Panofsky, one of the leading exponents of the iconological approach to painting, has written about painting in such a way as to leave no doubt that he believes it does contains certain truth claims or propositional assertions about the world. In his famous essay, *"Et in Arcadia Ego,"* which is a model of the sort of analysis he engages in as an iconologist, Panofsky is concerned with the Death theme in Watteau and Poussin. Here are a number of quotations from this essay:

> (1) [He says of Poussin's painting, *"Et in Arcadia Ego"*:] The transformation of a mere *memento mori* into the revelation of a metaphysical principle which connects the present and the future with the past and overthrows the limits of individuality, means that "Life" is conceived as transitory yet blessed with indestructible beauty and felicity; on the other hand, "Death" is seen as a preserver as well as a destroyer. From this emerges the magnificent conception of a cyclical succession which subordinates the existence of individuals to the inexorable laws of cosmic principles,

---

[14] From *Collected Poems*, published by Harcourt, Brace and Company; copyright, 1923, by E. E. Cummings. Reprinted by permission. (Eds.)

both natural and moral, endowing every stage of this existence, however transitory, with a substantial value of its own.

(2) [In summary of Poussin's art:] Thus Poussin's conception of life as a condition free though fatebound, dignified though pathetic, imperishable though variable, transpires even in a composition which seems to be nothing but the offshoot of a rather conventional allegorical tradition.

(3) Watteau's *Fêtes Champêtres*, too, may be called allegories of transience; however, they neither visualize the annihilation of the past, nor the persistence of ideal forms outlasting the destruction of matter. They depict the fading away of reality as such. Existence itself seems to be subject to transience; past, present, and future fuse into a phantasmagoric realm in which the borderline between illusion and reality, dream and wakefulness, nature and art, mirth and melancholy, love and loneliness, life and the continuous process of dying, are thoroughly obliterated.[15]

It is clear, I think, from the above quotations, that Panofsky believes that paintings embody not only single truth claims but even systems of them as they become basic *Weltanschauungen*. It may be that Panofsky is too grandiloquent in his reflections upon the truth claims of paintings; but there seems to be some sense in which these truth claims can be made in painting. The problem for aesthetics, which curiously enough is similar to Kant's problem of justifying science, is to show *how* these truth claims are possible.

In order to do this, I am convinced, we must give up the positivistic version of the distinction between emotive and referential language. Perhaps the whole distinction should be repudiated, but I should not like to commit myself on this point.

There are certain kinds of activity that the positivists have traditionally classified as *pure* emoting but that upon analysis can be seen to embody referential propositional assertions about the world that are true or false in the way in which ordinary empirical judgments are. Consider as an example the Christian ritualistic act of kneeling in prayer. Now, according to the positivist view, this act is pure emoting, the expression of feelings and attitudes, and an act which, linguistically, may enter into communication, but only in the sense of inducing similar feelings and attitudes (or perhaps even opposing ones) in the spectators around the worshiper. And, most importantly, the positivist maintains, there is nothing in the act that asserts anything or constitutes a truth claim.

That kneeling in prayer is the expression of a feeling or attitude, or that it can induce others to act, need not be denied; but that it is pure emoting, completely nonassertive and nonreferential in character can

---

[15] Erwin Panofsky, "Et in Arcadia Ego," *Philosophy and History, Essays Presented to Ernst Cassirer*, ed. Raymond Klibansky and H. J. Paton (Oxford: The Clarendon Press, 1936), pp. 240, 242, 247–248. Reprinted by permission. (Eds.)

be denied. Kneeling in prayer in a Christian ritualistic context includes also a referential propositional assertion or truth claim about the world. Specifically, the act itself includes, as *one* of its constituents, the assertion or claim that *there is a God Who is worthy of human respect.* Instead of affirming the proposition, "That God exists and is worthy of our respect," in ordinary verbal ways (i.e., in English, French, German, etc.), the worshiper gestures it as part of his total act of kneeling in prayer. His action is the medium of conveying the asserted proposition; and the assertional part of the action may be construed as a truth claim about the existence and nature of God. It will not do to say that the whole action is true or false, just as one cannot say that the usual method of speaking, which is after all an act, too, is true or false. It is only one aspect of the act, namely, the asserted proposition, spoken or gestured as the case may be, that is true or false.[17]

I should like to propose that in paintings where there are truth claims they are presented in ways that resemble the truth claims offered in certain ritualistic acts like kneeling in prayer in a Christian society. Painting can make certain truth claims mainly through its constituents of the symbol, the subject, or both working in relation to the plastic expressive elements.

Consider, to begin with, one of Hobbema's landscapes in which, it is said, there is being asserted that nature is the conflict between the old and the new. Is this a valid conception of the capacities of painting? I think that it is. In Hobbema, it is the subject and its traditional transparently symbolic associations that embody the truth claim. The subject of the landscape is usually the representation of old, decaying trees being contrasted with the representation of young, powerful-looking, new trees. We interpret this subject as a sign of certain objects and concepts; these concepts have certain traditionally associated meanings; these meanings comprise the assertional propositional claim that nature is the struggle between the old and the new, the decaying and the living.

In the "Resurrection," by Piero della Francesca, there is present, as one of the constituents, the truth claim that man is in ignorance and darkness whereas God is in Truth and Light. Without raising any question about the whole problem of verifying such a claim, which would constitute a problem even in the prose statement of such a claim, we may say that the picture contains this truth claim through the very simple device of flooding the representations of Christ and the sky with tremendous light, and leaving the representation of man

---

[16] We follow Sheffer and Lewis in distinguishing between propositions and assertions, and in regarding truth and falsity as attributes of assertions, not of propositions. See C. I. Lewis, *An Analysis of Knowledge and Valuation* (La Salle: The Open Court Publishing Company, 1946), pp. 48ff.

on the earth in relative shadow and darkness. All of these elements, with their transparently symbolic associations, add up to the assertional truth claim.

In the "Guernica," by Picasso, there is being asserted, among other things, that the victory of Fascism is the brutal destruction of everything. The painting asserts this through the bull, who symbolizes Fascism and who is relatively intact, and the other subjects—the soldier, the horse, the women, the children, and the houses—which are torn to pieces. All of these elements serve as a collective sign of the assertional proposition or truth claim regarding the nature of Fascism. One need only look at the painting to see that the artist is not wondering about the destructive character of Fascism, or denying it, or wishing it, or supposing it, but *asserting it*. The whole force of the painting leaves no doubt about the assertional character of the proposition, "That Fascism means the brutal destruction of everything."

Finally, one may say of Picasso's "Man with an All-Day Sucker" that it contains as one of its elements the truth claim that Fascism is the return to the infantile. This claim is made through the representation of a brutal-looking soldier (who is a transparent symbol of the Fascist), who is holding a sucker in the shape of a spear. The fact that the adult soldier is holding the weapon enables us to interpret the picture as claiming that Fascism is the return to the infantile, that is, the stage in which we lick all-day suckers.

MUSIC AND TRUTH CLAIMS

So much for the arts of literature and painting as they relate to the problem of referential language or truth claims. Our primary aim has been to offer a refutation of the extravagant views of the emotive theory. We have no desire to demonstrate that all art embodies truth claims; in fact, in our discussion of poetry, we presented certain examples of poetry in which no truth claims were made. Stated in its positive form, our thesis has been that in some of the arts, especially in literature and painting, among the many elements there are to be found, either directly or indirectly, either stated or gestured, certain asserted propositions which are true or false. The extent of these truth claims in the arts is still an open question, and an invitation to further aesthetic analysis. The whole problem of truth claims in music, for example, needs a tremendous overhauling along the lines we have suggested or perhaps along other lines made possible by the continuing growth of the discipline of semiotic. The present writer, unfortunately, has doubts about the linguistic capacities of music. That music is a language in the sense of a system of signs that has meaning to listeners, we have already shown,[17] but that music is a language in

---

[17] See pp. 110ff. of *Philosophy of the Arts*. (Eds.)

the sense of a system of signs that contains propositions in the ways that literature or painting do, we do not feel ready to accept. The position of J. W. N. Sullivan, in his book, *Beethoven: His Spiritual Development*, to the effect that music can embody a philosophy and that Beethoven's music does, while it is attractive and one would like to believe it, is open to serious criticisms of the sort mentioned already in our previous discussions of extreme heteronomy in music.[18] The most I am prepared to say, and this very tentatively, is that some music does contain *musical analogues* of assertions or truth claims. Consider, for example, Beethoven's last quartet, Opus 135. Many critics, even the composer himself, find in it the assertion that life is good or that affirmation of life is the answer to doubt. Perhaps this is too much to find in the music, but what one does find is the sequence of *musical* doubt and affirmation. The fourth and final movement begins slowly and is characterized in this beginning section by irresolution and hesitation within the musical sounds; this is followed by an allegro section in which all the musical doubt and irresolution give way to musical materials that are completely affirmative in their expressive character. Now, if we accept musical hesitation and affirmation as transparent symbols, we may say that this fourth movement embodies the contrast between doubt and affirmation, in which the latter comes after the former, as a kind of *reply* to it. But this is a musical reply, and the whole movement is at most an analogue of the claim that in life affirmation is the answer to doubt.

---

15. The Use of "Good" in Aesthetic Judgments

Helen Knight

I

I INTEND to speak about 'good' in such judgments as 'Most of Cézanne's pictures are good', '*Howard's End* is a good novel', 'This is a good film.' But the main points apply to 'beautiful' as much

From *Proceedings of the Aristotelian Society*, Volume XXXVI, 1935–36, pp. 147–160 (London: Harrison and Sons, Ltd.) Reprinted by courtesy of the Editor of the Aristotelian Society. Copyright 1935 by The Aristotelian Society.

[18] See pp. 112ff. of *Philosophy of the Arts*. (Eds.)

as to 'good.' It is largely a matter of choosing different illustrations for the same general point, and I have chosen 'good' in preference to 'beautiful' as I want to speak about works of art, and, in particular, about pictures. On the whole we commend the works of man for their goodness, and the works of nature for their beauty.

I am raising a philosophic question. When we get into philosophic difficulty about the use of 'good' we are puzzled by the difference between goodness and its criteria, the reasons for goodness—the difference, for example, between 'this is good' and 'this object balances that', 'this line repeats that', 'the placing of this figure brings out the psychological significance of the event.' We become interested in what differentiates the use of 'good' from the use of expressions for its criteria, we become interested in its generality.

This is the problem, and I shall try to show that we can only get light on it by considering the goodness-criteria relation. But this involves a significant denial. Many people have tried to solve their difficulty by giving a naturalistic analysis of 'good' or 'beautiful'. It is suggested, for example, that when anyone says that a work of art is good he means that he likes it, or that it satisfies a desire, or that it gives him a feeling of 'objectified self-affirmation.' But analysis throws no light at all on the goodness-criteria relation, and I shall try to show that no analysis will give us what we want. We shall also see that all naturalistic analyses misrepresent the situation in one way or other.

I will introduce my view by asking you to consider two different uses of 'good', one of which is also a group of uses. There is the use exemplified by 'good tennis player', 'good knitter', 'good Pekingese', 'good piece of steak', etc. We use 'good' in these cases for what is good of its kind. The goodness of these things depends on their satisfying the criteria of goodness for things of their kind. So this use embraces a group of *specific* uses. On the other hand, we have the *general* use exemplified in 'aesthetic experience is good', 'philosophic discussion is good.' We can bring out the contrast by comparing 'philosophic discussion is good' with 'that was a good philosophic discussion', we should use quite different arguments to establish each of these statements.

These uses are different—but in what respects? Certainly not because 'good' occupies different positions in the sentence. It makes no difference to our meaning whether we say 'that tennis player is good' or 'that's a good tennis player'. Whereas we do get the difference when we say 'that discussion was good' (as ordinarily used) and 'discussion is good' (but we might use 'that discussion was good' to exemplify the general use). The difference does not lie in the position of 'good', nor in another and far more important fact. For in *each* case we show the meaning of 'good' by considering its criteria—and not by giving an analysis. There is, however, this difference. Whenever we get a specific 'good' we can always use a certain type of expression—'is a good *picture*', 'is a good *knitter*', 'is a good *Pekingese*' etc.; and the words 'picture', 'knitter', and 'Pekingese' contribute to the meaning of the sentence. But if we try to put the general 'good' in this form we can only get 'is a good *thing*'; and 'is a good thing' means exactly the same as 'is good'. But I want in particular to notice another (though related) difference. It is highly plausible to suppose that my desire for aesthetic experience or philosophic discussion is a criterion for their goodness in the general sense; and, indeed, that my desire for *x* is a criterion for the goodness of *x* in this sense, whatever *x* may be. But it is not plausible to suppose that any of my mental states is a criterion for the goodness of Helen Wills' tennis. The contrast I am pointing to is this: On the one hand we get my desire as a criterion for the goodness of everything that is good in the general sense. On the other hand we get a number of completely different sets of criteria—criteria for tennis, for knitting, for Pekingese dogs, for pieces of steak, and so on. And this is a point I want to emphasize when I class the 'good' of aesthetic judgments among the specific uses.

When we say 'Cézanne's "Green Jar" is good', we are not using 'good' in the general, but in one of the specific senses. It belongs to the group exemplified by 'good tennis playing' and 'good Pekingese.' I shall try to show that this is the natural view to take. And I shall try to say as much as I can about what it involves. The main thing to consider is the goodness-criteria relation. This is the central fact, and explains the generality of 'good.' On the other hand, we must also consider the criteria specific to aesthetic goodness. I propose to discuss the goodness-criteria relation in a relatively simple case, and conclude this discussion with some general observations about the use of 'good.' But all this is extremely difficult, and I know that the discussion is most inadequate; I then hope to show that aesthetic goodness involves this relation. But why, it may be asked, has the point been overlooked? This is not surprising. The aesthetic situation is very complicated, and its complications have obscured the main structure of aesthetic reasoning. But if we see the structure in a simple case we may recognize it in a more complicated one. And accordingly I lay great stress on the analogy.

Suppose I am looking at a game of tennis and say 'that's a good player.' If someone asks me 'why?' or 'what do you mean?' I answer by pointing out features of his playing. I say, for example, that his strokes are swift, that his placing is accurate, and point to the speed of his footwork. In making these remarks I am showing that he satisfies the criteria. I am indicating features of his playing that are criteria for its goodness. And this is what my questioner expected. It is the only answer that any of us expects in our ordinary conversations. We give our meaning by pointing out criterion-characters.

But suppose that my questioner wants a philosophic discussion, and says that this answer neglects the generality of 'good.' It is clear that 'he's a good player' is not equivalent to any one of the reasons suggested above, nor to a group of such reasons. The mere fact of their being *reasons* shows that they are not equivalent, as no proposition is a reason for itself. But it is also obvious that 'he's a good player' says in a sense far less than 'his aim is accurate', and 'she's a good knitter' says far less than 'her knitting is even.' But though 'he's a good player' says less than *one* reason, yet in a sense it stretches over all.

It is at this point that analysis crops up. Suppose we persist in asking 'But what do we mean when we say his playing is good? what are we saying?' We no longer expect the normal answer. We want someone to say: 'I mean by "his playing is good" that it is so-and-so,' where 'so-and-so' is a set of words that provides an analysis. But such an answer, if it could be found, would not really satisfy us. For we want to understand the generality of 'good', and the key to this lies in the goodness-criteria relation. Thus at this point the question: what do we mean? is misleading. For neither an enumeration of criteria nor an analysis will give us what we want.

But let us consider what analysis might be suggested. We shall find the case of knitting quite instructive, for here I can see no candidate at all. It is plain that there just are different criteria, evenness, speed, capacity to do intricate patterns etc. In the case of tennis, someone might suggest 'has winning ability.' It would then be natural to retort: 'and what about style?' This is of course a criterion of goodness, though a steady and reliable player would be good without it. In winning ability and style we have simply found two criteria of a very general type. A player is good *because* of his style and *because* he is able to win. Let us suppose we are looking at two stylish players, neither of whom is able to win. One of them, we can see, is unlikely to improve, in spite of his style he is bad. But the other is promising, 'Look at his style,' we say, 'he is good even though he can't win.' These cases show us something about the goodness-criteria relation. Style is a criterion, but a player may be good without it; and a knitter may be good without speed. On the other hand, a player may have style and not be good, a knitter may be quick and not be good. And consider this: One player is good because of his smashing service and speed of returns, another because of his careful and unexpected placing of the ball, another because of his smashing service and spectacular backhand strokes, another because he never misses a ball. These variations are typical. We sometimes get one set of criteria, sometimes another; and the sets overlap, providing a number of different combinations. It is through considering such examples, and the more of them the better, that we get to know what the goodness-criteria relation is like. It is not, however, just a matter of collecting facts, but of seeing how elastic the relation is.

I shall now attempt to sum up some general points that I think have emerged about the use of 'good', and these contain as much as I can say about its generality. We have seen that the meaning of 'good' is determined by criteria. And this is to say: that the truth and falsity of 'he is a good so-and-so' depends on whether he possesses criterion-characters or not; and that the natural answer to the question, 'what do you mean?' lies in pointing out these characters. But, on the other hand, 'he is a good so-and-so' is not equivalent to any proposition which asserts the possession of a criterion-character, nor to a group of such propositions. This lack of equivalence is marked by the use of 'because' which introduces the criterion propositions. A clear way of stating the difference would be to give a great many cases in which goodness and criterion propositions are differently used. For example: 'he is good, but his placing is not accurate'; 'he is not good, but has a smashing service'; 'he is good, his service is smashing and his returns are speedy'; 'he is good, he is steady and reliable, his service is not smashing and his returns are not speedy.'

On different occasions, as we have seen, we judge by different criteria—'he is good because his service is smashing and his returns are speedy'; 'he is good because he is steady and reliable.' This is certainly not ambiguity. There are not several meanings of 'good' as there are two meanings of 'plain' or two meanings of 'see' when we distinguish 'seeing a physical object' from 'seeing a sense-datum'. The situation, as I have tried to show, is totally different. But none the less I should like to speak about variations in the meaning of 'good', to say that its meaning varies when we use different criteria. Some of the differences, I suggest, are striking enough to merit this description. I shall raise the point later on in connection with aesthetic judgments.

Let us now see how the meaning of 'good' in aesthetic judgments is determined by its criteria. It will be useful to look at a word like 'piquant.' Suppose I say that a certain woman is beautiful, and someone replies 'Not beautiful, but piquant.' I am quite likely to accept this correction, why? Because I see that her features are piquant as distinct from beautiful. And we might point out the marks of piquancy. We might say that her nose is *retroussé*, her chin pointed, her expression vivacious. But in any case we can see that her piquancy depends on her features or expression. And in distinguishing piquancy from beauty we imply that beauty depends on other features (though there may be overlapping).

This example is useful because 'piquant' is the same kind of word as 'good.' But the range of its criteria is narrower, and this makes its dependence on them easier to see. 'Good' is exactly the same kind of word as 'piquant' and 'beautiful', but its use is far wider. It is used with *this* set of criteria and with *that*; and so on through an extremely wide range of overlapping sets. On any *one* occasion it is used with one set only, but on this occasion with this set, on that occasion with that, and so on. This in a way drains it of meaning, it is empty as compared with 'piquant.' So we see the relation between 'piquant' and its criteria more readily, but with a little more attention we can see it just as clearly in the case of 'good.'

Suppose I say that Cézanne's 'Green Jar' is a good picture and someone asks me 'why?' or 'what do you mean?' I should answer by describing it. I should point out a number of facts about its organization, for example: that apple is placed so that it exactly balances the main mass on the right; the lines of tablecloth, knife, and shadows repeat each other; the diagonal of the knife counteracts the diagonals of the shadows. All these objects, I might continue, are exceedingly solid and the shadows exceedingly deep—each thing 'is infallibly in its place.' I might point out a number of important problems that Cézanne has solved; for example, that he combines a geometrical scheme with the variety we get in natural appearances. And finally I might allude to the profundity and gravity of the picture. In this description I have pointed out criterion-characters, the 'Green Jar' is good because it possesses them.

This is the type of reasoning that runs through critical writings. I shall give a few illustrations. Consider Reynolds' discussion of the principal lights in a picture.[1] He praises the 'Bacchus and Ariadne' of Titian. The figure of Ariadne dressed in blue and the sea behind her form a cold contrast to the mellow colours of the principal group. But by giving Ariadne a red scarf and one of the Bacchante some blue drapery Titian prevents a division of the picture into separate sections. On the other hand, Le Brun in 'The Tent of Darius' mismanages the light. The picture has a heavy air because the principal light falls on Statira who is dressed in pale blue. Reynolds then gives the 'Landscape in Moonlight' by Rubens as an example of modifying natural appearance for the sake of harmony. On the one hand Rubens introduces more colour contrast, and on the other hand modifies the natural brightness of the moon. The natural brightness could only be preserved by making everything else very dark. Rembrandt in his 'Man in Armour' preserves the natural brightness of the armour, and as a result the picture is too black. We get a similar type of criterion when

[1] *Discourses*. Seeley & Co., London, 1905, pp. 245–52.

Berenson praises Giotto for presenting just those lines, those lights and shadows which convey solidity,[2] and when Fry points out how Cézanne emphasizes just those aspects of colour which convey plastic form.[3] We get quite another type when Reynolds condemns Bernini's 'David' for the meanness of its expression,[4] and Delacroix points out that Millet's peasants are a little too ambitious—this, he explains, is because Millet only reads the Bible.[5]

We find in these cases the same kind of reasoning as in discussions about tennis—he is good because his returns are speedy, it is good because the red scarf and blue drapery preserve the balance. And the question 'what do you mean by saying it's good?' provokes the same kind of answer, 'I mean that the lines balance each other, that it combines geometric structure with variety, that it is profound.'

Let us now consider some cases in which I change my judgment. I decide that a picture is bad. Then someone points out its construction, and I see the picture in a new way. The figures had seemed a mere haphazard collection. I now see a diagonal movement in which the figures participate, and as I follow this movement the space recedes, giving a strong impression of depth. And I reverse my judgment. What determines the change? My perception of how the picture is constructed, my recognition of a criterion-character. Or take these cases. I believe that the 'Death of Chatterton' and the 'Last Goodbye' are good, the one because of its dramatic presentation, the other because of its pathos. But someone convinces me that the one is theatrical and the other sentimental. And I now decide that these pictures are bad.

It is worth while to notice that my *liking* a picture is never a criterion of its goodness. We never say 'this picture is good because I like it.' I fully admit that we value aesthetic experience because it includes enjoyment. It is obvious that liking is important, but we must not mistake its role. It is not a criterion. Nor is it true, as we may be inclined to think, that we always like what we judge to be good, and dislike what we judge to be bad. It is common to find indifference combined with approval—'I can't see anything in so-and-so, but I believe it's good.' And we also find liking combined with disapproval. I may have a taste for the sentimental, and like *East Lynne*, even if I know that *East Lynne* is sentimental and that sentimentality is bad. Or I may like a novel because it deals with a problem that interests me, and because I agree with its views. But I may believe that

[2] *The Italian Painters of the Renaissance.* The Clarendon Press, Oxford, 1930, pp. 70–71.
[3] *Cézanne.* Hogarth Press, London, 1927, pp. 39–40.
[4] *Discourses*, p. 71.
[5] *Journal*, Librairie Plon, Paris, 1893, vol. 2, p. 61.

its treatment of the problem is unsuited to the novel form. And in both these cases I condemn the novels for the very characters I like.

I have tried to show that the goodness of pictures depends on their possession of criterion-characters. We give reasons for goodness by pointing them out. The judgment 'this is good' or 'this is bad' depends on their presence or absence. And this means that we understand the 'good' of aesthetic judgments by understanding the goodness-criteria relation. Its meaning is determined by criterion-characters, but the proposition 'this is good' is not equivalent to any criterion proposition. And there are rules which determine the truth of the former in relation to the truth of the latter.

And now a few last words about analysis. It is irrelevant to our problem because it tells us nothing about the goodness-criteria relation. I believe we become increasingly convinced of this the more we consider this relation, and that desire for analysis dwindles away. We have indeed found a third alternative, previously overlooked. Our puzzle started when we became convinced that 'good' does not name an indefinable quality, and we tried to remove the puzzle by defining 'good' in naturalistic terms. We now see that 'good' may be indefinable and yet not stand for an indefinable quality, and that it has significance even though in one sense it stands for nothing.

We also see how naturalistic analyses distort the situation. Most of them select a state of mind such as our liking which is not even a criterion of goodness. In looking for such an analysis we tend to look for a mental state which constantly accompanies the judgment that a work of art is good or beautiful. We are struck by some one or other experience such as liking, satisfaction of desire, increased vitality, and analyse aesthetic judgments in terms of this experience. But let us suppose that we *do* find a mental state that constantly accompanies the judgment that a work of art is good or beautiful. What then? It will only provide us with a psychological generalization: whenever anyone judges a work of art to be good he always likes it or it always satisfies a desire, or it always increases his vitality. It does not solve any philosophic problem about the use of 'good.'

II

There are many points to notice about the criteria of aesthetic merit, and many problems to consider. I am passing over many of these, but certainly not because I think them of little importance. I shall first give examples to show the diversity of aesthetic criteria, and then consider variations in the use of 'good' to which this diversity leads. If we look at certain cases of disagreement from this point of view we shall be inclined to interpret them as linguistic differences.

One picture is good for one sort of thing, and another for something quite different. We may praise a water colour for its translucency and an oil for the thickness and richness of its impasto. We praise the brightness and clarity of an Impressionist painting, but do not condemn a Rembrandt for lacking these qualities. It is clear that we look for something different in each case. We praise a Botticelli for the poetry of its theme and a Degas for its realism. And how do we praise a realistic picture? We say that the artist has caught the exact pose, the kind of thing one might see at any moment. And the very banality of that post (in the case of Degas) is a merit. But we do not condemn Botticelli because we fail to meet his goddesses and nymphs as we walk through the street. On the contrary, we praise him for imagination of the ideal. And we praise him for his flowing rhythm, but do not condemn Byzantine art for being rigid, nor Cézanne for being ponderous. Suppose we are considering the work of a colourist, a member, let us say, of the Venetian school. We praise it for subtle nuances of colour and for atmospheric unity, the kind that obscures the contour of things. We praise it for richness of paint, for richness and vitality of effect. And if it fails in these respects we condemn it. But of course we do not condemn a fresco painting of the fifteenth century because it has none of these qualities. In this kind of painting we look for something quite different, for perfection in each part, for unity achieved by the balance of independent wholes, for simplicity in colour and thinness of paint, for its simple and dignified effect.

These examples show that there are a great many alternative standards. To a large extent these are set by the artist or school. An artist tries to produce a certain effect, and his purpose is shaped by a number of factors: the use of a certain medium (oil, tempera etc.), interest in a certain kind of appearance (sunlight, depth etc.), in a certain kind of form (classical, baroque, etc.), in a certain kind of subject (the poetic, the commonplace etc.). All these factors provide criteria, and each provides a large number of alternative criteria. I do not say that the artist's aim is our only critical measure, but it is extremely important and mainly responsible for the diversity of standards.

It is natural to suggest that we can classify criteria, or at least a great many of them, under the headings of form and representation. This classification is convenient and enlightening. But it may suggest misleading ideas. We may think, for example, that we class all formal criteria together because of a common property to which 'formal' refers. But the class of formal properties is heterogeneous. We praise a picture because the parts balance each other, because the colours are orchestrated, because the figures are solid, because the colours are brilliant. These are all formal criteria, but we do not class them together because of a common property. Classification is important, but it does not reduce the diversity of criteria.

I now want to discuss the diversity from the linguistic point of view.

We have seen that different pictures are good for different reasons. Accordingly when we say 'this picture is good' we are often judging by different criteria. We can translate this into a statement about language: when we say 'this picture is good' we are often using 'good' with different meanings. Only we must remember that 'good' is not ambiguous, and that the variations of meaning are distinctive.

These variations occur very frequently. We have already seen one reason for this; namely, that pictures are good by different criteria. But there is another reason, that some people *habitually* judge by certain criteria and not by others. It is a commonplace that some people always praise a picture for its form and others for its subject. Each set habitually selects criteria from another group, and, as we shall see, there are other cases. It may be a matter of ignorance. Without historical and technical training we do not know what artists are aiming at, and accordingly are ignorant of a great many criteria. But there is a far more curious reason. We *refuse* to use criteria of which we are well aware. And this is by no means uncommon. Suppose I say to someone that 'After Office Hours' is a good film, and he denies it. I then point out its competent acting, its slickness and smartness. He does not deny that it has these qualities, but answers 'that's not goodness.' But there are many different criteria of goodness in films and these are among them. His answer amounts to saying 'I don't want to accept these criteria of goodness—I don't want to use "good" in this way.' We also get more serious cases of this refusal. Thus Delacroix complains of the 'modern schools' who look on colour as an inferior and 'earthy' aspect of painting, and exhort artists to reject the technique of the colourist. Again what does this come to? 'We don't want to accept these criteria of goodness.' Even Reynolds maintains that the highest art requires simplicity, in fact monotony of colour, and must renounce the harmony of subtle nuances. This partly explains his depreciation of Tintoretto, Veronese and Rubens. And what does his criticism come to? 'I have *decided* to degrade these criteria, and in consequence these artists only paint "ornamental" pictures.'

The point then is this. Either through ignorance or prejudice many people habitually use 'good' with certain meanings and not with others. And when we look at the matter in this light we see that a great deal of aesthetic disagreement is linguistic. It is disagreement in the use of 'good.' Suppose that two people are looking at a picture by Picasso, the kind in which we get abstract treatment of actual objects. One of them says 'this is good' and the other 'this is bad.' The first is judging by its form, and the other points scornfully to the representation (or lack of it). The appropriate comment is, I suggest, 'They are using "good" with different meanings.' And this also applies to the dispute about 'After Office Hours.' But we need not only consider such complete disagreement. Delacroix, for example, places Rubens much higher than Reynolds places him, and this is partly because Delacroix is willing, in fact anxious, to accept colour criteria at their full value.

It is important to notice that when people disagree in this way they may completely agree about the nature of what they are discussing. The filmgoers may agree that 'After Office Hours' is competent in acting, smart and slick. Reynolds fully agrees with Delacroix that Rubens excels in colour technique. This agreement is significant, and fits in very happily with the linguistic explanation. Suppose, on the other hand, that Reynolds was disputing Rubens' excellence as a colourist. This would be a dispute of quite another kind. It would be a factual dispute about Rubens' technique.

There are two more points I must raise before concluding. I shall treat them both in a very sketchy manner, but cannot leave the subject without indicating the lines along which my answer to them would run.

The first is concerned with comparative judgments, 'this picture is better than that.' Such judgments are most profitable when we compare pictures that resemble each other pretty closely, two water colours, two impressionist paintings, two Baroque paintings, etc. In such cases we judge both pictures by the same criteria.

But what about the comparison of pictures which are good for different reasons? I believe that in some cases this would be nonsensical. It is nonsense to ask whether Raphael or Rembrandt is the better artist, whether rugged scenery is better than soft, or Gothic architecture than Norman. In these cases we can only state a preference for one or the other. But we *do* make comparative judgments where the criteria are different. Raphael's 'School of Athens' is better than a water colour by Crome or a cartoon by Max Beerbohm. But Crome and Beerbohm were aiming at completely different ends from Raphael, and their pictures may be perfect of their kind. The explanation of these comparative judgments is, I believe, that some criteria are higher than others. I mean by this simply that when pictures excel by some criteria we say they are better than if they excel by others. The criteria by which Raphael excels, such as space, composition, organization of groups, expressiveness, dignity, are among the very highest.

The second question is closely connected, and has probably been provoked by many of my statements. What is the guarantee of a criterion? What determines the truth of 'so-and-so is a criterion for goodness in pictures'? The guarantee, I would answer, lies in its being used as a criterion. Organization of groups, space composition, profundity etc., are criteria of goodness because they are used as such. But we

must face a difficulty. Who is it that uses them? It is true that some
are in general use. A large number of people would praise a picture
for its profundity. There is also the important fact that we often use
criteria without being able to name or distinguish them. But we must
acknowledge that some are only used by critics, and not even by all of
them. We must admit that criteria are not firmly fixed, like the points
(at any one time) of a Pekingese. But it completely misrepresents the
situation to say they are not fixed at all.

Perhaps I should also point out that the fixing of criteria is one
thing, and their use another. When we make aesthetic judgments we
are using criteria, and not talking about the circumstances in which
they are fixed. They are fixed by certain people who no doubt have
their reasons for preferring some to others. But we do not refer to
these facts in our aesthetic judgments.

I have been constantly harping in this paper on the judicial office of
aesthetic judgments, and feel that I must supply an antidote, for I have
no desire to exalt this office. I believe, it is true, that the judgments we
make in pointing out criteria are the most profitable judgments to
make. But we need not make them with judicial intent. It is far better
to say 'Cézanne was interested in that and that, we can find so-and-so
in his pictures.' The great thing is to discover what a work of art is like.

---

16. The Sensuous and the Sensual in Aesthetics

Arnold Berleant

AMONG ALL THE AREAS of cultural activity, the arts have occupied
a position of considerable dependence during most of the
course of the development of Western civilization. Indeed, the claim
of artistic expression to the status of equal merit with the other manifestations of the human creative genius is of comparatively recent occurrence and has rarely been freely allowed. More commonly, the arts
have been tolerated as a means of enhancing those beliefs and values
and their institutional expressions which have dominated intellectual

Reprinted by permission of the publisher and the author from *The Journal of Aesthetics and Art Criticism*, XXII:2 (Winter, 1964), 185–192.

activity and which were regarded as embodying unquestionable truth. So thoroughly has the belief in the subordinate role of the arts pervaded Western thought, moreover, that during recent times, when the arts have largely emancipated themselves from subservience to the church, state, and social interests, concepts under which much aesthetic discussion is conducted betray the extent to which aesthetic theory still remains bound to biases deriving from the inferior origins of the arts.

While the scope of critical inquiry that can be made in these directions is vast, we shall confine our remarks here to a traditional distinction which has become so deeply engrained in our thinking about the arts that it has acquired the position of a largely unquestioned postulate in most modern aesthetic theory. This is the distinction between the sensuous and the sensual as employed in characterizations of aesthetic experience and the objects which evoke it. The sensuous is commonly regarded as connoting the pleasurable attraction of the sensations of sight, hearing, and the other senses. The sensual, on the other hand, refers to that experience of the senses which is confined to bodily pleasures as contrasted with intellectual satisfaction, where appeal is to the "grosser" bodily sensations, particularly the sexual. Discrimination between these notions is commonly encountered in aesthetic theory and is maintained to be coterminous with the bounds of art, the sensuous being reluctantly admitted into the province of aesthetic experience and the sensual rejected.

While one hardly wonders at meeting this distinction among aesthetic theorists with a commitment to a religious or moral doctrine or to a spiritualistic metaphysic, it is more surprising to find it accepted without serious question by writers on aesthetics whose naturalistic or scientific bent might cause one to have expected otherwise.[1] Our object is to reveal how the restraining hand of the moral censor, gloved in metaphysical doctrine, is still a powerful force in aesthetic theory, an influence which exhibits itself in this commonly observed distinction. Moreover, we shall show that such a discrimination has a distorting influence on aesthetic theory in general, eliminat-

---

[1] Santayana, for example, distinguishes between physical and aesthetic pleasures. The former are lowly and call attention to the part of the body in which they arise, while in the latter the bodily organs do not capture our attention but direct it to an external object. Cf. *The Sense of Beauty* (New York, 1896), pp. 36–37. Dewey makes the distinction on similar grounds: "Any sensuous quality tends, because of its organic connections, to spread and fuse. When a sense quality remains on the relatively isolated plane on which it first emerges, it does so because of some special reaction, because it is cultivated for special reasons. It ceases to be sensuous and becomes sensual. This isolation of sense is not characteristic of esthetic objects, but of such things as narcotics, sexual orgasms, and gambling indulged in for the sake of the immediate excitement of sensation. In normal experience, a sensory quality is related to other qualities is such ways as to define an object." *Art as Experience* (New York, 1934), p. 124.

ing a large area of experience from the possibility of aesthetic perception of which it is intrinsically capable.

I

Irrespective of theoretical commitment, every treatment of aesthetic
issues involves reference to human experience. Independent of the
ontological status attributed to the art object, the relation of men to
it, in producing, appreciating, appraising it, is an experiential relation.
That this is a perceptual experience involving the various senses has
long been acknowledged, explicitly so since the formal establishment
of the discipline by the very name given it. In choosing the Greek
word *aesthesis*, Baumgartner, in the eighteenth century, made clear
the primary commitment of the theory of art to sensation, to sense
perception, and since that time aestheticians have continued to acknowledge the importance of the sensuous element in art. Among the
significant attempts to accord adequate recognition to this aspect of
art is Prall's concept of aesthetic surface, by which he meant the
sensuous surface of experience. Indeed, he went so far as to maintain
that "Experience is genuinely and characteristically aesthetic only
as it occurs in transactions with external objects of sense or with the
objects of sensuous imagination held clearly before the mind in intuition . . . , " and, " . . . the sensuous elements of experience in general
. . . are the very materials of beauty. . . . [T]hey are our first concern,
the primary subject matter of aesthetic theory." [2]

While we, like Prall, are not suggesting that such other fundamental
aspects of aesthetic experience as the formal and the conceptual
or significant are unimportant, they have perhaps been over-em-
phasized in recent discussion at the expense of the sensuous, possibly because of their greater adaptability to discourse and explication.
Although one can comment on the formal characteristics of a musical
work like *Wozzeck* or a Mondrian canvas, or advance another interpretation of *Ulysses*, one can hardly make someone *see* the colors in a
watercolor or an article of common use, *feel* the texture of cloth or
stone, or hear the sounds of a modern musical work regarded as
"offensive" by the prejudiced ear. [3]

---

[2] D. W. Prall, *Aesthetic Judgment* (New York, 1929), pp. 28, 56. Peirce's metaphysical category of firstness, by which he meant immediacy, feeling, quality, suchness,
corresponds to this feature of the aesthetic experience. Recently his three categories have
been adapted to a theory of art. Cf. Albert William Levi, "Peirce and Painting," *Philosophy and Phenomenological Research*, XXIII:1 (1962), 23–36.

[3] The neglect of the aesthetic appeal of art by the intellectualistic absorption in organization and meaning has occasionally been remarked upon. Hanslick was well aware of
this in the case of music: "The reason why people have failed to discover the beauties in
which pure music abounds, is, in great measure, to be found in the *underrating*, by the
older systems of aesthetics, of the *sensuous element*, and in its subordination to morality

At the time of endless talk about art, it would seem fitting to recall our attention to what is perhaps one of art's most characteristic features. For the distinctive quality of art is neither harmony,[4] unity in variety, aesthetic form, symbolic meaning, or the like, but rather what may be termed the *intrinsic perception of sensation,* either directly, as in painting, music, and sculpture, or indirectly, as in the case of the literary arts. For every perception is potentially aesthetic. When intellectual, moral, or emotional elements begin to obtrude, experience becomes less aesthetic and more cognitive, homiletic, or affective. Furthermore, recognition of the sensuousness of art emphasizes the particularity, the specificity of the aesthetic experience. The negation of *aesthetic* is, in every sense, *anaesthetic.*

II

In asserting the sensuousness of aesthetic perception, it is appropriate to consider, if briefly, the role of the senses in aesthetic experience. This is a topic which is usually given but passing attention in most treatments of the questions of aesthetics. The classic opinion that the aesthetic senses are the visual and the aural is dutifully echoed as a truth whose obviousness renders justification superfluous, after which attention is turned to seemingly more pressing matters. Yet this proposition is worth serious examination, if for no other reasons than that the senses are a necessary condition for most if not all aesthetic experience, and the bearing this has on the roles of the sensuous and the sensual in aesthetic perception.

The belief that sight and hearing are the aesthetic senses occurs in Greek philosophy, receiving the endorsement of Plato, Aristotle, and their later followers including Plotinus and Aquinas. This is no iso-

---

and feeling—in Hegel to the 'idea.' Every art sets out from the sensuous and operates within its limits. The theory relating to the expression of feelings ignores this fact, and disdainfully pushing aside the act of *hearing,* it passes on immediately to the *feelings.* Music, say they, is food for the soul, and the organ of hearing is beneath their notice." Eduard Hanslick, *The Beautiful in Music,* in *Problems in Aesthetics,* ed. M. Weitz (New York, 1959), p. 383.

The perceptive critic has not been the only one to remark upon the primacy of the aesthetic in art. While poetry is sensuous in its effect mainly indirectly through its ability to stimulate imaginative recollection, the poet, too, has engaged in similar observations: "Art bids us touch and taste and hear and see the world, and shrinks from what Blake calls mathematic form, from every abstract thing, from all that is the brain only, from all that is not a fountain jetting from the entire hopes, memories and sensations of the body. Its morality is personal, knows little of any general law. . . ." William Butler Yeats, in *The Creative Process,* ed. B. Ghiselin (New York, 1955), pp. 106–107.

[4] Although its meaning has been modified periodically, the philosophy of art has regarded harmony historically as the goal of artistic struggling and identical with beauty. Cf. K. E. Gilbert and H. Kuhn, *A History of Esthetics,* rev. ed. (Bloomington, Ind., 1954), pp. 186ff.

lated judgment, however. Following the rational bent of the dominant tradition of Greek thought, sight and hearing were regarded as the higher senses because they were held to be the senses most closely related to the operations of reason.[5] This belief complements the classical attitude which considers theoretical activity distinct from and superior to practical doing, and concurs with the Platonic metaphysic which relegates the material, the physical, to an inferior status, a belief which was reinforced during the centuries that the Christian influence was dominant in aesthetic theory. Since the organs of sight and hearing are distance receptors, detachment from direct contact with the physical may be retrained, for the other senses call attention to the body, so destroying the isolation of the contemplative mind. Thus the aristocratic attitude of classical Greek culture has been preserved: the conviction of the superiority of the essentially passive aloofness of the meditative spirit and contempt for the practical and manipulative.[6]

Indeed, this division between the distance receptors and the contact senses corresponds to the distinction between the sensuous and the sensual. The sensuous is admissable only when made safe by being perceived through the senses of sight and hearing, while the senses of taste, smell, and especially touch, are ineradicably suggestive of the sensual. In modern times, this view has obtained considerable prominence in aesthetics through the notions of psychical distance and disinterestedness. Thus, while it is sometimes allowed that the aesthetic attitude be taken toward any object of which we may be aware,[7] the enjoyment of some kinds of beauty has usually been regarded as possible only through the intervention of distance.[8] Only when the sensual has been depersonalized, removed from proximity, spiritualized, does it render itself aesthetically acceptable. Love as beauty, for example, has been held to demand the use of the principle of distance

[5] Ibid., pp. 117, 139.

[6] Cf. the brief but excellent discussion of some of these questions in Jerome Stolnitz, Aesthetics and Philosophy of Art Criticism (Boston, 1960), pp. 223–226. Dewey has suggested that the influence of this attitude of Greek culture does much to account for the late development of modern scientific knowledge and the methods by which it is acquired, since the latter have arisen out of the practical concerns, activities, and experiences of daily life.

[7] Ibid., pp. 39ff.

[8] "That the appeal of Art is sensuous, even sensual, must be taken as an indisputable fact. Puritanism will never be persuaded, and rightly so, that this is not the case. . . . [T]he whole sensual side of art is purified, spiritualized, 'filtered' . . . by Distance. The most sensual appeal becomes the translucent veil of an underlying spirituality, once the grossly personal and practical elements have been removed from it. And—a matter of special emphasis here—*this spiritual aspect of the appeal is the more penetrating, the more personal and direct its sensual appeal would have been* BUT FOR THE PRESENCE OF DISTANCE." Edward Bullough, " 'Psychical Distance' as a Factor in Art and an Esthetic Principle," in A Modern Book of Esthetics, ed. M. Rader, 3d ed. (1960), p. 410.

for its most complete development and fulfillment.[9] And, as might have been expected, transcending the physical presence entirely has been taken as affording the greater beauty.[10]

In such a way, aesthetic theory has become subservient to the tenets of a metaphysical position whose truth may well be questioned. Not only this. In addition to the a priori rejection of the possibility of aesthetic perception as involving the other senses, experience is distorted by categorizing it on the basis of the sense through which it is obtained. This is encountered in discussions in aesthetics which isolate the senses and associate them with specific art media. And since there are no major art forms corresponding to the senses of touch, taste, and smell, they are excluded from any role in aesthetic perception.

[9] "This limitation and restriction of amatory intercourse is demanded by the aesthetic rule of distance. In the long run the petty incidentals of physical presence menace the beauty of the visionary image that I have created of the human being I love. Insofar as beauty is of decisive significance in my love relationship—since, according to my understanding and interpretation, it is only thus that the primitive forms of sensuality acquire a content of infinite meaning—the destruction and obfuscation of the image created by the desire for beauty will cause the strength of love itself to wane and gradually disappear. For a short period, to be sure, the love object may be given to the lover, to touch and blissfully embrace, without any danger to the beauty of the love relationship. After all, the full sense of love includes a demand for the development of sensual desire. Even in a love formed on the basis of aesthetic values sensual desire must be accorded its due. It cannot be a question of mere beholding, of the kind of disinterested pleasure with which we meet dead works of art, and those living works of art that are and remain created forms for my artistic enthusiasm; for in the love relationship, a coming together and a fusion, with heavenly moments of passing intoxication, is of the essence; but the observance of the law of distance will reveal itself in the courage of leave-taking, in the consciously willed separation from the object of my love.

"Certainly, love is destined to die insofar as it is interwoven with the temporal fate of the senses. It has its moment of fulfillment in the most beautiful surrender and the attained understanding of the lovers, and then must necessarily wane in consequence of sickness, age, misunderstanding, and death. Nevertheless, the law of distance is able to counter certain dangers that threaten this beautiful relationship, and protect it from tiring and cooling off. For this, too, a certain keeping of distance, a concealment of emotional qualities from the object of love is required. The great value relations in life, love and friendship, should never be quite clear and transparent as we live them. We should spread over them the beautiful veil of illusion, and they should always hold a last residue of insolubility for us." George Mehlis, "The Aesthetic Problem of Distance," in Reflections on Art, ed. S. Langer (Baltimore: Johns Hopkins Press, 1958), pp. 84–85.

[10] "The pleasure of the present may be greater than the enjoyment of the past and the future; but the appearance of the unreal, of that which was or is to come, is more beautiful, because here the obstructive and weakening elements of embodiment have been replaced and enhanced by felicitous allusions and connections. Thus beauty gains by the distance of expectation, just as it gains by the distance of the past." To this, a fitting conclusion: "If, then, love itself has an aesthetic character, the feeling of love must also be controlled by the law of distance. Those who love only the beautiful, whose affections are destroyed by ugliness and bad taste, should be ever reminded of the law of distance; for profane proximity destroys the bliss of pure aloofness, as ugly frequency and intimacy annihilate the enjoyment of the rare and unknown." Ibid., pp. 87–88.

Both views commit an identical error. We are misled by thinking that since the various senses have their seats in specific bodily organs and areas, their signals are distinguishable on such grounds in actual perceptual situations. The ability to discriminate among the data of the various sense receptors results from selective experience and reflection and is not a spontaneous recognition. On the contrary, it is most usual for several or all of the senses to be involved in ordinary perception, although the fact usually comes as a surprise when this widespread misconception is revealed as such to an individual as a result of the impairment of one or another sense organ.[11] In like manner, characterizing art media on the basis of the sense through which they are perceived, as in describing music as an aural art and painting as a visual one, leads to gross distortion of aesthetic experience by making its major media conform to the several senses. It has been argued convincingly that sculpture, nominally a visual art, is not primarily visual in appeal but tactile,[12] and the sense of touch is appealed to in much graphic art, albeit indirectly, through the concern with texture, surface, and the like. Music, perhaps, fits this theory more easily than the other arts, but the experience of music is inseparable from its performance, and this introduces the influence of the visual spectacle.[13] The case of the theatrical arts hardly supports the theory of direct correspondence between major art and major sense, and the literary arts are inexplicable in its terms.

There is another explanation for the difficulty commonly alleged to exist in attaining an attitude of aesthetic sensitivity toward sensory experiences involving those senses requiring contact or close proximity for their employment. Activities involving these senses have frequently been excluded as possible occasions for aesthetic experience because of their failure to meet the criteria of aesthetic acceptability imposed by the "higher" senses. One of the more illustrative examples of this occurs in Plato's *Hippias Major*.[14] In proposing pleasure as a definition of the beautiful, Socrates restricts aesthetic pleasure to that

[11] . . . [M]any sense data apprehended as sight and sound are actually complex in origin, having been built by the combined action of eyes, ears and hands. . . . In experience our sense organs are seldom exercised separately but are simultaneously engaged in exploring objects which appeal to several senses at once. After the interrelations of the various qualities of experience have been learned . . . we can then get the complex of these qualities *indirectly* through the mediation of any one of the senses involved." Frances W. Herring, "Touch—the Neglected Sense," *JAAC*, VII (1949), 210. Cf. also pp. 200–201, 203.

[12] Cf., for example, Herring, pp. 206–207.

[13] Stravinsky's comment is worth citing: ". . . one *sees* music. An experienced eye follows, adjudges, sometimes unconsciously, the performer's least gesture." Quoted in Ernest Bacon, *Words on Music* (Syracuse, 1960), p. 21.

[14] The question of this dialogue's authenticity is irrelevant to the point here being made.

received through the senses of sight and hearing. Although it cannot be denied that pleasure is to be found in taste, love, and the like, these things may be termed pleasant, he argues, but hardly beautiful. " . . . [E]verybody would laugh at us if we should say that eating is not pleasant but is beautiful, and that a pleasant odour is not pleasant but is beautiful; and as to the act of sexual love, we should all, no doubt, contend that it is most pleasant, but that one must, if he perform it, do it so that no one else shall see, because it is most repulsive to see." [15] This is scarcely a surprising conclusion, since the major sensory channel through which love is experienced is not the visual but the tactile, not the distance but the contact receptors. Were the touch to be the standard for judging the aesthetic level of a pleasurable experience, the visual enjoyment of an object, then, would hardly prove passable.

Indeed, there is a powerful aesthetic appeal which touch, smell, and taste possess, an appeal which resides almost entirely in their immediate and direct sensuous attraction and not in their potentialities for meaning and for structural organization. Perhaps this sensuous immediacy limits us from developing art forms and techniques dependent largely on these senses that are on a par with those appealing to sight and hearing which do possess these potentialities, but such perceptual experience retains, nevertheless, a strong aesthetic quality as sensuously perceived, which often plays a part in aesthetic perception occurring mainly through the other senses.

It would seem that the most accurate resolution of the issue may be obtained through the recognition of the interrelated action of the senses and their connection with the total organism.[16] If we admit the continuity of man with nature, the constant transaction between the human organism and his natural surroundings, we are led to the conclusion that separation between man and nature, discrimination between the sensory data of the various receptors, between active involvement and passive contemplation, between the material and the spiritual and their opposing values, and the like, are products of a highly developed analysis which, in turn, is a consequence of traditional metaphysical commitments which are not beyond challenge. Direct aesthetic experience, on the other hand, is largely undifferentiated, and discussion of it must be made on its own terms, and not as a consequence of non-aesthetic convictions.

III

Although metaphysical opinions play a large part in the rejection of the sensual from aesthetic employment, moral beliefs closely related

[15] *Hippias Major*, trans. Fowler, 299A.
[16] Cf. the discussion by Dewey in *Art as Experience*, pp. 121ff.

to them are probably the major reason for this practice. To the imposition of distance is conjoined the rejection of the contact or lower
senses, especially touch, as vehicles of aesthetic enjoyment. Because
touch and the other contact senses are so closely associated with
physical pleasure, particularly erotic pleasure, their role in aesthetic
experience is proscribed. This argument is not altogether convincing.
however, as soon as we recognize that art media involving the visual
and auditory senses have also been regarded capable of erotic influence
and consequently requiring moral controls. From the time of Plato
to the present, music, literature, and the other arts have been regarded
with unabated suspicion on precisely these grounds. For while it has
been claimed that the intervention of distance is capable of allaying
the suspicions of the censor and rendering his activities superfluous,
theater, dance, sculpture, and music are acknowledged to have a
strong tendency to decrease distance and hence would seem to justify
the moralist's concern.[17]

For art, centering around the intrinsically perceived qualities of
sensory experience, turns men's eyes not to the glory of heaven but to
the glories of the earth. And yet not only to its beauties. By intensify-
ing our perceptual awareness, art can bring home to us directly, as can
perhaps no other medium, the uglinesses, the meanness, the unbear-
ables of life. Be it a conveyor of the sublime or the sordid, artistic
perception is a call to the world of natural existence of the present,
and hence, in this respect, is the least illusory of all our experience.
For nothing is as undoubtedly real as the direct experience of the
moment—the significant insight of empirical subjectivism.[18]

It is not the contention of the moral critic of art that we are denying, but its aesthetic relevance. There is an erotic appeal present in
certain forms of artistic expression which is integral to the work and
cannot be expunged without impairing, if not destroying, its aesthetic
merit. This is especially true of art employing the human figure, particularly the nude.[19] Yet the presence of powerful sensual appeal is

[17] Cf. Bullough, pp. 402–403.

[18] Cf. Irwin Edman, *Arts and the Man* (New York, 1949), pp. 39ff. Here, too, lies the
utility of distance for him who would pare art of any appeal to vital interests of all sorts:
". . . [E]xplicit references to organic affections, to the material existence of the body,
especially to sexual matters, lie normally below the Distance-limit, and can be touched
upon by Art only with special precautions. Allusions to social institutions of any degree
of personal importance—in particular, allusions implying any doubt as to their validity—
the questioning of some generally recognized ethical sanctions, references to topical subjects occupying public attention at the moment, and such like, are all dangerously near
the average limit and may at any time fall below it, arousing, instead of esthetic appreciation, concrete hostility or mere amusement." *Bullough*, p. 400.

[19] ". . . [T]he human body, as a nucleus, is rich in associations, and when it is turned
into art these associations are not entirely lost. . . . This is an aspect of the subject so obvious that I need hardly dwell on it; and yet some wise men have tried to close their eyes

hardly surprising, for probably no object is infused with such emotional meaning as the human body, and this is transferred with no effort to representations of and allusions to it. This does much to explain the perennial attraction the human form possesses for the artist, for, from neolithic cave painting to the art of the present, objects and matters of human interest have occupied the creative artist, and nothing has obsessed him more than the unquenchable appeal of the human figure.[20]

Not only does the form of the body have aesthetically sensuous attraction; the function of its members does as well. Is there not a beauty in the free and graceful movement of the body, a beauty which is perhaps bound up with its form? Such an appeal exists in the chance observations of daily life in addition to the art forms such as the dance and pantomime which take bodily movement for their materials. Here, as in architecture and design, lies the basis for challenging the religiously repeated exclusion of objects and activities of mainly practical significance from aesthetic enjoyment. Dewey's query is highly appropriate:

> Why is the attempt to connect the higher and ideal things of experience with basic vital roots so often regarded as betrayal of

---

to it. 'If the nude,' says Professor Alexander, 'is so treated that it raises in the spectator ideas or desires appropriate to the material subject, it is false art, and bad morals.' This high-minded theory is contrary to experience. In the mixture of memories and sensations aroused by Rubens' *Andromeda* or Renoir's *Bather* are many that are 'appropriate to the material subject.' And since these words of a famous philosopher are often quoted it is necessary to labor the obvious and say that no nude, however abstract, should fail to arouse in the spectator some vestige of erotic feeling, even though it be only the faintest shadow—and if it does not do so, it is bad art and false morals. The desire to grasp and be united with another human body is so fundamental a part of our nature that our judgment of what is known as 'pure form' is inevitably influenced by it; and one of the difficulties of the nude as a subject for art is that these instincts cannot lie hidden, as they do, for example, in our enjoyment of a piece of pottery, thereby gaining the force of sublimation, but are dragged into the foreground, where they risk upsetting the unity of responses from which a work of art derived its independent life. Even so, the amount of erotic content a work of art can hold in solution is very high. The temple sculptures of tenth-century India are an undisguised exaltation of physical desire; yet they are great works of art because their eroticism is part of their whole philosophy.

"Apart from biological needs, there are other branches of human experiences of which the naked body provides a vivid reminder—harmony, energy, ecstasy, humility, pathos; and when we see the beautiful results of such embodiments, it must seem as if the nude as a means of expression is of universal and external value. But this we know historically to be untrue." Kenneth Clarke, *The Nude*, (New York: Bollingen Foundation, 1953), pp. 28–29; quoted by permission of the Bollingen Foundation. Cf. also Herring, p. 208.

[20] ". . . [T]he body provides an inexhaustible source for a vocabulary of expressive forms, a vocabulary that is continually being enriched. Whether we consider the immense sensuous appeal of the living body, the equally powerful ascetic revulsion fom it as loathsome, or any of the host of intermediate experiences, we are compelled . . . to reckon with the response to the body as an integral and ineradicable component of artistic and aesthetic experience." Matthew Lipman, "The Aesthetic Presence of the Body," *JAAC*, XV (1957), p. 434. Cf. also p. 428.

their nature and denial of their value? Why is there repulsion
when the high achievements of fine art are brought into connection with common life, the life that we share with all living
creatures? Why is life thought of as an affair of low appetite, or
at its best a thing of gross sensation, and ready to sink from its
best to the level of lust and harsh cruelty? A complete answer to
the question would involve the writing of a history of morals that
would set forth the conditions that have brought about contempt
for the body, fear of the senses, and the opposition of flesh to
spirit.[21]

IV

What then, can we conclude about the significance for aesthetics
of the distinction between the sensuous and the sensual? Largely that
it is not a tenable one. The differentiation resembles those other
dichotomies that have had the intent of safe-guarding the interests,
the cherished domain of an institution or a tradition. The traditional
view in this instance sees aesthetic pleasure not as physical pleasure
but completely dissociated from it, and while the role of the senses
must be acknowledged, it is a role enacted on a spiritualized plane,
disembodied, "de-physicalized," as it were. Yet by admitting the
sensuous in the form of art to acceptable enjoyment, the time-
honored mind-body dualism of which this distinction is the aesthetic
manifestation destroys itself.[22] For the sensual enters with the sensuous, and in a vast area of aesthetic creation and experience the
sensual becomes a major if not predominant feature of its sensuous
appeal. Indeed, the two are often indistinguishable.

If we regard the sensual as continuous with the aesthetic, numerous
problems in aesthetic theory move closer to clarification and resolution, issues such as the significance of the nude in art, psychological
theorizing about the relation of the artist to sexuality, and especially
the place of the tactile and other contact senses in aesthetic experience.
For the tactile urge, undeveloped and unencouraged as it is, reveals
itself surreptitiously (as may be observed at any sculpture exhibit),
and becomes a fissure in the rock of aesthetic respectability. And by
thus acknowledging the physical more openly and involving it more
squarely in aesthetic experience, it becomes possible to explain differences of response to the same aesthetic stimuli through differences in
physical states of receptivity and sensitivity.

[21] Dewey, p. 20. Cf. also Chap. II in its entirety.

[22] "The moralist knows that sense is allied with emotion, impulse and appetition. So he
denounces the lust of the eye as part of the surrender of spirit to flesh. He identifies the
sensuous with the sensual and the sensual with the lewd. His moral theory is askew,
but at least he is aware that the eye is not an imperfect telescope designed for intellectual reception of material to bring about knowledge of distant objects." Dewey, p. 21.

What this interpretation suggests, then, is that aesthetic experience at its fullest and richest is experience by the whole man; the entire person is now involved in the aesthetic event. And instead of making aesthetic experience a "spiritual" communion of "kindred souls," effete and insubstantial, we have indicated how it may be revitalized by being brought into the world of natural events, universal in its inclusiveness—experience perhaps more fundamental, vital, and intrinsically significant than any other.

---

17. Method and Methodology in Literary Criticism

Eugene F. Kaelin

THE PROGRAM for instruction in any field of intellectual endeavor depends upon methods, and any discourse upon methods to be employed in the solution of an intellectual problem is rightfully termed "methodology." In the following, philosophical aesthetics will be interpreted as the methodology of criticism, which in turn is to be considered a method of art analysis. Instruction in literary criticism, therefore, must contain two elements: the laying down of a workable method of analysis (aesthetics), and *travaux pratiques* in the use of the method laid down (criticism). The distinction roughly parallels the usual educational distinction between theory and practice, which remains sound if the differenda do not lose contact in their separation. Accordingly, my thesis demands two sections: the first dedicated to what I take to be a methodologically sound aesthetic theory; and the second to an illustration of the theory in practice.

I

If the method sought is to be something other than general cultural history on the one hand, and is to yield specifically aesthetic results by treating its objects as something other than moral sermons or pseudoscientific and quasi-philosophical treatises on the other, it becomes imperative to conceive of some generally workable idea

Reprinted by permission from *The School Review*, LXXII:3 (Autumn, 1964), 289–308. Copyright 1964 by the University of Chicago.

of aesthetic expressions considered as a whole and then to proceed to an analysis of the particular case of literature. I shall arrange the general results into a small set of postulates.

Postulate 1.   Aesthetic expressions are context bound. There is no "meaning" for an gesture taken out of context, and no context can meaningfully take in the whole of the universe (everything that can be truthfully said). The universe of discourse defining the limits of significance for criticism is, therefore, what is usually referred to as the "work of art" or as the "object of criticism." In practice, this postulate limits critical sense to a single work of a single author and tends to concentrate attention rather than disperse it over the widest range possible. Thus it would be considered critical nonsense to refer to a work of art as "romantic" or "classical," since to classify the given work with others resembling it in one way or another leads the attention away from the specific romantic or classical quality of the given piece and places it on the class of objects of which the work is a member.

The temptation to classify, moreover, leads humanists to adopt the travesty of scientific minds, when, in character, they should be engaged not with facts, either particular or general, but with the experiencing of the quality, or value, of a given object. In a similar vein, Blaise Pascal distinguished between *l'esprit géométrique* and *l'esprit de finesse,* roughly between analysis and synthesis, which he thought proper for scientists and humanists, respectively. Following the rules of aesthetic positivism, Taine [1] and his disciples of our own day have illustrated the need for a peculiarly humanistic method, which cannot be attained without the maximum concentration on the specific values of a particular work. It is my hope that this method can be supplied by aesthetic theory.

Postulate 2.   The context of an aesthetic expression, and hence of its significance, is constructed uniquely and exhaustively by the network of relations set up by *the counters* of the given medium. I refer here to the medial symbols, markers, or elements with which the artist must think in solving his qualitative problems [2] and which, taken in

---

[1] See Hippolyte Taine, *Philosophie de l'art* (Paris: Hachette, 1906). The first lesson in this course of aesthetics contained three rules: to relate one work of an author with the others; to relate the total œuvre of an author with those of others; to relate the total œuvres of the various authors with the general climate of opinion under which each had been written in the first place. This method, called "modern" by Taine, is the one which more or less permeates education in the humanities today. Call it "the historical method" or "aesthetic positivism" or, more honestly, "cultural history," and the results are the same: Students are made aware of everything about a work of literary art except its own intrinsic values.

[2] See David Ecker, "The Artistic Process as Qualitative Problem Solving," *Journal of Aesthetics and Art Criticism,* XXI(1963), 283–90.

relation, form the sensuous surface of the work. In music, the medium is composed of sounds and silences, and anything that can be meaningfully said about music as an aesthetic expression must be traceable to sounds and silences. Painting, the visual medium, has for its context of significance anything that may be seen: lines and forms, colors and space; architecture, mass and force, etc. Although ultra-purists, those aestheticians who restrict artistic significance to the medial values alone, needlessly restrict the aesthetic context in that their music never has a program, their painting no subject, their architecture no function, the truth of the matter is that some music does have a program; some paintings, and very good ones at that, are figurative; and any piece of architecture having no function is no building at all. The problem to be conceived here is a "thickening of the surface."

When the sounds of nature are "pictured" in the sounds and silences of music, when the lines and forms of painting suggest recognizable forms of nature, when the masses and forces of structural concrete or steel permit and intensify the life within, the context of analysis must broaden to allow for the inclusion of this intellectual "depth." Representation of objects, suggestion of images, and conception of ideas—all depth qualities—may add considerably to and enrich the context of relatedness which is the artist's expression. In fact, if much of the musical medium and all of non-objective painting is a limited surface expression, it is not impossible to conceive of an expression without a sensuous surface.[3]

Since the marks on paper used to express mathematical truths are irrelevant to the value of the latter, mathematics in its ultra-purity could be considered a surfaceless aesthetic expression. The analytical trick in the case of a mathematical theorem as an art object would be to explain how the relatedness of abstract ideas could be experienced as a quality. This is a gift few mathematicians possess, and still fewer have been able to give coherent accounts of their process of thought: Einstein claimed to work with "visual phenomena and motor responses"; Poincaré wrote that his "aesthetic sense" enabled him to choose the most fruitful patterns of relatedness, especially when he had been frustrated for some time from finding the felicitous solution to his problem, which usually came when his mind was "idling." [4]

Since its medium is defined by spoken and written words and their attendant meanings, literature in its purity is a surface and depth art. Its surface is composed of the words as sounded or read, and its depth is the organized meanings given expression in the words. The word

[3] I borrow here the terminology of D. W. Prall (see his *Aesthetic Judgment* [New York: Thomas Y. Crowell Co., 1929], pp. 57–75).

[4] For the accounts each has given of his own creative approach to mathematics see *The Creative Process*, ed. Brewster Ghiselin (New York: Mentor Books, 1955).

"texture" is useful for the organization of the surface counters; and "structure" serves well for the depth.

Postulate 3. **The aesthetic expressiveness of a work of art is the experience of the relatedness of the surface counters and their representations, out of which the total context is constructed.** As indicated above, the work of art may be a surface expression only, hence non-objective; or it may be a depth expression in which an object, image, or idea is presented by means of the surface. Although literature, using words, is always a depth art, the relative values of the surface and depth may vary greatly: from a vary tense and musical surface that is poetry,

> In Xanadu did Kubla Khan
> A stately pleasure-dome decree

to the looser, more prosaic timbre of a symbolic narrative,

> Call me Ishmael. Some years ago—never mind how long precisely—having little or no money in my purse, and nothing particular to interest me on shore, I thought I would sail about a little and see the watery part of the world.

Both of the examples cited above have rhythm, a surface quality perceived whenever the words are read, aloud or in perceptive silence; and each rhythm is adapted to the necessities of the total work. In Coleridge's poetry, the musical values of the words dominate the sense; whereas the rhythm of Melville's prose sets one looking for an idea which is to follow.

In each case the surface serves the purpose of the total expressiveness of the piece; if ever one became unaware of the surface values, he could lay no claim to having experienced the work. The complete analysis of a literary work, of course, entails our ability to relate surface and depth, texture and structure, into a single experience. Being felt, or experienced, this expressiveness is not discursive; it is had or it is missed, but it cannot be rendered into words whose function it is to purvey information. Experience the difference between

> Man and plants are both natural events, subject to growth.

and

> The force that through the green fuse drives the flower
> Drives my green age . . .

and you will have experienced the difference between the use of words primarily to convey information (their discursive use) and the use of words to construct an aesthetic context (their non-discursive use).

So much for the general aesthetic postulates. The task now becomes that of considering the manner in which words are used non-discursively in the particular aesthetic contexts we call "literary."

The basic counters of the literary medium are the words; and, as noted above, the articulation of the words has a double effect. Perceptually, the words are sounds or marks on paper, and both of these features of words as articulated may go to constitute the texture of a literary work. But along with their perceptual values, be they aural or visual, one will find a second level of articulation: that of meaning. Any meanings represented constitute the depth of the work; and theoretically at least, there are no limits to the levels of meaning one can find as valid constituents of the aesthetic object.

The meanings may be denotative or connotative. The word "mother" denotes the class of women having borne a child and connotes precisely "woman having borne a child," if the meanings of words are limited to their conventional intension. Objectively considered, the connotations of a word are all the ideas or characteristics (and only those) necessary to define the class of objects denoted. These objective connotations (sometimes referred to as "comprehension" of the term) are theoretical limits and strictly possible only in the realm of mathematics and logic, whose entities are uniquely definable. To make up for this stricture, the literary artist has a whole range of subjective connotations with which to play. Witness the doggerel poem

> M is for the million things she gave me . . .

each line of which exploits one of the subjective connotations associated with the word "mother." Recall, too, Dame Edith Sitwell's dismay at one reader's inability to understand "Emily-colored hands," which according to the author was a misquotation. She later explained,

> I did not write "Emily-colored hands," a hideous phrase. I wrote "Emily-colored *primulas*," which to anyone who has progressed in poetry reading beyond the *White Cliffs of Dover* calls to mind the pink cheeks of young country girls.[5]

Whatever the limitations imposed upon the meanings of poetry by the use of a private language by obscurantist poets, the context in which the personally meaningful metaphors are used will further qualify, and thus limit, the meanings of literary expressions.

Every symbol, in fact, has its meaning, not externally, but inter-

[5] For some discussion of the use of connotation in the interpretation of poetry see Monroe C. Beardsley, *Aesthetics: Problems in the Philosophy of Criticism* (New York: Harcourt, Brace & Co., 1958), 149–52.

nally to the context of expression. A device for relating one level of significance in that context to another, the literary symbol serves to re-inforce the internal structure of a work. Faulkner's unbeatable three-legged horse, attended by the Negro boy possessing the gift of tongues, serves to relate the allegorical content of *The Fable*, the Christian myth, with the first-level events in the life of the unknown soldier. The soldier himself is a symbol for Christ, and to prove it obligingly disappears from his coffin after a three days' vigil by the mercenaries who were charged with the recovery of his body. The body was to be used for the purpose of commemorating the death of the soldier in the service of humanity, and the ceremonial was to be observed by all nations.

Symbolism is thus a literary technique for enriching the depth structures of a work; the greater the levels of significance, the greater the intensity of expression. Mechanically, symbolism is a relatively simple device: words are organized to represent objects; and the objects are related to represent ideas. On the higher levels of literary interpretation usually called "symbolic," one set of ideas may be so organized as to represent another, and so on. This is not to say that the aesthetic significance of the work is exhausted by an analysis of the various levels of meanings and their interrelations. The whole network of structural relations must be experienced in relation to the surface presenting the novel's depth. This experience is the total aesthetic expressivness of the literary work.

In the example to follow (Part II) I shall attempt to show how one event in a novel, for example, may be interpreted as a symbol for the very novel of which it is a single event. Although this process violates the logical theory of types (proscribing a reference by any set of symbols to itself), the art of literature is not limited to the techniques of logical expression and may indeed gain for wilfully breaking them.

It is useful for purposes of critical analysis to envisage the depth structures of novels and short stories as a function of character and plot, both of which are virtual "creations" [6] emerging from the articulation of connotative and denotative meanings. Moreover, they are not independent. Character depends upon the events which influence the lives of the fictional characters; and in a philosophical viewpoint allowing for a degree of personal freedom, the decisions and actions of the various characters may influence the course of events. In still other novels the events and the characters may be all but undistinguishable, as in *Molloy* by Beckett.

---

[6] This in opposition to George Santayana, who claimed that only the characters of literature were proper creations (see his *Sense of Beauty* [New York Modern Library, 1955], pp. 173–76).

The formal structures of character and plot [7] likewise allow the expression of serious philosophical ideas: morality and metaphysics, respectively. And these latter may be used as structural principles for integrating the structure of the story. Thus we find "naturalistic" stories in which the events determine the life of the characters, the whole being presented in reportorial style (e.g., Dreiser's *Sister Carrie*), and "humanistic" stories in which the characters qualify the nature of events (e.g., Cather's *My Ántonia*). An impressionistic style serves well to present a story based upon the metaphysics of subjective idealism, as in parts of Sartre's *Nausea;* and the symbolic mode of presentation fits well with the transcendental idealism of Melville's several novels, perhaps most clearly in *Moby Dick*.

This confluence of literary analysis and philosophical speculation has a second basis, the explanation of which will yield a further hermeneutical tool. Since the literary object is a closed context, inclosing within itself all the significance it bears, it is comparable in structure to the metaphysical concepts of "universe," "world," "cosmos," and the like. The author has constructed a unique universe, just as the metaphysician is trying to disclose the principle or principles upon which the structures of the "real" universe depend. Universe for universe, however, this basis of comparison affords no philosopher's stone to transmute bad into good literature.

The interpretative tool it does allow is the resultant necessity, when in doubt, to make a hypothesis for the description of a novel's structure. In some cases, this may not be necessary, depending upon the didactic purposes of the authors concerned (cf. Huxley's *Point Counterpoint*, in which the musical device is used to unify varied voices on a general hedonic theme); and, on the other hand, the individual interpreter may never succeed in discovering the unifying principle of even the most successfully unified work.

The source of an interpretative hypothesis may be anything: cultural history, the works of the same or other authors, philosophy, psychology, or what have you; but the rules of the game demand that the hypothesis be tried against the experienced events of the given universe—the facts of nature for the scientist or philosopher, and the facts of the narrative for the literary critic. And if one suggested hypothesis does not work, then the critic is authorized to discard it, sometimes in spite of what the author has claimed; and in the case of truly visionary authors, almost always in spite of the prevailing climate of opinion.

[7] Santayana's discussion contains the basis for the inclusion of plot and character as formal structures within an aesthetic context. Such an analysis vitiates the older distinction between "form" and "content."

But the successful unification of the structure is not "the meaning," the aesthetic significance of the piece. Criticism only begins when the depth has been understood in that the critic must yet relate, almost always in a second or third reading, what he has understood to the textural vehicle used by the author in presenting his universe of meaning. To use a trite example, the bite of wit and the ironic play of paradox can never be understood or felt without an understanding of the textural qualifications of the written or spoken message:

> "Do you love me, honey?"
> "I adore you, sweetheart."
> "How do you love me?"
> "In the pig's blue eye."

The last ironical response is enough to change anyone's honey into the bitterest of wormwood—depending upon the circumstances which surround the conversation, and, by filling in the context, qualify its meaning.

All the critic can do is to put a perceptive and imaginative individual into a receptive mood; he cannot verbalize the total expressiveness of the aesthetic object, which must be felt according to the patterning of human feeling determined by the textural-structural relations of the aesthetic context. If my description of this context is a workable methodological account of the method of criticism, that is the limit of the possibility of education within the literary medium. To move from

> "Yes, of course, if it's fine tomorrow," said Mrs. Ramsay. "But you'll have to be up with the lark," she added.

to

> It was done; it was finished. Yes, she thought, laying down her brush in extreme fatigue, I have had my vision.

is to perform a complicated score, and the art of teaching literature has for its end the realization of the values inherent in a novel's total context.

II

Virginia Woolf's *To the Lighthouse* opens in the middle of a conversation between a mother and son; and, while the father and the same son, accompanied by his favorite daughter and two other persons, land at a lighthouse off the Isles of Skye, the novel closes with an exclamation by an artist that her portrait is done. Thus, for the beginning and the end—of the novel, of a portrait, and of a planned trip, all of which, so related, become the same event in different perspective. But for a novel by Henry James of that title, this one might have been called *The Portrait of a Lady*.

The lady involved is Mrs. Ramsay, the mother of eight children and wife of an oafish metaphysician who had published his first book before the age of twenty-five and nothing thereafter. At the beginning of the novel she sits before a window knitting and incidentally posing for a picture with her youngest son, James. The boy has asked whether he might make a trip to the off-shore lighthouse just before the first written words of the novel. (The question, implied, is part of the novel's context.) The painter is one Lily Briscoe, whose work is being watched by the sympathetic critic, William Bankes. Through the window we are introduced into Mrs. Ramsey's world.

Everything there is not honey and light; but as Mrs. Ramsay looks out and Lily Briscoe looks in, the reader enjoys a double vision: the one perspective shows us the inner world of Mrs. Ramsay, whose actions are motivated by love and sympathy, and who, like the long, third stroke of the spinning beam of the lighthouse, becomes a principle by virtue of which other things are seen. What is seen through her constitutes a second set of objects presented to the reader's attention. The most important of these, of course, are James and his father.

Mrs. Ramsay knows by feeling, becoming one in intimacy with the objects she becomes conscious of. The not so dim analogue of carnal knowledge that is sexual union passes through Lily Briscoe's mind in her attempts to capture Mrs. Ramsay's personality:

> What art was there, known to love or cunning, by which one pressed through into those secret chambers? What device for becoming, like waters poured into one jar, inextricably the same, one with the object one adored? Could the body achieve, or the mind, subtly mingling in the intricate passages of the brain? or the heart? Could loving, as people called it, make her and Mrs. Ramsay one? for it was not knowledge but unity she desired, not inscriptions on tablets, nothing that could be written in any language known to men, but intimacy itself, which is knowledge, she thought, leaning her head on Mrs. Ramsay's knee.

If Lily could put that personality into the symbols of her own medium, what would it become? The answer, "a triangular purple shape," an abstract rendering of Mrs. Ramsay reading to James; so muses the critic, Bankes. Using his sympathy for an aesthetic object, he explains,

> Mother and child then—objects of universal veneration and in this case the mother was famous for her beauty—might be reduced . . . to a purple shadow without irreverence.

But Lily, wiser in the ways of intuition, corrects his naïveté:

> But the picture was not of them, she said. Or, not in his sense.
> There were other senses too in which one might reverence them.
> By a shadow here and a light there, for instance.

As the reader grasps the second level significance (the flashing light of
the lighthouse, if my hypothesis is correct), the author continues,

> Her tribute took that form if, as she vaguely supposed, a picture
> must be a tribute. A mother and child might be reduced to
> shadow without irreverence. A light here required a shadow there.

In that other universe, the one represented by the everyday, academic
lives of the Ramsays, the mother and child are merely shadows to the
failing light of the father. Here on vacation the values are reversed,
and the light is thrown off by the mother and son: The father doesn't
fit into the picture.

Receiving all of Mrs. Ramsay's affectionate sympathy and always
demanding more, he is incapable of reciprocating, bogged down like
David Hume into the mud of his own logic. His knowledge, about
"subjects and objects and the nature of reality," is all conceptual;
being general, and separated from its objects by the distance of the
signs he must use to think with, it is a good two degrees removed from
the reality he would like to describe. But to his wife his mind was of
the very first order:

> For if thought is like the keyboard of a piano, divided into so
> many notes, or like the alphabet is ranged in twenty-six letters all
> in order, then his splendid mind had no sort of difficulty in run-
> ning over those letters one by one, firmly and accurately, until it
> had reached, say, the letter Q. He reached Q. Very few people in
> the whole of England ever reach Q. . . . But after Q? What comes
> next? After Q there are a number of letters the last of which is
> scarcely visible to mortal eyes, but glimmers red in the distance.
> Z is only reached once by one man in a generation. Still, if he
> could reach R it would be something. Here at least was Q.

It comes as no surprise that Mr. Ramsay will dig in before he reaches
Z and continue smugly talking nonsense about "Locke, Hume, Berkeley, and the causes of the French Revolution"; nor yet that his young
son, who loves his mother, detests his father.

The first part of the book presents the events of one afternoon and
evening: Mrs. Ramsay's sitting, James's deception, Mr. Ramsay's
blundering into Lily Briscoe and William Bankes while reading
poetry, the engagement of Minta Doyle and Paul Rayley, the symbolic reading of The Fisherman and His Wife, the chaotic dinner
party of the family and their friends—academicians, lovers, painter,
poet, and critic, all presided over by Mrs. Ramsay, who alone makes a
single event of this curious gathering of unrelated passions. In keep-

ing with Mrs. Ramsay's distrust of the discursive intellect, this one moment in time resembles somewhat the picture-pasted pastiche her son James was making at her feet, cutting the images from an illustrated catalogue and putting them together to be seen all at once in a single act of vision. This is *how* we see through "The Window," Part I of the book.

In spite of her feelings for her son, however, Mrs. Ramsay is forced to acknowledge that the weather the next day would not permit a trip to the lighthouse. The pastiche of the events surrounding the Ramsays and viewed from "The Window" endures one half of a day; it takes up some 186 pages of writing.

The second part, "Time Passes," relates the events of ten years: the Great War, the death of Mrs. Ramsay, of her children Prue and Andrew, and the publication of a book of poems by Mr. Carmichael, the poet of the first part. The ten years' events consume a bare twenty-five pages of writing.

For the purposes of the story, then, the time of the clock is relatively unimportant, or more properly said, reduced to its strictest relevance in the lives of the individuals in the story. In explicating this hypothesis we shall discover the central phenomenon related in the novel.

The third part is an extended narrative of correlative events: James's piloting his father and sister to the lighthouse ten years after the first project and Lily Briscoe's final vision in the presence of Mr. Carmichael. Only artists (the painter and the poet) are permitted the ultimate realization. But, as Mrs. Ramsay muses in Part I, artists should marry critics and thus share their visions:

> Smiling, for it was an admirable idea, that had flashed upon her this very second—William and Lily should marry. . . .

In spite of the tauntings of that odious student of Mr. Ramsay's, who kept muttering that women couldn't paint, women couldn't write, Lily finishes her portrait when she discovers what was missing from that purple triangle (one of its necessary angles or sides, the father in sympathetic relation to mother and son), and Mrs. Woolf finishes her novel in the same stroke.

But what is the story about? A trip to a lighthouse, Lily's picture, Mrs. Ramsay's personality? Obviously, in one sense, about all three; but about none, in the same sense that Lily's picture is not about a mother and son, even as it is completed with the presence of the father. The novel must present, not represent, its object: it must be, not mean; and to do this the novelist must construct a single depth and express it through a surface which is of some interest in itself.

Now that main events of the story have been recounted, I may take the critic's privilege of constructing a hypothesis for giving a unified interpretation of the novel's depth. There are many hints to the structure, just as there are many "plants" for recognizing them. For example, the masculine and discursive intelligence of Mr. Ramsay and Charles Tansley, his student, is bound to evidence; and the evidential signs indicate to them that there will be no immediate trip to the lighthouse. This they know in their own manner of knowing. But the woman and the child feel or intuit more than they can conceptualize; the feminine intelligence that is close to instinct ignores the evidence and puts as indifferent the moment a given event is to take place. Tomorrow or ten years from now, what's the difference if the event actually takes place? The time of the clock is indifferent to the matter —save for the deception in the feelings of a small boy, always given in an immediate "now." Yet time is of the essence, and if time is not to be measured by a clock, then by some other, more accurate instrument, human consciousness.

Thus the divorce between masculine and feminine intelligence is strengthened by the split between naturalistic and psychological time. The time of the clock, the measure of natural events, is scientific and conceptual; that of the psyche, given by the impressions of consciousness, value-laden and empirical. In the difference lie the worlds of Mr. and Mrs. Ramsay, respectively.

His time is objective (independent of the events occuring within), and single; it is continuous, with no breaks, and infinitely divisible. As infinite, it cannot end; nor does it have a first instant. Further, it is homogeneous, that is, everywhere alike (whether at the Isles of Skye or Timbuctoo); and, last, it is isotropic, having the same physical properties in either direction. Time may occur as $+t$ or $-t$ in Mr. Ramsay's equations concerning the nature of the real world.

Mrs. Ramsay's time, psychological in essence, is relative, known through the felt changes in events: Something could be added or subtracted without changing its essential character, even the death of its perceiver. It is likewise plural, allowing for differences in psychological makeup (as between hers and her husband's and between hers and Charles Tansley's or even between hers and Lily Briscoe's). Since one instant may be more interesting than another (Parts I and III are more humanly significant than Part II), its span can be broken into a discontinuous series to emphasize the importance of a given event. But psychological time must start and end, and does so within the limits of expectation and memory. It is therefore finite. Its instants are non-homogeneous, since the now and the projected future are privileged moments: The events themselves determine the length of the moments. Finally, psychological time is anisotropic: As a dimension of experience it flows undirectionally from the future to the past.[8] Conceive this difference in temporal qualities, and you may perceive the difference between the personalities of Mr. and Mrs. Ramsay.

The last quality of psychological time, its flowing from the future to the past, enables us immediately to verify our temporal hypothesis. For psychological time to start, there must be an anticipated event; and with this event as an indefinite future each succeeding moment will become present until there is attained that one moment of initial projection of time that is now definitely past and in relation to which all prior events are past-anterior. I refer, of course to the opening conversation between Mrs. Ramsay and James, the past of the narrative with respect to the future, anticipated event, the voyage to the lighthouse.

The symbol of the lighthouse, then, becomes luminously clear: It is an enduring physical object (in everybody's world), an anticipated event in the lives of James and Mrs. Ramsay and thus, in anticipation, the moment when psychological time begins its (backward) flow; it is likewise the value which ultimately fulfils James's life (and by extension that of his mother, who has already passed away in Part II of the novel) and which enables Lily Briscoe to relate the life of Mr. to Mrs. Ramsay through the will and achievement of James.

The beginning of time, the lighthouse is likewise the measure of time (Mrs. Ramsay, recall, identifies herself with the third stroke of the rotating light); but that universe in which it is the beginning of time is different from that in which it is a measure. It is the beginning of time in the universe of Mrs. Ramsay and James; a measure in the one naturalistic universe shared by all the characters. As it rotates, the phases of its temporal passing are strictly analogous to the movements of all the timepieces, including Paul Rayley's gold watch, though the latter be discreetly hidden in a wash-leather bag.

The two times of the represented events within the novel necessitate a further unification in a single time of the novel itself, as formed by the novelist and as "per-formed" by a perceptive reader. For this over-all structure I may be permitted another hypothesis. In *Art as Experience*, John Dewey explains time as an organizing principle of an experience. (Remember that the experience I am interpreting is that of Mrs. Woolf's novel.)

> Time ceases to be either the endless and uniform flow of the succession of instantaneous points which some philosophers have asserted it to be. It, too, is the organized and organizing medium

[8] For these characteristics of the temporal distinctions I am indebted to my former teacher, A. C. Benjamin (see his *An Introduction to the Philosophy of Science* [New York: Macmillan Co., 1937], pp. 281–96).

of *the rhythmic ebb and flow of expectant impulse,* forward and retracted movement, resistance and suspense, with fulfillment and consummation. It is an ordering of growth and maturations. . . . Time as organization in change is growth, and growth signifies that a varied series of change enters upon intervals of pause and rest; of completions that become initial points of new processes of development. Like the soil, mind is fertilized while it lies fallow, until a new burst of bloom ensues.

When a flash of lightning illumines a dark landscape, there is a momentary recognition of objects. But the recognition itself is not a mere point in time. It is the focal culmination of long, slow processes of maturation. It is the manifestation of the continuity of an ordered temporal experience in a sudden discrete instant of climax. It is as meaningless in isolation as would be the drama of Hamlet were it confined to a single line or word with no context. But the phrase "the rest is silence" is infinitely pregnant as the conclusion of a drama enacted through development in time; so may be the momentary perception of a natural scene. Form, as it is present in the fine arts, is the art of making clear what is involved in the organization of space and time prefigured in every course of a developing life experience.[9]

It is no accident, of course, that Dewey's description of time as a formal organizational device corresponds, almost point for point, with Mrs. Woolf's novelistic structure. He was describing the form of a well-constructed experience, and she was presenting her readers with an example of the same phenomenon. All that is lacking is a critic to be able to perceive the relationship and to disclose to others what his perception has already disclosed to himself.

Texturally, the depth of the novel is reinforced by the surface. Noting the impressionism of her general style (to capture the glimpses of experience each character contributes to the novel), I shall restrict myself to the significance of Mrs. Woolf's use of parentheses and brackets.

One entire section of Part I (XIV) occurs within the parentheses indicating an abrupt breaking of the flow of events that mark off naturalistic time; they show the mind, like the soil, "fertilized while it lies fallow, until a new burst of bloom ensues." Other uses of parentheses mark switches in point of view, which indicate the multiplicity or plurality of (psychological) times of which the universe of the novel is constructed and through which the various characters live.

In Part II the more abrupt breaks of brackets are used to indicate the manner in which the naturalistic events of conceptual, clock time break into the psychological moments constituting the more signifi-

[9] John Dewey, *Art as Experience* (New York: Minton, Balch, 1934), pp. 23–24. (Italics mine.)

cant events of the novel's context. How surprising, for example, to read in the middle of the novel:

> [Mr. Ramsay, stumbling along a passage one dark morning, stretched his arms out, but Mrs. Ramsay having died rather suddenly the night before, his arms, though stretched out, remained empty.]

But this event too is only a new beginning in the realization of the first project to land at the lighthouse. United at last to her husband, in sympathy, some years following her death, Mrs. Ramsay lands at the lighthouse with him and their two youngest children; and one stretch of time comes to an end. The rest is silence.

The voyage, Mrs. Ramsay's portrait, and the novel are one and the same event; and with their completion time passes into timelessness. But this is in effect what the lighthouse has always symbolized as an enduring physical object in the rolling waves of the sea. The measure of time, itself timeless, the lighthouse is the point at which life passes over into art:

> Her horizon seemed to her limitless. There were all the places she had not seen; the Indian plains; she felt herself pushing aside the thick leather curtain of a church in Rome. This core of darkness could go anywhere, for no one saw it. They could not stop it, she thought, exulting. There was freedom, there was peace, there was, most welcome of all, a summoning together, a resting on a platform of stability. Not as oneself did one find rest ever . . ., but as a wedge of darkness. Losing personality, one lost the fret, the hurry, the stir; and there rose to her lips always some exclamation of triumph over life when things came together in this peace, this rest, this eternity; and pausing there she looked out to meet that stroke of the Lighthouse, the long steady stroke, the last of the three, which was her stroke. . . . Often she found herself sitting and looking, with her work in her hands until she became the things she looked at—that light, for example.

In this passage the roll of the sea, the phases of the light and the rhythm of the prose are unmistakably one.

Mr. Ramsay finally redeems himself by coming toward her in sympathy, the sympathy he could never give her alive, as she stood there, rigid in death, a platform of stability for all who have sympathy enough to know or to feel. Although he is not permitted to see it, the reader knows what the essence of Lily's picture must be.

In sum, I have been maintaining that the effective teaching of literature depends in the least upon two considerations. First, that teachers, and *a fortiori* teachers of teachers, become aesthetically more knowledgeable. Until they are capable of giving to their students a workable methodological approach to a particular art form, there will be no way of testing when claims to artistic knowledge are warranted; and the methodology of art criticism is the business of aesthetics. Second, until aestheticians themselves are capable of showing the bases for their own methodological prescriptions and defending them in actual criticism, teachers in the arts are not about to adopt their pronouncements. Literature remains one of the only major art forms to be taught by non-practitioners of the art. We have many painters who teach painting and sculptors, sculpture; but there are few successful writers who willingly take on the guise of writer-teacher, or even of writer in residence. Until, and even when they do, the methodology and the method of criticism will have to become a pre-requisite to education in the art.

I have tried to show that a contextualistic aesthetic provides a viable methodology, enabling a fruitful critical approach to literary analysis, and I would argue most emphatically for its inclusion in any program of education in the humanities. The other questions concerning the value of literature—its social importance, its value as a didactic tool, its "mirroring of the times in which it is written"—all seem to depend upon its validity as an artistic expression in the first instance. Training in aesthetic judgment is to the appreciation of the arts, whether by the artist or his audience, as the science of logic is to the making of sense in any field of discursive intelligence. And it is about time educators begin to make sense when talking about the arts. Anyone can be wrong; but to be wrong and not to know it, or not to know how to proceed in order to be right, is an indefensible educational posture.

PART FIVE
Philosophy

18. How I See Philosophy

Friedrich Waismann

I

W HAT PHILOSOPHY IS? [1] I don't know, nor have I a set formula
to offer. Immediately I sit down to contemplate the question I am flooded with so many ideas, tumbling over one another, that
I cannot do justice to all of them. I can merely make an attempt, a
very inadequate one, to sketch with a few strokes what the lie of the
land seems to me to be, tracing some lines of thoughts without entering upon a close-knit argument.

It is, perhaps, easier to say what philosophy is not than what it is.
The first thing, then, I should like to say is that philosophy, as it is
practised today, is very unlike science; and this in three respects: in
philosophy there are no proofs; there are no theorems; and there are
no questions which can be decided, Yes or No. In saying that there are
no proofs I do not mean to say that there are no arguments. Arguments certainly there are, and first-rate philosophers are recognized by
the originality of their arguments; only these do not work in the sort
of way they do in mathematics or in the sciences.

There are many things beyond proof: the existence of material
objects, of other minds, indeed of the external world, the validity of
induction, and so on. Gone are the days when philosophers were
trying to prove all sorts of things: that the soul is immortal, that this
is the best of all possible worlds and the rest, or to refute, by "irre-
futable" argument and with relish, materialism, positivism and what
not. Proof, refutation—these are dying words in philosophy (though
G. E. Moore still "proved" to a puzzled world that it exists. What can
one say to this—save, perhaps, that he is a great prover before the
Lord?).

But can it be *proved* that there are no proofs in philosophy? No; for
one thing, such a proof, if it were possible, would by its very existence

Reprinted by permission from *Contemporary British Philosophy*, edited by H. D.
Lewis, pp. 445–490 (London: George Allen and Unwin, Ltd., 1956).

[1] This article is in reply to a question put to me by the Editor (of *Contemporary
British Philosophy*).

establish what it was meant to confute. But why suppose the philosopher to have an I.Q. so low as to be unable to learn from the past?
Just as the constant failure of attempts at constructing a perpetual
motion has in the end led to something positive in physics, so the
efforts to construct a philosophical "system," going on for centuries
and going out of fashion fairly recently, tell their tale. This, I think, is
part of the reason why philosophers today are getting weaned from
casting their ideas into deductive moulds, in the grand style of
Spinoza.

What I want to show in this article is that it is quite wrong to look
at philosophy as though it had for its aim to provide theorems but had
lamentably failed to do so. The whole conception changes when one
comes to realize that what philosophers are concerned with is something different—neither discovering new propositions nor refuting
false ones nor checking and re-checking them as scientists do. For one
thing, proofs require premises. Whenever such premises have been
set up in the past, even tentatively, the discussion at once challenged
them and shifted to a deeper level. Where there are no proofs there
are no theorems either. (To write down lists of propositions "proved"
by Plato or Kant: a pastime strongly to be recommended.) Yet the
failure to establish a sort of Euclidean system of philosophy based on
some suitable "axioms" is, I submit, neither a mere accident nor a
scandal but deeply founded in the nature of philosophy.

Yet there are questions; (and arguments). Indeed, a philosopher is
a man who senses as it were hidden crevices in the build of our concepts where others only see the smooth path of commonplaceness
before them.

Questions but no answers? Decidedly odd. The oddness may lessen
when we take a look at them at closer range. Consider two famous
examples: Achilles and the tortoise, and the astonishment of St.
Augustine when confronted with the fact of memory. He is amazed,
not at some striking feat of memory, but at there being such a thing
as memory at all. A sense-impression, say a smell or a taste, floats
before us and disappears. One moment it is here and the next it is
gone. But in the galleries of the memory, pale copies of it are stored up
after its death. From there I can drag them out when and as often as
I wish, like, and yet strangely unlike, the original—unlike in that they
are not perishable like the momentary impression: what was transitory
has been arrested and has achieved duration. But who can say how
this change comes about?

Here the very fact of memory feels mystifying in a way in which
ordinary questions asking for information do not; and *of course* it is
not a factual question. What is it?

From Plato to Schopenhauer philosophers are agreed that the

source of their philosophizing is wonder. What gives rise to it is nothing recondite and rare but precisely those things which stare us in the face: memory, motion, general ideas. (Plato: What does "horse" mean? A single particular horse? No, for it may refer to *any* horse; *all* the horses, the total class? No, for we may speak of this or that horse. But if it means neither a single horse nor all horses, what *does* it mean?) The idealist is shaken in just the same way when he comes to reflect that he has, in Schopenhauer's words, "no knowledge of the sun but only of an eye that sees a sun, and no knowledge of the earth but only of a hand that feels an earth." Can it be, then, that nothing whatever is known to us except our own consciousness?

In looking at such questions, it seems as if the mind's eye were growing dim and as if everything, even that which ought to be absolutely clear, was becoming oddly puzzling and unlike its usual self. To bring out what seems to be peculiar to these questions one might say that they are not so much questions as tokens of a profound uneasiness of mind. Try for a moment to put yourself into the frame of mind of which Augustine was possessed when he asked: How is it possible to measure time? Time consists of past, present and future. The past can't be measured, it is gone; the future can't be measured, it is not yet here; and the present can't be measured, it has no extension. Augustine knew of course how time is measured and this was not his concern. What puzzled him was how it is *possible* to measure time, seeing that the past hour cannot be lifted out and placed alongside the present hour for comparison. Or look at it this way: what is measured is in the past, the measuring in the present: how can that be?

The philosopher as he ponders over some such problem has the appearance of a man who is deeply disquieted. He seems to be straining to grasp something which is beyond his powers. The words in which such a question presents itself do not quite bring out into the open the real point—which may, perhaps more aptly, be described as the recoil from the incomprehensible. If, on a straight railway journey, you suddenly come in sight of the very station you have just left behind, there will be terror, accompanied perhaps by slight giddiness. That is exactly how the philosopher feels when he says to himself, "Of course time can be measured; but how *can* it?" It is as though, up to now, he had been passing heedlessly over the difficulties, and now, all of a sudden, he notices them and asks himself in alarm, "But how can that be?" That is a sort of question which we only ask when it is the very facts themselves which confound us, when something about them strikes us as preposterous.

Kant, I fancy, must have felt something of the sort when he suddenly found the existence of geometry a puzzle. Here we have propositions as clear and transparent as one would wish, prior, it seems, to all experience; at the same time they apply miraculously to the real world. How is that possible? Can the mind, unaided by experience, in some dark manner actually fathom the properties of real things? Looked upon in this way, geometry takes on a disturbing air.

We all have our moments when something quite ordinary suddenly strikes us as queer—for instance, when time appears to us as a curious thing. Not that we are often in this frame of mind; but on some occasions, when we look at things in a certain way, unexpectedly they seem to change as though by magic: they stare at us with a puzzling expression, and we begin to wonder whether they can possibly be the things we have known all our lives.

"Time flows" we say—a natural and innocent expression, and yet one pregnant with danger. It flows "equably," in Newton's phrase, at an even rate. What can this mean? When something moves, it moves with a definite speed (and speed means: rate of change in time). To ask with what speed time moves, i.e. to ask how quickly time changes in time, is to ask the unaskable. It also flows, again in Newton's phrase, "without relation to anything external." How are we to figure that? Does time flow on irrespective of what happens in the world? Would it flow on even if everything in heaven and on earth came to a sudden standstill as Schopenhauer believed? For if this were not so, he said, time would have to stop with the stopping of the clock and move with the clock's movement. How odd: time flows at the same rate and yet without speed; and perhaps even without anything to occur in it? The expression is puzzling in another way. "I can never catch myself being in the past or in the future," someone might say; "whenever I think or perceive or breathe the word 'now,' I am in the present; therefore I am *always* in the present." In saying this, he may think of the present moment as a bridge as it were from which he is looking down at the "river of time." Time is gliding along underneath the bridge, but the "now" does not take part in the motion. What was future passes into the present (is just below the bridge) and then into the past, while the onlooker, the "self" or the "I," is always in the present. "Time flows *through* the 'now,'" he may feel to be a quite expressive metaphor. Yes, it sounds all right—until he suddenly comes to his senses and, with a start, realizes, "But surely the moment flies?" (Query: How to succeed in wasting time? Answer: In this way, for instance—by trying, with eyes closed or staring vacantly in front of oneself, to catch the present moment as it is flitting by.) He may come now to look at matters in a different way. He sees himself advancing through time towards the future, and with this goes a suggestion of being active, just as at other times he may see himself floating down the stream whether he likes it or not. "What exactly is it that is moving—the events in time or the present moment?" he may wonder. In the first case, it looks to him as if time were moving while he stands still; in the second case as if he were moving through time. "How exactly is it," he may say in a dubious voice, "am I always in the present? Is the present always eluding me?" Both ring true in a way; but they contradict each other. Again, does it make sense to ask, "At what time is the present moment?" Yes, no doubt; but how *can* it, if the "now" is but the fixed point from which the dating of any event ultimately receives its sense?

So he is pulled to and fro: "I am always in the present, yet it slips through my fingers; I am going forward in time—no, I am carried down the stream." He is using different pictures, each in its way quite appropriate to the occasion; yet when he tries to apply them jointly they clash. "What a queer thing time must be," he may say to himself with a puzzled look on his face, "what after all *is* time?"—expecting, half-expecting perhaps, that the answer will reveal to him time's hidden essence. Ranged beyond the intellectual are deeper levels of uneasiness—terror of the inevitability of time's passage, with all the reflections upon life that this forces upon us. Now all these anxious doubts release themselves in the question, "What is time?" (*En passant* this is a hint that *one* answer will never do—will never remove all these doubts that break out afresh on different levels and yet are expressed in the same form of words.)

As we all know what time is and yet cannot say what it is it feels mystifying; and precisely because of its elusiveness it catches our imagination. The more we look at it the more we are puzzled: it seems charged with paradoxes. "What is time? What is this being made up of movement only without anything that is moving?" (Schopenhauer). How funny to have it bottled up! "I've got here in my hand the most potent, the most enigmatic, the most fleeting of all essences —Time." (Logan Pearsall Smith of an hour-glass.) For Shelley it is an "unfathomable sea! whose waves are years," a "shoreless flood," for Proust—well, why not leave something to the reader?

But isn't the answer to this that what mystifies us lies in the *noun* form "the time"? Having a notion embodied in the form of a noun almost irresistibly makes us turn round to look for what it is "the name of." We are trying to catch the shadows cast by the opacities of speech. A wrong analogy absorbed into the forms of our language produces mental discomfort; (and the feeling of discomfort, when it refers to language, is a profound one). "All sounds, all colors . . . evoke indefinite and yet precise emotions, or, as I prefer to think, call down among us certain disembodied powers whose footsteps over our hearts we call emotions" (W. B. Yeats).

Yet the answer is a prosaic one: don't ask what time is but how the *word* "time" is being used. Easier said than done; for if the philosopher rectifies the use of language, ordinary language has "the advantage of being in possession of declensions," to speak with Lichtenberg, and thus renews its spell over him, luring him on into the shadow chase. It is perhaps only when we turn to languages of a widely different grammatical structure that the way towards such possibilities of interpretation is entirely barred. "It is highly probable that philosophers within the domain of the Ural-Altaic languages (where the subject-concept is least developed) will look differently 'into the world' and be found on paths of thought different from those of the Indo-Europeans or Mussulmans" (Nietzsche).

II

It may be well at this point to remind ourselves that the words "question" and "answer," "problem" and "solution" are not always used in their most trite sense. It is quite obvious that we often have to do something very different to find the way out of a difficulty. A problem of politics is solved by adopting a certain line of action, the problems of novelists perhaps by the invention of devices for presenting the inmost thoughts and feelings of their characters; there is the painter's problem of how to suggest depth or movement on the canvas, the stylistic problem of expressing things not yet current, not yet turned into cliché; there are a thousand questions of technology which are answered, not by the discovery of some truth, but by a practical achievement; and there is of course the "social question." In philosophy, the real problem is not to find the answer to a given question but to find a sense for it.

To see in what the "solution" of such a "problem" consists let us start with Achilles who, according to Zeno, is to this day chasing the tortoise. Suppose that Achilles runs twice as fast as the tortoise. If the tortoise's start is 1, Achilles will have to cover successively 1, $\frac{1}{2}$, $\frac{1}{4}$, $\frac{1}{8}$, . . . ; this series is endless: so he can never catch the tortoise. "Nonsense!" (a mathematician's voice), "the sum of the infinite series is finite, namely 2, and that settles it." Though perfectly true, his remark is not to the point. It does not remove the sting from the puzzle, the disconcerting idea, namely, that however far we go in the series there is always a next term, that the lead the tortoise has in the race, though naturally getting smaller and smaller, yet never ceases to be: there *can* be no moment when it is strictly zero. It is *this* feature of the case, I suggest, that we do not understand and which throws us into a state of confusion.

But look at it this way. Suppose that we apply the same sort of argument to a minute, then we shall have to argue in some such way as this. Before the minute can be over the first half of it must elapse, then one-quarter of it, then one-eighth of it, and so on *ad infinitum*. This being an endless process, the minute can never come to an end. Immediately we have the argument in this form, the blunder leaps to the eye: we have been confusing two senses of "never," a temporal and a non-temporal one. While it is quite correct to say that the sequence 1, ½, ¼, ⅛, . . . never ends, this sense of the word "never" has nothing whatever to do with time. All it means is that there is no last term in the series, or (what comes to the same) that to any term, no matter how far out in the sequence, a successor can be constructed according to the simple rule "halve it": that is meant here by "never"; whereas in saying, for instance, that man will never find out anything to avert death, "never" is meant in the sense "at no time." It is clear that the mathematical assertion concerning the possibility of going on in the sequence by forming new terms according to the rule does not state anything about actual occurrences in time. The mistake should really be obvious: in saying that, since the start is getting progressively smaller and yet can never cease to be, Achilles can never catch the tortoise, we jump from the mathematical, *non*-temporal to the temporal sense. Had there been two different words in our language to mark these senses the confusion could never have arisen, and the world would be poorer for one of its most attractive paradoxes. But the same word is as a matter of course used with different meanings. Result: something like a conjuring trick. While our attention is diverted, while, "in our mind's eye," we stare fixedly at Achilles as he is speeding along, with each big bound diminishing his distance from the tortoise, the one sense is so innocuously palmed off for the other as to escape notice.

This way of bringing out the fallacy also holds when the other key term is used for presenting the puzzle. As there will "always" be a next term in the sequence, i.e. a next step in the scheme of subdividing the race-course (the word "always" looking just as spotless and innocent) we readily fall into the trap of concluding that the tortoise will "always" be ahead of Achilles, eternally to be chased by his pursuer.

Many are the types of bewilderment: there is the obsessional doubt —can I ever know that other people have experiences, that they see, hear and feel as I do? Can I be sure that memory does not always deceive me? Are there really material objects and not only sense-impressions "of" them? There is the doubtlike uneasiness—what sort of being is possessed by numbers? There is the anxiety-doubt—are we really free? This doubt has taken many different forms one of which I shall single out for discussion—the question, namely, whether the law of excluded middle, when it refers to statements in the future tense, forces us into a sort of logical Predestination. A typical argument is this. If it is true now that I shall do a certain thing tomorrow, say, jump into the Thames, then no matter how fiercely I resist, strike out with hands and feet like a madman, when the day comes I cannot help jumping into the water; whereas, if this prediction is false now, then whatever efforts I may make, however many times I may nerve and brace myself, look down at the water and say to myself, "One, two, three—," it is impossible for me to spring. Yet that the prediction is either true or false is itself a necessary truth, asserted by the law of excluded middle. From this the startling consequence seems to follow that it is already now decided what I shall do tomorrow, that indeed the entire future is somehow fixed, logically preordained. Whatever I do and whichever way I decide, I am merely moving along lines clearly marked in advance which lead me towards my appointed lot. We are all, in fact, marionettes. If we are not prepared to swallow *that*, then— and there is a glimmer of hope in the "then"—there is an alternative open to us. We need only renounce the law of excluded middle for statements of this kind, and with it the validity of ordinary logic, and all will be well. Descriptions of what will happen are, at present, neither true nor false. (This sort of argument was actually propounded by Lukasiewicz in favor of a three-valued logic with "possible" as a third truth-value alongside "true" and "false.")

The way out is clear enough. The asker of the question has fallen into the error of so many philosophers: of giving an answer before stopping to consider the question. For is he clear what he is asking? He seems to suppose that a statement referring to an event in the future is at present undecided, neither true nor false, but that when the event happens the proposition enters into a sort of new state, that of being true. But how are we to figure the change from "undecided" to "true"? Is it sudden or gradual? At what moment does the statement "it will rain tomorrow" begin to be true? When the first drop falls to the ground? And supposing that it will not rain, when will the statement begin to be false? Just at the end of the day, at 12 p.m. sharp? Supposing that the event *has* happened, that the statement *is* true, will it remain so forever? If so, in what way? Does it remain uninterruptedly true, at every moment of day and night? Even if there were no one about to give it any thought? Or is it true only at the moments when it is being thought of? In that case, how long does it remain true? For the duration of the thought? We wouldn't know how to answer these questions; this is due not to any particular ignorance or stupidity on our part but to the fact that something has gone wrong with the way the words "true" and "false" are applied here.

If I say, "It is true that I was in America," I am saying that I was

in America and no more. That in uttering the words "It is true
that—" I take responsibility upon myself is a different matter that
does not concern the present argument. The point is that in making
a statement prefaced by the words "It is true that" I do not *add* anything to the factual information I give you. *Saying* that something is
true is not *making* it true: cp. the criminal lying in court, yet every
time he is telling a lie protesting, his hand on his heart, that he is
telling the truth.

What is characteristic of the use of the words "true" and "false"
and what the pleader of logical determinism has failed to notice is
this. "It is true" and "it is false," while they certainly have the force
of asserting and denying, are not descriptive. Suppose that someone
says, "It is true that the sun will rise tomorrow" all it means is that
the sun will rise tomorrow: he is not regaling us with an extra-descrip-
tion of the trueness of what he says. But supposing that he were to
say instead, "It is true *now* that the sun will rise tomorrow," this
would boil down to something like "The sun will rise tomorrow now";
which is nonsense. To ask, as the puzzle-poser does, "Is it true or false
now that such-and-such will happen in the future?" is not the sort of
question to which an answer can be given: which *is* the answer.

This sheds light on what has, rather solemnly, been termed the
"timelessness of truth." It lies in this that the clause "it is true that—"
does not allow of inserting a date. To say of a proposition like "Dia-
mond is pure carbon" that it is true on Christmas Eve would be just
as poor a joke as to say that it is true in Paris and not in Timbuctoo.
(This does not mean that we cannot say in certain circumstances,
"Yes, it was true in those days" as this can clearly be paraphrased
without using the word "true.")

Now it begins to look a bit less paradoxical to say that when a
philosopher wants to dispose of a question the one thing he must not
do is: to give an answer. A philosophic question is not solved: it *dissolves.* And in what does the "dissolving" consist? In making the
meaning of the words used in putting the question so clear to ourselves that we are released from the spell it casts on us. Confusion was
removed by calling to mind the use of language or, so far as the use
can be distilled into rules, the rules: it therefore *was* a confusion about
the use of language, or a confusion about rules. It is here that philosophy and grammar meet.

There is one further point that needs elucidation. When we say
of a given assertion, e.g. "It is raining," that it is true we can hardly
escape the impression that we say something "about" the assertion,
namely, that it has the property of trueness. To make such a statement seems, then, to say *more* than what was asserted originally,
namely, that it is raining and that this assertion is true. That, how-

ever, leads to queer consequences. For in which sense does it say more? Consider first under which circumstances it would be appropriate to say of two given propositions that the one says "more" than the other. "This is red" says more than "this is colored" for the obvious reason that anyone can conclude from the first statement to the second but no one reversely; similarly "today is Tuesday" says more than "today is a weekday." The criterion, then, suggests itself that, given two propositions p and q, p says more than q, if $\sim p$. q is meaningful and p. $\sim q$ contradictory. The holder of the view that "p is true" says more than p (p standing e.g. for "It is raining"), may now be challenged to explain what he means by that. Is he using the word "more" in the sense just explained? If so, the curious consequence ensues that it must *make sense* to assert the conjunction $\sim p$. q, that is in our case. "It is not true that it is raining and it is raining." Since this obviously is not what he had in mind, what *does* he mean? We are not contradicting him; we merely remind him of how these words have always been used by him, in non-philosophical contexts that is, and then point out that, if he still wants to use them in this sense, to say what he wanted to say lands him in an absurdity. All we do is to make him aware of his own practice. We abstain from any assertion. It is for him to explain what he means. Not that he cannot do it. In ascribing truth to a given statement, he might say, he wants to express perhaps either (i) that it is "in accordance with fact" or something of the sort; or (ii) that he *knows* that it is true. In the first case he is faced with the same dilemma, namely, that it must make sense to say, "It is not in accordance with the facts that it is raining and it is raining"; in the second fresh difficulties are breaking out. For one thing, the words "it is true that—," when uttered by different people, would then mean different things; for another, and this is more fatal to the advocate of fatalism, in construing the words in this sense, he cuts the ground from under his own feet. No one would then be worried by the question whether, supposing that it is false now that he will write a certain letter tomorrow, it follows that it will really be impossible for him to write that letter, that this line of conduct is barred to him, logically barred. For since "it is false now" means in the new sense "he doesn't know yet" nothing follows and the whole question evaporates.

My reason for going into this tangle at some length is that the method applied in unravelling it presents some interesting features. First, we don't *force* our interlocutor. We leave him free to choose, accept or reject any way of using his words. He may depart from ordinary usage—language is not untouchable—if it is only in this way that he can explain himself. He may even use an expression one time in this, another time in that, way. The only thing we insist upon is that he should be aware of what he is doing. If we strictly adhere to this method—going over the argument, asking him at each step whether he is willing to use an expression in a certain way, if not, offering him alternatives, but leaving the decisions to him and only pointing out what their consequences are—no dispute can arise. Disputes arise only if certain steps in this procedure are omitted so that it looks as if we had made an assertion, adding to the world's woes a new apple of discord. This would be the true way of doing philosophy undogmatically. The difficulty of this method lies in presenting the subject in a manner which can easily be taken in—in arranging the cases and the ways in which they are connected through intermediate links so that we can gain a clear synoptic view of the whole.

Second, we do not use arguments in order to prove or disprove any "philosophic view." As we have no views we can afford to look at things as they are.

Next, we only describe; we do not "explain." An explanation, in the sense of a deductive proof, cannot satisfy us because it pushes the question "Why just these rules and no other ones?" only one stage back. In following that method, we do not *want* to give reasons. All we do is to describe a use or tabulate rules. In doing this, we are not making any discoveries: there is nothing to be discovered in grammar. Grammar is autonomous and not dictated by reality. Giving reasons, bound as it is to come to an end and leading to something which cannot further be explained, *ought* not to satisfy us. In grammar we never ask the question "why?"

But isn't the result of this that philosophy itself "dissolves"? Philosophy eliminates those questions which *can* be eliminated by such a treatment. Not all of them, though: the metaphysician's craving that a ray of light may fall on the mystery of the existence of this world, or on the incomprehensible fact that it is comprehensible, or on the "meaning of life"—even if such questions *could* be shown to lack a clear meaning or to be devoid of meaning altogether, they are *not silenced*. It does nothing to lessen the dismay they rouse in us. There is something cheap in "debunking" them. The heart's unrest is not to be stilled by logic. Yet philosophy is not dissolved. It derives its weight, its grandeur, from the significance of the questions it destroys. It overthrows idols, and it is the importance of these idols which gives philosophy its importance.

Now it can perhaps be seen why the search for answers fitting the moulds of the questions fails, is *bound* to fail. They are not real questions asking for information but "muddles felt as problems" (Wittgenstein) which wither away when the ground is cleared. If philosophy advances, it is not by adding new propositions to its list, but rather by transforming the whole intellectual scene and, as a consequence of this, by reducing the number of questions which befog and bedevil us. Philosophy so construed is one of the great liberating forces. Its task is, in the words of Frege, "to free the spirit from the tyranny of words by exposing the delusions which arise, almost inevitably, through the use of a word language."

III

What, only criticism and no meat? The philosopher a fog dispeller? If that were all he was capable of I would be sorry for him and leave him to his devices. Fortunately, this is not so. For one thing, a philosophic question, if pursued far enough, may lead to something positive—for instance, to a more profound understanding of language. Take the sceptical doubts as to material objects, other minds, etc. The first reaction is perhaps to say: these doubts are idle. Ordinarily, when I doubt whether I shall finish this article, after a time my doubt comes to an end. I cannot go on doubting forever. It's the destiny of doubt to die. But the doubts raised by the sceptic never die. Are they doubts? Are they pseudo-questions? They appear so only when judged by the twin standards of common sense and common speech. The real trouble lies deeper: it arises from the sceptic casting doubt on the very facts which underlie the use of language, those permanent features of experience which make concept formation possible, which in fact are precipitated in the use of our most common words. Suppose that you see an object in front of you quite clearly, say, a pipe, and when you are going to pick it up it melts into thin air, then you may feel, "Lord, I'm going mad" or something of the sort (unless the whole situation is such that you have reason to suspect that it was some clever trick). But what, the sceptic may press now, if such experiences were quite frequent? Would you be prepared to *dis*solve the connection between different sense experiences which form the hard core of our idea of a solid object, to *un*do what language has done—to part with the category of thing-hood? And would you then be living in a phenomenalist's paradise with color patches and the other paraphernalia of the sense-datum theory, in a disobjected, desubstantialized world? To say in such circumstances, "Look, it's just tabling now" would be a joke (for even in the weakened verb forms "tabling," "chairing," an element of the thing-category lingers on). That is why the sceptic struggles to express himself in a language which is not fit for this purpose. He expresses himself misleadingly when he says that he doubts such-and-such *facts*: his doubts cut so deep that they affect the fabric of language itself. For what he doubts is already embodied in the very forms of speech, e.g. in what is condensed in the use of thing-words. The moment he tries to penetrate those deep-sunken layers, he undermines the language in which he ventilates his qualms—with the result that he seems to be talking nonsense. He is not. But in order to make his doubts fully expressible, language would first have to go into the melting-pot. (We can get a glimmering of what is needed from modern science where all the long-established categories—thinghood, causality, position—had to be revolutionized. This required nothing less than the construction of some new language, not the expression of new facts with the old one.)

If we look at the matter in this way the attitude of the sceptic is seen in a new light. He considers possibilities which lie far outside the domain of our current experience. If his doubts are taken seriously, they turn into observations which cast a new and searching light on the subsoil of language, showing what possibilities are open to our thought (though not to ordinary language), and what paths might have been pursued if the texture of our experience were different from what it is. These problems are not spurious: they make us aware of the vast background in which any current experiences are embedded, and to which language has adapted itself; thus they bring out the unmeasured sum of experience stored up in the use of our words and syntactical forms.

For another thing, a question may decide to go in for another career than dissolving: it may pass into science. Frege, for instance, was prompted to his inquiries by philosophical motives, namely, to find a definite answer to the question about the nature of arithmetical truths—whether they are analytic or synthetic, a priori or a posteriori. Starting from this question and pursuing it with all possible rigor, he was led to unearth a whole mine of problems of a scientific nature; and proceeding along these lines, he came to fashion a new instrument, a logic, which in delicacy and range and power far surpassed anything that went by this name before, a subject revealing to this day new and unexpected depths. True, the question from which Frege set out was not too clearly defined owing to the imprecise nature of the Kantian terms in which it was expressed.

A whole chapter might be written on the fate of questions, their curious adventures and transformations—how they change into others and in the process remain, and yet do not remain, the same. The original question may split and multiply almost like a character in a dream play. To mention just a few examples: can logic be characterized completely in a formal way, i.e. without bringing in any extraneous ideas such as the use of language and all that goes with it? Can arithmetic be characterized in any such way, entirely "from within"? Or will any interpretation include some Erdenrest of the empiric? These questions have given rise to extensive research on mathematical interpretation of formal systems. The query how far logical intuition is correct has got ramified into a bunch of questions pertaining to the theory of logical types, the axiom of choice, etc., indeed to a far more fundamental issue, namely, whether ordinary logic itself is "right" as contrasted with the system of inferences evolved by the intuitionists. Or again, are there undecidable questions in mathematics, not in the restricted sense of Gödel, but undecidable in an absolute sense? Are there natural limits to generalization? It is interesting to watch how from a question of this sort, not too precise, somewhat blurred, new and better defined questions detach themselves, the parent question—in Frege's case philosophic *par excellence*—giving rise to a scientist's progeny.

Now something else must be noted—how these questions become, not only precise, but clear (which is not the same thing). To illustrate, can the infinity represented by all natural numbers be compared with the infinity represented by all points in space? That is, can the one be said to be less than, or equal to, the other? When it was first asked, the question had no clear sense—perhaps no sense at all. Yet it guided G. Cantor in his ingenious search. Before set theory was discovered—or should I rather say "invented"?—the question acted as a sort of signpost pointing vaguely to some so far uncharted region of thought. It is perhaps best characterized by saying that it guides our imagination in a given direction, stimulates research along new lines. Such questions do not "dissolve": they are solved, only not in the existing system of thought but rather by constructing a new conceptual system—such as set theory—where the intended and faintly anticipated sense finds its full realization. They are therefore of the nature of incitements to the building of such systems, they point from the not-yet-meaningful to the meaningful.

The question is the first groping step of the mind in its journeyings that lead towards new horizons. The genius of the philosopher shows itself nowhere more strikingly than in the new kind of question he brings into the world. What distinguishes him and gives him his place is the passion of questioning. That his questions are at times not so clear is perhaps of not so much moment as one makes of it. There is nothing like clear thinking to protect one from making discoveries. It is all very well to talk of clarity, but when it becomes an obsession it is liable to nip the living thought in the bud. This, I am afraid, is one of the deplorable results of Logical Positivism, not foreseen by its founders, but only too striking in some of its followers. Look at these people, gripped by a clarity neurosis, haunted by fear, tongue-tied, asking themselves continually, "Oh dear, now does this make perfectly good sense?" Imagine the pioneers of science, Kepler,

Newton, the discoverers of non-Euclidean geometry, of field physics, the unconscious, matter waves or heaven knows what, imagine them asking themselves this question at every step—this would have been the surest means of sapping any creative power. No great discoverer has acted in accordance with the motto, "Everything that can be said can be said clearly." And some of the greatest discoveries have even emerged from a sort of primordial fog. (Something to be said for the fog. For my part, I've always suspected that clarity is the last refuge of those who have nothing to say.)

The great mind is the great questioner. An example in point is Kant's problem "How is geometry possible?" The way to its solution was only opened up through the rise of the "axiomatic method." Seeing that the axioms of geometry are capable of an indefinite number of different interpretations and that the particular way they may be interpreted is irrelevant to deductive purposes, Hilbert separated what belongs to the logical form of the axioms from what belongs to their intuitional (or other) content and turned the whole question by saying: a point, a straight line, etc., may be anything that satisfies the axioms. As the business of deduction hinges only on the relations in which the basic terms stand to each other and not on the "content" we associate with them, and as these relations are fully set out in the axioms, the axioms in their totality determine what a "point," a "line," etc., is so far as it is sufficient for deductive needs. Through the rise of this technique it became apparent that the word "geometry," as understood by Kant, covers, in fact, two totally different sciences, mathematical and physical geometry. It was the failure to distinguish between them that produced Kant's perplexity. "So far as the laws of mathematics refer to reality, they are not certain; and so far as they are certain, they do not refer to reality" (Einstein). Kant's credit lies in having *seen* that there is a problem, not in having solved it.

But here a new problem presents itself: How do we know what will satisfy a given question? More generally: How does the answer fit the question? Questions of the current sort ("What is the right time?") show already by their form what sort of answer to expect. They are, so to speak, cheques with a blank to be filled; yet not always so: Augustine's question, "How is it possible to measure time?" or Kant's question, "How is geometry possible?" do not trace out the form of the answer. There is no *obvious* link between question and answer, any more than there is in the case of asking "What is a point?" When Hilbert's idea—that the axioms of geometry jointly provide the "implicit definition" of the basic terms—was first propounded it came totally unexpected; no one had ever thought of that before; on the contrary, many people had an uneasy feeling as if this were a way of evading the issue rather than an answer, amongst them no less a man than Frege. He thought the problem still unsolved.

Now is there anything one can do to make a man like Frege see that the axiomatic method provides the correct answer? Can it, for example, be *proved* to him? The point to which attention must now be drawn, though it should really be obvious, is that such a proof cannot be given, and it cannot because he, the asker, has first to be turned round to see the matter differently. What is required is a change of the entire way of thinking. Indeed, anyone who is puzzled by this problem and yet refuses to accept Hilbert's solution only betrays that he has got stuck in the groove hollowed out by the form in which the question is put. "A point is—" he begins and then stops. What is to be done to help him to get out of the groove or, better still, to make him shift for himself when he feels "cramped" in it, is a *discussion*, not a proof.

Frege behaves not so very unlike a man mystified by the question, "What is time?" We may suggest converting the latter into the question how the word "time" is being used (which would bring him down to earth). But aren't we cheating him? We seem to be holding out the answer to *one* question, but not to that one which he was asking. He may suspect that we are trying to fob him off with the second best we have in store, his original question still remaining an enigma. Similarly Frege: he considered it a scandal that the questions "What is a point?" "What is a number?" were still unanswered.

In either of these cases, the aim of a discussion, in the absence of a proof, can only be to change the asker's attitude. We may, for instance, scrutinize similar, or partially similar, cases, point out that the form of the answer is not always that of the question; by going patiently over such cases, the vast background of analogies against which the question is seen will slowly change. The turning up of a wide field of language loosens the position of certain standards which are so ingrained that we do not see them for what they are; and if we do this in an effective manner, a mind like Frege's will be released from the obsession of seeking strainingly for an answer to fit the mould. Arguments are used in such a discussion, not as proofs though but rather as means to make him see things he had not noticed before: e.g. to dispel wrong analogies, to stress similarities with other cases and in this way to bring about something like a shift of perspective. However, there is no way of proving him wrong or bullying him into mental acceptance of the proposal: when all is said and done the decision is his.

But here more is at stake than loosening a cramped position—

it is a question of escaping the domination of linguistic forms. How often are we merely following the channels carved out by numberless repetition of the same modes of expression—as when we say, unsuspectingly, "Time flows" and are, when confronted (say) with Augustine's paradox, suddenly shocked out of complacency. Existing language, by offering us only certain stereotyped moulds of expression, creates habits of thought which it is almost impossible to break. Such a mold is, e.g. the actor-action scheme of the Indo-European languages. How deep their influence is can perhaps be surmised from Descartes' conclusion from thinking to the presence of an agent, an ego, different from the thinking, that does the thinking—a conclusion so natural and convincing to us because it is supported by the whole weight of language. Frege's obsession with the question "What is a number?" is another case. As we can speak of "*the* number five," five, Frege argued, must be the proper name of an entity, a sort of Platonic crystal, indicated by means of the definite article. (A Chinese pupil of mine once informed me that Frege's question is unaskable in Chinese, "five" being used there only as a numeral in contexts like "five friends," "five boats," etc.). Again, when we say of a given statement that it is true, we seem to be saying something "about" it—evidence of the power of the subject-predicate cliché. Indeed, so strong is the temptation to construe it in this way, namely, as a statement about a statement, that the idea of a different interpretation scarcely occurs to us. It is important to notice that in doing so we assimilate the expression to analogical forms; but it is no less important to notice that none of these analogies needs to be present to our minds: it is enough if they make themselves felt in a dim, inarticulated way. Such patterns have an effect on us like thousands of explicit analogies: they act upon us, one might say, like a field of force, a language field, that draws our mental gaze in a certain direction. And, I venture to add, it is precisely because of the fleeting, half-formed, shadow-like nature of these analogies that it is almost impossible to escape their influence. If we are taken in by them, it is our fault. A philosopher, instead of preaching the righteousness of ordinary speech, should learn to be on his guard against the pitfalls ever present in its forms. To use a picture: just as a good swimmer must be able to swim up-stream, so the philosopher should master the unspeakably difficult art of thinking up-speech, against the current of clichés.

Now for another point. When we dissuade a man like Frege from his search, we seem to be hindering him from reaching the aim he set out to reach. Does our discussion clash, then, with his search? And, if so, in which way? First of all, in no clearly definable way; for he is not yet clearly aware what he is aiming at, and the discussion brings him gradually to see things in a different light. How is this change brought about? Well, he first saw the question in analogy with other ones, and these analogies are, one by one, destroyed; or rather, in the course of the discussion they are seen to be misleading. In proportion as the whole conceptual background changes, he comes to see that something is wrong with the way he puts his question, that the attainment of his object is no longer satisfying. It is not that he gives up because he has tried very hard, but in vain, and has now got tired: no, he gives up because he "sees" the question differently. And in what does *this* consist? Well, in the fact that he is now well aware of the analogies which were misleading him, that he sees the question against a different linguistic background (a "figure" sometimes changes when it is seen against a different "ground"), that a certain strain disappears and that he says, with a sigh of relief, "Yes, that's it."

The philosopher contemplates things through the prism of language and, misled (say) by some analogy, suddenly sees things in a new strange light. We can cope with these problems only by digging down to the soil from which they spring. What we do is to light up the mental background from which the question has detached itself; in a clearer perception of some of the crucial concepts the question transforms itself into another one. Not that it has been answered in the current sense. Rather we have removed the factors that prompted the question by a more profound and penetrating analysis. The essence of this process is that it leads the questioner on to some new aspect— and leads him with his spontaneous consent. He agrees to be thus led and therefore ends by abandoning his search. We cannot constrain anyone who is unwilling to follow the new direction of a question; we can only extend the field of vision of the asker, loosen his prejudices, guide his gaze in a new direction: but all this can be achieved only with his consent.

By our critical analysis we try to counteract the influence of the language field, or (what comes to the same) we may help the questioner to gain a deeper insight into the nature of what he is seeking first of all—make him see the build of the concepts and the moulds in which he expresses the question. What matters is more like changing his outlook than proving to him some theorem; or more like increasing his insight. Insight cannot be lodged in a theorem, and this is the deeper reason why the deductive method is doomed to fail: insight cannot be demonstrated by proof.

What it comes to in the end is that the asker of the question, in the course of the discussion, has to make a number of *decisions*. And this makes the philosophical procedure so unlike a logical one. He compares, for instance, the case before him with analogous ones and has to *judge* how far these analogies hold. That is, it is for him to decide how far he is willing to accept these analogies: he has not, like a slave, to follow blindly in their track.

Science is rich in questions of this type. They are not scientific questions properly and yet they exercise scientists; they are philosophic questions and yet they do not exercise philosophers.

What I have wanted to say in this section and have not said, or only half-said:

(1) Philosophy is not only criticism of language: so construed, its aim is too narrow. It is criticizing, dissolving and stepping over *all* prejudices, loosening all rigid and constricting moulds of thought, no matter whether they have their origin in language or somewhere else.

(2) What is essential in philosophy is the breaking through to a *deeper insight*—which is something positive—not merely the dissipation of fog and the exposure of spurious problems.

(3) Insight cannot be lodged in a theorem, and it can therefore not be demonstrated.

(4) Philosophic arguments are, none of them, logically *compelling*: they really screen what actually happens—the quiet and patient undermining of categories over the whole field of thought.

(5) Their purpose is to open our eyes, to bring us to see things in a new way—from a wider standpoint unobstructed by misunderstandings.

(6) The essential difference between philosophy and logic is that logic *constrains* us while philosophy leaves us free: in a philosophic discussion we are led, step by step, to change our angle of vision, e.g. to pass from one way of putting a question to another, and this with our spontaneous agreement—a thing profoundly different from deducing theorems from a given set of premises. Misquoting Cantor one might say: the essence of philosophy lies in its freedom.

IV

There is a notion that philosophy is an exercise of the intellect and that philosophic questions can be settled by argument, and conclusively if one only knew how to set about it. What seems to me queer, however, is that I cannot find any really good hard argument; and more than that, the example just discussed must make it doubtful whether any compelling argument *can* be found. Out of this plight I incline to come to a new and somewhat shocking conclusion: that the thing cannot be done. No philosopher has ever proved anything. The whole claim is spurious. What I have to say is simply this. Philosophic arguments are not deductive; therefore they are not rigorous; and therefore they don't prove anything. Yet they have force.

Before going into the matter, I want to show, quite summarily first, how unplausible the view is that rigorous arguments are applied in philosophy. A first alarming sign can perhaps already be seen in the notorious fact that the ablest minds disagree, that what is indisputable to the one seems to have no force in the eyes of the other. In a clear system of thought such differences are impossible. That they exist in philosophy is weighty evidence that the arguments have none of the logical rigor they have in mathematics and the exact sciences.

Next, arguments, in the way they are thought of, must contain inferences, and inferences must start somewhere. Now where is the philosopher to look for his premises? To science? Then he will "do" science, not philosophy. To statements of everyday life? To particular ones? Then he will never be able to advance a single step beyond them. To general statements? If so, a number of questions raise their ugly heads. By what right does he pass from "some" to "all"? ("To Generalize is to be an Idiot," W. Blake.) Can he be sure that his premises are stated with such clarity and precision that not a ghost of a doubt can creep in? Can he be sure that they contain meat, are not analytic, vacuous, definitions in disguise and the like? Can he be sure that they are true? (How *can* he?) And even supposing, what is not the case, that all these requirements could be met, there is still another task looming before him when it comes to developing the consequences: can he be sure how to operate with the terms? (How *can* he?) I am not letting out a secret when I say that the ordinary rules of logic often break down in natural speech— a fact usually hushed up by logic books. Indeed, the words of common language are so elastic that anyone can stretch their sense to fit his own whims; and with this their "logic" is queered. (Plenty of scope for a "natural logic"; we know that we are *unhappy*; so we *are* unhappy. We *know* that we are unhappy; so we are *great*. Pascal. "If she had perished, she had perished:" does this entail that she has not perished? If so, by what rule? "If I believed that I should be very silly indeed:" does this, or does this not, entail that I don't believe it? Natural language holds logical problems of its own, lots of them.)

This brings me to another point. Ordinary language simply has not got the "hardness," the logical hardness, to cut axioms in it. It needs something like a metallic substance to carve a deductive system out of it such as Euclid's. But common speech? If you begin to draw inferences it soon begins to go "soft" and fluffs up somewhere. You may just as well carve cameos on a cheese soufflé. (My point is: language is plastic, yielding to the will to express, even at the price of some obscurity. Indeed, how could it ever express anything that does not conform to the cliché? If logicians had their way, language would become as clear and transparent as glass, but also as brittle as glass: and what would be the good of making an axe of glass that breaks the moment you use it?) But language is not hard. And that is why it is dangerous in philosophy to hunt for premises instead of just going over the ground, standing back and saying: look.

Most philosophic arguments, to ignore constructions à la Spinoza, hinge on such points as what "can" and what "cannot" be said or what sort of question it is "proper" and what sort of question it would be "inappropriate" to ask. Much skill and ingenuity has been spent in elucidating such questions as to whether a certain metaphor is "natural," a certain diction "fitting." It would not be right to burke the point that considerations such as these, while apparently pertaining to matters of style, contribute in fact largely to the forcefulness of an argument, indeed play a very real and decisive part in the way they make us look at the subject. In going over, examining and comparing the various modes of expression that center around certain key notions, for instance, "imagination," "memory," "pleasure," we catch the first glimpse of what is sometimes called the "logic" of these notions. Now can any of these things be proved? Can it be proved, for example, that a certain diction is "fitting"? (Remember, no such thing as a definition of a "well-formed formula.") No philosopher has ever made so much as an attempt. Everyone uses words in this way and he leaves it at that; and rightly so. For what sort of reasons *could* he give anyway? Here already, at the very threshold, the idea of a philosophic proof begins to ring hollow.

"Ah, but the ordinary use of language." All right; but even so, it is not that one "cannot" use language differently. To illustrate: "frozen music"—does this "tell" you anything? Perhaps not; yet a saying like "Architecture is frozen music" (Goethe) drives the point home. To say "The arms are full of blunted memories" sounds odd, until you come upon it in Proust's context. The "will to understand" does not even flinch before those bogies of the logician, contradictions: it transforms them, wresting a new sense from the apparent nonsense. ("Dark with excess of light," "the luminous gloom of Plato"—just to remind the reader of two examples of Coleridge.) There are about 303 reasons why we sometimes express ourselves in a contradiction, and understandably so.

Result: it cannot even be proved that a given expression is natural, a metaphor fitting, a question proper (or unaskable), a collocation of words expressive (or devoid of meaning). Nothing of the sort can be demonstrated.

Two other points reinforce what has been said. What we sometimes do in a philosophical discussion is not argue at all but simply raise lots of questions—a method brilliantly employed by Ryle. Indeed, a volley of perplexing questions can certainly not be described as an argument and *a fortiori* not as a logical one, yet it is no less effective in making one turn back in recoil to consider one's views. Lastly, though on the surface the philosopher seems to be engaged in much the same thing as a logician is, for instance, in testing an argument for any loose links in it or in building up an argument, this should not mislead us. For if he were to construct rigorous proofs, where are the theorems established by them? What has he to show as the fruit of his labors?

I have not raised any of these questions wantonly; they force themselves on everyone who tries to arrive at a clear and unbiased view of the matter. Should these difficulties not have their origin in the nature of philosophy itself?

V

I proceed now to consider philosophic arguments, especially those which are regarded as constituting a decisive advance, to see whether they give us any reason for modifying the view advocated here. There are only a few classical cases. One of them is Hume's celebrated argument to show that the relation of cause and effect is intrinsically different from that of ground and consequence. Now in what does this "proof" consist? He *reminds* us of what we have always known: that, while it is self-contradictory to assert the ground and deny the consequence, no such contradiction arises in assuming that a certain event, the "cause," may be followed not by its usual effect but by some other event. If it is asked "Is this a proof?" what is one to say? It certainly is not the sort of proof to be found in a deductive system. Much the same applies to Berkeley's argument when he tells us that, try as he might, he cannot call up in his mind an abstract idea of a triangle, of just a triangle with no particular shape, any more than he can conceive the idea of a man without qualities. Is this a proof? He points out the obvious. (Only it wants a genius to see it.)

To take my own argument against logical fatalism, it is not strict. The decisive step consists in following a certain analogy with other cases. It is analogical, not logical. Similarly the argument used against Zeno is not conclusive. (I have no space to enlarge upon that.)

Now for two more examples, one of the current sort of argument applied today by philosophers, the other taken from Aristotle.

When we say of someone that he "sees" or "hears" an aeroplane, or "descries," "detects" a lark in the sky, or again that he "tastes" or "smells" roast pork, we do not ascribe to him an activity. That "seeing" is not a sort of doing can be illustrated, e.g. by calling attention to the fact that we don't use the continuous present tense. We say "I see the clock," not "I am seeing the clock" (save G. E. Moore, who, oddly enough, regularly says that he "is seeing his right hand"), whereas it is perfectly correct to say "I am looking at the clock, listening to its ticking," and so in the other cases. Again, while it is proper to say "I have forgotten to post the letter," no one would say "I have forgotten to see the letter-box." There is no sense in asking you, when you look at me, whether your seeing is easy or difficult, quick or slowish, careful or heedless, whether you see me deliberately and whether you have now finished seeing me. So, it is argued, perceiving is not a doing (an argument used by myself in lectures).

The point to be labored is that this argument is not conclusive. Odd as it sounds, "I have finished seeing you" *may* be said, though only in very special circumstances. A man with impaired eyesight who, unable to take in the shape as a whole, has perhaps to scan the face bit by bit in search of some characteristic marks might say, and understandably, "Now I have finished seeing you." We too are occasionally in a not much better position, as when, in magnesium light, we look at some scene, and afterwards complain, "Too quick, I couldn't take it in." It would seem then that there is no more than a difference in degree between this case and the normal ones. Odd cases, certainly; but what would you think of a mathematician whose theorems collapse when applied to slightly out-of-the-way curves?

For my next example I choose pleasure. Aristotle, in criticizing Plato, pointed out that if pleasure were a process going on in time I could enjoy something swiftly or slowly—an argument which is almost a bombshell in its destructive power. Certainly, to speak in such terms is very odd and sounds absurd. Yet, If I strain my imagination, I can perhaps bring myself to conceive of a set of circumstances under which it would not be entirely unnatural to say such a thing. In listening to music, for example, when I am following a slow and gentle movement, my enjoying it appears in some respects to be different from what I get when listening to an exciting piece of music. The very quality of my enjoyment seems to change as if something of the slow and gentle or of the wild, intoxicating flow of the music had entered into it. If I say, in the one case, that I was enjoying it leisurely like basking in the sun or sipping wine, in the other that I was suddenly carried away, breathlessly following its onrush and enjoying it like a storm at sea—does this sound like sheer nonsense? So there does seem to be a time factor in pleasure.

Amongst the most powerful weapons in the philosopher's armory are *reductio ad absurdum* and infinite regress arguments. Before proceeding to an appraisal of these forms of reasoning, it will be well to consider how they work in their home land, mathematics.

Let me choose as a typical case the proof that $\sqrt{2}$ is irrational. If it were a rational number, we could find two integers m and n such that

$$m^2 = 2n^2 \tag{1}$$

We may then argue as follows. As m^2 is even, m must be even; hence $m = 2m_1$. Substitution yields

$$2m_1^2 = n^2. \tag{2}$$

As n^2 is even, n must be even; hence $n = 2n_1$. Substitution yields

$$m_1^2 = 2n_1^2. \tag{3}$$

If, then, two integers m and n exist which stand in the relation (1), they must have halves which stand in exactly the same relation (3), and these must have halves which stand in the same relation, and so on *ad infinitum*; which is plainly impossible, m and n being finite. Therefore the tentative assumption (1) cannot hold, and $\sqrt{2}$ cannot be rational. Q.E.D. This is the prototype of a refutation by infinite regress.

Arguments of this type have been applied outside mathematics. However, when I come to look at them a bit more closely I begin to hesitate. An example will illustrate my doubts. An argument propounded against the use of mechanical models is this. If the elastic properties of matter can be explained as being due to electric forces with which the molecules act on each other, it surely is pointless to explain the action of the electric forces as being due to the elastic properties of a mechanical medium, the "ether." To do this is to go round in a circle: elasticity is explained in terms of electric force, and electric force in terms of elasticity; while the attempt to break out of the circle by supposing that the elasticity of the ether is due to "electric forces" acting between the ether particles and these to the elastic properties of a second-order ether is to be pushed into an infinite series of reduction steps. Thus the mechanistic program is faced with a dilemma both horns of which are equally fatal.

A formidable argument—or is it? I can well imagine an undaunted champion of the lost cause retort: "Not a bit of a regress. Yes, the ether is elastic, not, however, in the sense in which a spring is: while elasticity of matter can be reduced to electric force, elasticity of the ether, being an ultimate postulate of the theory, cannot be reduced any further." And with this the argument falls to the ground.

But this is unconvincing, it will be said. I agree; I am not such an imbecile as to plead for retaining mechanical models and the rest. My point is only to see whether this "refutation" is compelling. *It*

isn't. The advocate of models is not forcibly dislodged from his position. There is, it would seem, always a way of getting out of the
dilemma—of wriggling out if you like—which foils the argument.
What is shown in it is merely that to cling to models of this sort
becomes, in the circumstances, very unnatural. But to say that something is unnatural is not to say that it is logically impossible: yet
this is what the argument should establish. In the mathematical proof
cited above no loophole was left for wriggling out. The whole deduction was a "chain of adamant"—precisely the sort of thing the argument under review is not.

Consider now a similar argument. There cannot be any such thing
as volitions, it has been said. Volitions were called in by theorists
to provide causes not only for what we (intentionally) do but also
for mental processes or operations such as controlling an impulse,
paying heed to something, and the like. As a consequence of this,
acts of will were supposed to be the sort of thing the presence of
which makes an action "voluntary," or which—somehow, in some
unfathomable way—"gets itself translated" into a bodily or mental
act. In fine, volitions were thought of as causes as well as effects of
other, mental or physical, occurrences. Now the dilemma: if my
pulling of the trigger were the result of a mental act of "willing to
pull the trigger," what of this mental act itself? Was it willed or unwilled? If unwilled, it cannot be called voluntary and therefore not
a volition; if willed, then we must suppose, according to the theory,
that it results from a prior act, namely, "willing to will to pull the
trigger," and that from another *ad infinitum*, leaving no possibility
for me ever to start.

Brilliant as the argument is, the point to be brought up here is
only whether it is logically fatal. Does it really prove that the assumption of acts of willing involves an infinite regress? A believer in
such acts need not be cowed into submission. To ask of volitions
whether they are themselves voluntary or involuntary acts, he may
say, is plain nonsense. Only an *action* can be voluntary or involuntary, not an act of will. It is just the point that an act of will is an
act of will and does not issue from any anterior act of will, any
more than, in order to recall a thing I must first recall what I want
to recall, and before I can even do that I must recall that I want to
recall what I want to recall, and so on *ad infinitum*. Just as I can
recall a thing without need to call in an act of recalling what I want
to recall, so my pulling the trigger may be the direct result of an
act of will without the latter issuing from a parent act of will. Thus
the whole argument apparently crumbles away.

This is meant not to belittle the argument or detract from its
force, but only to get clear as to *what sort* of force it has. If it were

conclusive, it would, with its destructive power, do away with a good many more acts and states of mind, not only with volitions—with intending and desiring, for instance. Indeed, precisely similar arguments can be constructed "to deal with them." Intention: though clearly not the sort of thing to be classed as a simple "act," it yet seems somehow to "connect" with what goes on in us before we carry it into action—such as considering, planning, hesitating, choosing. I may, let us say, intend to find a flaw in a given argument, and when I subsequently turn it over in my mind, this will be the result of my intention. Some mental operations, then, *can* arise from an intention, they are "intended." So what of the intention itself? Is it intended or unintended? If the intention is not intended, it is not the intention, and if it is intended it must be due to another intention, and this to yet another *ad infinitum*. Similarly in the case of desire. Suppose that I feel a desire for a certain thing, is this desire itself desired or undesired? Either answer lands us in absurdities.

If the strength of the argument were to lie in its structure it would, with its devastating effect, apply after the exchange of some of its terms for other ones, e.g. "volition" for "intention"—provided, of course, that certain other circumstances essential to the reasoning are the same. Yet, while the first argument sounds, to say the least, very plausible, no one will be duped by its caricatures. So if it *has* any force it cannot owe it to its structure and consequently cannot be of a logical sort. It is meant to refute the existence of a kind of mental thrust; but then we should remember that to prove the non-existence of something is always a precarious business. "No one has ever proved the non-existence of Apollo or Aphrodite" it has been observed; too much weight, then, need perhaps not be laid on this particular case. What is disturbing, however, is the ease with which arguments can be cast into pseudo-deductive moulds. And it is this fact to which I wish to call attention by examining the argument. As has been shown in the preceding discussion, it is not an isolated case. No philosophic argument ends with a Q.E.D. However forceful, it never forces. There is no bullying in philosophy, neither with the stick of logic nor with the stick of language.

VI

In throwing such strong doubts on the power of arguments as used by philosophers I may seem to deny them any value whatever. But such is not my intention. Even if they are lacking in logical rigor this certainly has not prevented an original thinker from using them successfully, or from bringing out something not seen before or not seen so clearly. So in the case I have discussed: something *is* seen in that argument, something *is* made clear, though perhaps not quite in the sense intended by the arguer. If so, something very important has been left out from the picture.

Perhaps our objections have been doing injustice to philosophic arguments. They were, quite mistakenly as I hope to have shown, supposed to be proofs and refutations in a strict sense. But what the philosopher does is something else. *He builds up a case.* First, he makes you see all the weaknesses, disadvantages, shortcomings of a position; he brings to light inconsistencies in it or points out how unnatural some of the ideas underlying the whole theory are by pushing them to their farthest consequences; and this he does with the strongest weapons in his arsenal, reduction to absurdity and infinite regress. On the other hand, he offers you a new way of looking at things not exposed to those objections. In other words, he submits to you, like a barrister, all the facts of his case, and you are in the position of the judge. You look at them carefully, go into the details, weigh the pros and cons and arrive at a verdict. But in arriving at a verdict you are not following a deductive highway, any more than a judge in the High Court does. Coming to a decision, though a rational process, is very unlike drawing conclusions from given premises, just as it is very unlike doing sums. A judge has to judge, we say, implying that he has to use discernment in contrast to applying, machine-like, a set of mechanical rules. There are no computing machines for doing the judge's work nor could there be any—a trivial yet significant fact. When the judge reaches a decision this may be, and in fact often is, a rational result, yet not one obtained by deduction; it does not simply follow from such-and-such: what is required is insight, judgment. Now in arriving at a verdict, you are like a judge in this that you are not carrying out a number of formal logical steps: you have to use discernment, e.g. to descry the pivotal point. Considerations such as these make us see what is already apparent in the use of "rational," that this term has a wider range of application than what can be established deductively. To say that an argument can be rational and yet not deductive is not a sort of contradiction as it would inevitably be in the opposite case, namely, of saying that a deductive argument need not be rational.

This alters the whole picture. The point to be emphasized is that a philosopher may see an important truth and yet be unable to demonstrate it by formal proof. But the fact that his arguments are not logical does nothing to detract from their rationality. To return to our previous example, the argument used against volition, though it is not what it professes to be, logically destructive, nevertheless has a force difficult to resist. Now to what is this due? It does not need much acumen to find the answer. It is the whole arrangement of so many felicitous examples, preceding the argument, and their masterly analysis, which breathes life into its bare bones; aided greatly by the fact that the connection between a mental thrust and a bodily movement is allowed to remain a mystery. The unsatisfactoriness of this position, together with the amassing of hosts of unanswerable questions and very striking examples—this makes the argument so convincing.

What do you find in reading Ryle or Wittgenstein? Lots of examples with little or no logical bone in between. Why so many examples? They speak for themselves; they usually are more transparent than the trouble maker; each one acts as an analogy; together they light up the whole linguistic background with the effect that the case before us is seen in the light they produce. Indeed, examples aptly arranged are often more convincing and, above all, of a more lasting effect than an argument which is anyhow spidery. Not that the "proofs" proffered are valueless: a *reductio ad absurdum* always points to a knot in thought, and so does an infinite regress. But they *point* only. The real strength lies in the examples. All the proofs, in a good book on philosophy, could be dispensed with, without its losing a whit of its convincingness. To seek, in philosophy, for rigorous proofs is to seek for the shadow of one's voice.

In order to forestall misinterpretations which will otherwise certainly arise I have to concede one point: arguments on a small scale, containing a few logical steps only, may be rigorous. The substance of my remarks is that the conception of a whole philosophical view —from Heraclitus to Nietzsche or Bradley—is never a matter of logical steps. A *weltanschauung* like any of these or even a new approach like that of Wittgenstein is never "arrived at," in particular it is not deduced, and once found it can neither be proved nor refuted by strictly logical reasoning; though arguments may play a part in making them acceptable. But some authors have disdained even that.

The one remaining question to be asked is this: if the philosopher's views cannot be derived from any premises how has he ever arrived at them? How can he get to a place to which no road is leading? This leads to a new and deeper problem.

VII

To ask, "What is your aim in philosophy?" and to reply, "To show the fly the way out of the fly-bottle" is . . . well, honor where it is due, I suppose what I was going to say; except perhaps this. There is something deeply exciting about philosophy, a fact not intelligible on such a negative account. It is not a matter of "clarifying thoughts" nor of "the correct use of language" nor of any other of these damned things.

What is it? Philosophy is many things and there is no formula to cover them all. But if I were asked to express in one single word what is its most essential feature I would unhesitatingly say: vision. At the heart of any philosophy worth the name is vision and it is from there it springs and takes its visible shape. When I say "vision" I mean it: I do not want to romanticize. What is characteristic of philosophy is the piercing of that dead crust of tradition and convention, the breaking of those fetters which bind us to inherited preconceptions so as to attain a new and broader way of looking at things. It has always been felt that philosophy should reveal to us what is hidden. (I am not quite insensitive to the dangers of such a view.) Yet from Plato to Moore and Wittgenstein every great philosopher was led by a sense of vision: without it no one could have given a new direction to human thought or opened windows into the not-yet-seen. Though he may be a good technician, he will not leave his marks on the history of ideas. What is decisive is a new way of seeing and, what goes with it, the will to transform the whole intellectual scene. This is the real thing and everything else is subservient to it.

Suppose that a man revolts against accepted opinion, that he feels "cramped" in its categories; a time may come when he believes, rightly or wrongly, that he has freed himself of these notions; when he has that sense of sudden growth in looking back at the prejudices which held him captive; or a time when he believes, rightly or wrongly, that he has reached a vantage point from which things can be seen to be arranged in clear and orderly patterns while difficulties of long standing dissolve as though by magic. If he is of a philosophic cast of mind he will argue this out with himself and then, perhaps, try to impart what has dawned on him to others. The arguments he will offer, the attacks he will make, the suggestions he will advance are all devised for one end: to win other people over to his own way of looking at things, to change the whole climate of opinion. Though to an outsider he appears to advance all sorts of arguments, this is not the decisive point. What is decisive is that he has seen things from a new angle of vision. Compared to that everything else is secondary. Arguments come only afterwards to lend support to what he has seen. "Big words, not every philosopher, etc.:" but where should one get one's bearings if not from the masters? And besides, once tradition has given way there is always ample scope for specialists to reduce some "pockets of resistance." Unpalatable though it may be, behind the arguments so well-planned, so neat and logical, something else is at work, a will to transform the entire way of thinking. In arguing for his view, the philosopher will, almost against his will, have to undermine current categories and clichés of thinking by exposing the fallacies which underly the established views he is attacking; and not only this, he may go so far as to question the canons of satisfactoriness themselves. In this sense, philosophy is the re-testing of the standards. In every philosopher lives something of the reformer. That is the reason why any advance in science when it touches the standards is felt to be of philosophic significance, from Galileo to Einstein and Heisenberg.

If there is any truth in this, the relation of logic and philosophy appears in a new light. What is at issue is not a conflict between a formal and a less formal or informal logic, nor between the behavior of technical and everyday concepts, but something radically different. It is the difference between drawing a conclusion and seeing, or making one see, a new aspect.

To put the matter in a nutshell, a philosophic argument does more and does less than a logical one: less in that it never establishes anything conclusively; more in that, if successful, it is not content to establish just one isolated point of truth, but effects a change in our whole mental outlook so that, as a result of that, myriads of such little points are brought into view or turned out of sight, as the case may be. Are illustrations necessary? Once Hume had exposed the fallacies of his predecessors when dealing with the notion of causality he had made it impossible for anyone to think along the lines of Spinoza whose world looks to us strange as the moon. Suppose that you look at a picture-puzzle: at first you can see in it only a maze of lines; then, suddenly, you recognize a human face. Can you now, having discovered the face, see the lines as before? Clearly not. As with the maze of lines, so with the muddle cleared up by Hume: to recapture the mood of the past, to travel back into the fog has become impossible—one of the big difficulties of understanding history of philosophy. It is for the same reason that the rise of the linguistic technique in our day has put an end to the great speculative systems of the past.

A philosophy is an attempt to unfreeze habits of thinking, to replace them by less stiff and restricting ones. Of course, these may in time themselves harden, with the result that they clog progress: Kant, the *Alleszermalmer* to his contemporaries, yet proudly upholding his table of categories—which appear to us unduly narrow. The liberator of yesterday may turn into the tyrant of tomorrow.

It can now be seen that the philosopher is not doing what the logician does only less competently but doing something altogether different. A philosophic argument is not an *approximation* of a logical one nor is the latter the ideal the philosopher is striving for. Such an account totally misdescribes what really takes place. Philosophy is not an exercise in formal logic, philosophic arguments are not chains of logical inference, only bungled ones, nor can they by any effort be recast into deductive moulds. What is being confused here is the scientist's aim to find new truths and the philosopher's aim to gain insight. As the two things are so entirely out of scale it is small wonder that the philosopher cannot move in the logician's armor. Not even if the logician himself is fighting the battle. The clash over the law of excluded middle in mathematics is a clash between two parties, each in possession of clear and precisely defined concepts. Yet there seems to be no way of settling the dispute by cogent argument. If it were true that philosophical troubles arise from the loose nature of our everyday concepts, why should such conflicts break out in the exactest of the sciences?

There have never been any absolutely cogent reasons for parting with the law of excluded middle, accepting Darwinism, giving up the Ptolemaic system or renouncing the principle of causality. If any of these things could be demonstrated how does it come that there are always partisans of the "lost causes"? Are they like the unlucky circle-squarers, wasting their time in trying to do what has been shown to be logically impossible? The truth is that conflicts of this type cannot be resolved, not entirely, either by adducing factual evidence or by logical demonstration. Both sides, of course, bring up arguments in the combat but they are not decisive. These are battles never lost and never won irrevocably. It is a typical situation, a recurrent theme in the history of human thought.

Whenever science arrives at a crucial stage where the fundamental notions become uncertain and are held as it were in solution, disputes of an odd kind are breaking out. The mere fact that leading scientists, in spite of differences in temperament, outlook, etc., take part in them, feel bound to do so, should make us reflect. Now what the protagonists avowedly or unavowedly are trying to do is to win their fellow scientists over to their own way of thinking; and to the degree to which their arguments are attempts at changing the whole intellectual attitude they take on a philosophical character. Is this coincidence?

VIII

I have so far spoken of "seeing a new aspect" without making an attempt to explain the term. I hope now to do so, though only perfunctorily, by giving one or two illustrations. There is a sort of paradox connected with the idea of certain discoveries. Descartes, for instance, was the discoverer of analytic geometry. But could he seek for it? To say that he spent years looking for it sounds downright absurd. What we are inclined to say in such a case is: to seek for analytic geometry is not possible—first because it was not seen and then because it was seen. But if he could not seek, how could he find? This leads us straight to the heart of the matter.

Consider first an entirely imaginary case. In the propositional calculus, as it was built up by Frege, two primitive ideas occur, "not" and "or." It was later discovered by Sheffer that the whole calculus can be based on one single idea (his "stroke" function). Of what kind was this discovery? Suppose that Frege, by a curious chance, had written all his logical axioms in the form

$$\sim(\ldots)\vee\sim(\ldots)$$

i.e. as a sum of two negations, but had none the less mistakenly believed that *two* symbols were required for expressing these laws, namely "$\sim$" and "$\vee$." Imagine now that someone else looking at these formulae is struck by what, on our assumption, has escaped Frege, namely that they all have one and the same structure and require therefore only one symbol. In what exactly does his discovery consist? In his *seeing* the formulae in a new way, in his reading a new structure into them. What matters is his apprehension: so long as he does not see the structure of a new system in the old one he has not got it. Anyone may look at the formulae and yet not perceive what Sheffer has perceived, the occurrence of an identical structure. *This* is the discovery, not the introducing of a special symbol for a combination of the old ones. It would have been quite enough, for instance, had Sheffer merely pointed out the constant recurrence of this structure in all the laws without providing his "stroke"; that is inessential.

This example may illustrate what is meant by the "seeing of a new aspect." Seeing such an aspect is often the core of a new discovery. If you look at the formulae, the moment you notice the new structure in them they suddenly seem to change—a phenomenon akin to seeing a figure, say, a drawn cube differently, now as solid and protruding, now as hollow and receding. The one pattern suddenly "jumps" into the other. Similarly in our case, though there are also differences; thus the new aspect, once it has dawned, can steadily be held in mind and has not that perceptual instability. The apprehension of a new pattern in the formulae seems to hold in it actually more of a visual experience, anyhow to be more closely akin to it than it might at first appear. Seeing and interpreting, looking and thinking seem as it were to fuse here.

If it is now asked whether it is possible for anyone to *seek* for the new aspect, what is one to reply? Well, that something *can* be seen in a new way is seen only when it *is* seen in this way. That an aspect is possible is seen only when the aspect has already flashed and not before: that's why the finding cannot be anticipated, not even by the greatest genius. It always comes unbidden and, as it would seem, in a sudden flash.

To take another case, is the calculation

$$(5+3)^2 = 5^2 + 2\cdot5\cdot3 + 3^2$$

at the same time a proof that

$$(2+3)^2 = 2^2 + 2 \cdot 2 \cdot 3 + 3^2 \quad ?$$

Yes and no—depending on how you look at it. (Does it strike you that the 2 in the middle term is a "structural" 2, deriving not from the special numbers but from the general form of the operation?) A man, while reckoning with special numbers only, may yet conceivably do algebra if he sees the special sums in a new way, as the expressions of a general law. (Discovery of algebra as the discovery of an aspect of numerical calculation.)

What goes for these more or less trivial cases goes for Descartes and also for Einstein and Hilbert. They were unable to seek, Einstein for a conceptual gap in the idea of simultaneity, Hilbert for the axiomatic method. Though these discoveries are of a different order altogether, the principle underlying them is the same. None of them has ever "arrived" at his view because he was never travelling. They did not seek, they found (like Picasso). And that is so wrong with the whole way in which such discoveries are so often presented—as if they were the result of a "method" or "procedure," as if the great men arrived at their solutions by drawing logical inferences. This leaves out the most essential thing—the flashing of a new aspect which is *non*-inferential. The moments of seeing cannot be foreseen, any more than they can be planned, forced, controlled, or summoned by will-power.

Is there any truth in what I am saying? I shall not argue. Instead, let me remind you of some observations which will be familiar to you. It is notorious that a philosophy is not made, it grows. You don't choose a puzzle, you are shocked into it. Whoever has pondered some time over some dark problem in philosophy will have noticed that the solution, when it comes, comes with a suddenness. It is not through working very hard towards it that it is found. What happens is rather that he suddenly sees things in a new light—as if a veil had been lifted that screened his view, or as if the scales had fallen from his eyes, leaving him surprised at his own stupidity not to have seen what was there quite plain before him all the time. It is less like finding out something and more, like maturing, outgrowing preconceived notions.

To give just one example of vision in philosophy: Wittgenstein saw through a big mistake of his time. It was then held by most philosophers that the nature of such things as hoping and fearing, or intending, meaning and understanding could be discovered through introspection, while others, in particular psychologists, sought to arrive at an answer by experiment, having only obscure notions as to what their results meant. Wittgenstein changed the whole approach by saying: what these words mean shows itself in the way they are used—the nature of understanding reveals itself in grammar, not in experiment. This was at the time quite a revelation and came to him, so far as I remember, suddenly.

The view advocated here is that at the living center of every philosophy is a vision and that it should be judged accordingly. The really important questions to be discussed in the history of philosophy are not whether Leibniz or Kant were consistent in arguing as they did but rather what lies behind the systems they have built. And here I want to end with a few words on metaphysics.

To say that metaphysics is nonsense *is* nonsense. It fails to acknowledge the enormous part played at least in the past by those systems. Why this is so, why they should have such a hold over the human mind I shall not undertake here to discuss. Metaphysicians, like artists, are the antennae of their time: they have a flair for feeling which way the spirit is moving. (There is a Rilke poem about it.) There is something visionary about great metaphysicians as if they had the power to see beyond the horizons of their time. Take, for instance, Descartes' work. That it has given rise to endless metaphysical quibbles is certainly a thing to hold against it. Yet if we attend to the spirit rather than to the words I am greatly inclined to say that there is a certain grandeur in it, a prophetic aspect of the comprehensibility of nature, a bold anticipation of what has been achieved in science at a much later date. The true successors of Descartes were those who translated the spirit of this philosophy into deeds, not Spinoza or Malebranche but Newton and the mathematical description of nature. To go on with some hairsplitting as to what substance is and how it should be defined was to miss the message. It was a colossal mistake. A philosophy is there to be lived out. What goes into the word dies, what goes into the work lives.

---

19.   The Teaching of Philosophy

G. C. Fields

WE HAVE NOT, I think, hitherto on these occasions devoted any of our formal meetings to the discussion of the teaching of Philosophy. Yet it seems a pity, when so many teachers of Philosophy

From *Proceedings of the Aristotelian Society*, Supplementary Volume XVI, 1937, pp. 1–19, "The Inaugural Address" (London: Harrison and Sons., Ltd.). Reprinted by courtesy of the Editor of the Aristotelian Society. Copyright 1937 by The Aristotelian Society.

are gathered together, that they should not from time to time take the opportunity of exchanging experiences on the technical problems of their professional work. I propose to offer you a few reflections on the subject that have occurred to me as the result of such experience as I have had. And if at times I may seem to speak somewhat dogmatically, this is merely for the sake of brevity. I am very far from feeling dogmatic on any question of teaching methods in our subject.

I suppose our views on these problems will be largely governed by our views of what Philosophy is and why it should be taught. But it is clear that if I embarked on an exposition of my views on these matters it would exhaust the time and space allotted to me long before I had come within sight of my proper subject. I may, perhaps, be permitted to refer to my paper on "The Examination of Assumptions," which originally appeared in the Aristotelian Society's *Proceedings* three years ago, for a summary account of my own view of what Philosophy is. My view is, to put it in a few words, that philosophical thinking consists in an examination of the general assumptions made and a criticism of the categories used primarily, at any rate, in other kinds of thinking. Whenever we consciously and explicitly accept or reject any particular assumption or set of assumptions we have, so far, adopted a philosophical view. But we may be content with a minimum or aim at a maximum amount of this. In the first case, we carry on the examination and selection of assumptions just so far as seems to us to have an immediate bearing on our thinking in some other line of thought in which our primary interest lies. We should not, normally, describe this as having a philosophy. We should probably only begin to use such a term when we had approximated some way to the latter extreme. In this, we try to carry our examination as far as we can, with the ultimate aim of arriving at a systematic set of assumptions, the only one which we can adopt consistently in all our thinking. Any claim to have attained this I should call a metaphysical theory, positive or negative. And, of course, there are many intermediate stages between the minimum and the maximum.

The other preliminary question brings us more nearly to the main subject. Why do we teach Philosophy? What results can we hope for and ought we to aim at? This is a question that seems to present itself with particular urgency to those of us who teach in the modern Universities. In the older Universities a subject that has the prestige of a long-established tradition behind it can much more easily be taken for granted as a desirable object of study. But in a modern University we always have to be prepared to justify our existence. I must confess that this seems to me, on the whole, a healthier state of things, though it can be at times an uncomfortable one.

It is clear that in many subjects the answer to the question why we teach them is simple. We teach Chemistry, for instance, in order to produce chemists. We cannot, however, give such a simple answer for Philosophy. Certainly we do not expect that more than a minute proportion of our students will earn their living by teaching or researching in the subject. And I do not think that we can or ought to expect any considerable proportion of them to become expert metaphysicians, moral philosophers or logicians. I do not wish to depreciate the value of these activities. But I cannot feel that one could justify the claims made for the study of Philosophy in Universities if this were its sole or principal aim. There are, of course, those who believe that, at any rate, metaphysical and ethical theories are necessarily meaningless and impossible. One representative of this school, the late Professor Schlick, wrote that, if his views were accepted, "the result would be that no more books would be written about Philosophy, but all books would be written in a philosophical manner." I do not believe the theory. But as a practical guide to the teacher I think this epigram contains a great deal of value. I, at any rate, should be perfectly satisfied if the students who went out from my department never thought any more about Philosophy but thought about all other subjects in a philosophical manner.

The main justification, then, for the teaching of Philosophy should be looked for in the effect it has on the rest of the thinking of those who study it. If we want metaphysicians or logicians as well we must look for them to be thrown up from time to time as by-products of this process. I think we could confidently hope to get quite as many as we wanted that way. Those who have a natural ability for these studies can be safely left to look after themselves. Indeed, it is my own conviction that a philosophical education that is primarily directed towards influencing people's thinking on other subjects is also the training most likely to produce sound philosophers in the more technical sense. A certain number of these will be needed to keep up the supply of teachers in the subject. For I think experience shows that the training of people to think philosophically about other subjects needs the stimulus of minds who have carried their philosophical thinking a good way beyond the minimum, as described above. And this will serve as a warning against supposing that, if my view of the value of teaching Philosophy is accepted, it would mean that at every stage in the study of the subject we should check ourselves the moment it seemed that our speculations were going beyond what could have an obvious and immediate effect on the rest of our thinking. No subject could produce its educational effect under these conditions. Once started on these studies we have to go wherever the wind of the argument leads us. But these considerations, if true, should be used to determine our line of approach to the subject, and the general framework of the curriculum and methods of teaching.

The question what qualities in the rest of our thinking we should expect to be developed by the study of Philosophy is not very easy to answer in general terms and the answer might vary in individual cases. But as a rule, I should at least hope that the person trained in Philosophy would be distinguished by his readiness to detect and criticise the underlying and unexpressed assumptions of any argument or train of thought, his own or other people's. I should hope, also, that he would be more careful and precise about the meanings of the terms he used than the average person. At the same time, he would learn to bear in mind Aristotle's warning against demanding a greater degree of precision and exactness than the particular subject-matter admitted. And I should hope that he would develop a high standard of logical form, of coherence and connectedness in argument. As a result of the combination of these, I should hope, also, that he would develop a certain catholicity of outlook, which would show itself, among other ways, in a critical caution about accepting the assumptions and methods of one specialized branch of thought, however successful it might be in its own field, as of universal application. There are other results, too, which might be produced. Some of them, though real enough, are difficult to put into precise language. But those I have mentioned may suffice as examples of the kind of result one might hope for from the study of Philosophy.

How, then, would a teacher of Philosophy who starts from this point of view, proceed? To begin with, I think, he would observe the existence of two rival temptations that beset all teachers of Philosophy. One arises from an excess, and the other from a defect of the interest in the bearing of Philosophy on the rest of life, which, in the right degree, is his most essential qualification. On the one hand, there is the danger of becoming the preacher of a particular gospel. The other danger is just as serious, though perhaps less obvious and less readily admitted. And that is the danger of becoming an instructor in the rules of a game played for its own sake, without reference to anything outside it.

Of these tendencies, the first seems to me to show a truer appreciation of the position and duties of the philosopher than the latter. But it is none the less an error. The object of teaching Philosophy is to make people think philosophically, to examine their assumptions and to criticise their categories. And, whether this process is carried on to the maximum or stops short at the minimum, an essential feature of it is that it is a process which has to be carried on by each man for himself. It is hardly ever possible in Philosophy to hand over our results to someone else, apart from the processes by which we arrived at them. We can, of course, hope to persuade other people of the truth of our views. But we can only do it by trying to lead them through somewhat the same processes of thought until they come to see them for themselves. And it is extremely improbable that we can start with a student entirely untrained in philosophical thinking, and hope in two or three years intermittent contact with him to lead him to the point we have reached, perhaps, after many years of reflexion.

It is a standing temptation to anyone who has a philosophy of his own to try to get it accepted more rapidly than is possible through the slow process of philosophical thinking. But what happens if that attempt is made is that it gets accepted, if at all, through the eloquence or authority or personality of the teacher, or the prestige of being the up-to-date or most advanced view, or the attraction of party loyalty to a particular school. And then it is something very different from what it was to its originator. Indeed, it often becomes little more than the ability to pronounce certain formulæ, on the appropriate occasions, which have become devoid of the greater part of their meaning. I remember many years ago hearing from a very much senior colleague an account of lectures at Glasgow in the days of Edward Caird. Caird would begin by developing, in the approved manner, first his thesis, and then his antithesis, until at some point the excitement of the students would get too much for them and they would burst out, in chorus, "And it's resolved into a higher unity." I will leave it to the representatives of the schools of thought current at the present day to examine their consciences and ask themselves whether their influence may not at times be producing a similar result now.

I certainly do not mean to suggest that the teacher of Philosophy should conceal his own opinions or avoid making a positive pronouncement on any question. But I am sure that he should not make this the centre of his teaching. There is a natural tendency to exaggerate both the importance and the certainty of one's own beliefs. And when a teacher does expound his own opinions he must be careful to present them merely as one among many theories which are or have been held. But, in my opinion, if a teacher takes seriously his task of bringing the student to see how philosophical problems and philosophical theories arise, he will find he has exhausted most of the time at his disposal before he has reached the stage of expounding and advocating his own positive theories at all.

The opposite temptation is more subtle, and few people are likely to yield to it so completely. But a tendency in that direction can be observed from time to time at all periods. It arises partly, I think, from the modesty of philosophers in that they do not wish to be placed in a position where they have to pronounce an opinion on any subject which might possibly be regarded as in the domain of another specialist. Partly, also, it arises from their pride, which leads them to wish to mark off some field which will be all their own and in which they can speak with unquestioned authority. But if I am right in my view of the nature of philosophical thinking it is obviously impossible for it ever to attain this degree of independence and self-sufficiency. And in attempting to do so the philosopher may easily cut himself off from everything that gives substance and meaning to his speculations.

I do not wish to arouse unnecessary controversy by looking for traces of this tendency in contemporary developments of philosophical activity. I think I can find a sufficiently good illustration in the old-fashioned Formal Logic, which can safely be attacked as it has so few friends left to defend it. I am thinking of it as it was taught to elementary students in my own young days. But judging by my experience as an examiner I should suspect that in some places very similar methods have been pursued much more recently. One interesting thing about Formal Logic is, if I am not mistaken, that it was originally constructed very largely, at any rate, with the practical aim of enabling people to see through certain fallacies and sophisms which really did puzzle them in Aristotle's day. Partly because it did its work so well a great many of these no longer afford any difficulty to us at all. Yet in Formal Logic we go on learning how to deal with them while no help is given us against all the numerous other fallacies and sophisms, which really do affect our thinking nowadays.

One thing this suggests to me is that we should begin Logic—or whatever we call the study which aims at doing what the original Logic intended to do—with a study of fallacies. And these should be fallacies of a kind which people are actually in the habit of committing. They should not be artificially constructed for the purpose of showing how, if we thought in some way in which we are not in the least likely to think, we should be breaking certain rules. Similarly when we get on to analysing propositions and arguments we should start with those which really contain some obscurity or possibility of misunderstanding. It is important at the outset to make the students feel that there is some point in the analysis, and that it is not a mere exercise of ingenuity in discovering all the possible ways in which a proposition or argument could be re-stated or re-arranged. The danger is that many quick-witted students like exercises in ingenuity and can come to enjoy Formal Logic almost as much as cross-word puzzles. But I find it hard to believe that any student at the Formal Logic stage really believes that what he is learning has any bearing on the rest of his thinking. The teachers make efforts from time to time to show that there is a possible connexion. But it generally requires more ingenuity and effort to make this connexion than it would to correct the faults of his thinking without the intervention of Formal Logic at all.

Where the student, who starts thus, really does begin to think philosophically is when he begins to examine and criticise the assumptions of Formal Logic and to see its inadequacies and limitations. But it seems rather a waste of time to instruct him in any detail in this study just in order to show where it is wrong. For the rest, it seems to me that if there is any place for Formal Logic it is as a chapter in the history of Greek Philosophy. But a great proportion of the detail would be superfluous however it was treated.

The first task of the teacher of Philosophy is to lead his students to see that philosophical problems arise out of the rest of our thinking. Most people would probably be prepared to admit this in a general way. But where, as it seems to me, so many of us fail is in not realizing what a lot of time and effort is needed to do this. I have certainly known many students from many Universities who have completed their course successfully without any but the vaguest realisation of this. Most of their philosophical studies seemed to them to the end either a game or a self-contained field of knowledge to be pursued, if at all, for its own sake. Yet I think it is a matter of history that all serious and important philosophical speculation has begun because people were puzzled about something in the rest of their thinking and turned to a philosophical examination of their assumptions in order to throw light on this. And that is the way I should like to see all students begin.

One of the difficulties in the way of this is that the students themselves are very often impatient of this ground work. They want to get on straight away to the great theories, or even to the construction of systems themselves. And that is also, if I may venture to say so, the fault of a great many amateurs in Philosophy. They want to get a philosophy without philosophical thinking and, too often, they want this philosophy as a relaxation from their own problems, not as something which arises out of them. The business man, for instance, who takes up Philosophy, is very rarely interested in examining the assumptions, say, of his own code of business ethics, on which he might make most valuable contributions. He wants to construct a theory of the nature of reality, to solve the problem of Free Will, or, at a lower level, to find a short book which will explain clearly the philosophy of Spinoza or Bergson.

I suggest, then, that a great deal of philosophical teaching tends to start much too far forward. A considerable proportion of the introductory stages should be devoted, not to expounding a system of rules or general principles and then looking for possible applications of them, but to examining typical arguments in large number. We should choose those in which the possibility of obscurity, error or differences of opinion was most obviously present, and we should try to extract the unexpressed assumptions in them. General conclusions, classifications and the like should be led up to gradually, and put forward tentatively and provisionally. And at this stage the examples will be chosen without much system from whatever sources are most likely to provide matter that will be of interest to our students. Even when at a later stage we attack the more defined branches of our subject the same line of approach may be followed. In Ethics, for instance, we could start with some actual moral controversy, particularly if we can find one which has been a subject of public discussion. Another approach which I have often found stimulating is to start an examination of some of the common moral generalizations with which we are familiar,—"You mustn't blame him, because he's never had a chance," "There's no merit in a thing if you like doing it," and the like.

When we do make some use of this method of approach we tend, generally, to look for our examples in the kind of experience that is open to everyone, our ordinary everyday thinking. But that is rather an arbitrary line to draw. And I suggest that we rarely make enough use of the material to be found in the other University or pre-University studies of our students, their history, their economics, or, if the teacher of Philosophy feels qualified to use this material, their natural science. I feel it to be of the utmost importance that the student should be provided with a constant flow of material on which to exercise his powers of philosophical criticism. And this has led me to the conclusion, which I know arouses strong opposition among some of my colleagues, that Philosophy should always be taught, throughout the undergraduate stage, in combination with some other subject. For preference one would choose a subject in which there was a good deal of controversy. But almost any subject can provide some material for philosophical examination of assumptions. I remember hearing a distinguished archæologist, the late Professor Eric Peet, say that one of the books that most needed writing was one on the Logic of Archæology. This principle has, of course, long been an established tradition at Oxford. But it was not adopted there in the first place as a matter of conscious policy. And it has been very slow to secure acceptance elsewhere.

But this practice in the examination of assumptions which have come, more or less, within his own experience is only one part of the work that should be required of the student. I doubt whether the ordinary student has either the material or the intellectual energy to keep it up continuously. At any rate, I am sure that he will only do it effectively if his realization of the possibilities of the process is enlarged by a knowledge of how other people have tried to do it. And here we come to the vexed question of the place in philosophical training of the study of the works of other philosophers and of the history of Philosophy.

I believe, for the reasons just indicated, that this study is an essential part of a course in Philosophy, which should be very largely based on it. The antithesis that I have heard made between teaching students to think for themselves and teaching them what other people have thought seems to me a false one. At any rate, I should maintain that we cannot hope to teach students to think effectively for themselves without showing them how other people have attempted the task. Nor, in fact, does any teacher of Philosophy really attempt to do so. If he does not make use of the work of the great thinkers of the past, he uses instead his own work and perhaps those of his immediate associates. Yet I do not think that we can assume that there is any special educational value in the choice, as our historical period, of the history of thought during the last ten years in our own particular University, even if it is combined with minute textual criticism of the works of our distinguished colleagues.

It cannot, however, be denied that it is possible to teach the history of Philosophy in a way which lends some colour to the reproach implied in the above-mentioned antithesis. I can remember examining in one University institution in which the students showed a really remarkable capacity for saying the right things in a reasonably small compass about Locke, Berkeley, Hume, Descartes, Leibniz, Spinoza, and even Malebranche and Geulincx. Yet when they were asked a question which demanded some expression of their own opinions they were quite incapable of giving any answer except a neat summary of what had been said on the subject by various past thinkers. As thus taught, the history of Philosophy can become, like Formal Logic, just a game played for its own sake, quite detached not only from the rest of experience but from the rest of Philosophy also.

The historical approach to the teaching of Philosophy is, indeed, beset with pitfalls. One of them is the danger of forgetting that it is an approach to Philosophy and not a subject by itself. I always feel suspicious of this when I see "History of Philosophy" set down as one of the subjects in the curriculum. Closely allied to this is the idea that the well-trained student should have "covered the ground" in Philosophy, to use a well-worn academic phrase, and that he has not been turned out properly qualified in the subject unless he knows something to say about any philosopher of any importance who has ever written. But, in my view, the object of studying past writers is to see how they came to raise their problems and to understand the processes by which they reached their conclusions. It is obviously impossible to do this within the limits of a student course for more than a very small number of thinkers. To attempt to go beyond this results finally in giving the student a few well-chosen formulæ about each philosopher, and a few standard headings under which they can be classed. And if this conveys any meaning to him at all, it is at any rate something very different from what the theories meant to those who first conceived them. I think the same should be made to apply to the student's reading. General histories of Philosophy doubtless have a certain value as books of reference for the professional. But they should, in my opinion, be passed, like A-films, for exhibition to adults only.

All general rules of conduct admit of exceptions. But I think we should allow very few exceptions to the rule that a student should never be told about a philosopher without having to read some of his works. On the other hand, just as a student cannot be expected to know something about every philosopher, so it would be equally unreasonable to expect him to know everything about some one philosopher. I think the conventional method of choosing one or two typical works for study will produce the results we want, if judiciously applied. We must remember that our aim is not to enable the student to answer all possible questions that can be raised about the interpretation of any particular philosopher, but to show by illustrations how various important problems arise and can be treated.

In using these works we find ourselves, once more, between the Scylla and Charybdis of two opposed dangers. On the one hand, we may find ourselves treating the particular work as a self-contained whole, which can be discussed, in the light of our own situation and general assumptions, as a theory which has to be accepted as right or rejected as wrong. This may be the end at which we should ultimately aim, though I do not, personally, believe that any serious philosophical theory can be simply rejected as just wrong. But, in any case, the first essential is to lead the student to see how the thinker in question came to think as he did. This can rarely be done by studying his arguments alone, essential though that is. We must also understand something of the situation from which his speculations arose. This will involve some knowledge of previous or contemporary philosophers; perhaps we may find an exception to the rule forbidding us to tell the student about a philosopher's theories without making him read some of the works in a case such as this. Sometimes, too, we may have to explain something about other thinkers, not generally described as philosophers in the modern sense. I doubt, for instance, whether we could really make Descartes or Locke intelligible without saying something about Galileo or Newton.

It may also at times be necessary to say something about political and social conditions. It is impossible, for instance, to expound Plato's *Republic* satisfactorily without reference to political movements and institutions in ancient Greece. But what is important, above all, is to be able to give some account of what a seventeenth century writer called "the climate of thought" of the period, the current interests, ideas and assumptions which are not fully expressed in any one writer of the time but can be seen, to a greater or lesser degree, to lie behind the thought of all of them. This is really the material from which the philosopher of any age starts. And I regard the ability to bring this out for whatever period one is concerned with as one of the great tests of the capacity for philosophical teaching.

All this may seem rather a formidable programme. But I am sure that the attempt must be made to fulfil it. And it is easy to exaggerate the difficulties of the task. Every teacher, who is serious about his duties, has to learn how to carry his treatment of a subject just as far as is necessary for his immediate purposes and no further, and it is a test of his worth to be able to be summary without being superficial.

It is possible, however, to carry this too far. And then we fall into the opposite error of treating a thinker of the past merely historically, that is, as nothing but the product of a set of circumstances which only occurred once and, in the nature of things, cannot be repeated. I need not labour the point that this treatment fails to do justice to the thinker concerned, for we should probably all claim that our own philosophical beliefs, at any rate, were something more than the transient product of temporary historical circumstances. But the purely historical treatment misses, also, the educational advantages of the approach through history. The first step in learning to think philosophically is to become conscious and critical of our own assumptions. And it is a great stimulus to this to study the thought of an age in which the assumptions were not the same as our own. But if they were merely different and had no point of resemblance we could not come to understand them at all. It is the identity in difference which is the really instructive thing. It is the realization of this which leads us on to the further stage of philosophical thought, when we begin to ask which of our assumptions we cannot help making, and which can be modified or dispensed with altogether.

I have put this in very general terms. I will try to illustrate it by instances taken from the study of Plato's *Republic*, which I still believe to be one of the best introductions to Philosophy that one can find. The "climate of thought" in Plato's time seems to me to have been unlike enough to our own to stimulate our thought and not so unlike as merely to produce bewilderment. If we think of the political discussions it is fairly easy to see that it would be foolish to discuss Plato's proposals as if they were embodied in a Bill presented for acceptance or rejection to the House of Commons at the present moment. It would be equally unreasonable to say that they were applied to a different situation and therefore had no interest for us nowadays. It is when we are forced to ask what and how much in the discussions of the *Republic* can be applied to our own times that we get our first lesson in the analysis of political ideas and situations. It is, no doubt, theoretically possible to learn how to analyse our own political ideas without any knowledge of those of any other age. But in practice I do not believe that there is any such valuable stimulus to this analysis as the comparison between the two.

I do not want to drag out this discussion of details. But I should like to illustrate my argument further by reference to one special point. That is the use of general terms in the analysis of which so great a part of philosophical thinking consists. I can illustrate this best, perhaps, from certain ethical terms. When we begin to read Plato or Aristotle we find them using certain terms which we translate by "justice" or "virtue." A great deal of their use of those terms may seem to us quite ordinary and familiar. But sometimes we find them using them, or arguing about them, in a way which seems very queer and unnatural, or, indeed, almost unintelligible, as when Plato speaks of "the art called justice." I generally tell my students that, while it is quite possible that Plato's arguments were wrong, it is in the highest degree improbable that they were not even plausible. And if they seem so to anyone reading them in a translation or in the original with the conventional translations in mind, we must consider whether the word in question conveyed quite the same meaning to Plato and his readers as its nearest equivalent in English does to us. In fact, we must try to think what the word must have conveyed to them for the argument to have been capable of taking anyone in. I cannot think of any such effective way of starting students thinking about how words are used. I may add, as a record of personal experience, that I now think, contrary to my former opinion, that it is quite possible to get this result by studying the book in a translation. But I am not so certain that this is possible if the teacher has no knowledge of the original.

I have dwelt at some length on the historical method of approach. But I wish to make it clear that I do not regard this as a satisfactory method by itself, and I think the historical element in a philosophical course may easily become too predominant. The other approach, which I outlined earlier, must be pursued concurrently with it. For that is directly concerned with the end of philosophical teaching while the other is only a means. Yet I still maintain that it is an indispensable means. And it has other incidental advantages. It may prevent the students being too much at the mercy of the special point of view or the special phraseology of their particular teacher. Perhaps it may yet save us from the situation towards which at the moment we seem to be drifting, in which philosophers of different Universities, or even of different groups in the same University, are ceasing to be intelligible to each other at all.

Apart from these general considerations, I find little that I feel called upon to say about the details of the curriculum, the divisions of subjects, and the like. Obviously in an undergraduate course one cannot hope to "do Philosophy," and it would be a great mistake to attempt to cover too much ground. But what selection shall be made and in what order the different parts shall be taken seems to me a comparatively minor matter. Any of the usually recognized branches of Philosophy can be used as a stimulant for philosophical thinking. Perhaps, students, on the whole, tend to have their interest more easily aroused by some question than by others. But this varies considerably, and it would not be safe to lay down any general rule. In a small University, in which the teaching is in the hands of two or three people and adjustments in the curriculum can easily be made, there is a lot to be said for being guided to some extent by the special interests of the teachers. Other things being equal, they are more likely to stimulate their students to think philosophically about the subjects in which they have been specially concerned themselves. But there are obvious limits to this.

There is, I think, a good deal more to say about the methods of imparting instruction, the lecture, the seminar, the tutorial. And here I have to bear testimony to a definite change in my own opinions. I used to think that the lecture was the least valuable part of the instruction, and could probably, indeed, be dispensed with altogether, while the tutorial, as I knew it, seemed to me almost the perfection of educational method. I now think that there is a great deal more to be said for the lecture and a great deal less for the tutorial system than I thought then. But, in saying this, I wish to challenge the assumption that there is necessarily a sharp dividing line between the two. The lecture need not be a lecture and nothing more. If the lecturer has got on the right terms with his hearers it can be freely interspersed with questions and discussion. Of course, numbers affect this to some extent. There is obviously a limit beyond which this is impossible. But I know from experience that a quite lively discussion can develop in a class of forty to fifty and in a really small class one ought not to know whether one is giving a lecture or leading a discussion.

On the other hand, a so-called tutorial can, and often does, develop into a monologue. Nor is this necessarily a criticism of it. For we should probably all recognize that the serious presentation of a philosophical point of view needs to be worked up to gradually and developed at length. In spite of Socrates, the method of question and answer can only take us a little way. I have been greatly struck by observing how often a student, who shows himself quick and clever in questions and brief discussion, fails entirely if set to develop a continuous and systematic train of argument. And those who are quick, but less clever, can often lead off the discussion into endless irrelevant side-issues. On the other hand, I have also known students who seemed unwilling to say anything, and could hardly be got to answer questions. And yet, if left to themselves to work in their own way, they ended up by producing absolutely first-class presentations of a coherent point of view. This surely shows a much higher degree of philosophical ability than the former.

The continuous piece of exposition, whether we call it a lecture or anything else, is necessary for the teacher to be able to present his views fairly. It is necessary for the student because the ability to follow a continuous argument and to judge it as a whole is a most essential part of his training. It may be asked why this should not be derived from reading books. And that, no doubt, is a very necessary part of his work. But I think a good lecturer can supply a great deal that can not be got very easily from books. He can adjust his lectures to the rest of the scheme of study and the special needs of the students. If he is skilful he can do a good deal of adjustment even during the lecture. I believe it to be possible to develop a sort of sense of how the audience is responding as one proceeds and to modify the exposition accordingly. Further, the most valuable form of questioning and discussion is that which arises out of a systematic exposition of an argument and is directed towards elucidating or criticising points in it.

Of course, there are lectures which could very easily be replaced by books. Broadly speaking, I should say that the more the lecture consists in the statement of facts and the giving of information the more superfluous it is. And it follows from that, again contrary to what I used to think, that in Philosophy, where the need for the mere giving of information is at the minimum, there is a greater place for the lecture than in most other subjects. It hardly needs saying, of course, that the kind of lecture that ought to be given must be determined by each lecturer for himself with these considerations in mind.

There is also the other equally essential side of the process of education, the expression by the student of his own difficulties and his own opinions. This can be done to a great extent verbally. And, as indicated above, I believe the most valuable form of this is when it is done spontaneously, as the student finds his own difficulties and develops his own opinions and wants to express them. He may do this to some extent with his teachers and they will do well to encourage it as far as possible. But I am not sure that he does not gain a good deal more by discussion with his fellow-students.

Besides this, I think all teachers would recognize that a certain amount of practice in writing is essential. This is the great strength of the tutorial system, as I knew it at Oxford, and as I suppose it still exists. But, in spite of this great and incontestable advantage, I do not feel that this system is beyond criticism. I am certain that it often tends to put too great a strain on the tutors. And I am inclined to think it generally demands more written work than is really profitable from the students. The contribution of the tutors consists, very often, largely of developing their own views on the question. This becomes, in fact, a rather informal kind of lecture, which is quite unnecessarily repeated over and over again to a series of students, when it could just as effectively be delivered once to the whole lot taken together. Even the criticisms of the essays can very often perfectly well be given in that way. But, in any case, really effective criticism of the essays, which might produce improvement in the method of exposition, seems to me to demand a more careful study of the essays in question than is possible by simply hearing them read aloud. If I want to criticize an essay effectively I find I have to read it through first by myself, and then, after an interval, go over it again carefully with the student. But, of course, it would not be possible to deal in this way with anything like the number of essays that the tutorial system demands, unless one were to give up all one's other activities for this.

These, then, are some of the reflections which have occurred to me in connexion with our pedagogical problems. There are a number of other questions, both of principle and detail, which it would be interesting to discuss. We might, for instance, raise the general question what the qualities are which are most required in a teacher of Philosophy. Are they the same as those which are likely to produce the most original contributions to constructive philosophical theory? Perhaps, such questions as these are too delicate to raise in the present audience. But I should like to end with a plea for a careful consideration of the educational problems of philosophical studies, a more careful consideration than, I think, we have hitherto been inclined to give.

SELECTED BIBLIOGRAPHY

AYER, A. J., editor, *Logical Positivism*. Glencoe, Ill.: The Free Press, 1959.

BANDMAN, BERTRAM, *The Place of Reason in Education*. Columbus, Ohio: The Ohio State University Press, 1967.

BROADBECK, M., editor, *Readings in the Philosophy of the Social Sciences*. New York: The Macmillan Company, 1968.

CARNEY, JAMES D. and RICHARD K. SCHEER, *Fundamentals of Logic*. New York: The Macmillan Company, 1964.

COHEN, M. R. and ERNEST NAGEL, *An Introduction to Logic and Scientific Method*. New York: Harcourt, Brace & World, Inc., 1934.

ELAM, S., editor, *Education and the Structure of Knowledge*. Chicago: Rand McNally & Company, 1964.

FEIGL, H. and MAY BROADBECK, editors, *Readings in the Philosophy of Science*. New York: Appleton-Century-Crofts, 1953.

FORD, G. W. and LAWRENCE PUGNO, editors, *The Structure of Knowledge and the Curriculum*. Chicago: Rand McNally & Company, 1964.

HOSPERS, J., *An Introduction to Philosophical Analysis*, Second editon. Englewood Cliffs, N.J.: Prentice-Hall, Inc., 1967.

LOUCH, A. R., *Explanation and Human Action*. Oxford: Basil Blackwell & Mott, Ltd., 1966.

NAGEL, E., *The Structure of Science*. New York: Harcourt, Brace & World, Inc., 1961.

OPPENHEIMER, J. ROBERT, *The Open Mind*. New York: Simon and Schuster, Inc., 1955.

QUINE, W. V. O., *Methods of Logic*. New York: Holt, Rinehart & Winston, Inc., 1950.

RORTY, R., editor, *The Linguistic Turn*. Chicago: Chicago University Press, 1967.

SCHEFFLER, I., editor, *Philosophy and Education*. First edition. Boston: Allyn & Bacon, Inc., 1958.

SOMMERHOFF, G., *Analytical Biology*. London: Oxford University Press, 1950.

Theory and Practice in Historical Study: A Report of the Committee on Historiography. New York: Social Science Research Council, 1942.

TOULMIN, S., *The Philosophy of Science*. London: Hutchinson University Library, 1953.

WEITZ, M., editor, *Problems in Aesthetics*. New York: The Macmillan Company, 1959.

YOUNG, J. W., *Lectures on the Fundamental Concepts of Algebra and Geometry*. New York: The Macmillan Company, 1911.

Index

385